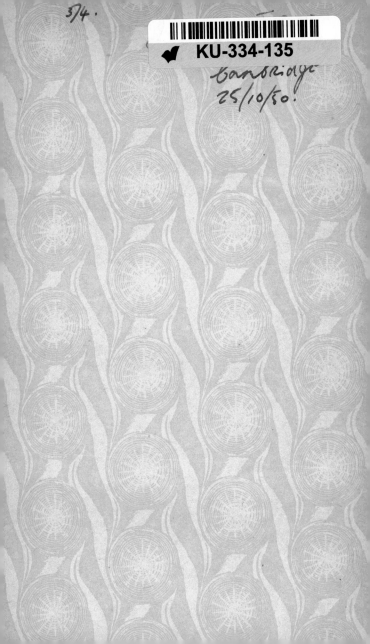

Everyman, I will go with thee, and be thy guide,
In thy most need to go by thy side.

REFLECTIONS ON
THE FRENCH REVOLUTION

EDMUND BURKE

LONDON: J. M. DENT & SONS LTD.
NEW YORK: E. P. DUTTON & CO. INC.

X 139/12 m

INTRODUCTION

ALTHOUGH there have been critics who place Edmund Burke
at the summit of English prose-writers, it is hardly to be gain-
said that he belongs more to the history of politics and to the
history of thought, than to that of pure literature. Apart from
his personal characteristics, the essential magnanimity of his
nature, his kindly and sympathetic disposition towards struggling aspirants like Crabbe, and his utter freedom from self-
seeking in an age of almost universal corruption, which make
him a conspicuous and memorable figure in the history of
eighteenth-century politics, in which he was so thoroughly
engrossed, his commanding eminence is due to the fact that he
was the first to rebut the conception made dominant by Locke,
that every man's thought was a sufficient authority for himself,
that the individual reason is a competent and sufficient guide
to truth. Burke argued on the contrary that society is an
organic whole in which each mind is a particular growth, conditioned by the rest, and incapable of fully living if it detaches
itself from the rest. Hence the great value which he set upon
custom and traditional opinion, the consensus of thought as
opposed to individual judgment. All through his career he
attacked unsparingly the assertion of individual, or, as he called
it, critical opinion, as against the permanent convictions of
society.

This conception is connected with a widespread movement in
European thought and literature during the early nineteenth
century, a movement partly reactionary as tending to revive
mediæval forms of belief and views of society simply because in
the Middle Ages the authority of custom and tradition had been
paramount. We see another phase of the movement in the
Catholic reaction on the Continent at the beginning of the nineteenth century, and in the "Oxford Movement" in England a
generation later. Similarly in philosophy comes the change
from Locke's idea of the single mind to that of mankind as the
starting point, and so in theology the change from Transcen-
dence or Deism (God conceived as existing apart from and
independent of the world) to Immanence (God conceived as a

world soul), which, when unqualified, becomes **Pantheism**. This change is illustrated by Wordsworth. And not only in thought, but in style does Burke serve as a link between the two centuries: he unites the powerful understanding, the clear and luminous construction, the sanity of judgment of the earlier age, with the passionate imagination, the fervid eloquence and the glowing colour which we associate with the romantic movement of the early nineteenth century.

With this clue in our hands we may more easily trace the story of Burke's writings, and especially come to some understanding of the apparent inconsistency between his attitude to the American and the French Revolutions. One may start, indeed, with the *Vindication of Natural Society* (published, like the *Essay on the Sublime and the Beautiful*, in 1751). This book professed to be a "letter to a lord, by a late noble writer," viz. Bolingbroke, and Bolingbroke's style is so deftly imitated that many accepted the book as from his hand. In truth it was a marvellous piece of satire, which took its rise from the current discussions on "natural" and "revealed" religion. Burke's endeavour was to show that the same arguments which Bolingbroke had used in favour of natural religion could be used with equal success in favour of natural as against "artificial" society. For one absurdity in religion he undertook to produce a hundred in political law and institution. His book is a great plea for the recognition of collective as well as individual reason, and he asserts that all that is regarded as excellent and venerable, nay society itself, would tumble to ruin, if the practice of all moral duties and the constitution of the social order, rested upon their being submitted to the unrestrained criticism of every individual. Thus even at this early date we may trace Burke's love of order, the same ardent zeal for constitutional forms of accepted rule, and the same appeal to the general and traditional sense of national life that we find in the speeches and writings of his mature manhood.

We find the same thread, in spite of the tangles of verbosity, detail, and ephemeral interests, running through the *Observations on the Present State of the Nation* (1769) and the *Thoughts on the Causes of the Present Discontents* (1770). Burke's contribution to the serious problems raised by the triangular disagreement between king, advisers, and people, was as full of political principles as the contribution made in the *Letters of Junius* was devoid of them. Its main contention is that the study of political conditions with a view to solving the problems they involve must be accompanied by a study of social conditions. He goes behind the political constitution to the state of society upon which the validity of the constitution depends, examining the elements which constitute national strength and the different classes who contribute towards national prosperity, and showing the futility of a government which ignores these primary conditions and attempts to rule through a parliament half of whose members are simply creatures of the court and out of all relation with the real constituents of a nation.

When the American question came to the front, Burke saw clearly that the question of liberty in America was closely connected with the question of liberty in England, and that the resistance of the colonists to the arbitrary proposals of the English Government was only another phase of the resistance offered by the people of the home country. Burke and those who were with him felt that the New Englanders were fighting their battles and that the suppression of liberty there would have the same consequences at home. We shall see that it was this particular regard for the interests of England that guided Burke twenty years later in his views of the French Revolution. In his speeches on American Taxation, and on Conciliation with America, and in his *Letter to the Citizens of Bristol* (1774–5) he opposes the arbitrary contention of the English Government— that the king had sovereign right over the colonies and might therefore do as he pleased with them. To this claim Burke did not reply as Rousseau might have done, that if the sovereign had rights the people also had rights. Instead of this he rejected decisively the whole conception of rights as a ground of political action. A right is merely an abstract metaphysical conception which can never be imposed upon society without disaster. Political problems must be solved along other lines than this, by large and wise considerations of expediency. The sovereign may have a "right" to tax the colonists, but it is surely inexpedient to assert the right which abstrusely exists. Laws must grow out of customs, not glaringly contradict and oppose them.

The American Revolution was succeeded on the stage of English politics by the problem of the East India Company, and its impeachment and trial in the person of Warren Hastings. But long before the curtain had rung down upon that episode, the outbreak of the French Revolution had taken place. In its beginnings it was an effort to reform extraordinary abuses, social and political, within the limits of the existing monarchy. The abolition of the monarchy, when it came, was mainly the work of the emigrants who had fled from France and, by threatening invasion, drove the Republicans to the final step. Sheridan and Fox, like most English folk, recognized this moderation of the first stages and welcomed the movement, but Burke from the outset took another view. He gave his *Reflections* to the English people as a warning, and brought about a complete change of English national sentiment. With fiery partisanship he applied the disastrous consequences of the disorderly method in which the French pursued freedom, to his own country, and filled his countrymen with panic. He broke off not only all public co-operation, but even personal relations, with his old friend and colleague, Fox. Abroad the book had a success as great as at home. The Revolutionists themselves read it, the French king translated it, Catherine of Russia congratulated the author; while nearer home the Tories, till now Burke's implacable foes, lavished their favours upon their old-time opponent, and even George III praised the work and recommended everybody to read it.

By his own party Burke was naturally accused of treason to his former position and principles, though even then there were a few observers who saw that in reality there was no inconsistency and that Burke was no renegade. Coleridge, for instance, pointed out that in Burke's attitude to the revolutions in America and France the principles were the same, the deductions from them the same, but the practical influences opposite though equally legitimate. As Lord Morley points out, Burke "changed his front, but not his basis," he is from beginning to end repugnant to the critical spirit, to all inquiry into the origin of opinions, In such inquiry he saw an inevitable risk of a breach of order, and with all his largeness for liberty, *i.e.* the opportunity of full development of faculty, he would never consent to secure it at the cost of order. "Liberty," said Montesquieu, Burke's political father, "does not consist in doing what one pleases . . . liberty can only consist in being able to do what one ought to do." Now in the case of America it was plainly the English Government that had attempted a breach of order by trying to enforce an abstract right of sovereignty. In the case of France, on the other hand, he was convinced that it was the people who were responsible for the breach, by the violent proceedings which had initiated the Revolution. The real charge that we can bring against Burke here is not one of inconsistency, but of inadequate knowledge (he partly admits this, see p. 133). He knew far less of the social state of France than of the conditions of either France or America, and totally ignored the existence in France of the oppressive abuses that constituted the case of the French people against their government. He forgot his own assertion that "revolutions are not created by the people, they spring from irresistible need, they are not fomented, but when they come they are irresistible." The knowledge that Burke lacked was put before the English people in the following year (1791) by Arthur Young, whose *Travels in France* is an intimate picture of the feudal exactions that prevailed in France down to the Revolution. Though a more momentous contribution to the philosophy of the great upheaval, it came too late to influence a people inflamed by the denunciatory eloquence of Burke.

Hartley Coleridge (*Essays*, i. 134), writing of Shakespeare, says, that he is one of those "who build the commonweal, not on the shifting shoals of expedience, or the incalculable tides of popular will, but on the sure foundations of the divine purpose, demonstrated by the great and glorious ends of rational being; who deduce the rights and duties of men, not from the animal nature, in which neither right nor duty can inhere, not from a state of nature which never existed, nor from an arbitrary contract which never took place in the memory of men nor angels, but from the complex life of the soul and the body, defined by reason and conscience, expounded and ratified by revelation." The words might have been written of Burke.

It has often been pointed out that Burke's literary style was conditioned by his rhetoric. It began with his selection of Bolingbroke as a model and was maintained by his own unceasing exercise in the oratorical arena. Yet his rhetoric always inclined more to the written than the spoken form, and though this may not have pleased him it has preserved his work better than that of the ordinary orator and debater. Such is the judgment of Professor Saintsbury, who goes on to enumerate certain qualities of Burke's style and method, and in particular what is technically known as Amplification, "the faculty of building up an argument or a picture by a succession of complementary strokes, not added at haphazard, but growing out of and on to one another." The *Reflections* perhaps displays a less orderly arrangement than some of the earlier works, but for compensation there is a greater rush of thought and rhetoric. "In his ornaments, whether of idea or of imagery, Burke is better worth studying than almost any other English writer. In simile and trope generally, he is, though often wonderfully brilliant, distinctly uncertain, quite untrustworthy in the direction of humour, and in some of his more forcible images apt even to be positively disgusting. On the other hand, his grandeur seldom falls into the grandiose, and the magical effect of more imaginative passages (of which the famous one about Marie Antoinette is only the stock example) has never been exceeded in political writing. Epigram he can occasionally manage with great effect, but it is not by any means so specially and definitely his weapon as imaginative argument, and the marshalling of vast masses of complicated detail into properly rhetorical battalions or (to alter the image) mosaic pictures of enduring beauty."

Sir Leslie Stephen found in Burke's style a praiseworthy "flexibility"; but Sir Edmund Gosse compares it to "a robe of brocaded damask, splendid, sumptuous, and appropriate to noble public occasions, but scarcely flexible." To be a perfect prose-writer, a man must play sometimes upon thrilling and soul-subduing instruments, but Burke never takes the trumpet from his lips. It has been said that he greatly admired Dryden's prose and tried to imitate it, but the only striking resemblance between the two is the elaborate art with which the parts of the sentences are balanced and adjusted. "In the class of declamatory writers," says Sir Edmund, "Burke stands easily first; his tracts and orations do not speak reflectively, with the still small voice which the cloistered student loves, but in resonant accents, so that even in the study their effect is completed to the imagination by cries of defiance or rounds of applause from an unseen audience."

To return to the *Reflections*, in which, if the reader seeks a narrative history of the French Revolution, he will seek in vain. Its ostensible *raison d'être* was an address given by the Rev. Dr. Richard Price, a Nonconformist minister of some note, to a harmless body called the Revolutionary Society, and a sermon by the same gentleman *On the Love of our Country*. Burke takes far more notice of these productions than they merit, but they are the grit around which he built up his pearl. Price had been lauding the proceedings in France (as far as they had gone in 1789) as a conspicuous vindication of the "rights" of the governed. Burke sets out to show that the English liberties which Price was so proud of were not first achieved at the Revolution of 1688, but were essentially an English inheritance, and, further, that between the orderly procedure of England in 1688 and the disorderly action of France a century later there was a whole world of difference. He says that Price misrepresents English sentiment, and goes on to sketch a true picture of the English political system, comparing it at different points with the French. He proposes four heads—the Church, the monarchy, the aristocracy, and the democracy; the first gets most attention, the last, none at all. For when, after an interval in which he was otherwise engaged, Burke set to writing the second part of his *Reflections*, he took up at once the policy of the Revolutionist party, and after denying that the National Assembly had any right at all to legislate, he adversely criticizes what they had done in matters legislative, executive, judicial, military, and financial. Throughout the whole book it is evident that his prime concern is for his own country—"Whenever our neighbour's house is on fire, it cannot be amiss for the engines to play a little on our own."

The rest of Burke's life is a record of his increasingly passionate hostility to the Revolution. His subsequent writings, *A Letter to a Member of the National Assembly* and *An Appeal from the New to the Old Whigs*, and especially the *Letters on a Regicide Peace*, show the old eloquence and imagination, but are sadly lacking in the old sagacity, clear judgment, and power of marshalling facts. The execution of the French king in January 1793, which apparently justified all Burke's antagonism to the Revolution, raised him to the height of his influence, and was followed by an outburst of national passion.

About this time (1794) Burke lost his only son Richard, a blow that fell heavily upon him. He was roused from his despondency by an attack made by the Duke of Bedford upon the pension drawn by Burke from the Government. In his *Letter to a Noble Lord* his earlier gifts of calm and clear reasoning reappear. The letter in this respect stands in marked contrast to what we can only describe as the frenzy of the *Letters on a Regicide Peace*, letters whose course was interrupted—after two of them had appeared, though four were written—by the author's death on July 9, 1797.

LEADING DATES IN BURKE'S LIFE

1729, Jan. Birth in Dublin. His father was a Protestant attorney; his first schoolmaster was Abraham Shackleton.

1743–8. At Trinity College, Dublin.

1750. Enters the Middle Temple, London.

1756. Marriage. First publications.

1759. Plans the *Annual Register*.

1761. Private secretary to Gerard Hamilton, Chief Secretary for Ireland.

1765. Private secretary to Lord Rockingham, and M.P. for Wendover.

1769–70. Writings on home politics.

1773. Visit to France.

1774–80. M.P. for Bristol.

1774–5. Writings and speeches on the American Revolution.

1781–94. M.P. for Malton.

1782–3. Paymaster of the Forces.

1786. Leads the impeachment of Warren Hastings.

1790 ff. Writings on the French Revolution.

1797, July 9. Death.

Burke's character and temper, conversational ability and other personal qualities are reflected in Boswell's *Johnson*, Fanny Burney's *Diary*, and other memoirs of the period. Mr. E. J. Payne, in the Clarendon Press edition of *Burke's Select Works* (Vol. II), has an admirable essay on the *Reflections*, and Lord Morley's monograph in the English Men of Letters Series is, of course, known to every reader as the indispensable handbook to any adequate study of Burke.

A Vindication of Natural Society (Letter), 1756; A Philosophical Enquiry into the Origin of our Ideas of the Sublime and the Beautiful, 1756, 2nd edition; Discourse concerning Taste, 1757; A Short Account of a Short Administration, 1766; Observations on a Short Publication intituled "The Present State of the Nation," 1769; Thoughts on the Causes of the Present Discontents, 1770; Speech on American Taxation, 1774; Speech on Conciliation with America, 1775, 1778; Letters to the Sheriffs of Bristol, 1777; Speech on Economic Reform, 1780; On Fox's East India Bill, 1784; On the Debts of the Nabob of Arcot, 1785; Articles of Charge against Warren Hastings, 1786; Reflections on the Revolution in France, 1790; new edition, 1793; Appeal from the New to the Old Whigs, 1791; Letter to the Empress of Russia, 1791 (in Collected Works); Letter on the Penal Laws (to Lord Kenmare), 1782, 1785; ed. H. C. Clifford, 1824; Letter to Sir Hercules Langrishe, M.P., 1792; Speeches on the Impeachment of Warren Hastings, with Introduction, 1792; Observations on the Conduct of the Minority (Letter to the Duke of Portland), 1793, published 1797 under the title "Fifty-four Articles of Impeachment against the Right Hon. C. F. Fox"; Thoughts and Details on Scarcity, presented to W. Pitt, 1795; A Letter to a Noble Lord, etc., 1796; Letters I and II on a Regicide Peace, 1796 (two other letters have been published in Collected Works); Hints for an Essay on the Drama (Collected Works); An Essay towards an Abridgement of the English History (Collected Works). Other Letters, Notes, and fragments are published in the Collected Works.

The "Annual Register" was started by Burke in 1759. His contributions to it continued for many years.

Works: 3 vols., 1792; complete in 8 vols., 1827; 16 vols. (Laurence and King), first 8 vols., 1803, 1808, with a Life, 1823; edition completed with addition of posthumous works, 1827; first 12 vols. of this edition, reissued in 2 vols., with Biographical Notice, 1834; "Works and Correspondence," 8 vols., 1852; Bohn's "British Classics," with Prior's Life, and two supplementary vols. of Speeches, 1853; Edition in progress (New Universal Library), 1905, etc.; with Introduction by Judge Willis (World's Classics), 1906, etc.

Boston Editions of Works: 7 vols., 1806–27; 9 vols., 1839 (includes "Account of European Settlements in America," and Correspondence with Dr. Laurence, not in earlier English editions); 12 vols., revised edition, 1865–7.

Speeches and Letters: Collection of Speeches, 1777; 4 vols., 1816; 1854 with Memoir.

Letters: ed. by Earl Fitzwilliam and Sir R. Bourke, 4 vols., 1844.

Letters and Speeches on Irish Affairs, ed. M. Arnold, 1881; Speeches on American Taxation, and Conciliation with America, etc., ed. F. G. Selby, 1895; ed. A. D. Innes (Pitt Press Series), 1906.

Life: Charles MacCormick, 1798; Robert Bisset, 1798, 1800; Sir James Prior, 1824, 2nd edition enlarged, 1826; revised in Bohn (see above); George Croly, 1840; MacKnight, "History of the Life and Times of Edmund Burke," 1858; Hon. J. Napier (Lecture), 1862; J. Morley, "Burke, a Historical Study," 1867; in "English Men of Letters," 1879; E. A. Pankhurst, "A Study of the Life and Character, etc.," 1886; W. Willis, "Edmund Burke, the Story of his Life" (Lecture), 1889; B. F. Brooke, "Edmund Burke, a Literary Essay," 1897; G. A. Chadwick, 1902; T. D. Pillans, 1905; A. P. I. Samuel, "The Early Life, Correspondence, and Writings of Edmund Burke," 1923.

CONTENTS

REFLECTIONS

ON

THE REVOLUTION IN FRANCE

AND

ON THE PROCEEDINGS IN CERTAIN SOCIETIES IN LONDON RELATIVE
TO THAT EVENT

IN A LETTER

INTENDED TO HAVE BEEN SENT TO A GENTLEMAN IN PARIS

1790

IT may not be unnecessary to inform the reader, that the following Reflections had their origin in a correspondence between the Author and a very young gentleman at Paris, who did him the honour of desiring his opinion upon the important transactions, which then, and ever since, have so much occupied the attention of all men. An answer was written some time in the month of October, 1789; but it was kept back upon prudential considerations. That letter is alluded to in the beginning of the following sheets. It has since been forwarded to the person to whom it was addressed. The reasons for the delay in sending it were assigned in a short letter to the same gentleman. This produced on his part a new and pressing application for the Author's sentiments.

The Author began a second and more full discussion on the subject. This he had some thoughts of publishing early in the last spring; but, the matter gaining upon him, he found that what he had undertaken not only far exceeded the measure of a letter, but that its importance required rather a more detailed consideration than at that time he had any leisure to bestow upon it. However, having thrown down his first thoughts in the form of a letter, and, indeed, when he sat down to write, having intended it for a private letter, he found it difficult to change the form of address, when his sentiments had grown into a greater extent, and had received another direction. A different plan, he is sensible, might be more favourable to a commodious division and distribution of his matter.

———————

DEAR SIR,

You are pleased to call again, and with some earnestness, for my thoughts on the late proceedings in France. I will not give you reason to imagine that I think my sentiments of such value as to wish myself to be solicited about them. They are of too little consequence to be very anxiously either communicated or withheld. It was from attention to you, and to you only, that I hesitated at the time when you first desired to receive them. In the first letter I had the honour to write to you, and which at length I send, I wrote neither for, nor from, any description of men; nor shall I in this. My errors, if any, are my own. My reputation alone is to answer for them.

You see, Sir, by the long letter I have transmitted to you, that though I do most heartily wish that France may be animated by a spirit of rational liberty, and that I think you bound, in all honest policy, to provide a permanent body in which that spirit may reside, and an effectual organ by which it may act, it is my misfortune to entertain great doubts concerning several material points in your late transactions.

You imagined, when you wrote last, that I might possibly be reckoned among the approvers of certain proceedings in France, from the solemn public seal of sanction they have received from two clubs of gentlemen in London, called the Constitutional Society, and the Revolution Society.

I certainly have the honour to belong to more clubs than one, in which the constitution of this kingdom, and the principles of the glorious Revolution, are held in high reverence, and I reckon myself among the most forward in my zeal for maintaining that constitution and those principles in their utmost purity and vigour. It is because I do so that I think it necessary for me that there should be no mistake. Those who cultivate the memory of our Revolution, and those who are attached to the constitution of this kingdom, will take good care how they are involved with persons, who under the pretext of zeal towards the Revolution and constitution too frequently wander from their true principles; and are ready on every occasion to depart from the firm but cautious and deliberate spirit which produced the one, and which presides in the other. Before I proceed to answer the more material particulars in your letter, I shall beg leave to give you such information as I have been able to obtain of the two clubs which have thought proper, as bodies, to interfere in the concerns of France; first assuring you, that I am not, and that I have never been, a member of either of those societies.

The first, calling itself the Constitutional Society, or Society for Constitutional Information, or by some such title, is, I believe, of seven or eight years' standing. The institution of this society appears to be of a charitable, and so far of a laudable nature: it was intended for the circulation, at the expense of the members, of many books, which few others would be at the expense of buying; and which might lie on the hands of the booksellers, to the great loss of a useful body of men. Whether the books, so charitably circulated, were ever as charitably read, is more than I know. Possibly several of them have been exported to France; and, like goods not in request here, may with you have found a market. I have heard much talk of the lights to be drawn from books that are sent from hence. What improvements they have had in their passage (as it is said some liquors are meliorated by crossing the sea) I cannot tell: but I never heard a man of common judgment, or the least degree of information, speak a word in praise of the greater part of the publications circulated by that society; nor have their proceedings been accounted, except by some of themselves, as of any serious consequence.

Your National Assembly seems to entertain much the same opinion that I do of this poor charitable club. As a nation, you reserved the whole stock of your eloquent acknowledgments for the Revolution Society; when their fellows in the Constitutional were, in equity, entitled to some share. Since you have selected the Revolution Society as the great object of your national thanks and praises, you will think me excusable in making its late conduct the subject of my observations. The National Assembly of France has given importance to these gentlemen by adopting them: and they return the favour, by acting as a committee in England for extending the principles of the National Assembly. Henceforward we must consider them as a kind of privileged persons; as no inconsiderable members in the diplomatic body. This is one among the revolutions which have given splendour to obscurity, and distinction to undiscerned merit. Until very lately I do not recollect to have heard of this club. I am quite sure that it never occupied a moment of my thoughts; nor, I believe, those of any person out of their own set. I find, upon inquiry, that on the anniversary of the Revolution in 1688, a club of dissenters, but of what denomination I know not, have long had the custom of hearing a sermon in one of their churches; and that afterwards they spent the day cheerfully, as other clubs do, at the tavern. But I never heard that any public measure, or political system, much less that the merits of the constitution of any foreign nation, had been the subject of a formal proceeding at their festivals; until, to my inexpressible surprise, I found them in a sort of public capacity, by a congratulatory address, giving an authoritative sanction to the proceedings of the National Assembly in France.

In the ancient principles and conduct of the club, so far at least as they were declared, I see nothing to which I could take exception. I think it very probable, that, for some purpose, new members may have entered among them; and that some truly Christian politicians, who love to dispense benefits, but are careful to conceal the hand which distributes the dole, may have made them the instruments of their pious designs. Whatever I may have reason to suspect concerning private management, I shall speak of nothing as of a certainty but what is public.

For one, I should be sorry to be thought, directly or indirectly, concerned in their proceedings. I certainly take my full share, along with the rest of the world, in my individual and private capacity, in speculating on what has been done, or is doing, on the public stage, in any place ancient or modern; in the republic of Rome, or the republic of Paris; but having no general apostolical mission, being a citizen of a particular state, and being bound up, in a considerable degree, by its public will, I should think it at least improper and irregular for me to open a formal public correspondence with the actual government of a foreign nation, without the express authority of the government under which I live.

I should be still more unwilling to enter into that correspondence under anything like an equivocal description, which to many, unacquainted with our usages, might make the address, in which I joined, appear as the act of persons in some sort of corporate capacity, acknowledged by the laws of this kingdom, and authorized to speak the sense of some part of it. On account of the ambiguity and uncertainty of unauthorized general descriptions, and of the deceit which may be practised under them, and not from mere formality, the House of Commons would reject the most sneaking petition for the most trifling object, under that mode of signature to which you have thrown open the folding doors of your presence chamber, and have ushered into your National Assembly with as much ceremony and parade, and with as great a bustle of applause, as if you had been visited by the whole representative majesty of the whole English nation. If what this society has thought proper to send forth had been a piece of argument, it would have signified little whose argument it was. It would be neither the more nor the less convincing on account of the party it came from. But this is only a vote and resolution. It stands solely on authority; and in this case it is the mere authority of individuals, few of whom appear. Their signatures ought, in my opinion, to have been annexed to their instrument. The world would then have the means of knowing how many they are; who they are; and of what value their opinions may be, from their personal abilities, from their knowledge, their experience, or their lead and authority in this state. To me, who am but a plain man, the proceeding looks a little too refined, and too ingenious; it has too much the air of a political stratagem, adopted for the sake of giving, under a high-sounding name, an importance to the public declarations of this club, which, when the matter came to be closely inspected, they did not altogether so well deserve. It is a policy that has very much the complexion of a fraud.

I flatter myself that I love a manly, moral, regulated liberty as well as any gentleman of that society, be he who he will; and perhaps I have given as good proofs of my attachment to that cause, in the whole course of my public conduct. I think I envy liberty as little as they do, to any other nation. But I cannot stand forward, and give praise or blame to anything which relates to human actions, and human concerns, on a simple view of the object, as it stands stripped of every relation, in all the nakedness and solitude of metaphysical abstraction. Circumstances (which with some gentlemen pass for nothing) give in reality to every political principle its distinguishing colour and discriminating effect. The circumstances are what render every civil and political scheme beneficial or noxious to mankind. Abstractedly speaking, government, as well as liberty, is good; yet could I, in common sense, ten years ago, have felicitated France on her enjoyment of a government (for she then had a government) without inquiry what the nature of that government was, or how it was administered? Can I now congratulate the same nation upon its freedom? Is it because liberty in the abstract may be classed amongst the blessings of mankind, that I am seriously to felicitate a madman, who has escaped from the protecting restraint and wholesome darkness of his cell, on his restoration to the enjoyment of light and liberty? Am I to congratulate a highwayman and murderer, who has broke prison, upon the recovery of his natural rights? This would be to act over again the scene of the criminals condemned to the galleys, and their heroic deliverer, the metaphysic knight of the sorrowful countenance.

When I see the spirit of liberty in action, I see a strong principle at work; and this, for a while, is all I can possibly know of it. The wild *gas*, the fixed air, is plainly broke loose: but we ought to suspend our judgment until the first effervescence is a little subsided, till the liquor is cleared, and until we see something deeper than the agitation of a troubled and frothy surface. I must be tolerably sure, before I venture publicly to congratulate men upon a blessing, that they have really received one. Flattery corrupts both the receiver and the giver; and adulation is not of more service to the people than to kings. I should therefore suspend my congratulations on the new liberty of France, until I was informed how it had been combined with government; with public force; with the discipline and obedience of armies; with the collection of an effective and well-distributed revenue; with morality and religion; with the solidity of property; with peace and order; with civil and social manners. All these (in their way) are good things too; and, without them, liberty is not a benefit whilst it lasts, and is not likely to continue long. The effect of liberty to individuals is, that they may do what they please: we ought to see what it will please them to do, before we risk congratulations, which may be soon turned into complaints. Prudence would dictate this in the case of separate, insulated, private men; but liberty, when men act in bodies, is *power*. Considerate people, before they declare themselves, will observe the use which is made of *power;* and particularly of so trying a thing as *new* power in *new* persons, of whose principles, tempers, and dispositions they have little or no experience, and in situations, where those who appear the most stirring in the scene may possibly not be the real movers.

All these considerations, however, were below the transcendental dignity of the Revolution Society. Whilst I continued in the country, from whence I had the honour of writing to you, I had but an imperfect idea of their transactions. On my coming to town, I sent for an account of their proceedings, which had been published by their authority, containing a sermon of Dr. Price, with the Duke de Rochefoucault's and the Archbishop of Aix's letter, and several other documents annexed. The whole of that publication, with the manifest design of connecting the affairs of France with those of England, by drawing us into an imitation of the conduct of the National Assembly, gave me a considerable degree of uneasiness. The effect of that conduct upon the power, credit, prosperity, and tranquillity of France, became every day more evident. The form of constitution to be settled, for its future polity, became more clear. We are now in a condition to discern, with tolerable exactness, the true nature of the object held up to our imitation. If the prudence of reserve and decorum dictates silence in some circumstances, in others prudence of a higher order may justify us in speaking our thoughts. The beginnings of confusion with us in England are at present feeble enough; but, with you, we have seen an infancy, still more feeble, growing by moments into a strength to heap mountains upon mountains, and to wage war with heaven itself. Whenever our neighbour's house is on fire, it cannot be amiss for the engines to play a little on our own. Better to be despised for too anxious apprehensions, than ruined by too confident a security.

Solicitous chiefly for the peace of my own country, but by no means unconcerned for yours, I wish to communicate more largely what was at first intended only for your private satisfaction. I shall still keep your affairs in my eye, and continue to address myself to you. Indulging myself in the freedom of epistolary intercourse, I beg leave to throw out my thoughts, and express my feelings, just as they arise in my mind, with very little attention to formal method. I set out with the proceedings of the Revolution Society; but I shall not confine myself to them. Is it possible I should? It appears to me as if I were in a great crisis, not of the affairs of France alone, but of all Europe, perhaps of more than Europe. All circumstances taken together, the French Revolution is the most astonishing that has hitherto happened in the world. The most wonderful things are brought about in many instances by means the most absurd and ridiculous; in the most ridiculous modes; and, apparently, by the most contemptible instruments. Everything seems out of nature in this strange chaos of levity and ferocity, and of all sorts of crimes jumbled together with all sorts of follies. In viewing this monstrous tragi-comic scene, the most opposite passions necessarily succeed, and sometimes mix with each other in the mind; alternate contempt and indignation; alternate laughter and tears; alternate scorn and horror.

It cannot, however, be denied, that to some this strange

scene appeared in quite another point of view. Into them it inspired no other sentiments than those of exultation and rapture. They saw nothing in what has been done in France, but a firm and temperate exertion of freedom : so consistent, on the whole, with morals and with piety as to make it deserving not only of the secular applause of dashing Machiavelian politicians, but to render it a fit theme for all the devout effusions of sacred eloquence.

On the forenoon of the 4th of November last, Doctor Richard Price, a non-conforming minister of eminence, preached at the dissenting meeting-house of the Old Jewry, to his club or society, a very extraordinary miscellaneous sermon, in which there are some good moral and religious sentiments, and not ill expressed, mixed up in a sort of porridge of various political opinions and reflections ; but the Revolution in France is the grand ingredient in the cauldron. I consider the address transmitted by the Revolution Society to the National Assembly, through Earl Stanhope, as originating in the principles of the sermon, and as a corollary from them. It was moved by the preacher of that discourse. It was passed by those who came reeking from the effect of the sermon, without any censure or qualification, expressed or implied. If, however, any of the gentlemen concerned shall wish to separate the sermon from the resolution, they know how to acknowledge the one, and to disavow the other. They may do it : I cannot.

For my part, I looked on that sermon as the public declaration of a man much connected with literary caballers, and intriguing philosophers ; with political theologians, and theological politicians, both at home and abroad. I know they set him up as a sort of oracle ; because, with the best intentions in the world, he naturally *philippizes*, and chants his prophetic song in exact unison with their designs.

That sermon is in a strain which I believe has not been heard in this kingdom, in any of the pulpits which are tolerated or encouraged in it, since the year 1648 ; when a predecessor of Dr. Price, the Rev. Hugh Peters, made the vault of the king's own chapel at St. James's ring with the honour and priviiege of the saints, who, with the "high praises of God in their mouths, and a *two*-edged sword in their hands, were to execute judgment on the heathen, and punishments upon the *people;* to bind their *kings* with chains, and their *nobles* with fetters of iron." [1]   Few harangues from the pulpit, except in the days of your league in France, or in the days of our Solemn League and Covenant in England, have ever breathed less of the spirit of moderation than this lecture in the Old Jewry.   Supposing, however, that something like moderation were visible in this political sermon; yet politics and the pulpit are terms that have little agreement.   No sound ought to be heard in the church but the healing voice of Christian charity.   The cause of civil liberty and civil government gains as little as that of religion by this confusion of duties.   Those who quit their proper character, to assume what does not belong to them, are, for the greater part, ignorant both of the character they leave, and of the character they assume.   Wholly unacquainted with the world in which they are so fond of meddling, and inexperienced in all its affairs, on which they pronounce with so much confidence, they have nothing of politics but the passions they excite.   Surely the church is a place where one day's truce ought to be allowed to the dissensions and animosities of mankind.

This pulpit style, revived after so long a discontinuance, had to me the air of novelty, and of a novelty not wholly without danger.   I do not charge this danger equally to every part of the discourse.   The hint given to a noble and reverend lay-divine, who is supposed high in office in one of our universities,[2] and other lay-divines "of *rank* and literature," may be proper and seasonable, though somewhat new.   If the noble *Seekers* should find nothing to satisfy their pious fancies in the old staple of the national church, or in all the rich variety to be found in the well-assorted warehouses of the dissenting congregations, Dr. Price advises them to improve upon nonconformity; and to set up, each of them, a separate meeting-house upon his own particular principles.[3]   It is some-

---

   [1] Psalm cxlix.
   [2] Discourse on the Love of our Country, Nov. 4th, 1789, by Dr. Richard Price, 3rd edition, pp. 17 and 18.
   [3] "Those who dislike that mode of worship which is prescribed by public authority, ought, if they can find *no* worship *out* of the church

what remarkable that this reverend divine should be so earnest for setting up new churches, and so perfectly indifferent concerning the doctrine which may be taught in them. His zeal is of a curious character. It is not for the propagation of his own opinions, but of any opinions. It is not for the diffusion of truth, but for the spreading of contradiction. Let the noble teachers but dissent, it is no matter from whom or from what. This great point once secured, it is taken for granted their religion will be rational and manly. I doubt whether religion would reap all the benefits which the calculating divine computes from this "great company of great preachers." It would certainly be a valuable addition of nondescripts to the ample collection of known classes, genera and species, which at present beautify the *hortus siccus* of dissent. A sermon from a noble duke, or a noble marquis, or a noble earl, or baron bold, would certainly increase and diversify the amusements of this town, which begins to grow satiated with the uniform round of its vapid dissipations. I should only stipulate that these new *Mess-Johns* in robes and coronets should keep some sort of bounds in the democratic and levelling principles which are expected from their titled pulpits. The new evangelists will, I dare say, disappoint the hopes that are conceived of them. They will not become, literally as well as figuratively, polemic divines, nor be disposed so to drill their congregations, that they may, as in former blessed times, preach their doctrines to regiments of dragoons and corps of infantry and artillery. Such arrangements, however favourable to the cause of compulsory freedom, civil and religious, may not be equally conducive to the national tranquillity. These few restrictions I hope are no great stretches of intolerance, no very violent exertions of despotism.

But I may say of our preacher, "*utinam nugis tota illa dedisset tempora sævitiæ.*"—All things in this his fulminating bull are not of so innoxious a tendency. His doctrines affect our constitution in its vital parts. He tells the

---

which they approve, *to set up a separate worship for themselves;* and by doing this, and giving an example of a rational and manly worship, men of *weight* from their *rank* and literature may do the greatest service to society and the world."—P. 18, Dr. Price's Sermon.

Revolution Society in this political sermon, that his Majesty "is almost the *only* lawful king in the world, because the *only* one who owes his crown to the *choice of his people*." As to the kings of *the world*, all of whom (except one) this archpontiff of the *rights of men*, with all the plenitude, and with more than the boldness, of the papal deposing power in its meridian fervour of the twelfth century, puts into one sweeping clause of ban and anathema, and proclaims usurpers by circles of longitude and latitude, over the whole globe, it behoves them to consider how they admit into their territories these apostolic missionaries, who are to tell their subjects they are not lawful kings. That is their concern. It is ours, as a domestic interest of some moment, seriously to consider the solidity of the *only* principle upon which these gentlemen acknowledge a king of Great Britain to be entitled to their allegiance.

This doctrine, as applied to the prince now on the British throne, either is nonsense, and therefore neither true nor false, or it affirms a most unfounded, dangerous, illegal, and unconstitutional position. According to this spiritual doctor of politics, if his Majesty does not owe his crown to the choice of his people, he is no *lawful king*. Now nothing can be more untrue than that the crown of this kingdom is so held by his Majesty. Therefore if you follow their rule, the king of Great Britain, who most certainly does not owe his high office to any form of popular election, is in no respect better than the rest of the gang of usurpers, who reign, or rather rob, all over the face of this our miserable world, without any sort of right or title to the allegiance of their people. The policy of this general doctrine, so qualified, is evident enough. The propagators of this political gospel are in hopes that their abstract principle (their principle that a popular choice is necessary to the legal existence of the sovereign magistracy) would be overlooked, whilst the king of Great Britain was not affected by it. In the mean time the ears of their congregations would be gradually habituated to it, as if it were a first principle admitted without dispute. For the present it would only operate as a theory, pickled in the preserving juices of pulpit eloquence, and laid by for future use. *Condo et compono quæ mox depromere possim.* By this policy, whilst our government is soothed with a reservation in its favour, to which it has no claim, the security, which it has in common with all governments, so far as opinion is security, is taken away.

Thus these politicians proceed, whilst little notice is taken of their doctrines; but when they come to be examined upon the plain meaning of their words, and the direct tendency of their doctrines, then equivocations and slippery constructions come into play. When they say the king owes his crown to the choice of his people, and is therefore the only lawful sovereign in the world, they will perhaps tell us they mean to say no more than that some of the king's predecessors have been called to the throne by some sort of choice; and therefore he owes his crown to the choice of his people. Thus, by a miserable subterfuge, they hope to render their proposition safe, by rendering it nugatory. They are welcome to the asylum they seek for their offence, since they take refuge in their folly. For, if you admit this interpretation, how does their idea of election differ from our idea of inheritance? And how does the settlement of the crown in the Brunswick line derived from James the First come to legalize our monarchy, rather than that of any of the neighbouring countries? At some time or other, to be sure, all the beginners of dynasties were chosen by those who called them to govern. There is ground enough for the opinion that all the kingdoms of Europe were, at a remote period, elective, with more or fewer limitations in the objects of choice. But whatever kings might have been here, or elsewhere, a thousand years ago, or in whatever manner the ruling dynasties of England or France may have begun, the king of Great Britain is, at this day, king by a fixed rule of succession, according to the laws of his country; and whilst the legal conditions of the compact of sovereignty are performed by him (as they are performed), he holds his crown in contempt of the choice of the Revolution Society, who have not a single vote for a king amongst them, either individually or collectively; though I make no doubt they would soon erect themselves into an electoral college, if things were ripe to give effect to their claim. His Majesty's heirs and successors, each in his time and order, will come to the crown with the same contempt of their choice with which his Majesty has succeeded to that he wears.

Whatever may be the success of evasion in explaining away the gross error of *fact*, which supposes that his Majesty (though he holds it in concurrence with the wishes) owes his crown to the choice of his people, yet nothing can evade their full explicit declaration, concerning the principle of a right in the people to choose; which right is directly maintained, and tenaciously adhered to. All the oblique insinuations concerning election bottom in this proposition, and are referable to it. Lest the foundation of the king's exclusive legal title should pass for a mere rant of adulatory freedom, the political divine proceeds dogmatically to assert,[1] that, by the principles of the Revolution, the people of England have acquired three fundamental rights, all which, with him, compose one system, and lie together in one short sentence; namely, that we have acquired a right,

1. "To choose our own governors."
2. "To cashier them for misconduct."
3. "To frame a government for ourselves."

This new, and hitherto unheard-of, bill of rights, though made in the name of the whole people, belongs to those gentlemen and their faction only. The body of the people of England have no share in it. They utterly disclaim it. They will resist the practical assertion of it with their lives and fortunes. They are bound to do so by the laws of their country, made at the time of that very Revolution which is appealed to in favour of the fictitious rights claimed by the society which abuses its name.

These gentlemen of the Old Jewry, in all their reasonings on the Revolution of 1688, have a Revolution which happened in England about forty years before, and the late French Revolution, so much before their eyes, and in their hearts, that they are constantly confounding all the three together. It is necessary that we should separate what they confound. We must recall their erring fancies to the *acts* of the Revolution which we revere, for the discovery of its true *principles*. If the *principles* of the Revolution of 1688 are anywhere to be found, it is in the statute called the *Declaration of Right*. In that most wise, sober, and

[1] P. 34, Discourse on the Love of our Country, by Dr. Price.

considerate declaration, drawn up by great lawyers and great statesmen, and not by warm and inexperienced enthusiasts, not one word is said, nor one suggestion made, of a general right "to choose our own *governors;* to cashier them for misconduct; and to *form* a government for *ourselves*."

This Declaration of Right (the act of the 1st of William and Mary, sess. 2, ch. 2) is the corner-stone of our constitution, as reinforced, explained, improved, and in its fundamental principles for ever settled. It is called "An Act for declaring the rights and liberties of the subject, and for *settling* the *succession* of the crown." You will observe, that these rights and this succession are declared in one body, and bound indissolubly together.

A few years after this period, a second opportunity offered for asserting a right of election to the crown. On the prospect of a total failure of issue from King William, and from the Princess, afterwards Queen Anne, the consideration of the settlement of the crown, and of a further security for the liberties of the people, again came before the legislature. Did they this second time make any provision for legalizing the crown on the spurious revolution principles of the Old Jewry? No. They followed the principles which prevailed in the Declaration of Right; indicating with more precision the persons who were to inherit in the Protestant line. This act also incorporated, by the same policy, our liberties, and an hereditary succession in the same act. Instead of a right to choose our own governors, they declared that the *succession* in that line (the Protestant line drawn from James the First) was absolutely necessary "for the peace, quiet, and security of the realm," and that it was equally urgent on them "to maintain a *certainty in the succession* thereof, to which the subjects may safely have recourse for their protection." Both these acts, in which are heard the unerring, unambiguous oracles of revolution policy, instead of countenancing the delusive, gipsy predictions of a "right to choose our governors," prove to a demonstration how totally adverse the wisdom of the nation was from turning a case of necessity into a rule of law.

Unquestionably there was at the Revolution, in the person of King William, a small and a temporary deviation

from the strict order of a regular hereditary succession;
but it is against all genuine principles of jurisprudence to
draw a principle from a law made in a special case, and
regarding an individual person. *Privilegium non transit
in exemplum.* If ever there was a time favourable for
establishing the principle, that a king of popular choice
was the only legal king, without all doubt it was at the
Revolution. Its not being done at that time is a proof that
the nation was of opinion it ought not to be done at any
time. There is no person so completely ignorant of our
history as not to know, that the majority in parliament of
both parties were so little disposed to anything resembling
that principle, that at first they were determined to place
the vacant crown, not on the head of the Prince of Orange,
but on that of his wife Mary, daughter of King James,
the eldest born of the issue of that king, which they
acknowledged as undoubtedly his. It would be to repeat a
very trite story, to recall to your memory all those circumstances which demonstrated that their accepting King
William was not properly a *choice;* but to all those who
did not wish, in effect, to recall King James, or to deluge
their country in blood, and again to bring their religion,
laws, and liberties into the peril they had just escaped, it
was an act of *necessity,* in the strictest moral sense in
which necessity can be taken.

In the very act, in which for a time, and in a single case,
parliament departed from the strict order of inheritance,
in favour of a prince, who, though not next, was however
very near, in the line of succession, it is curious to observe
how Lord Somers, who drew the bill called the Declaration
of Right, has comported himself on that delicate occasion.
It is curious to observe with what address this temporary
solution of continuity is kept from the eye; whilst all that
could be found in this act of necessity to countenance the
idea of an hereditary succession is brought forward, and
fostered, and made the most of, by this great man, and
by the legislature who followed him. Quitting the dry,
imperative style of an act of parliament, he makes the
Lords and Commons fall to a pious, legislative ejaculation,
and declare, that they consider it "as a marvellous providence, and merciful goodness of God to this nation, to
preserve their said Majesties' *royal* persons, most happily

to reign over us *on the throne of their ancestors*, for which, from the bottom of their hearts, they return their humblest thanks and praises."—The legislature plainly had in view the act of recognition of the first Queen Elizabeth, chap. 3rd, and of that of James the First, chap. 1st, both acts strongly declaratory of the inheritable nature of the crown, and in many parts they follow, with a nearly literal precision, the words and even the form of thanksgiving which is found in these old declaratory statutes.

The two houses, in the act of King William, did not thank God that they had found a fair opportunity to assert a right to choose their own governors, much less to make an election the *only lawful* title to the crown. Their having been in a condition to avoid the very appearance of it, as much as possible, was by them considered as a providential escape. They threw a politic, well-wrought veil over every circumstance tending to weaken the rights, which in the meliorated order of succession they meant to perpetuate; or which might furnish a precedent for any future departure from what they had then settled for ever. Accordingly, that they might not relax the nerves of their monarchy, and that they might preserve a close conformity to the practice of their ancestors, as it appeared in the declaratory statutes of Queen Mary [1] and Queen Elizabeth, in the next clause they vest, by recognition, in their Majesties, *all* the legal prerogatives of the crown, declaring, "that in them they are most *fully*, rightfully, and *entirely* invested, incorporated, united, and annexed." In the clause which follows, for preventing questions, by reason of any pretended titles to the crown, they declare (observing also in this the traditionary language, along with the traditionary policy of the nation, and repeating as from a rubric the language of the preceding acts of Elizabeth and James), that on the preserving "a *certainty* in the succession thereof, the unity, peace, and tranquillity of this nation doth, under God, wholly depend."

They knew that a doubtful title of succession would but too much resemble an election; and that an election would be utterly destructive of the "unity, peace, and tranquillity of this nation," which they thought to be considerations of some moment. To provide for these objects, and therefore

---

[1] 1st Mary, sess. 3, ch. 1.

to exclude for ever the Old Jewry doctrine of "a right to choose our own governors," they follow with a clause containing a most solemn pledge, taken from the preceding act of Queen Elizabeth, as solemn a pledge as ever was or can be given in favour of an hereditary succession, and as solemn a renunciation as could be made of the principles by this society imputed to them. "The Lords spiritual and temporal, and Commons, do, in the name of all the people aforesaid, most humbly and faithfully submit *themselves, their heirs and posterities for ever;* and do faithfully promise that they will stand to, maintain, and defend their said Majesties, and also the *limitation of the crown*, herein specified and contained, to the utmost of their powers," etc., etc.

So far is it from being true, that we acquired a right by the Revolution to elect our kings, that if we had possessed it before, the English nation did at that time most solemnly renounce and abdicate it, for themselves, and for all their posterity for ever. These gentlemen may value themselves as much as they please on their Whig principles; but I never desire to be thought a better Whig than Lord Somers; or to understand the principles of the Revolution better than those by whom it was brought about; or to read in the Declaration of Right any mysteries unknown to those whose penetrating style has engraved in our ordinances, and in our hearts, the words and spirit of that immortal law.

It is true, that, aided with the powers derived from force and opportunity, the nation was at that time, in some sense, free to take what course it pleased for filling the throne; but only free to do so upon the same grounds on which they might have wholly abolished their monarchy, and every other part of their constitution. However, they did not think such bold changes within their commission. It is indeed difficult, perhaps impossible, to give limits to the mere *abstract* competence of the supreme power, such as was exercised by parliament at that time; but the limits of a *moral* competence, subjecting, even in powers more indisputably sovereign, occasional will to permanent reason, and to the steady maxims of faith, justice, and fixed fundamental policy, are perfectly intelligible, and perfectly binding upon those who exercise any authority, under any name, or under any title, in the state. The House of Lords, for instance, is not morally competent to dissolve the House of Commons; no, nor even to dissolve itself, nor to abdicate, if it would, its portion in the legislature of the kingdom. Though a king may abdicate for his own person, he cannot abdicate for the monarchy. By as strong, or by a stronger reason, the House of Commons cannot renounce its share of authority. The engagement and pact of society, which generally goes by the name of the constitution, forbids such invasion and such surrender. The constituent parts of a state are obliged to hold their public faith with each other, and with all those who derive any serious interest under their engagements, as much as the whole state is bound to keep its faith with separate communities. Otherwise competence and power would soon be confounded, and no law be left but the will of a prevailing force. On this principle the succession of the crown has always been what it now is, an hereditary succession by law: in the old line it was a succession by the common law; in the new by the statute law, operating on the principles of the common law, not changing the substance, but regulating the mode, and describing the persons. Both these descriptions of law are of the same force, and are derived from an equal authority, emanating from the common agreement and original compact of the state, *communi sponsione reipublicæ*, and as such are equally binding on king and people too, as long as the terms are observed, and they continue the same body politic.

It is far from impossible to reconcile, if we do not suffer ourselves to be entangled in the mazes of metaphysic sophistry, the use both of a fixed rule and an occasional deviation; the sacredness of an hereditary principle of succession in our government, with a power of change in its application in cases of extreme emergency. Even in that extremity (if we take the measure of our rights by our exercise of them at the Revolution), the change is to be confined to the peccant part only; to the part which produced the necessary deviation; and even then it is to be effected without a decomposition of the whole civil and political mass, for the purpose of originating a new civil order out of the first elements of society.

A state without the means of some change is without

the means of its conservation. Without such means it might even risk the loss of that part of the constitution which it wished the most religiously to preserve. The two principles of conservation and correction operated strongly at the two critical periods of the Restoration and Revolution, when England found itself without a king. At both those periods the nation had lost the bond of union in their ancient edifice; they did not, however, dissolve the whole fabric. On the contrary, in both cases they regenerated the deficient part of the old constitution through the parts which were not impaired. They kept these old parts exactly as they were, that the part recovered might be suited to them. They acted by the ancient organized states in the shape of their old organization, and not by the organic *moleculæ* of a disbanded people. At no time, perhaps, did the sovereign legislature manifest a more tender regard to that fundamental principle of British constitutional policy, than at the time of the Revolution, when it deviated from the direct line of hereditary succession. The crown was carried somewhat out of the line in which it had before moved; but the new line was derived from the same stock. It was still a line of hereditary descent; still an hereditary descent in the same blood, though an hereditary descent qualified with Protestantism. When the legislature altered the direction, but kept the principle, they showed that they held it inviolable.

On this principle, the law of inheritance had admitted some amendment in the old time, and long before the era of the Revolution. Some time after the conquest great questions arose upon the legal principles of hereditary descent. It became a matter of doubt, whether the heir *per capita* or the heir *per stirpes* was to succeed; but whether the heir *per capita* gave way when the heirdom *per stirpes* took place, or the Catholic heir when the Protestant was preferred, the inheritable principle survived with a sort of immortality through all transmigrations— *multosque per annos stat fortuna domus, et avi numerantur avorum.* This is the spirit of our constitution, not only in its settled course, but in all its revolutions. Whoever came in, or however he came in, whether he obtained the crown by law, or by force, the hereditary succession was either continued or adopted.

The gentlemen of the Society for Revolutions see nothing in that of 1688 but the deviation from the constitution; and they take the deviation from the principle for the principle. They have little regard to the obvious consequences of their doctrine, though they must see, that it leaves positive authority in very few of the positive institutions of this country. When such an unwarrantable maxim is once established, that no throne is lawful but the elective, no one act of the princes who preceded this era of fictitious election can be valid. Do these theorists mean to imitate some of their predecessors, who dragged the bodies of our ancient sovereigns out of the quiet of their tombs? Do they mean to attaint and disable backwards all the kings that have reigned before the Revolution, and consequently to stain the throne of England with the blot of a continual usurpation? Do they mean to invalidate, annul, or to call into question, together with the titles of the whole line of our kings, that great body of our statute law which passed under those whom they treat as usurpers? to annul laws of inestimable value to our liberties—of as great value at least as any which have passed at or since the period of the Revolution? If kings, who did not owe their crown to the choice of their people, had no title to make laws, what will become of the statute *de tallagio non concedendo?*—of the *Petition of Right?*—of the act of *habeas corpus?* Do these new doctors of the rights of men presume to assert, that King James the Second, who came to the crown as next of blood, according to the rules of a then unqualified succession, was not to all intents and purposes a lawful king of England, before he had done any of those acts which were justly construed into an abdication of his crown? If he was not, much trouble in parliament might have been saved at the period these gentlemen commemorate. But King James was a bad king with a good title, and not an usurper. The princes who succeeded according to the act of parliament which settled the crown on the Electress Sophia and on her descendants, being Protestants, came in as much by a title of inheritance as King James did. He came in according to the law, as it stood at his accession to the crown; and the princes of the House of Brunswick came to the inheritance of the crown, not by election, but by the law, as it stood at their several accessions of Protestant descent and inheritance, as I hope I have shown sufficiently.

The law, by which this royal family is specifically destined to the succession, is the act of the 12th and 13th of King William. The terms of this act bind "us and our *heirs*, and our *posterity*, to them, their *heirs*, and their *posterity*," being Protestants, to the end of time, in the same words as the Declaration of Right had bound us to the heirs of King William and Queen Mary. It therefore secures both an hereditary crown and an hereditary allegiance. On what ground, except the constitutional policy of forming an establishment to secure that kind of succession which is to preclude a choice of the people for ever, could the legislature have fastidiously rejected the fair and abundant choice which our country presented to them, and searched in strange lands for a foreign princess, from whose womb the line of our future rulers were to derive their title to govern millions of men through a series of ages?

The Princess Sophia was named in the Act of Settlement of the 12th and 13th of King William, for a *stock* and root of *inheritance* to our kings, and not for her merits as a temporary administratrix of a power, which she might not, and in fact did not, herself ever exercise. She was adopted for one reason, and for one only, because, says the act, "the most excellent Princess Sophia, Electress and Duchess Dowager of Hanover, is *daughter* of the most excellent Princess Elizabeth, late Queen of Bohemia, *daughter* of our late *sovereign lord* King James the First, of happy memory, and is hereby declared to be the next in *succession* in the Protestant line," etc., etc.; "and the crown shall continue to the *heirs* of her body, being Protestants." This limitation was made by parliament, that through the Princess Sophia an inheritable line not only was to be continued in future, but (what they thought very material) that through her it was to be connected with the old stock of inheritance in King James the First; in order that the monarchy might preserve an unbroken unity through all ages, and might be preserved (with safety to our religion) in the old approved mode by descent, in which, if our liberties had been once endangered, they had often, through all storms and struggles of prerogative and privilege, been preserved. They did well. No experience has taught us, that in any other course or method than that of an *hereditary crown* our liberties can be regularly perpetuated and preserved sacred as our *hereditary right*. An irregular, convulsive movement may be necessary to throw off an irregular, convulsive disease. But the course of succession is the healthy habit of the British constitution. Was it that the legislature wanted, at the act for the limitation of the crown in the Hanoverian line, drawn through the female descendants of James the First, a due sense of the inconveniences of having two or three, or possibly more, foreigners in succession to the British throne? No!—they had a due sense of the evils which might happen from such foreign rule, and more than a due sense of them. But a more decisive proof cannot be given of the full conviction of the British nation, that the principles of the Revolution did not authorize them to elect kings at their pleasure, and without any attention to the ancient fundamental principles of our government, than their continuing to adopt a plan of hereditary Protestant succession in the old line, with all the dangers and all the inconveniences of its being a foreign line full before their eyes, and operating with the utmost force upon their minds.

A few years ago I should be ashamed to overload a matter, so capable of supporting itself, by the then unnecessary support of any argument; but this seditious, unconstitutional doctrine is now publicly taught, avowed, and printed. The dislike I feel to revolutions, the signals for which have so often been given from pulpits; the spirit of change that is gone abroad; the total contempt which prevails with you, and may come to prevail with us, of all ancient institutions, when set in opposition to a present sense of convenience, or to the bent of a present inclination : all these considerations make it not unadvisable, in my opinion, to call back our attention to the true principles of our own domestic laws; that you, my French friend, should begin to know, and that we should continue to cherish them. We ought not, on either side of the water, to suffer ourselves to be imposed upon by the counterfeit wares which some persons, by a double fraud, export to you in illicit bottoms, as raw commodities of British growth, though wholly alien to our soil, in order afterwards to smuggle them back again into this country, manufactured after the newest Paris fashion of an improved liberty.

The people of England will not ape the fashions they have never tried, nor go back to those which they have found mischievous on trial. They look upon the legal hereditary succession of their crown as among their rights, not as among their wrongs; as a benefit, not as a grievance; as a security for their liberty, not as a badge of servitude. They look on the frame of their commonwealth, *such as it stands*, to be of inestimable value; and they conceive the undisturbed succession of the crown to be a pledge of the stability and perpetuity of all the other members of our constitution.

I shall beg leave, before I go any further, to take notice of some paltry artifices, which the abettors of election, as the only lawful title to the crown, are ready to employ, in order to render the support of the just principles of our constitution a task somewhat invidious. These sophisters substitute a fictitious cause, and feigned personages, in whose favour they suppose you engaged, whenever you defend the inheritable nature of the crown. It is common with them to dispute as if they were in a conflict with some of those exploded fanatics of slavery, who formerly maintained, what I believe no creature now maintains, "that the crown is held by divine, hereditary and indefeasible right."—These old fanatics of single arbitrary power dogmatized as if hereditary royalty was the only lawful government in the world, just as our new fanatics of popular arbitrary power maintain that a popular election is the sole lawful source of authority. The old prerogative enthusiasts, it is true, did speculate foolishly, and perhaps impiously too, as if monarchy had more of a divine sanction than any other mode of government; and as if a right to govern by inheritance were in strictness *indefeasible* in every person, who should be found in the succession to a throne, and under every circumstance, which no civil or political right can be. But an absurd opinion concerning the king's hereditary right to the crown does not prejudice one that is rational, and bottomed upon solid principles of law and policy. If all the absurd theories of lawyers and divines were to vitiate the objects in which they are conversant, we should have no law and no religion left in the world. But an absurd theory on one side of a question forms no justification for alleging a false fact, or promulgating mischievous maxims, on the other.

The second claim of the Revolution Society is "a right of cashiering their governors for *misconduct.*" Perhaps the apprehensions our ancestors entertained of forming such a precedent as that "of cashiering for misconduct," was the cause that the declaration of the act, which implied the abdication of King James, was, if it had any fault, rather too guarded, and too circumstantial.[1] But all this guard, and all this accumulation of circumstances, serves to show the spirit of caution which predominated in the national councils in a situation in which men irritated by oppression, and elevated by a triumph over it, are apt to abandon themselves to violent and extreme courses : it shows the anxiety of the great men who influenced the conduct of affairs at that great event to make the Revolution a parent of settlement, and not a nursery of future revolutions.

No government could stand a moment, if it could be blown down with anything so loose and indefinite as an opinion of "*misconduct.*" They who led at the Revolution grounded the virtual abdication of King James upon no such light and uncertain principle. They charged him with nothing less than a design, confirmed by a multitude of illegal overt acts, to *subvert the Protestant church and state,* and their *fundamental,* unquestionable laws and liberties : they charged him with having broken the *original contract* between king and people. This was more than *misconduct.* A grave and overruling necessity obliged them to take the step they took, and took with infinite reluctance, as under that most rigorous of all laws. Their trust for the future preservation of the constitution was not in future revolutions. The grand policy of all their regulations was to render it almost impracticable for any

---

1 "That King James the Second, having endeavoured to *subvert the constitution* of the kingdom by breaking the *original contract* between king and people, and, by the advice of Jesuits, and other wicked persons, having violated the *fundamental* laws, and *having withdrawn himself out of the kingdom,* hath *abdicated* the government, and the throne is thereby *vacant.*"

*B 460

future sovereign to compel the states of the kingdom to have again recourse to those violent remedies. They left the crown what, in the eye and estimation of law, it had ever been, perfectly irresponsible. In order to lighten the crown still further, they aggravated responsibility on ministers of state. By the statute of the 1st of King William, sess. 2nd, called "*the act for declaring the rights and liberties of the subject, and for settling the succession to the crown,*" they enacted, that the ministers should serve the crown on the terms of that declaration. They secured soon after the *frequent meetings of parliament*, by which the whole government would be under the constant inspection and active control of the popular representative and of the magnates of the kingdom. In the next great constitutional act, that of the 12th and 13th of King William, for the further limitation of the crown, and *better* securing the rights and liberties of the subject, they provided, "that no pardon under the great seal of England should be pleadable to an impeachment by the Commons in parliament." The rule laid down for government in the Declaration of Right, the constant inspection of parliament, the practical claim of impeachment, they thought infinitely a better security not only for their constitutional liberty, but against the vices of administration, than the reservation of a right so difficult in the practice, so uncertain in the issue, and often so mischievous in the consequences, as that of "cashiering their governors."

Dr. Price, in his sermon,[1] condemns very properly the practice of gross, adulatory addresses to kings. Instead of this fulsome style, he proposes that his Majesty should be told, on occasions of congratulation, that "he is to consider himself as more properly the servant than the sovereign of his people." For a compliment, this new form of address does not seem to be very soothing. Those who are servants in name, as well as in effect, do not like to be told of their situation, their duty, and their obligations. The slave, in the old play, tells his master, "*Hæc commemoratio est quasi exprobratio.*" It is not pleasant as compliment; it is not wholesome as instruction. After all, if the king were to bring himself to echo this new kind of address, to adopt it in terms, and even to take the

[1] Pp. 22–24.

appellation of Servant of the People as his royal style, how either he or we should be much mended by it, I cannot imagine. I have seen very assuming letters, signed, Your most obedient, humble servant. The proudest denomination that ever was endured on earth took a title of still greater humility than that which is now proposed for sovereigns by the Apostle of Liberty. Kings and nations were trampled upon by the foot of one calling himself "the Servant of Servants"; and mandates for deposing sovereigns were sealed with the signet of "the Fisherman."

I should have considered all this as no more than a sort of flippant, vain discourse, in which, as in an unsavoury fume, several persons suffer the spirit of liberty to evaporate, if it were not plainly in support of the idea, and a part of the scheme, of "cashiering kings for misconduct." In that light it is worth some observation.

Kings, in one sense, are undoubtedly the servants of the people, because their power has no other rational end than that of the general advantage; but it is not true that they are, in the ordinary sense, (by our constitution at least,) anything like servants; the essence of whose situation is to obey the commands of some other, and to be removable at pleasure. But the king of Great Britain obeys no other person; all other persons are individually, and collectively too, under him, and owe to him a legal obedience. The law, which knows neither to flatter nor to insult, calls this high magistrate, not our servant, as this humble divine calls him, but "*our sovereign Lord the king*"; and we, on our parts, have learned to speak only the primitive language of the law, and not the confused jargon of their Babylonian pulpits.

As he is not to obey us, but as we are to obey the law in him, our constitution has made no sort of provision towards rendering him, as a servant, in any degree responsible. Our constitution knows nothing of a magistrate like the *Justicia* of Arragon; nor of any court legally appointed, nor of any process legally settled, for submitting the king to the responsibility belonging to all servants. In this he is not distinguished from the Commons and the Lords; who, in their several public capacities, can never be called to an account for their conduct; although the Revolution Society chooses to assert, in direct opposition to one of the wisest and most beautiful parts of our constitution, that "a king is no more than the first servant of the public, created by it, *and responsible to it.*"

Ill would our ancestors at the Revolution have deserved their fame for wisdom, if they had found no security for their freedom, but in rendering their government feeble in its operations and precarious in its tenure; if they had been able to contrive no better remedy against arbitrary power than civil confusion. Let these gentlemen state who that *representative* public is to whom they will affirm the king, as a servant, to be responsible. It will be then time enough for me to produce to them the positive statute law which affirms that he is not.

The ceremony of cashiering kings, of which these gentlemen talk so much at their ease, can rarely, if ever, be performed without force. It then becomes a case of war, and not of constitution. Laws are commanded to hold their tongues amongst arms; and tribunals fall to the ground with the peace they are no longer able to uphold. The Revolution of 1688 was obtained by a just war, in the only case in which any war, and much more a civil war, can be just. "Justa bella quibus *necessaria.*" The question of dethroning, or, if these gentlemen like the phrase better, "cashiering kings," will always be, as it has always been, an extraordinary question of state, and wholly out of the law; a question (like all other questions of state) of dispositions, and of means, and of probable consequences, rather than of positive rights. As it was not made for common abuses, so it is not to be agitated by common minds. The speculative line of demarcation, where obedience ought to end, and resistance must begin, is faint, obscure, and not easily definable. It is not a single act, or a single event, which determines it. Governments must be abused and deranged indeed, before it can be thought of; and the prospect of the future must be as bad as the experience of the past. When things are in that lamentable condition, the nature of the disease is to indicate the remedy to those whom nature has qualified to administer in extremities this critical, ambiguous, bitter potion to a distempered state. Times, and occasions, and provocations will teach their own lessons. The wise will determine from the gravity of the case; the irritable, from sensibility to oppression; the high-minded, from disdain and indignation at abusive power in unworthy hands; the brave and bold, from the love of honourable danger in a generous cause: but, with or without right, a revolution will be the very last resource of the thinking and the good.

The third head of right, asserted by the pulpit of the Old Jewry, namely, the "right to form a government for ourselves," has, at least, as little countenance from anything done at the Revolution, either in precedent or principle, as the two first of their claims. The Revolution was made to preserve our *ancient* indisputable laws and liberties, and that *ancient* constitution of government which is our only security for law and liberty. If you are desirous of knowing the spirit of our constitution, and the policy which predominated in that great period which has secured it to this hour, pray look for both in our histories, in our records, in our acts of parliament, and journals of parliament, and not in the sermons of the Old Jewry, and the after-dinner toasts of the Revolution Society. In the former you will find other ideas and another language. Such a claim is as ill-suited to our temper and wishes as it is unsupported by any appearance of authority. The very idea of the fabrication of a new government is enough to fill us with disgust and horror. We wished at the period of the Revolution, and do now wish, to derive all we possess as *an inheritance from our forefathers*. Upon that body and stock of inheritance we have taken care not to inoculate any scion alien to the nature of the original plant. All the reformations we have hitherto made have proceeded upon the principle of reverence to antiquity; and I hope, nay I am persuaded, that all those which possibly may be made hereafter, will be carefully formed upon analogical precedent, authority, and example.

Our oldest reformation is that of Magna Charta. You will see that Sir Edward Coke, that great oracle of our law, and indeed all the great men who follow him, to Blackstone,[1] are industrious to prove the pedigree of our liberties. They endeavour to prove, that the ancient charter, the Magna Charta of King John, was connected with another positive charter from Henry I., and that both the one and the other were nothing more than a reaffirmance

[1] See Blackstone's Magna Charta, printed at Oxford, 1759.

of the still more ancient standing law of the kingdom. In the matter of fact, for the greater part, these authors appear to be in the right; perhaps not always; but if the lawyers mistake in some particulars, it proves my position still the more strongly; because it demonstrates the powerful prepossession towards antiquity, with which the minds of all our lawyers and legislators, and of all the people whom they wish to influence, have been always filled; and the stationary policy of this kingdom in considering their most sacred rights and franchises as an *inheritance*.

In the famous law of the 3rd of Charles I., called the *Petition of Right*, the parliament says to the king, "Your subjects have *inherited* this freedom," claiming their franchises not on abstract principles "as the rights of men," but as the rights of Englishmen, and as a patrimony derived from their forefathers. Selden, and the other profoundly learned men, who drew this Petition of Right, were as well acquainted, at least, with all the general theories concerning the "rights of men," as any of the discoursers in our pulpits, or on your tribune; full as well as Dr. Price, or as the Abbé Sieyes. But, for reasons worthy of that practical wisdom which superseded their theoretic science, they preferred this positive, recorded, *hereditary* title to all which can be dear to the man and the citizen, to that vague speculative right, which exposed their sure inheritance to be scrambled for and torn to pieces by every wild, litigious spirit.

The same policy pervades all the laws which have since been made for the preservation of our liberties. In the 1st of William and Mary, in the famous statute, called the Declaration of Right, the two Houses utter not a syllable of "a right to frame a government for themselves." You will see, that their whole care was to secure the religion, laws, and liberties, that had been long possessed, and had been lately endangered. "Taking [1] into their most serious consideration the *best* means for making such an establishment, that their religion, laws, and liberties might not be in danger of being again subverted," they auspicate all their proceedings, by stating as some of those *best* means, "in the *first place*" to do "as their *ancestors in like cases have usually* done for vindicating their *ancient* rights and

[1] 1 W. and M.

liberties, to *declare*" ;—and then they pray the king and queen, "that it may be *declared* and enacted, that *all and singular* the rights and liberties *asserted and declared*, are the true *ancient* and indubitable rights and liberties of the people of this kingdom."

You will observe, that from Magna Charta to the Declaration of Right, it has been the uniform policy of our constitution to claim and assert our liberties, as an *entailed inheritance* derived to us from our forefathers, and to be transmitted to our posterity; as an estate specially belonging to the people of this kingdom, without any reference whatever to any other more general or prior right. By this means our constitution preserves a unity in so great a diversity of its parts. We have an inheritable crown; an inheritable peerage; and a House of Commons and a people inheriting privileges, franchises, and liberties, from a long line of ancestors.

This policy appears to me to be the result of profound reflection; or rather the happy effect of following nature, which is wisdom without reflection, and above it. A spirit of innovation is generally the result of a selfish temper and confined views. People will not look forward to posterity, who never look backward to their ancestors. Besides, the people of England well know, that the idea of inheritance furnishes a sure principle of conservation and a sure principle of transmission; without at all excluding a principle of improvement. It leaves acquisition free; but it secures what it acquires. Whatever advantages are obtained by a state proceeding on these maxims, are locked fast as in a sort of family settlement; grasped as in a kind of mortmain for ever. By a constitutional policy, working after the pattern of nature, we receive, we hold, we transmit our government and our privileges, in the same manner in which we enjoy and transmit our property and our lives. The institutions of policy, the goods of fortune, the gifts of providence, are handed down to us, and from us, in the same course and order. Our political system is placed in a just correspondence and symmetry with the order of the world, and with the mode of existence decreed to a permanent body composed of transitory parts; wherein, by the disposition of a stupendous wisdom, moulding together the great mysterious incorporation of the human race, the whole, at one time, is never old, or middle-aged, or young, but, in a condition of unchangeable constancy, moves on through the varied tenor of perpetual decay, fall, renovation, and progression. Thus, by preserving the method of nature in the conduct of the state, in what we improve, we are never wholly new; in what we retain, we are never wholly obsolete. By adhering in this manner and on those principles to our forefathers, we are guided not by the superstition of antiquarians, but by the spirit of philosophic analogy. In this choice of inheritance we have given to our frame of polity the image of a relation in blood; binding up the constitution of our country with our dearest domestic ties; adopting our fundamental laws into the bosom of our family affections; keeping inseparable, and cherishing with the warmth of all their combined and mutually reflected charities, our state, our hearths, our sepulchres, and our altars.

Through the same plan of a conformity to nature in our artificial institutions, and by calling in the aid of her unerring and powerful instincts, to fortify the fallible and feeble contrivances of our reason, we have derived several other, and those no small benefits, from considering our liberties in the light of an inheritance. Always acting as if in the presence of canonized forefathers, the spirit of freedom, leading in itself to misrule and excess, is tempered with an awful gravity. This idea of a liberal descent inspires us with a sense of habitual native dignity, which prevents that upstart insolence almost inevitably adhering to and disgracing those who are the first acquirers of any distinction. By this means our liberty becomes a noble freedom. It carries an imposing and majestic aspect. It has a pedigree and illustrating ancestors. It has its bearings, and its ensigns armorial. It has its gallery of portraits; its monumental inscriptions; its records, evidences, and titles. We procure reverence to our civil institutions on the principle upon which nature teaches us to revere individual men; on account of their age, and on account of those from whom they are descended. All your sophisters cannot produce anything better adapted to preserve a rational and manly freedom than the course that we have pursued, who have chosen our nature rather than our speculations, our breasts rather than our inventions, for the great conservatories and magazines of our rights and privileges.

You might, if you pleased, have profited of our example, and have given to your recovered freedom a correspondent dignity. Your privileges, though discontinued, were not lost to memory. Your constitution, it is true, whilst you were out of possession, suffered waste and dilapidation; but you possessed in some parts the walls, and, in all, the foundations, of a noble and venerable castle. You might have repaired those walls; you might have built on those old foundations. Your constitution was suspended before it was perfected; but you had the elements of a constitution very nearly as good as could be wished. In your old states you possessed that variety of parts corresponding with the various descriptions of which your community was happily composed; you had all that combination, and all that opposition of interests, you had that action and counteraction, which, in the natural and in the political world, from the reciprocal struggle of discordant powers, draws out the harmony of the universe. These opposed and conflicting interests, which you considered as so great a blemish in your old and in our present constitution, interpose a salutary check to all precipitate resolutions. They render deliberation a matter not of choice, but of necessity; they make all change a subject of *compromise*, which naturally begets moderation; they produce *temperaments* preventing the sore evil of harsh, crude, unqualified reformations; and rendering all the headlong exertions of arbitrary power, in the few or in the many, for ever impracticable. Through that diversity of members and interests, general liberty had as many securities as there were separate views in the several orders; whilst by pressing down the whole by the weight of a real monarchy, the separate parts would have been prevented from warping, and starting from their allotted places.

You had all these advantages in your ancient states; but you chose to act as if you had never been moulded into civil society, and had everything to begin anew. You began ill, because you began by despising everything that belonged to you. You set up your trade without a capital. If the last generations of your country appeared without much lustre in your eyes, you might have passed them by, and derived your claims from a more early race of ancestors. Under a pious predilection for those ancestors, your imaginations would have realized in them a standard of virtue and wisdom, beyond the vulgar practice of the hour : and you would have risen with the example to whose imitation you aspired. Respecting your forefathers, you would have been taught to respect yourselves. You would not have chosen to consider the French as a people of yesterday, as a nation of low-born servile wretches until the emancipating year of 1789. In order to furnish, at the expense of your honour, an excuse to your apologists here for several enormities of yours, you would not have been content to be represented as a gang of Maroon slaves, suddenly broke loose from the house of bondage, and therefore to be pardoned for your abuse of the liberty to which you were not accustomed, and ill fitted. Would it not, my worthy friend, have been wiser to have you thought, what I, for one, always thought you, a generous and gallant nation, long misled to your disadvantage by your high and romantic sentiments of fidelity, honour, and loyalty; that events had been unfavourable to you, but that you were not enslaved through any illiberal or servile disposition; that in your most devoted submission, you were actuated by a principle of public spirit, and that it was your country you worshipped, in the person of your king? Had you made it to be understood, that in the delusion of this amiable error you had gone farther than your wise ancestors; that you were resolved to resume your ancient privileges, whilst you preserved the spirit of your ancient and your recent loyalty and honour; or if, diffident of yourselves, and not clearly discerning the almost obliterated constitution of your ancestors, you had looked to your neighbours in this land, who had kept alive the ancient principles and models of the old common law of Europe meliorated and adapted to its present state—by following wise examples you would have given new examples of wisdom to the world. You would have rendered the cause of liberty venerable in the eyes of every worthy mind in every nation. You would have shamed despotism from the earth, by showing that freedom was not only reconcilable, but, as when well disciplined it is, auxiliary to law. You would have had an unoppressive but a productive revenue. You would have had a flourishing commerce to feed it. You would have had a free constitution; a potent monarchy; a disciplined army; a reformed and venerated clergy; a mitigated but spirited nobility, to lead your virtue, not to overlay it; you would have had a liberal order of commons, to emulate and to recruit that nobility; you would have had a protected, satisfied, laborious, and obedient people, taught to seek and to recognise the happiness that is to be found by virtue in all conditions; in which consists the true moral equality of mankind, and not in that monstrous fiction, which, by inspiring false ideas and vain expectations into men destined to travel in the obscure walk of laborious life, serves only to aggravate and embitter that real inequality, which it never can remove; and which the order of civil life establishes as much for the benefit of those whom it must leave in a humbe state, as those whom it is able to exalt to a condition more splendid, but not more happy. You had a smooth and easy career of felicity and glory laid open to you, beyond anything recorded in the history of the world; but you have shown that difficulty is good for man.

Compute your gains: see what is got by those extravagant and presumptuous speculations which have taught your leaders to despise all their predecessors, and all their contemporaries, and even to despise themselves, until the moment in which they became truly despicable. By following those false lights, France has bought undisguised calamities at a higher price than any nation has purchased the most unequivocal blessings! France has bought poverty by crime! France has not sacrificed her virtue to her interest, but she has abandoned her interest, that she might prostitute her virtue. All other nations have begun the fabric of a new government, or the reformation of an old, by establishing originally, or by enforcing with greater exactness, some rites or other of religion. All other people have laid the foundations of civil freedom in severer manners, and a system of a more austere and masculine morality. France, when she let loose the reins of regal authority, doubled the licence of a ferocious dissoluteness in manners, and of an insolent irreligion in opinions and practices; and has extended through all ranks of life, as if she were communicating some privilege, or laying open some secluded benefit, all the unhappy corruptions that usually were the disease of wealth and power. This is one of the new principles of equality in France.

France, by the perfidy of her leaders, has utterly disgraced the tone of lenient council in the cabinets of princes, and disarmed it of its most potent topics. She has sanctified the dark, suspicious maxims of tyrannous distrust; and taught kings to tremble at (what will hereafter be called) the delusive plausibilities of moral politicians. Sovereigns will consider those, who advise them to place an unlimited confidence in their people, as subverters of their thrones; as traitors who aim at their destruction, by leading their easy good-nature, under specious pretences, to admit combinations of bold and faithless men into a participation of their power. This alone (if there were nothing else) is an irreparable calamity to you and to mankind. Remember that your parliament of Paris told your king, that, in calling the states together, he had nothing to fear but the prodigal excess of their zeal in providing for the support of the throne. It is right that these men should hide their heads. It is right that they should bear their part in the ruin which their counsel has brought on their sovereign and their country. Such sanguine declarations tend to lull authority asleep; to encourage it rashly to engage in perilous adventures of untried policy; to neglect those provisions, preparations, and precautions, which distinguish benevolence from imbecility; and without which no man can answer for the salutary effect of any abstract plan of government or of freedom. For want of these, they have seen the medicine of the state corrupted into its poison. They have seen the French rebel against a mild and lawful monarch, with more fury, outrage, and insult, than ever any people has been known to rise against the most illegal usurper,, or the most sanguinary tyrant. Their resistance was made to concession; their revolt was from protection; their blow was aimed at a hand holding out graces, favours, and immunities.

This was unnatural. The rest is in order. They have found their punishment in their success. Laws overturned; tribunals subverted; industry without vigour; commerce expiring; the revenue unpaid, yet the people impoverished; a church pillaged, and a state not relieved;

civil and military anarchy made the constitution of the kingdom; everything human and divine sacrificed to the idol of public credit, and national bankruptcy the consequence; and, to crown all, the paper securities of new, precarious, tottering power, the discredited paper securities of impoverished fraud and beggared rapine, held out as a currency for the support of an empire, in lieu of the two great recognized species that represent the lasting, conventional credit of mankind, which disappeared and hid themselves in the earth from whence they came, when the principle of property, whose creatures and representatives they are, was systematically subverted.

Were all these dreadful things necessary? Were they the inevitable results of the desperate struggle of determined patriots, compelled to wade through blood and tumult, to the quiet shore of a tranquil and prosperous liberty? No! nothing like it. The fresh ruins of France, which shock our feelings wherever we can turn our eyes, are not the devastation of civil war; they are the sad but instructive monuments of rash and ignorant counsel in time of profound peace. They are the display of inconsiderate and presumptuous, because unresisted and irresistible, authority. The persons who have thus squandered away the precious treasure of their crimes, the persons who have made this prodigal and wild waste of public evils (the last stake reserved for the ultimate ransom of the state), have met in their progress with little, or rather with no opposition at all. Their whole march was more like a triumphal procession, than the progress of a war. Their pioneers have gone before them, and demolished and laid everything level at their feet. Not one drop of *their* blood have they shed in the cause of the country they have ruined. They have made no sacrifices to their projects of greater consequence than their shoe-buckles, whilst they were imprisoning their king, murdering their fellow-citizens, and bathing in tears, and plunging in poverty and distress, thousands of worthy men and worthy families. Their cruelty has not even been the base result of fear. It has been the effect of their sense of perfect safety, in authorizing treasons, robberies, rapes, assassinations, slaughters, and burnings, throughout their harassed land. But the cause of all was plain from the beginning.

This unforced choice, this fond election of evil, would appear perfectly unaccountable, if we did not consider the composition of the National Assembly : I do not mean its formal constitution, which, as it now stands, is exceptionable enough, but the materials of which, in a great measure, it is composed, which is of ten thousand times greater consequence than all the formalities in the world. If we were to know nothng of this Assembly but by its title and function, no colours could paint to the imagination anything more venerable. In that light the mind of an inquirer, subdued by such an awful image as that of the virtue and wisdom of a whole people collected into a focus, would pause and hesitate in condemning things even of the very worst aspect. Instead of blameable, they would appear only mysterious. But no name, no power, no function, no artificial institution whatsoever, can make the men of whom any system of authority is composed any other than God, and nature, and education, and their habits of life have made them. Capacities beyond these the people have not to give. Virtue and wisdom may be the objects of their choice; but their choice confers neither the one nor the other on those upon whom they lay their ordaining hands. They have not the engagement of nature, they have not the promise of revelation, for any such powers.

After I had read over the list of the persons and descriptions selected into the *Tiers Etat*, nothing which they afterwards did could appear astonishing. Among them, indeed, I saw some of known rank; some of shining talents; but of any practical experience in the state, not one man was to be found. The best were only men of theory. But whatever the distinguished few may have been, it is the substance and mass of the body which constitutes its character, and must finally determine its direction. In all bodies, those who will lead, must also, in a considerable degree, follow. They must conform their propositions to the taste, talent, and disposition, of those whom they wish to conduct : therefore, if an assembly is viciously or feebly composed in a very great part of it, nothing but such a supreme degree of virtue as very rarely appears in the world, and for that reason cannot enter into calculation, will prevent the men of talent disseminated through it from becoming only the expert instruments of absurd projects! If, what is the more likely event, instead of that unusual degree of virtue, they should be actuated by sinister ambition, and a lust of meretricious glory, then the feeble part of the Assembly, to whom at first they conform, becomes in its turn the dupe and instrument of their designs. In this political traffic, the leaders will be obliged to bow to the ignorance of their followers, and the followers to become subservient to the worst designs of their leaders.

To secure any degree of sobriety in the propositions made by the leaders in any public assembly, they ought to respect, in some degree perhaps to fear, those whom they conduct. To be led any otherwise than blindly, the followers must be qualified, if not for actors, at least for judges; they must also be judges of natural weight and authority. Nothing can secure a steady and moderate conduct in such assemblies, but that the body of them should be respectably composed, in point of condition in life, of permanent property, of education, and of such habits as enlarge and liberalize the understanding.

In the calling of the states-general of France, the first thing that struck me, was a great departure from the ancient course. I found the representation for the third estate composed of six hundred persons. They were equal in number to the representatives of both the other orders. If the orders were to act separately, the number would not, beyond the consideration of the expense, be of much moment. But when it became apparent that the three orders were to be melted down into one, the policy and necessary effect of this numerous representation became obvious. A very small desertion from either of the other two orders must throw the power of both into the hands of the third. In fact, the whole power of the state was soon resolved into that body. Its due composition became therefore of infinitely the greater importance.

Judge, Sir, of my surprise, when I found that a very great proportion of the Assembly (a majority, I believe, of the members who attended) was composed of practitioners in the law. It was composed, not of distinguished magistrates, who had given pledges to their country of their science, prudence, and integrity; not of leading advocates, the glory of the bar; not of renowned professors in universities;—but for the far greater part, as it must in such a number, of the inferior, unlearned, mechanical, merely instrumental members of the profession. There were distinguished exceptions; but the general composition was of obscure provincial advocates, of stewards of petty local jurisdictions, country attorneys, notarys, and the whole train of the ministers of municipal litigation, the fomenters and conductors of the petty war of village vexation. From the moment I read the list, I saw distinctly, and very nearly as it has happened, all that was to follow.

The degree of estimation in which any profession is held becomes the standard of the estimation in which the professors hold themselves. Whatever the personal merits of many individual lawyers might have been, and in many it was undoubtedly very considerable, in that military kingdom no part of the profession had been much regarded, except the highest of all, who often united to their professional offices great family splendour, and were invested with great power and authority. These certainly were highly respected, and even with no small degree of awe. The next rank was not much esteemed; the mechanical part was in a very low degree of repute.

Whenever the supreme authority is vested in a body so composed, it must evidently produce the consequences of supreme authority placed in the hands of men not taught habitually to respect themselves; who had no previous fortune in character at stake; who could not be expected to bear with moderation, or to conduct with discretion, a power, which they themselves, more than any others, must be surprised to find in their hands. Who could flatter himself that these men, suddenly, and, as it were, by enchantment, snatched from the humblest rank of subordination, would not be intoxicated with their unprepared greatness? Who could conceive that men, who are habitually meddling, daring, subtle, active, of litigious dispositions and unquiet minds, would easily fall back into their old condition of obscure contention, and laborious, low, and unprofitable chicane? Who could doubt but that, at any expense to the state, of which they understood nothing, they must pursue their private interests which they understood but too well? It was not an event depending on chance, or contingency. It was inevitable; it was necessary; it was planted in the nature of things. They must *join* (if their capacity did not permit them to *lead*) in any project which could procure to them a *litigious constitution;* which could lay open to them those innumerable lucrative jobs, which follow in the train of all great convulsions and revolutions in the state, and particularly in all great and violent permutations of property. Was it to be expected that they would attend to the stability of property, whose existence had always depended upon whatever rendered property questionable, ambiguous, and insecure? Their objects would be enlarged with their elevation, but their disposition and habits, and mode of accomplishing their designs, must remain the same.

Well! but these men were to be tempered and restrained by other descriptions, of more sober and more enlarged understandings. Were they then to be awed by the supereminent authority and awful dignity of a handful of country clowns, who have seats in that Assembly, some of whom are said not to be able to read and write? and by not a greater number of traders, who, though somewhat more instructed, and more conspicuous in the order of society, had never known anything beyond their counting-house. No! both these descriptions were more formed to be overborne and swayed by the intrigues and artifices of lawyers, than to become their counterpoise. With such a dangerous disproportion, the whole must needs be governed by them. To the faculty of law was joined a pretty considerable proportion of the faculty of medicine. This faculty had not, any more than that of the law, possessed in France its just estimation. Its professors, therefore, must have the qualities of men not habituated to sentiments of dignity. But supposing they had ranked as they ought to do, and as with us they do actually, the sides of sick beds are not the academies for forming statesmen and legislators. Then came the dealers in stocks and funds, who must be eager, at any expense, to change their ideal paper wealth for the more solid substance of land. To these were joined men of other descriptions, from whom as little knowledge of, or attention to, the interests of a great state was to be expected, and as little regard to the stability of any institution; men formed to be instruments, not controls. Such in general was the composition of the

Tiers État in the National Assembly; in which was scarcely to be perceived the slightest traces of what we call the natural landed interest of the country.

We know that the British House of Commons, without shutting its doors to any merit in any class, is, by the sure operation of adequate causes, filled with everything illustrious in rank, in descent, in hereditary and in acquired opulence, in cultivated talents, in military, civil, naval, and politic distinction, that the country can afford. But supposing, what hardly can be supposed as a case, that the House of Commons should be composed in the same manner with the *Tiers État* in France, would this dominion of chicane be borne with patience, or even conceived without horror? God forbid I should insinuate anything derogatory to that profession, which is another priesthood, administrating the rights of sacred justice. But whilst I revere men in the functions which belong to them, and would do as much as one man can do to prevent their exclusion from any, I cannot, to flatter them, give the lie to nature. They are good and useful in the composition; they must be mischievous if they preponderate so as virtually to become the whole. Their very excellence in their peculiar functions may be far from a qualification for others. It cannot escape observation, that when men are too much confined to professional and faculty habits, and as it were inveterate in the recurrent employment of that narrow circle, they are rather disabled than qualified for whatever depends on the knowledge of mankind, on experience in mixed affairs, on a comprehensive, connected view of the various, complicated, external and internal interests, which go to the formation of that multifarious thing called a state.

After all, if the House of Commons were to have a wholly professional and faculty composition, what is the power of the House of Commons, circumscribed and shut in by the immovable barriers of laws, usages, positive rules of doctrine and practice, counterpoised by the House of Lords, and every moment of its existence at the discretion of the crown to continue, prorogue, or dissolve us? The power of the House of Commons, direct or indirect, is indeed great; and long may it be able to preserve its greatness, and the spirit belonging to true greatness, at the full; and it will do so, as long as it can keep the breakers of law in India from becoming the makers of law for England. The power, however, of the House of Commons, when least diminished, is as a drop of water in the ocean, compared to that residing in a settled majority of your National Assembly. That Assembly, since the destruction of the orders, has no fundamental law, no strict convention, no respected usage to restrain it. Instead of finding themselves obliged to conform to a fixed constitution, they have a power to make a constitution which shall conform to their designs. Nothing in heaven or upon earth can serve as a control on them. What ought to be the heads, the hearts, the dispositions, that are qualified, or that dare, not only to make laws under a fixed constitution, but at one heat to strike out a totally new constitution for a great kingdom, and in every part of it, from the monarch on the throne to the vestry of a parish? But—"*fools rush in where angels fear to tread.*" In such a state of unbounded power for undefined and undefinable purposes, the evil of a moral and almost physical inaptitude of the man to the function must be the greatest we can conceive to happen in the management of human affairs.

Having considered the composition of the third estate as it stood in its original frame, I took a view of the representatives of the clergy. There too it appeared, that full as little regard was had to the general security of property, or to the aptitude of the deputies for their public purposes, in the principles of their election. That election was so contrived, as to send a very large proportion of mere country curates to the great and arduous work of new-modelling a state; men who never had seen the state so much as in a picture; men who knew nothing of the world beyond the bounds of an obscure village; who, immersed in hopeless poverty, could regard all property, whether secular or ecclesiastical, with no other eye than that of envy; among whom must be many who, for the smallest hope of the meanest dividend in plunder, would readily join in any attempts upon a body of wealth, in which they could hardly look to have any share, except in a general scramble. Instead of balancing the power of the active chicaners in the other assembly, these curates must necessarily become the active coadjutors, or at best the passive instruments, of those by whom they had been habitually guided in their petty village concerns. They too could hardly be the most conscientious of their kind, who, presuming upon their incompetent understanding, could intrigue for a trust which led them from their natural relation to their flocks, and their natural spheres of action, to undertake the regeneration of kingdoms. This preponderating weight, being added to the force of the body of chicane in the *Tiers État*, completed that momentum of ignorance, rashness, presumption, and lust of plunder, which nothing has been able to resist.

To observing men it must have appeared from the beginning, that the majority of the Third Estate, in conjunction with such a deputation from the clergy as I have described, whilst it pursued the destruction of the nobility, would inevitably become subservient to the worst designs of individuals in that class. In the spoil and humiliation of their own order these individuals would possess a sure fund for the pay of their new followers. To squander away the objects which made the happiness of their fellows, would be to them no sacrifice at all. Turbulent, discontented men of quality, in proportion as they are puffed up with personal pride and arrogance, generally despise their own order. One of the first symptoms they discover of a selfish and mischievous ambition, is a profligate disregard of a dignity which they partake with others. To be attached to the subdivision, to love the little platoon we belong to in society, is the first principle (the germ as it were) of public affections. It is the first link in the series by which we proceed towards a love to our country, and to mankind. The interest of that portion of social arrangement is a trust in the hands of all those who compose it; and as none but bad men would justify it in abuse, none but traitors would barter it away for their own personal advantage.

There were in the time of our civil troubles in England (I do not know whether you have any such in your Assembly in France), several persons like the then Earl of Holland, who by themselves or their families had brought an odium on the throne, by the prodigal dispensation of its bounties towards them, who afterwards joined in the rebellions arising from the discontents of which they were themselves the cause; men who helped to subvert that throne to which they owed, some of them, their existence, others all that power which they employed to ruin their benefactor. If any bounds are set to the rapacious demands of that sort of people, or that others are permitted to partake in the objects they would engross, revenge and envy soon fill up the craving void that is left in their avarice. Confounded by the complication of distempered passions, their reason is disturbed; their views become vast and perplexed; to others inexplicable; to themselves uncertain. They find, on all sides, bounds to their unprincipled ambition in any fixed order of things. But in the fog and haze of confusion all is enlarged, and appears without any limit.

When men of rank sacrifice all ideas of dignity to an ambition without a distinct object, and work with low instruments and for low ends, the whole composition becomes low and base. Does not something like this now appear in France? Does it not produce something ignoble and inglorious? a kind of meanness in all the prevalent policy? a tendency in all that is done to lower along with individuals all the dignity and importance of the state? Other revolutions have been conducted by persons, who, whilst they attempted or affected changes in the commonwealth, sanctified their ambition by advancing the dignity of the people whose peace they troubled. They had long views. They aimed at the rule, not at the destruction, of their country. They were men of great civil and great military talents, and if the terror, the ornament of their age. They were not like Jew brokers, contending with each other who could best remedy with fraudulent circulation and depreciated paper the wretchedness and ruin brought on their country by their degenerate councils. The compliment made to one of the great bad men of the old stamp (Cromwell) by his kinsman, a favourite poet of that time, shows what it was he proposed, and what indeed to a great degree he accomplished, in the success of his ambition :

> " Still as *you* rise, the *state* exalted too,
> Finds no distemper whilst 'tis changed by *you ;*
> Changed like the world's great scene, when without noise
> The rising sun night's *vulgar* lights destroys."

These disturbers were not so much like men usurping

power, as asserting their natural place in society. Their rising was to illuminate and beautify the world. Their conquest over their competitors was by outshining them. The hand that, like a destroying angel, smote the country, communicated to it the force and energy under which it suffered. I do not say (God forbid), I do not say, that the virtues of such men were to be taken as a balance to their crimes: but they were some corrective to their effects. Such was, as I said, our Cromwell. Such were your whole race of Guises, Condés, and Colignis. Such the Richelieus, who in more quiet times acted in the spirit of a civil war. Such, as better men, and in a less dubious cause, were your Henry the Fourth and your Sully, though nursed in civil confusions, and not wholly without some of their taint. It is a thing to be wondered at, to see how very soon France, when she had a moment to respire, recovered and emerged from the longest and most dreadful civil war that ever was known in any nation. Why? Because among all their massacres, they had not slain the *mind* in their country. A conscious dignity, a noble pride, a generous sense of glory and emulation, was not extinguished. On the contrary, it was kindled and inflamed. The organs also of the state, however shattered, existed. All the prizes of honour and virtue, all the rewards, all the distinctions remained. But your present confusion, like a palsy, has attacked the fountain of life itself. Every person in your country, in a situation to be actuated by a principle of honour, is disgraced and degraded, and can entertain no sensation of life, except in a mortified and humiliated indignation. But this generation will quickly pass away. The next generation of the nobility will resemble the artificers and clowns, and money-jobbers, usurers, and Jews, who will be always their fellows, sometimes their masters. Believe me, Sir, those who attempt to level, never equalise. In all societies, consisting of various descriptions of citizens, some description must be uppermost. The levellers therefore only change and pervert the natural order of things; they load the edifice of society, by setting up in the air what the solidity of the structure requires to be on the ground. The associations of tailors and carpenters, of which the republic (of Paris, for instance) is composed, cannot be equal to the situation, into which, by the worst of usurpations, an usurpation on the prerogatives of nature, you attempt to force them.

The Chancellor of France at the opening of the States, said, in a tone of oratorical flourish, that all occupations were honourable. If he meant only, that no honest employment was disgraceful, he would not have gone beyond the truth. But in asserting that anything is honourable, we imply some distinction in its favour. The occupation of a hair-dresser, or of a working tallow-chandler, cannot be a matter of honour to any person—to say nothing of a number of other more servile employments. Such descriptions of men ought not to suffer oppression from the state; but the state suffers oppression, if such as they, either individually or collectively, are permitted to rule. In this you think you are combating prejudice, but you are at war with nature.[1]

I do not, my dear Sir, conceive you to be of that sophistical, captious spirit, or of that uncandid dulness, as to require, for every general observation or sentiment, an explicit detail of the correctives and exceptions, which reason will presume to be included in all the general propositions which come from reasonable men. You do not imagine, that I wish to confine power, authority, and distinction to blood, and names, and titles. No, Sir. There is no qualification for government but virtue and wisdom, actual or presumptive. Wherever they are actually found, they have, in whatever state, condition, profession or trade, the passport of Heaven to human place and

---

1 Ecclesiasticus, chap. xxxviii. verses 24, 25. "The wisdom of a learned man cometh by opportunity of leisure : and he that hath little business shall become wise."—"How can he get wisdom that holdeth the plough, and that glorieth in the goad ; that driveth oxen ; and is occupied in their labours ; and whose talk is of bullocks ?"

Ver. 27. "So every carpenter and work-master that laboureth night and day," etc.

Ver. 33. "They shall not be sought for in public counsel, nor sit high in the congregation : they shall not sit on the judge's seat, nor understand the sentence of judgment ; they cannot declare justice and judgment, and they shall not be found where parables are spoken."

Ver. 34. "But they will maintain the state of the world."

I do not determine whether this book be canonical, as the Gallican church (till lately) has considered it, or apocryphal, as here it is taken. I am sure it contains a great deal of sense and truth.

honour. Woe to the country which would madly and impiously reject the service of the talents and virtues, civil, military, or religious, that are given to grace and to serve it; and would condemn to obscurity everything formed to diffuse lustre and glory around a state! Woe to that country too, that, passing into the opposite extreme, considers a low education, a mean contracted view of things, a sordid, mercenary occupation, as a preferable title to command! Everything ought to be open; but not indifferently to every man. No rotation; no appointment by lot; no mode of election operating in the spirit of sortition, or rotation, can be generally good in a government conversant in extensive objects. Because they have no tendency, direct or indirect, to select the man with a view to the duty, or to accommodate the one to the other. I do not hesitate to say, that the road to eminence and power from obscure condition, ought not to be made too easy, nor a thing too much of course. If rare merit be the rarest of all rare things, it ought to pass through some sort of probation. The temple of honour ought to be seated on an eminence. If it be opened through virtue, let it be remembered too, that virtue is never tried but by some difficulty and some struggle.

Nothing is a due and adequate representation of a state, that does not represent its ability, as well as its property. But as ability is a vigorous and active principle, and as property is sluggish, inert, and timid, it never can be safe from the invasions of ability, unless it be, out of all proportion, predominant in the representation. It must be represented too in great masses of accumulation, or it is not rightly protected. The characteristic essence of property, formed out of the combined principles of its acquisition and conservation, is to be *unequal*. The great masses therefore which excite envy, and tempt rapacity, must be put out of the possibility of danger. Then they form a natural rampart about the lesser properties in all their gradations. The same quantity of property, which is by the natural course of things divided among many, has not the same operation. Its defensive power is weakened as it is diffused. In this diffusion each man's portion is less than what, in the eagerness of his desires, he may flatter himself to obtain by dissipating the accumulations of others. The plunder of the few would indeed give but a share inconceivably small in the distribution to the many. But the many are not capable of making this calculation; and those who lead them to rapine never intend this distribution.

The power of perpetuating our property in our families is one of the most valuable and interesting circumstances belonging to it, and that which tends the most to the perpetuation of society itself. It makes our weakness subservient to our virtue; it grafts benevolence even upon avarice. The possessors of family wealth, and of the distinction which attends hereditary possession (as most concerned in it), are the natural securities for this transmission. With us the House of Peers is formed upon this principle. It is wholly composed of hereditary property and hereditary distinction; and made therefore the third of the legislature; and, in the last event, the sole judge of all property in all its subdivisions. The House of Commons too, though not necessarily, yet in fact, is always so composed, in the far greater part. Let those large proprietors be what they will, and they have their chance of being amongst the best, they are, at the very worst, the ballast in the vessel of the commonwealth. For though hereditary wealth, and the rank which goes with it, are too much idolized by creeping sycophants, and the blind, abject admirers of power, they are too rashly slighted in shallow speculations of the petulant, assuming, shortsighted coxcombs of philosophy. Some decent, regulated pre-eminence, some preference (not exclusive appropriation) given to birth, is neither unnatural, nor unjust, nor impolitic.

It is said, that twenty-four millions ought to prevail over two hundred thousand. True; if the constitution of a kingdom be a problem of arithmetic. This sort of discourse does well enough with the lamp-post for its second: to men who *may* reason calmly, it is ridiculous. The will of the many and their interest must very often differ; and great will be the difference when they make an evil choice. A government of five hundred country attorneys and obscure curates is not good for twenty-four millions of men, though it were chosen by eight-and-forty millions; nor is it the better for being guided by a dozen of persons of quality, who have betrayed their trust in order to obtain that power. At present, you seem in everything to have strayed out of the high road of nature. The property of France does not govern it. Of course property is destroyed, and rational liberty has no existence. All you have got for the present is a paper circulation and a stock-jobbing constitution: and, as to the future, do you seriously think that the territory of France, upon the republican system of eighty-three independent municipalities (to say nothing of the parts that compose them), can ever be governed as one body, or can ever be set in motion by the impulse of one mind? When the National Assembly has completed its work, it will have accomplished its ruin. These commonwealths will not long bear a state of subjection to the republic of Paris. They will not bear that this one body should monopolize the captivity of the king, and the dominion over the Assembly calling itself national. Each will keep its own portion of the spoil of the church to itself; and it will not suffer either that spoil, or the more just fruits of their industry, or the natural produce of their soil, to be sent to swell the insolence, or pamper the luxury, of the mechanics of Paris. In this they will see none of the equality, under the pretence of which they have been tempted to throw off their allegiance to their sovereign, as well as the ancient constitution of their country. There can be no capital city in such a constitution as they have lately made. They have forgot, that when they framed democratic governments, they had virtually dismembered their country. The person, whom they persevere in calling king, has not power left to him by the hundredth part sufficient to hold together this collection of republics. The republic of Paris will endeavour indeed to complete the debauchery of the army, and illegally to perpetuate the Assembly, without resort to its constituents, as the means of continuing its despotism. It will make efforts, by becoming the heart of a boundless paper circulation, to draw everything to itself; but in vain. All this policy in the end will appear as feeble as it is now violent.

If this be your actual situation, compared to the situation to which you were called, as it were by the voice of God and man, I cannot find it in my heart to congratulate you on the choice you have made, or the success which has attended your endeavours. I can as little recommend to any other nation a conduct grounded on such principles, and productive of such effects. That I must leave to those who can see farther into your affairs than I am able to do, and who best know how far your actions are favourable to their designs. The gentlemen of the Revolution Society, who were so early in their congratulations, appear to be strongly of opinion that there is some scheme of politics relative to this country, in which your proceedings may, in some way, be useful. For your Dr. Price, who seems to have speculated himself into no small degree of fervour upon this subject, addresses his auditory in the following very remarkable words : " I cannot conclude without recalling *particularly* to your recollection a consideration which I have *more than once alluded to*, and which probably your thoughts have *been all along anticipating ;* a consideration with which my *mind is impressed more than I can express.* I mean the consideration of the *favourableness of the present times to all exertions in the cause of liberty.*"

It is plain that the mind of this *political* preacher was at the time big with some extraordinary design ; and it is very probable that the thoughts of hs audience, who understood him better than I do, did all along run before him in his reflection, and in the whole train of consequences to which it led.

Before I read that sermon, I really thought I had lived in a free country ; and it was an error I cherished, because it gave me a greater liking to the country I lived in. I was indeed aware, that a jealous, ever-waking vigilance, to guard the treasure of our liberty, not only from invasion, but from decay and corruption, was our best wisdom, and our first duty. However, I considered that treasure rather as a possession to be secured, than as a prize to be contended for. I did not discern how the present time came to be so very favourable to all *exertions* in the cause of freedom. The present time differs from any other only by the circumstance of what is doing in France. If the example of that nation is to have an influence on this, I can easily conceive why some of their proceedings which have an unpleasant aspect, and are not quite reconcilable to humanity, generosity, good faith, and justice, are palliated with so much milky good-nature towards the actors, and borne with so much heroic fortitude towards the sufferers. It is certainly not prudent to discredit the authority of an example we mean to follow. But allowing this, we are led to a very natural question: What is that cause of liberty, and what are those exertions in its favour, to which the example of France is so singularly auspicious? Is our monarchy to be annihilated, with all the laws, all the tribunals, and all the ancient corporations of the kingdom? Is every land-mark of the country to be done away in favour of a geometrical and arithmetical constitution? Is the House of Lords to be voted useless? Is episcopacy to be abolished? Are the church lands to be sold to Jews and jobbers; or given to bribe new-invented municipal republics into a participation in sacrilege? Are all the taxes to be voted grievances, and the revenue reduced to a patriotic contribution, or patriotic presents? Are silver shoe-buckles to be substituted in the place of the land tax and the malt tax, for the support of the naval strength of this kingdom? Are all orders, ranks, and distinctions to be confounded, that out of universal anarchy, joined to national bankruptcy, three or four thousand democracies should be formed into eighty-three, and that they may all, by some sort of unknown attractive power, be organized into one? For this great end is the army to be seduced from its discipline and its fidelity, first by every kind of debauchery, and then by the terrible precedent of a donative in the increase of pay? Are the curates to be seduced from their bishops, by holding out to them the delusive hope of a dole out of the spoils of their own order? Are the citizens of London to be drawn from their allegiance by feeding them at the expense of their fellow-subjects? Is a compulsory paper currency to be substituted in the place of the legal coin of this kingdom? Is what remains of the plundered stock of public revenue to be employed in the wild project of maintaining two armies to watch over and to fight with each other? If these are the ends and means of the Revolution Society, I admit they are well assorted; and France may furnish them for both with precedents in point.

I see that your example is held out to shame us. I know that we are supposed a dull, sluggish race, rendered passive by finding our situation tolerable, and prevented by a mediocrity of freedom from ever attaining to its full perfection. Your leaders in France began by affecting to admire, almost to adore, the British constitution; but as they advanced, they came to look upon it with a sovereign contempt. The friends of your National Assembly amongst us have full as mean an opinion of what was formerly thought the glory of their country. The Revolution Society has discovered that the English nation is not free. They are convinced that the inequality in our representation is a "defect in our constitution *so gross and palpable*, as to make it excellent chiefly in *form* and *theory*." [1] That a representation in the legislature of a kingdom is not only the basis of all constitutional liberty in it, but of "*all legitimate government; that without it a government* is nothing but an *usurpation;*"—that "when the representation is *partial*, the kingdom possesses liberty only *partially;* and if extremely partial, it gives only a *semblance;* and if not only extremely partial, but corruptly chosen, it becomes a *nuisance*." Dr. Price considers this inadequacy of representation as our *fundamental grievance;* and though, as to the corruption of this semblance of representation, he hopes it is not yet arrived to its full perfection of depravity, he fears that "nothing will be done towards gaining for us this *essential blessing*, until some *great abuse of power* again provokes our resentment, or some *great calamity* again alarms our fears, or perhaps till the acquisition of a *pure and equal representation by other countries*, whilst we are *mocked* with the *shadow*, kindles our shame." To this he subjoins a note in these words: "A representation chosen chiefly by the treasury, and a *few* thousands of the *dregs* of the people, who are generally paid for their votes."

You will smile here at the consistency of those democratists, who, when they are not on their guard, treat the humbler part of the community with the greatest contempt, whilst, at the same time, they pretend to make them the depositories of all power. It would require a long discourse to point out to you the many fallacies that lurk in the generality and equivocal nature of the terms "inadequate representation." I shall only say here, in justice to that old-fashioned constitution, under which we have long

[1] Discourse on the Love of our Country, 3rd edit. p. 39.

prospered, that our representation has been found perfectly adequate to all the purposes for which a representation of the people can be desired or devised. I defy the enemies of our constitution to show the contrary. To detail the particulars in which it is found so well to promote its ends, would demand a treatise on our practical constitution. I state here the doctrine of the Revolutionists, only that you and others may see what an opinion these gentlemen entertain of the constitution of their country, and why they seem to think that some great abuse of power, or some great calamity, as giving a chance for the blessing of a constitution according to their ideas, would be much palliated to their feelings; you see *why they* are so much enamoured of your fair and equal representation, which being once obtained, the same effects might follow. You see they consider our House of Commons as only "a semblance," "a form," "a theory," "a shadow," "a mockery," perhaps "a nuisance."

These gentlemen value themselves on being systematic; and not without reason. They must therefore look on this gross and palpable defect of representation, this fundamental grievance (so they call it), as a thing not only vicious in itself, but as rendering our whole government absolutely *illegitimate*, and not at all better than a downright *usurpation*. Another revolution, to get rid of this illegitimate and usurped government, would of course be perfectly justifiable, if not absolutely necessary. Indeed their principle, if you observe it with any attention, goes much further than to an alteration in the election of the House of Commons; for, if popular representation, or choice, is necessary to the *legitimacy* of all government, the House of Lords is, at one stroke, bastardized and corrupted in blood. That house is no representative of the people at all, even in "semblance or in form." The case of the crown is altogether as bad. In vain the crown may endeavour to screen itself against these gentlemen by the authority of the establishment made on the Revolution. The Revolution which is resorted to for a title, on their system, wants a title itself. The Revolution is built, according to their theory, upon a basis not more solid than our present formalities, as it was made by a House of Lords, not representing any one but themselves; and by a House of Commons exactly such as the present, that is, as they term it, by a mere "shadow and mockery" of representation.

Something they must destroy, or they seem to themselves to exist for no purpose. One set is for destroying the civil power through the ecclesiastical; another, for demolishing the ecclesiastic through the civil. They are aware that the worst consequences might happen to the public in accomplishing this double ruin of church and state; but they are so heated with their theories, that they give more than hints, that this ruin, with all the mischiefs that must lead to it and attend it, and which to themselves appear quite certain, would not be unacceptable to them, or very remote from their wishes. A man amongst them of great authority, and certainly of great talents, speaking of a supposed alliance between church and state, says, "perhaps *we must wait for the fall of the civil powers* before this most unnatural alliance be broken. Calamitous no doubt will that time be. But what convulsion in the political world ought to be a subject of lamentation, if it be attended with so desirable an effect?" You see with what a steady eye these gentlemen are prepared to view the greatest calamities which can befall their country.

It is no wonder therefore, that with these ideas of everything in their constitution and government at home, either in church or state, as illegitimate and usurped, or at best as a vain mockery, they look abroad with an eager and passionate enthusiasm. Whilst they are possessed by these notions, it is vain to talk to them of the practice of their ancestors, the fundamental laws of their country, the fixed form of a constitution, whose merits are confirmed by the solid test of long experience, and an increasing public strength and national prosperity. They despise experience as the wisdom of unlettered men; and as for the rest, they have wrought under ground a mine that will blow up, at one grand explosion, all examples of antiquity, all precedents, charters, and acts of parliament. They have "the rights of men." Against these there can be no prescription; against these no agreement is binding: these admit no temperament and no compromise: anything withheld from their full demand is so much of fraud and injustice. Against these their rights of men let no government look for security in the length of its continuance, or in the justice and lenity of its administration. The objections of these speculatists, if its forms do not quadrate with their theories, are as valid against such an old and beneficent government, as against the most violent tyranny, or the greenest usurpation. They are always at issue with governments, not on a question of abuse, but a question of competency, and a question of title. I have nothing to say to the clumsy subtilty of their political metaphysics. Let them be their amusement in the schools.—"Illa *se jactat in aula—Æolus, et clauso ventorum carcere regnet.*" —But let them not break prison to burst like a *Levanter*, to sweep the earth with their hurricane, and to break up the fountains of the great deep to overwhelm us.

Far am I from denying in theory, full as far is my heart from withholding in practice (if I were of power to give or to withhold), the *real* rights of men. In denying their false claims of right, I do not mean to injure those which are real, and are such as their pretended rights would totally destroy. If civil society be made for the advantage of man, all the advantages for which it is made become his right. It is an institution of beneficence; and law itself is only beneficence acting by a rule. Men have a right to live by that rule; they have a right to do justice, as between their fellows, whether their fellows are in public function or in ordinary occupation. They have a right to the fruits of their industry; and to the means of making their industry fruitful. They have a right to the acquisitions of their parents; to the nourishment and improvement of their offspring; to instruction in life, and to consolation in death. Whatever each man can separately do, without trespassing upon others, he has a right to do for himself; and he has a right to a fair portion of all which society, with all its combinations of skill and force, can do in his favour. In this partnership all men have equal rights; but not to equal things. He that has but five shillings in the partnership, has as good a right to it, as he that has five hundred pounds has to his larger proportion. But he has not a right to an equal dividend in the product of the joint stock; and as to the share of power, authority, and direction which each individual ought to have in the management of the state, that I must deny to be amongst the direct original rights of man in civil society; for I have in my contemplation the civil social man, and no other. It is a thing to be settled by convention.

If civil society be the offspring of convention, that convention must be its law. That convention must limit and modify all the descriptions of constitution which are formed under it. Every sort of legislative, judicial, or executory power are its creatures. They can have no being in any other state of things; and how can any man claim under the conventions of civil society, rights which do not so much as suppose its existence? rights which are abolutely repugnant to it? One of the first motives to civil society, and which becomes one of its fundamental rules, is, *that no man should be judge in his own cause.* By this each person has at once divested himself of the first fundamental right of uncovenanted man, that is, to judge for himself, and to assert his own cause. He abdicates all right to be his own governor. He inclusively, in a great measure, abandons the right of self-defence, the first law of nature. Men cannot enjoy the rights of an uncivil and of a civil state together. That he may obtain justice, he gives up his right of determining what it is in points the most essential to him. That he may secure some liberty, he makes a surrender in trust of the whole of it.

Government is not made in virtue of natural rights, which may and do exist in total independence of it; and exist in much greater clearness, and in a much greater degree of abstract perfection : but their abstract perfection is their practical defect. By having a right to everything they want everything. Government is a contrivance of human wisdom to provide for human *wants*. Men have a right that these wants should be provided for by this wisdom. Among these wants is to be reckoned the want, out of civil society, of a sufficient restraint upon their passions. Society requires not only that the passions of individuals should be subjected, but that even in the mass and body, as well as in the individuals, the inclinations of men should frequently be thwarted, their will controlled, and their passions brought into subjection. This can only be done *by a power out of themselves;* and not, in the exercise of its function, subject to that will and to those passions which it is its office to bridle and subdue. In this sense the restraints on men, as well as their liberties, are to be reckoned among their rights. But as the liberties and the restrictions vary with times and circumstances, and admit of infinite modifications, they cannot be settled upon any abstract rule; and nothing is so foolish as to discuss them upon that principle.

The moment you abate anything from the full rights of men, each to govern himself, and suffer any artificial, positive limitation upon those rights, from that moment the whole organization of government becomes a consideration of convenience. This it is which makes the constitution of a state, and the due distribution of its powers, a matter of the most delicate and complicated skill. It requires a deep knowledge of human nature and human necessities, and of the things which facilitate or obstruct the various ends, which are to be pursued by the mechanism of civil institutions. The state is to have recruits to its strength, and remedies to its distempers. What is the use of discussing a man's abstract right to food or medicine? The question is upon the method of procuring and administering them. In that deliberation I shall always advise to call in the aid of the farmer and the physician, rather than the professor of metaphysics.

The science of constructing a commonwealth, or renovating it, or reforming it, is, like every other experimental science, not to be taught *à priori*. Nor is it a short experience that can instruct us in that practical science; because the real effects of moral causes are not always immediate; but that which in the first instance is prejudicial may be excellent in its remoter operation; and its excellence may arise even from the ill effects it produces in the beginning. The reverse also happens: and very plausible schemes, with very pleasing commencements, have often shameful and lamentable conclusions. In states there are often some obscure and almost latent causes, things which appear at first view of little moment, on which a very great part of its prosperity or adversity may most essentially depend. The science of government being therefore so practical in itself, and intended for such practical purposes, a matter which requires experience, and even more experience than any person can gain in his whole life, however sagacious and observing he may be, it is with infinite caution that any man ought to venture upon pulling down an edifice, which has answered in any tolerable degree for ages the common purposes of society, or on building it up again, without having models and patterns of approved utility before his eyes.

These metaphysic rights entering into common life, like rays of light which pierce into a dense medium, are, by the laws of nature, refracted from their straight line. Indeed in the gross and complicated mass of human passions and concerns, the primitive rights of men undergo such a variety of refractions and reflections, that it becomes absurd to talk of them as if they continued in the simplicity of their original direction. The nature of man is intricate; the objects of society are of the greatest possible complexity: and therefore no simple disposition or direction of power can be suitable either to man's nature, or to the quality of his affairs. When I hear the simplicity of contrivance aimed at and boasted of in any new political constitutions, I am at no loss to decide that the artificers are grossly ignorant of their trade, or totally negligent of their duty. The simple governments are fundamentally defective, to say no worse of them. If you were to contemplate society in but one point of view, all these simple modes of polity are infinitely captivating. In effect each would answer its single end much more perfectly than the more complex is able to attain all its complex purposes. But it is better that the whole should be imperfectly and anomalously answered, than that, while some parts are provided for with great exactness, others might be totally neglected, or perhaps materially injured, by the overcare of a favourite member.

The pretended rights of these theorists are all extremes: and in proportion as they are metaphysically true, they are morally and politically false. The rights of men are in a sort of *middle*, incapable of definition, but not impossible to be discerned. The rights of men in governments are their advantages; and these are often in balances between differences of good; in compromises sometimes between good and evil, and sometimes between evil and evil. Political reason is a computing principle; adding, subtracting, multiplying, and dividing, morally and not metaphysically, or mathematically, true moral denominations.

By these theorists the right of the people is almost always sophistically confounded with their power. The body of the community, whenever it can come to act, can meet with no effectual resistance; but till power and right are the same, the whole body of them has no right inconsistent with virtue, and the first of all virtues, prudence. Men have no right to what is not reasonable, and to what is not for their benefit; for though a pleasant writer said, *Liceat perire poetis*, when one of them, in cold blood, is said to have leaped into the flames of a volcanic revolution, *Ardentem frigidus Ætnam insiluit*, I consider such a frolic rather as an unjustifiable poetic licence, than as one of the franchises of Parnassus; and whether he were poet, or divine, or politician, that chose to exercise this kind of right, I think that more wise, because more charitable, thoughts would urge me rather to save the man, than to preserve his brazen slippers as the monuments of his folly.

The kind of anniversary sermons to which a great part of what I write refers, if men are not shamed out of their present course, in commemorating the fact, will cheat many out of the principles, and deprive them of the benefits, of the revolution they commemorate. I confess to you, Sir, I never liked this continual talk of resistance, and revolution, or the practice of making the extreme medicine of the constitution its daily bread. It renders the habit of society dangerously valetudinary; it is taking periodical doses of mercury sublimate, and swallowing down repeated provocatives of cantharides to our love of liberty.

This distemper of remedy, grown habitual, relaxes and wears out, by a vulgar and prostituted use, the spring of that spirit which is to be exerted on great occasions. It was in the most patient period of Roman servitude that themes of tyrannicide made the ordinary exercise of boys at school—*cum perimit sævos classis numerosa tyrannos*. In the ordinary state of things, it produces in a country like ours the worst effects, even on the cause of that liberty which it abuses with the dissoluteness of an extravagant speculation. Almost all the high-bred republicans of my time have, after a short space, become the most decided, thorough-paced courtiers; they soon left the business of a tedious, moderate, but practical resistance, to those of us whom, in the pride and intoxication of their theories, they have slighted as not much better than Tories. Hypocrisy, of course, delights in the most sublime speculations; for, never intending to go beyond speculation, it costs nothing to have it magnificent. But even in cases where rather levity than fraud was to be suspected in these ranting speculations, the issue has been much the same. These professors, finding their extreme principles not applicable to cases which call only for a qualified, or, as I may say, civil and legal resistance, in such cases employ no resistance at all. It is with them a war or a revolution, or it is nothing. Finding their schemes of politics not adapted to the state of the world in which they live, they often come to think lightly of all public principle; and are ready, on their part, to abandon for a very trivial interest what they find of very trivial value. Some indeed are of more steady and persevering natures; but these are eager politicians out of parliament, who have little to tempt them to abandon their favourite projects. They have some change in the church or state, or both, constantly in their view. When that is the case, they are always bad citizens, and perfectly unsure connexions. For, considering their speculative designs as of infinite value, and the actual arrangement of the state as of no estimation, they are at best indifferent about it. They see no merit in the good, and no fault in the vicious, management of public affairs; they rather rejoice in the latter, as more propitious to revolution. They see no merit or demerit in any man, or any action, or any political principle, any further than as they may forward or retard their design of change : they therefore take up, one day, the most violent and stretched prerogative, and another time the wildest democratic ideas of freedom, and pass from the one to the other without any sort of regard to cause, to person, or to party..

In France you are now in the crisis of a revolution, and in the transit from one form of government to another— you cannot see that character of men exactly in the same situation in which we see it in this country. With us it is militant; with you it is triumphant; and you know how it can act when its power is commensurate to its will. I would not be supposed to confine those observations to any description of men, or to comprehend all men of any description within them—No! far from it. I am as incapable of that injustice, as I am of keeping terms with those who profess principles of extremities; and who, under the name of religion, teach little else than wild and dangerous politics. The worst of these politics of revolution is this : they temper and harden the breast, in order to prepare it for the desperate strokes which are sometimes used in extreme occasions. But as these occasions may never arrive, the mind receives a gratuitous taint; and the moral sentiments suffer not a little, when no political purpose is served by the deprivation. This sort of people are so taken up with their theories about the rights of man, that they have totally forgotten his nature. Without opening one new avenue to the understanding, they have succeeded in stopping up those that lead to the heart. They have perverted in themselves, and in those that attend to them, all the well-placed sympathies of the human breast.

This famous sermon of the Old Jewry breathes nothing but this spirit through all the political part. Plots, massacres, assassinations, seem to some people a trivial price for obtaining a revolution. A cheap, bloodless reformation, a guiltless liberty, appear flat and vapid to their taste. There must be a great change of scene; there must be a magnificent stage effect; there must be a grand spectacle to rouse the imagination, grown torpid with the lazy enjoyment of sixty years' security, and the still unanimating repose of public prosperity. The preacher found them all in the French Revolution. This inspires a juvenile warmth through his whole frame. His enthusiasm kindles as he advances; and when he arrives at his peroration it is in a full blaze. Then viewing, from the Pisgah of his pulpit, the free, moral, happy, flourishing, and glorious state of France, as in a bird's-eye landscape of a promised land, he breaks out into the following rapture :

"What an eventful period is this! I am *thankful* that I have lived to it; I could almost say, *Lord, now lettest thou thy servant depart in peace, for mine eyes have seen thy salvation.* I have lived to see a *diffusion* of knowledge, which has undermined superstition and error.—I have lived to see *the rights of men* better understood than ever; and nations panting for liberty which seemed to have lost the idea of it.—I have lived to see *thirty millions of people*, indignant and resolute, spurning at slavery, and demanding liberty with an irresistible voice. *Their king led in triumph, and an arbitrary monarch surrendering himself to his subjects."* [1]

Before I proceed further, I have to remark, that Dr. Price seems rather to overvalue the great acquisitions of light which he has obtained and diffused in this age. The last century appears to me to have been quite as much enlightened. It had, though in a different place, a triumph as memorable as that of Dr. Price; and some of the great preachers of that period partook of it as eagerly as he has done in the triumph of France. On the trial of the Rev. Hugh Peters for high treason, it was deposed, that when King Charles was brought to London for his trial, the Apostle of Liberty in that day conducted the *triumph*. "I saw," says the witness, "his Majesty in the coach with six horses, and Peters riding before the king, *triumphing.*" Dr. Price, when he talks as if he had made a discovery, only follows a precedent; for, after the commencement of the king's trial, this precursor, the same Dr. Peters, concluding a long prayer at the Royal Chapel at Whitehall (he had very triumphantly chosen his place), said, "I have prayed and preached these twenty years; and now I may say with old Simeon, *Lord, now lettest thou thy servant depart in peace, for mine eyes have seen thy salvation."* [2] Peters had not the fruits of his prayer; for he neither departed so soon as he wished, nor in peace. He became (what I heartily hope none of his followers may be in this country) himself a sacrifice to the triumph which he led as pontiff. They dealt at the Restoration, perhaps, too hardly with this poor good man. But we owe it to his

[1] Another of these reverend gentlemen, who was witness to some of the spectacles which Paris has lately exhibited, expresses himself thus: —"*A king dragged in submissive triumph by his conquering subjects,* is one of those appearances of grandeur which seldom rise in the prospect of human affairs, and which, during the remainder of my life, I shall think of with wonder and gratification." These gentlemen agree marvellously in their feelings.

[2] State Trials, vol. ii. pp. 360, 363.

memory and his sufferings, that he had as much illumination, and as much zeal, and had as effectually undermined all *the superstition and error* which might impede the great business he was engaged in, as any who follow and repeat after him, in this age, which would assume to itself an exclusive title to the knowledge of the rights of men, and all the glorious consequences of that knowledge.

After this sally of the preacher of the Old Jewry, which differs only in place and time, but agrees perfectly with the spirit and letter of the rapture of 1648, the Revolution Society, the fabricators of governments, the heroic band of *cashierers of monarchs*, electors of sovereigns, and leaders of kings in triumph, strutting with a proud consciousness of the diffusion of knowledge, of which every member had obtained so large a share in the donative, were in haste to make a generous diffusion of the knowledge they had thus gratuitously received. To make this bountiful communication, they adjourned from the church in the Old Jewry to the London Tavern; where the same Dr. Price, in whom the fumes of his oracular tripod were not entirely evaporated, moved and carried the resolution, or address of congratulation, transmitted by Lord Stanhope to the National Assembly of France.

I find a preacher of the gospel profaning the beautiful and prophetic ejaculation, commonly called "*nunc dimittis*," made on the first presentation of our Saviour in the temple, and applying it, with an inhuman and unnatural rapture, to the most horrid, atrocious, and afflicting spectacle that perhaps ever was exhibited to the pity and indignation of mankind. This "*leading in triumph*," a thing in its best form unmanly and irreligious, which fills our preacher with such unhallowed transports, must shock, I believe, the moral taste of every well-born mind. Several English were the stupified and indignant spectators of that triumph. It was (unless we have been strangely deceived) a spectacle more resembling a procession of American savages, entering into Onondaga, after some of their murders called victories, and leading into hovels hung round with scalps, their captives, overpowered with the scoffs and buffets of women as ferocious as themselves, much more than it resembled the triumphal pomp of a civilized, martial nation;—if a civilized nation, or any men who had a sense of generosity, were capable of a personal triumph over the fallen and afflicted.

This, my dear Sir, was not the triumph of France. I must believe that, as a nation, it overwhelmed you with shame and horror. I must believe that the National Assembly find themselves in a state of the greatest humiliation in not being able to punish the authors of this triumph, or the actors in it; and that they are in a situation in which any inquiry they may make upon the subject must be destitute even of the appearance of liberty or impartiality. The apology of that assembly is found in their situation; but when we approve what they *must* bear, it is in us the degenerate choice of a vitiated mind.

With a compelled appearance of deliberation, they vote under the dominion of a stern necessity. They sit in the heart, as it were, of a foreign republic: they have their residence in a city whose constitution has emanated neither from the charter of their king, nor from their legislative power. There they are surrounded by an army not raised either by the authority of their crown, or by their command; and which, if they should order to dissolve itself, would instantly dissolve them. There they sit, after a gang of assassins had driven away some hundreds of the members; whilst those who held the same moderate principles, with more patience or better hope, continued every day exposed to outrageous insults and murderous threats. There a majority, sometimes real, sometimes pretended, captive itself, compels a captive king to issue as royal edicts, at third hand, the polluted nonsense of their most licentious and giddy coffee-houses. It is notorious, that all their measures are decided before they are debated. It is beyond doubt, that under the terror of the bayonet, and the lamp-post, and the torch to their houses, they are obliged to adopt all the crude and desperate measures suggested by clubs composed of a monstrous medley of all conditions, tongues, and nations. Among these are found persons, in comparison of whom Catiline would be thought scrupulous, and Cethegus a man of sobriety and moderation. Nor is it in these clubs alone that the public measures are deformed into monsters. They undergo a previous distortion in academies, intended as so many seminaries for these clubs, which are set up in all the places of public resort. In these meetings of all sorts, every counsel, in proportion as it is daring, and violent, and perfidious, is taken for the mark of superior genius. Humanity and compassion are ridiculed as the fruits of superstition and ignorance. Tenderness to individuals is considered as treason to the public. Liberty is always to be estimated perfect as property is rendered insecure. Amidst assassination, massacre, and confiscation, perpetrated or meditated, they are forming plans for the good order of future society. Embracing in their arms the carcases of base criminals, and promoting their relations on the title of their offences, they drive hundreds of virtuous persons to the same end, by forcing them to subsist by beggary or by crime.

The assembly, their organ, acts before them the farce of deliberation with as little decency as liberty. They act like the comedians of a fair before a riotous audience; they act amidst the tumultuous cries of a mixed mob of ferocious men, and of women lost to shame, who, according to their insolent fancies, direct, control, applaud, explode them; and sometimes mix and take their seats amongst them; domineering over them with a strange mixture of servile petulance and proud, presumptuous authority. As they have inverted order in all things, the gallery is in the place of the house. This assembly, which overthrows kings and kingdoms, has not even the physiognomy and aspect of a grave legislative body—*nec color imperii, nec frons ulla senatûs.* They have a power given to them, like that of the evil principle, to subvert and destroy; but none to construct, except such machines as may be fitted for further subversion and further destruction.

Who is it that admires, and from the heart is attached to, national representative assemblies, but must turn with horror and disgust from such a profane burlesque, and abominable perversion of that sacred institute? Lovers of monarchy, lovers of republics, must alike abhor it. The members of your assembly must themselves groan under the tyranny of which they have all the shame, none of the direction, and little of the profit. I am sure many of the members who compose even the majority of that body must feel as I do, notwithstanding the applauses of the Revolution Society. Miserable king! miserable assembly! How must that assembly be silently scandalized with those of their members, who could call a day which seemed to blot the sun out of heaven, "*un beau jour!*"[1] How must they be inwardly indignant at hearing others, who thought fit to declare to them, "that the vessel of the state would fly forward in her course towards regeneration with more speed than ever," from the stiff gale of treason and murder, which preceded our preacher's triumph! What must they have felt, whilst, with outward patience, and inward indignation, they heard of the slaughter of innocent gentlemen in their houses, that "the blood spilled was not the most pure!" What must they have felt, when they were besieged by complaints of disorders which shook their country to its foundations, at being compelled coolly to tell the complaints, that they were under the protection of the law, and that they would address the king (the captive king) to cause the laws to be enforced for their protection; when the enslaved ministers of that captive king had formally notified to them, that there were neither law, nor authority, nor power left to protect! What must they have felt at being obliged, as a felicitation on the present new year, to request their captive king to forget the stormy period of the last, on account of the great good which *he* was likely to produce to his people; to the complete attainment of which good they adjourned the practical demonstrations of their loyalty, assuring him of their obedience, when he should no longer possess any authority to command!

This address was made with much good nature and affection, to be sure. But among the revolutions in France must be reckoned a considerable revolution in their ideas of politeness. In England we are said to earn manners at second-hand from your side of the water, and that we dress our behaviour in the frippery of France. If so, we are still in the old cut; and have not so far conformed to the new Parisian mode of good breeding, as to think it quite in the most refined strain of delicate compliment (whether in condolence or congratulation) to say, to the most humiliated creature that crawls upon the earth, that great public benefits are derived from the murder of his servants, the attempted assassination of himself and of his wife, and the

[1] 6th of October, 1789.

mortification, disgrace, and degradation, that he has personally suffered. It is a topic of consolation which our ordinary of Newgate would be too humane to use to a criminal at the foot of the gallows. I should have thought that the hangman of Paris, now that he is liberalized by the vote of the National Assembly, and is allowed his rank and arms in the herald's college of the rights of men, would be too generous, too gallant a man, too full of the sense of his new dignity, to employ that cutting consolation to any of the persons whom the *leze nation* might bring under the administration of his *executive power*.

A man is fallen indeed, when he is thus flattered. The anodyne draught of oblivion, thus drugged, is well calculated to preserve a galling wakefulness, and to feed the living ulcer of a corroding memory. Thus to administer the opiate potion of amnesty, powdered with all the ingredients of scorn and contempt, is to hold to his lips, instead of "the balm of hurt minds," the cup of human misery full to the brim, and to force him to drink it to the dregs.

Yielding to reasons, at least as forcible as those which were so delicately urged in the compliment on the new year, the king of France will probably endeavour to forget these events and that compliment. But history, who keeps a durable record of all our acts, and exercises her awful censure over the proceedings of all sorts of sovereigns, will not forget either those events or the era of this liberal refinement in the intercourse of mankind. History will record, that on the morning of the 6th of October, 1789, the king and queen of France, after a day of confusion, alarm, dismay, and slaughter, lay down, under the pledged security of public faith, to indulge nature in a few hours of respite, and troubled, melancholy repose. From this sleep the queen was first startled by the voice of the sentinel at her door, who cried out to her to save herself by flight——that this was the last proof of fidelity he could give——that they were upon him, and he was dead. Instantly he was cut down. A band of cruel ruffians and assassins, reeking with his blood, rushed into the chamber of the queen, and pierced with a hundred strokes of bayonets and poniards the bed, from whence this persecuted woman had but just time to fly almost naked, and, through ways unknown to the murderers, had escaped to seek refuge at the feet of a king and husband, not secure of his own life for a moment.

This king, to say no more of him, and this queen, and their infant children (who once would have been the pride and hope of a great and generous people), were then forced to abandon the sanctuary of the most splendid palace in the world, which they left swimming in blood, polluted by massacre, and strewed with scattered limbs and mutilated carcases. Thence they were conducted into the capital of their kingdom. Two had been selected from the unprovoked, unresisted, promiscuous slaughter, which was made of the gentlemen of birth and family who composed the king's body guard. These two gentlemen, with all the parade of an execution of justice, were cruelly and publicly dragged to the block, and beheaded in the great court of the palace. Their heads were stuck upon spears, and led the procession; whilst the royal captives who followed in the train were slowly moved along, amidst the horrid yells, and shrilling screams, and frantic dances, and infamous contumelies, and all the unutterable abominations of the furies of hell, in the abused shape of the vilest of women. After they had been made to taste, drop by drop, more than the bitterness of death, in the slow torture of a journey of twelve miles, protracted to six hours, they were, under a guard, composed of those very soldiers who had thus conducted them through this famous triumph, lodged in one of the old palaces of Paris, now converted into a bastile for kings.

Is this a triumph to be consecrated at altars? to be commemorated with grateful thanksgiving? to be offered to the divine humanity with fervent prayer and enthusiastic ejaculation?—These Theban and Thracian orgies, acted in France, and applauded only in the Old Jewry, I assure you, kindle prophetic enthusiasm in the minds but of very few people in this kingdom: although a saint and apostle, who may have revelations of his own, and who has so completely vanquished all the mean superstitions of the heart, may incline to think it pious and decorous to compare it with the entrance into the world of the Prince of Peace, proclaimed in a holy temple by a venerable sage, and not long before not worse announced by the voice of angels to the quiet innocence of shepherds.

At first I was at a loss to account for this fit of unguarded transport. I knew, indeed, that the sufferings of monarchs make a delicious repast to some sort of palates. There were reflections which might serve to keep this appetite within some bounds of temperance. But when I took one circumstance into my consideration, I was obliged to confess, that much allowance ought to be made for the society, and that the temptation was too strong for common discretion; I mean, the circumstance of the Io Pæan of the triumph, the animating cry which called "for *all* the BISHOPS to be hanged on the lamp-posts," [1] might well have brought forth a burst of enthusiasm on the foreseen consequences of this happy day. I allow to so much enthusiasm some little deviation from prudence. I allow this prophet to break forth into hymns of joy and thanksgiving on an event which appears like the precursor of the millennium, and the projected fifth monarchy, in the destruction of all church establishments. There was, however (as in all human affairs there is), in the midst of this joy, something to exercise the patience of these worthy gentlemen, and to try the long-suffering of their faith. The actual murder of the king and queen, and their child, was wanting to the other auspicious circumstances of this "*beautiful day.*" The actual murder of the bishops, though called for by so many holy ejaculations, was also wanting. A group of regicide and sacrilegious slaughter was indeed boldly sketched, but it was only sketched. It unhappily was left unfinished, in this great history-piece of the massacre of innocents. What hardy pencil of a great master, from the school of the rights of men, will finish it, is to be seen hereafter. The age has not yet the complete benefit of that diffusion of knowledge that has undermined superstition and error; and the king of France wants another object or two to consign to oblivion, in consideration of all the good which is to arise from his own sufferings, and the patriotic crimes of an enlightened age. [2]

1 Tous les Évêques à la lanterne.
2 It is proper here to refer to a letter written upon this subject by an eye-witness. That eye-witness was one of the most honest, intelligent, and eloquent members of the National Assembly, one of the most active and zealous reformers of the state. He was obliged to secede from the assembly; and he afterwards became a voluntary exile, on account of the horrors of this pious triumph, and the dispositions of men, who,

Although this work of our new light and knowledge did not go to the length that in all probability it was intended

profiting of crimes, if not causing them, have taken the lead in public affairs.

Extract of M. de Lally Tollendal's Second Letter to a Friend.

"Parlons du parti que j'ai pris; il est bien justifié dans ma conscience.—Ni cette ville coupable, ni cette assemblée plus coupable encore, ne meritoient que je me justifie; mais j'ai à cœur que vous, et les personnes qui pensent comme vous, ne me condamnent pas.—Ma santé, je vous jure, me rendoit mes fonctions impossibles; mais même en les mettant de côté il a été au-dessus de mes forces de supporter plus long-tems l'horreur que me causoit ce sang,—ces têtes—cette reine *presque égorgée*,—ce roi,—amené *esclave*,—entrant à Paris, au milieu de ses assassins, et précédé des têtes des ses malheureux grades—ces perfides janissaires, ces assassins, ces femmes cannibales, ce cri de TOUS LES ÉVÊQUES À LA LANTERNE, dans le moment où le roi entre sa capitale avec deux évêques de son conseil dans sa voiture—un *coup de fusil,* que j'ai vu tirer dans un *des carosses de la reine*. M. Bailly appellant cela *un beau jour,*—l'assemblée ayant déclaré froidement le matin, qu'il n'étoit pas de sa dignité d'aller toute entière environner le roi—M. Mirabeau disant impunément dans cette assemblée que le vaisseau de l'état, loins d'être arrêté dans sa course, s'élanceroit avec plus de rapidité que jamais vers sa régénération—M. Barnave, riant avec lui, quand des flots de sang couloient autour de nous—le vertueux Mounier[1] échappant par miracle à vingt assassins, qui avoient voulu faire de sa tête un trophée de plus : Voilà ce qui me fit jurer de ne plus mettre le pied *dans cette caverne d'Anthropophages* [the National Assembly] où je n'avois plus de force d'élever la voix, où depuis six semaines je l'avois élevée en vain.

"Moi, Mounier, et tous les honnêtes gens, ont pensé que le dernier effort à faire pour le bien étoit d'en sortir. Aucune idée de crainte ne s'est approchée de moi. Je rougirois de m'en défendre. J'avois encore reçu sur la route de la part de ce peuple, moins coupable que ceux qui l'ont enivré de fureur, des acclamations, et des applaudissements, dont d'autres auroient été flattés, et qui m'ont fait frémir. C'est à l'indignation, c'est à l'horreur, c'est aux convulsions physiques, que le seul aspect du sang me fait éprouver que j'ai cédé. On brave une seul mort; on la brave plusieurs fois, quand elle peut être utile. Mais aucune puissance sous le Ciel, mais aucune opinion publique ou privée n'ont le droit de me condamner à souffrir inutilement mille supplices par minute, et à perir de désespoir, de rage, au milieu des *triomphes,* du crime que je n'ai pu arrêter. Ile me proscriront, ils confisqueront mes biens. Je labourerai la terre, et je ne les verrai plus.—Voilà ma justification. Vous pourrez la lire, la montrer, la laisser copier ; tant pis pour ceux qui ne la comprendront pas ; ce ne sera alors moi qui auroit eu tort de la leur donner."

This military man had not so good nerves as the peaceable gentle-

[1] N.B. Mr. Mounier was then speaker of the National Assembly. He has since been obliged to live in exile, though one of the firmest assertors of liberty.

it should be carried, yet I must think that such treatment of any human creatures must be shocking to any but those who are made for accomplishing revolutions. But I cannot stop here. Influenced by the inborn feelings of my nature, and not being illuminated by a single ray of this new-sprung modern light, I confess to you, Sir, that the exalted rank of the persons suffering, and particularly the sex, the beauty, and the amiable qualities of the descendant of so many kings and emperors, with the tender age of royal infants, insensible only through infancy and innocence of the cruel outrages to which their parents were exposed, instead of being a subject of exultation, adds not a little to my sensibility on that most melancholy occasion.

I hear that the august person, who was the principal object of our preacher's triumph, though he supported himself, felt much on that shameful occasion. As a man, it became him to feel for his wife and his children, and the faithful guards of his person, that were massacred in cold blood about him; as a prince, it became him to feel for the strange and frightful transformation of his civilized subjects, and to be more grieved for them than solicitous for himself. It derogates little from his fortitude, while it adds infinitely to the honour of his humanity. I am very sorry to say it, very sorry indeed, that such personages are in a situation in which it is not becoming in us to praise the virtues of the great.

I hear, and I rejoice to hear, that the great lady, the other object of the triumph, has borne that day (one is interested that beings made for suffering should suffer well), and that she bears all the succeeding days, that she bears the imprisonment of her husband, and her own captivity, and the exile of her friends, and the insulting adulation of addresses, and the whole weight of her accumulated wrongs, with a serene patience, in a manner suited to her rank and race, and becoming the offspring of a sovereign distinguished for her piety and her courage: that, like her, she has lofty sentiments; that she feels with the dignity of a Roman matron; that in the last extremity she will

men of the Old Jewry.—See Mons. Mounier's narrative of these transactions; a man also of honour, and virtue, and talents, and therefore a fugitive.

save herself from the last disgrace; and that, if she must fall, she will fall by no ignoble hand.

It is now sixteen or seventeen years since I saw the queen of France, then the dauphiness, at Versailles; and surely never lighted on this orb, which she hardly seemed to touch, a more delightful vision. I saw her just above the horizon, decorating and cheering the elevated sphere she just began to move in,—glittering like the morning-star, full of life, and splendour, and joy. Oh! what a revolution! and what a heart must I have to contemplate without emotion that elevation and that fall! Little did I dream when she added titles of veneration to those of enthusiastic, distant, respectful love, that she should ever be obliged to carry the sharp antidote against disgrace concealed in that bosom; little did I dream that I should have lived to see such disasters fallen upon her in a nation of gallant men, in a nation of men of honour, and of cavaliers. I thought ten thousand swords must have leaped from their scabbards to avenge even a look that threatened her with insult. But the age of chivalry is gone. That of sophisters, economists, and calculators, has succeeded; and the glory of Europe is extinguished for ever. Never, never more shall we behold that generous loyalty to rank and sex, that proud submission, that dignified obedience, that subordination of the heart, which kept alive, even in servitude itself, the spirit of an exalted freedom. The unbought grace of life, the cheap defence of nations, the nurse of manly sentiment and heroic enterprise, is gone! It is gone, that sensibility of principle, that chastity of honour, which felt a stain like a wound, which inspired courage whilst it mitigated ferocity, which ennobled whatever it touched, and under which vice itself lost half its evil, by losing all its grossness.

This mixed system of opinion and sentiment had its origin in the ancient chivalry; and the principle, though varied in its appearance by the varying state of human affairs, subsisted and influenced through a long succession of generations, even to the time we live in. If it should ever be totally extinguished, the loss I fear will be great. It is this which has given its character to modern Europe. It is this which has distinguished it under all its forms of government, and distinguished it to its advantage, from the states of Asia, and possibly from those states which flourished in the most brilliant periods of the antique world. It was this, which, without confounding ranks, had produced a noble equality, and handed it down through all the gradations of social life. It was this opinion which mitigated kings into companions, and raised private men to be fellows with kings. Without force or opposition, it subdued the fierceness of pride and power; it obliged sovereigns to submit to the soft collar of social esteem, compelled stern authority to submit to elegance, and gave a dominating vanquisher of laws to be subdued by manners.

But now all is to be changed. All the pleasing illusions, which made power gentle and obedience liberal, which harmonized the different shades of life, and which, by a bland assimilation, incorporated into politics the sentiments which beautify and soften private society, are to be dissolved by this new conquering empire of light and reason. All the decent drapery of life is to be rudely torn off. All the superadded ideas, furnished from the wardrobe of a moral imagination, which the heart owns, and the understanding ratifies, as necessary to cover the defects of our naked, shivering nature, and to raise it to dignity in our own estimation, are to be exploded as a ridiculous, absurd, and antiquated fashion.

On this scheme of things, a king is but a man, a queen is but a woman; a woman is but an animal, and an animal not of the highest order. All homage paid to the sex in general as such, and without distinct views, is to be regarded as romance and folly. Regicide, and parricide, and sacrilege, are but fictions of superstition, corrupting jurisprudence by destroying its simplicity. The murder of a king, or a queen, or a bishop, or a father, are only common homicide; and if the people are by any chance, or in any way, gainers by it, a sort of homicide much the most pardonable, and into which we ought not to make too severe a scrutiny.

On the scheme of this barbarous philosophy, which is the offspring of cold hearts and muddy understandings, and which is as void of solid wisdom as it is destitute of all taste and elegance, laws are to be supported only by their own terrors, and by the concern which each individual may find in them from his own private speculations, or can spare to them from his own private interests. In the groves of *their* academy, at the end of every vista, you see nothing but the gallows. Nothing is left which engages the affections on the part of the commonwealth. On the principles of this mechanic philosophy, our institutions can never be embodied, if I may use the expression, in persons; so as to create in us love, veneration, admiration, or attachment. But that sort of reason which banishes the affections is incapable of filling their place. These public affections, combined with manners, are required sometimes as supplements, sometimes as correctives, always as aids to law. The precept given by a wise man, as well as a great critic, for the construction of poems, is equally true as to states : —*Non satis est pulchra esse poemata, dulcia sunto*. There ought to be a system of manners in every nation, which a well-formed mind would be disposed to relish. To make us love our country, our country ought to be lovely.

But power, of some kind or other, will survive the shock in which manners and opinions perish; and it will find other and worse means for its support. The usurpation which, in order to subvert ancient institutions, has destroyed ancient principles, will hold power by arts similar to those by which it has acquired it. When the old feudal and chivalrous spirit of *fealty*, which, by freeing kings from fear, freed both kings and subjects from the precautions of tyranny, shall be extinct in the minds of men, plots and assassinations will be anticipated by preventive murder and preventive confiscation, and that long roll of grim and bloody maxims, which form the political code of all power, not standing on its own honour, and the honour of those who are to obey it. Kings will be tyrants from policy, when subjects are rebels from principle.

When ancient opinions and rules of life are taken away, the loss cannot possibly be estimated. From that moment we have no compass to govern us; nor can we know distinctly to what port we steer. Europe, undoubtedly, taken in a mass, was in a flourishing condition the day on which your revolution was completed. How much of that prosperous state was owing to the spirit of our old manners and opinions is not easy to say; but as such causes cannot be indifferent in their operation, we must presume, that, on the whole, their operation was beneficial.

We are but too apt to consider things in the state in which we find them, without sufficiently adverting to the causes by which they have been produced, and possibly may be upheld. Nothing is more certain, than that our manners, our civilization, and all the good things which are connected with manners and with civilization, have, in this European world of ours, depended for ages upon two principles; and were indeed the result of both combined; I mean the spirit of a gentleman, and the spirit of religion. The nobility and the clergy, the one by profession, the other by patronage, kept learning in existence, even in the midst of arms and confusions, and whilst governments were rather in their causes, than formed. Learning paid back what it received to nobility and to priesthood; and paid it with usury, by enlarging their ideas, and by furnishing their minds. Happy if they had all continued to know their indissoluble union, and their proper place! Happy if learning, not debauched by ambition, had been satisfied to continue the instructor, and not aspired to be the master! Along with its natural protectors and guardians, learning will be cast into the mire, and trodden down under the hoofs of a swinish multitude.[1]

If, as I suspect, modern letters owe more than they are always willing to own to ancient manners, so do other interests which we value full as much as they are worth. Even commerce, and trade, and manufacture, the gods of our economical politicians, are themselves perhaps but creatures; are themselves but effects, which, as first causes, we choose to worship. They certainly grew under the same shade in which learning flourished. They too may decay with their natural protecting principles. With you, for the present at least, they all threaten to disappear together. Where trade and manufactures are wanting to a people, and the spirit of nobility and religion remains, sentiment supplies, and not always ill supplies, their place; but if commerce and the arts should be lost in an experiment to try how well a state may stand without these old

[1] See the fate of Bailly and Condorcet, supposed to be here particularly alluded to. Compare the circumstances of the trial and execution of the former with this prediction.

fundamental principles, what sort of a thing must be a nation of gross, stupid, ferocious, and, at the same time, poor and sordid, barbarians, destitute of religion, honour, or manly pride, possessing nothing at present, and hoping for nothing hereafter?

I wish you may not be going fast, and by the shortest cut, to that horrible and disgustful situation. Already there appears a poverty of conception, a coarseness and vulgarity, in all the proceedings of the Assembly and of all their instructors. Their liberty is not liberal. Their science is presumptuous ignorance. Their humanity is savage and brutal.

It is not clear, whether in England we learned those grand and decorous principles and manners, of which considerable traces yet remain, from you, or whether you took them from us. But to you, I think, we trace them best. You seem to me to be—*gentis incunabula nostræ.* France has always more or less influenced manners in England; and when your fountain is choked up and polluted, the stream will not run long, or not run clear, with us, or perhaps with any nation. This gives all Europe, in my opinion, but too close and connected a concern in what is done in France. Excuse me, therefore, if I have dwelt too long on the atrocious spectacle of the 6th of October, 1789, or have given too much scope to the reflections which have arisen in my mind on occasion of the most important of all revolutions, which may be dated from that day, I mean a revolution in sentiments, manners, and moral opinions. As things now stand, with everything respectable destroyed without us, and an attempt to destroy within us every principle of respect, one is almost forced to apologize for harbouring the common feelings of men.

Why do I feel so differently from the Reverend Dr. Price, and those of his lay flock who will choose to adopt the sentiments of his discourse?—For this plain reason—because it is *natural* I should; because we are so made, as to be affected at such spectacles with melancholy sentiments upon the unstable condition of mortal prosperity, and the tremendous uncertainty of human greatness; because in those natural feelings we learn great lessons; because in events like these our passions instruct our reason; because when kings are hurled from their thrones by the Supreme Director of this great drama, and become the objects of insult to the base, and of pity to the good, we behold such disasters in the moral, as we should behold a miracle in the physical, order of things. We are alarmed into reflection; our minds (as it has long since been observed) are purified by terror and pity; our weak, unthinking pride is humbled under the dispensations of a mysterious wisdom. Some tears might be drawn from me, if such a spectacle were exhibited on the stage. I should be truly ashamed of finding in myself that superficial, theatric sense of painted distress, whilst I could exult over it in real life. With such a perverted mind, I could never venture to show my face at a tragedy. People would think the tears that Garrick formerly, or that Siddons not long since, have extorted from me, were the tears of hypocrisy; I should know them to be the tears of folly.

Indeed the theatre is a better school of moral sentiments than churches, where the feelings of humanity are thus outraged. Poets who have to deal with an audience not yet graduated in the school of the rights of men, and who must apply themselves to the moral constitution of the heart, would not dare to produce such a triumph as a matter of exultation. There, where men follow their natural impulses, they would not bear the odious maxims of a Machiavelian policy, whether applied to the attainment of monarchical or democratic tyranny. They would reject them on the modern, as they once did on the ancient stage, where they could not bear even the hypothetical proposition of such wickedness in the mouth of a personated tyrant, though suitable to the character he sustained. No theatric audience in Athens would bear what has been borne, in the midst of the real tragedy of this triumphal day; a principal actor weighing, as it were in scales hung in a shop of horrors,—so much actual crime against so much contingent advantage,—and after putting in and out weights, declaring that the balance was on the side of the advantages. They would not bear to see the crimes of new democracy posted as in a ledger against the crimes of old despotism, and the book-keepers of politics finding democracy still in debt, but by no means unable or unwilling to pay the balance. In the theatre, the first intuitive glance, without any elaborate process of reasoning, will show, that this method of political computation would justify every extent of crime. They would see, that on these principles, even where the very worst acts were not perpetrated, it was owing rather to the fortune of the conspirators, than to their parsimony in the expenditure of treachery and blood. They would soon see, that criminal means once tolerated are soon preferred. They present a shorter cut to the object than through the highway of the moral virtues. Justifying perfidy and murder for public benefit, public benefit would soon become the pretext, and perfidy and murder the end; until rapacity, malice, revenge, and fear more dreadful than revenge, could satiate their insatiable appetites. Such must be the consequences of losing, in the splendour of these triumphs of the rights of men, all natural sense of wrong and right.

But the reverend pastor exults in this " leading in triumph," because truly Louis the Sixteenth was "an arbitrary monarch "; that is, in other words, neither more nor less than because he was Louis the Sixteenth, and because he had the misfortune to be born king of France, with the prerogatives of which, a long line of ancestors, and a long acquiescence of the people, without any act of his, had put him in possession. A misfortune it has indeed turned out to him, that he was born king of France. But misfortune is not crime, nor is indiscretion always the greatest guilt. I shall never think that a prince, the acts of whose whole reign were a series of concessions to his subjects, who was willing to relax his authority, to remit his prerogatives, to call his people to a share of freedom, not known, perhaps not desired, by their ancestors; such a prince, though he should be subjected to the common frailties attached to men and to princes, though he should have once thought it necessary to provide force against the desperate designs manifestly carrying on against his person, and the remnants of his authority; though all this should be taken into consideration, I shall be led with great difficulty to think he deserves the cruel and insulting triumph of Paris and of Dr. Price. I tremble for the cause of liberty, from such an example to kings. I tremble for the cause of humanity, in the unpunished outrages of the most wicked of mankind. But there are some people of that low and degenerate fashion of mind, that they look up with a sort of complacent awe and admiration to kings, who know to keep firm in their seat, to hold a strict hand over their subjects, to assert their prerogative, and, by the awakened vigilance of a severe despotism, to guard against the very first approaches of freedom. Against such as these they never elevate their voice. Deserters from principle, listed with fortune, they never see any good in suffering virtue, nor any crime in prosperous usurpation.

If it could have been made clear to me, that the king and queen of France (those I mean who were such before the triumph) were inexorable and cruel tyrants, that they had formed a deliberate scheme for massacring the National Assembly (I think I have seen something like the latter insinuated in certain publications), I should think their captivity just. If this be true, much more ought to have been done, but done, in my opinion, in another manner. The punishment of real tyrants is a noble and awful act of justice; and it has with truth been said to be consolatory to the human mind. But if I were to punish a wicked king, I should regard the dignity in avenging the crime. Justice is grave and decorous, and in its punishments rather seems to submit to a necessity, than to make a choice. Had Nero, or Agrippina, or Louis the Eleventh, or Charles the Ninth, been the subject; if Charles the Twelfth of Sweden, after the murder of Patkul, or his predecessor Christina, after the murder of Monaldeschi, had fallen into your hands, Sir, or into mine, I am sure our conduct would have been different.

If the French king, or king of the French (or by whatever name he is known in the new vocabulary of your constitution), has in his own person, and that of his queen, really deserved these unavowed, but unavenged, murderous attempts, and those frequent indignities more cruel than murder, such a person would ill deserve even that subordinate executory trust, which I understand is to be placed in him; nor is he fit to be called chief in a nation which he has outraged and oppressed. A worse choice for such an office in a new commonwealth, than that of a deposed tyrant, could not possibly be made. But to degrade and insult a man as the worst of criminals, and afterwards to trust him in your highest concerns, as a faithful, honest, and zealous servant, is not consistent with reasoning, nor prudent in policy, nor safe in practice. Those who could make such an appointment must be guilty of a more flagrant breach of trust than any they have yet committed against the people. As this is the only crime in which your leading politicians could have acted inconsistently, I conclude that there is no sort of ground for these horrid insinuations. I think no better of all the other calumnies.

In England, we give no credit to them. We are generous enemies: we are faithful allies. We spurn from us with disgust and indignation the slanders of those who bring us their anecdotes with the attestation of the flower-de-luce on their shoulder. We have Lord George Gordon fast in Newgate; and neither his being a public proselyte to Judaism, nor his having, in his zeal against catholic priests and all sorts of ecclesiastics, raised a mob (excuse the term, it is still in use here) which pulled down all our prisons, have preserved to him a liberty, of which he did not render himself worthy by a virtuous use of it. We have rebuilt Newgate, and tenanted the mansion. We have prisons almost as strong as the Bastile, for those who dare to libel the queens of France. In this spiritual retreat, let the noble libeller remain. Let him there meditate on his Thalmud, until he learns a conduct more becoming his birth and parts, and not so disgraceful to the ancient religion to which he has become a proselyte; or until some persons from your side of the water, to please your new Hebrew brethren, shall ransom him. He may then be enabled to purchase, with the old boards of the synagogue, and a very small poundage on the long compound interest of the thirty pieces of silver (Dr. Price has shown us what miracles compound interest will perform in 1790 years), the lands which are lately discovered to have been usurped by the Gallican church. Send us your Popish archbishop of Paris, and we will send you our Protestant Rabbin. We shall treat the person you send us in exchange like a gentleman and an honest man, as he is; but pray let him bring with him the fund of his hospitality, bounty, and charity; and, depend upon it, we shall never confiscate a shilling of that honourable and pious fund, nor think of enriching the treasury with the spoils of the poor-box.

To tell you the truth, my dear Sir, I think the honour of

our nation to be somewhat concerned in the disclaimer of the proceedings of this society of the Old Jewry and the London Tavern. I have no man's proxy. I speak only for myself, when I disclaim, as I do with all possible earnestness, all communion with the actors in that triumph, or with the admirers of it. When I assert anything else, as concerning the people of England, I speak from observation, not from authority; but I speak from the experience I have had in a pretty extensive and mixed communication with the inhabitants of this kingdom, of all descriptions and ranks, and after a course of attentive observation, began early in life, and continued for nearly forty years. I have often been astonished, considering that we are divided from you but by a slender dyke of about twenty-four miles, and that the mutual intercourse between the two countries has lately been very great, to find how little you seem to know of us. I suspect that this is owing to your forming a judgment of this nation from certain publications, which do, very erroneously, if they do at all, represent the opinions and dispositions generally prevalent in England. The vanity, restlessness, petulance, and spirit of intrigue, of several petty cabals, who attempt to hide their total want of consequence in bustle and noise, and puffing, and mutual quotation of each other, makes you imagine that our contemptuous neglect of their abilities is a mark of general acquiescence in their opinions. No such thing, I assure you. Because half a dozen grasshoppers under a fern make the field ring with their importunate chink, whilst thousands of great cattle, reposed beneath the shadow of the British oak, chew the cud and are silent, pray do not imagine that those who make the noise are the only inhabitants of the field; that, of course, they are many in number; or that, after all, they are other than the little, shrivelled, meagre, hopping, though loud and troublesome, insects of the hour.

I almost venture to affirm, that not one in a hundred amongst us participates in the "triumph" of the Revolution Society. If the king and queen of France, and their children, were to fall into our hands by the chance of war, in the most acrimonious of all hostilities (I deprecate such an event, I deprecate such hostilities), they would be treated with another sort of triumphal entry into London. We formerly have had a king of France in that situation; you have read how he was treated by the victor in the field; and in what manner he was afterwards received in England. Four hundred years have gone over us; but I believe we are not materially changed since that period. Thanks to our sullen resistance to innovation, thanks to the cold sluggishness of our national character, we still bear the stamp of our forefathers. We have not (as I conceive) lost the generosity and dignity of thinking of the fourteenth century; nor as yet have we subtilized ourselves into savages. We are not the converts of Rousseau; we are not the disciples of Voltaire; Helvetius has made no progress amongst us. Atheists are not our preachers; madmen are not our lawgivers. We know that *we* have made no discoveries, and we think that no discoveries are to be made, in morality; nor many in the great principles of government, nor in the ideas of liberty, which were understood long before we were born, altogether as well as they will be after the grave has heaped its mould upon our presumption, and the silent tomb shall have imposed its law on our pert loquacity. In England we have not yet been completely embowelled of our natural entrails; we still feel within us, and we cherish and cultivate, those inbred sentiments which are the faithful guardians, the active monitors of our duty, the true supporters of all liberal and manly morals. We have not been drawn and trussed, in order that we may be filled, like stuffed birds in a museum, with chaff and rags and paltry blurred shreds of paper about the rights of man. We preserve the whole of our feelings still native and entire, unsophisticated by pedantry and infidelity. We have real hearts of flesh and blood beating in our bosoms. We fear God; we look up with awe to kings; with affection to parliaments; with duty to magistrates; with reverence to priests; and with respect to nobility.[1] Why? Because when such ideas are brought

---

[1] The English are, I conceive, misrepresented in a letter published in one of the papers, by a gentleman thought to be a dissenting minister. —When writing to Dr. Price of the spirit which prevails at Paris, he says: "The spirit of the people in this place has abolished all the proud *distinctions* which the *king* and *nobles* had usurped in their minds; whether they talk of *the king, the noble, or the priest,* their whole language is that of the most *enlightened and liberal amongst the English.*" If this gentleman means to confine the terms *enlightened and*

before our minds, it is *natural* to be so affected; because all other feelings are false and spurious, and tend to corrupt our minds, to vitiate our primary morals, to render us unfit for rational liberty; and by teaching us a servile, licentious, and abandoned insolence, to be our low sport for a few holidays, to make us perfectly fit for, and justly deserving of, slavery, through the whole course of our lives.

You see, Sir, that in this enlightened age I am bold enough to confess, that we are generally men of untaught feelings; that instead of casting away all our old prejudices, we cherish them to a very considerable degree, and, to take more shame to ourselves, we cherish them because they are prejudices; and the longer they have lasted, and the more generally they have prevailed, the more we cherish them. We are afraid to put men to live and trade each on his own private stock of reason; because we suspect that this stock in each man is small, and that the individuals would do better to avail themselves of the general bank and capital of nations and of ages. Many of our men of speculation, instead of exploding general prejudices, employ their sagacity to discover the latent wisdom which prevails in them. If they find what they seek, and they seldom fail, they think it more wise to continue the prejudice, with the reason involved, than to cast away the coat of prejudice, and to leave nothing but the naked reason; because prejudice, with its reason, has a motive to give action to that reason, and an affection which will give it permanence. Prejudice is of ready application in the emergency; it previously engages the mind in a steady course of wisdom and virtue, and does not leave the man hesitating in the moment of decision, sceptical, puzzled, and unresolved. Prejudice renders a man's virtue his habit; and not a series of unconnected acts. Through just prejudice, his duty becomes a part of his nature.

Your literary men, and your politicians, and so do the whole clan of the enlightened among us, essentially differ in these points. They have no respect for the wisdom of others; but they pay it off by a very full measure of confidence in their own. With them it is a sufficient motive to

liberal to one set of men in England, it may be true. It is not generally so.

destroy an old scheme of things, because it is an old one. As to the new, they are in no sort of fear with regard to the duration of a building run up in haste; because duration is no object to those who think little or nothing has been done before their time, and who place all their hopes in discovery. They conceive, very systematically, that all things which give perpetuity are mischievous, and therefore they are at inexpiable war with all establishments. They think that government may vary like modes of dress, and with as little ill effect: that there needs no principle of attachment, except a sense of present conveniency, to any constitution of the state. They always speak as if they were of opinion that there is a singular species of compact between them and their magistrates, which binds the magistrate, but which has nothing reciprocal in it, but that the majesty of the people has a right to dissolve it without any reason, but its will. Their attachment to their country itself is only so far as it agrees with some of their fleeting projects; it begins and ends with that scheme of polity which falls in with their momentary opinion.

These doctrines, or rather sentiments, seem prevalent with your new statesmen. But they are wholly different from those on which we have always acted in this country.

I hear it is sometimes given out in France, that what is doing among you is after the example of England. I beg leave to affirm, that scarcely anything done with you has originated from the practice or the prevalent opinions of this people, either in the act or in the spirit of the proceeding. Let me add, that we are as unwilling to learn these lessons from France, as we are sure that we never taught them to that nation. The cabals here, who take a sort of share in your transactions, as yet consist of but a handful of people. If unfortunately by their intrigues, their sermons, their publications, and by a confidence derived from an expected union with the counsels and forces of the French nation, they should draw considerable numbers into their faction, and in consequence should seriously attempt anything here in imitation of what has been done with you, the event, I dare venture to prophesy, will be, that, with some trouble to their country, they will soon accomplish their own destruction. This people refused to change their law in remote ages from respect to the infallibility of popes; and they will not now alter it from a pious implicit faith in the dogmatism of philosophers; though the former was armed with the anathema and crusade, and though the latter should act with the libel and the lamp-iron.

Formerly your affairs were your own concern only. We felt for them as men; but we kept aloof from them, because we were not citizens of France. But when we see the model held up to ourselves, we must feel as Englishmen, and feeling, we must provide as Englishmen. Your affairs, in spite of us, are made a part of our interest; so far at least as to keep at a distance your panacea, or your plague. If it be a panacea, we do not want it. We know the consequences of unnecessary physic. If it be a plague, it is such a plague that the precautions of the most severe quarantine ought to be established against it.

I hear on all hands that a cabal, calling itself philosophic, receives the glory of many of the late proceedings; and that their opinions and systems are the true actuating spirit of the whole of them. I have heard of no party in England, literary or political, at any time, known by such a description. It is not with you composed of those men, is it? whom the vulgar, in their blunt, homely style, commonly call atheists and infidels? If it be, I admit that we too have had writers of that description, who made some noise in their day. At present they repose in lasting oblivion. Who, born within the last forty years, has read one word of Collins, and Toland, and Tindal, and Chubb, and Morgan, and that whole race who called themselves Freethinkers? Who now reads Bolingbroke? Who ever read him through? Ask the booksellers of London what is become of all these lights of the world. In as few years their few successors will go to the family vault of "all the Capulets." But whatever they were, or are, with us, they were and are wholly unconnected individuals. With us they kept the common nature of their kind, and were not gregarious. They never acted in corps, or were known as a faction in the state, nor presumed to influence in that name or character, or for the purposes of such a faction, on any of our public concerns. Whether they ought so to exist, and so be permitted to act, is another question. As such cabals have not existed in England, so neither has the spirit of them had any influence in establishing the original frame of our constitution, or in any one of the several reparations and improvements it has undergone. The whole has been done under the auspices, and is confirmed by the sanctions, of religion and piety. The whole has emanated from the simplicity of our national character, and from a sort of native plainness and directness of understanding, which for a long time characterized those men who have successively obtained authority amongst us. This disposition still remains; at least in the great body of the people.

We know, and what is better, we feel inwardly, that religion is the basis of civil society, and the source of all good and of all comfort.[1] In England we are so convinced of this, that there is no rust of superstition, with which the accumulated absurdity of the human mind might have crusted it over in the course of ages, that ninety-nine in a hundred of the people of England would not prefer to impiety. We shall never be such fools as to call in an enemy to the substance of any system to remove its corruptions, to supply its defects, or to perfect its construction. If our religious tenets should ever want a further elucidation, we shall not call on atheism to explain them. We shall not light up our temple from that unhallowed fire. It will be illuminated with other lights. It will be perfumed with other incense, than the infectious stuff which is imported by the smugglers of adulterated metaphysics. If our ecclesiastical establishment should want a revision, it is not avarice or rapacity, public or private, that we shall employ for the audit, or receipt, or application of its consecrated revenue. Violently condemning neither the Greek nor the Armenian, nor, since heats are subsided, the Roman system of religion, we prefer the Protestant; not because we think it has less of the Christian religion in it, but because, in our judgment, it has more. We are Protestants, not from indifference, but from zeal.

We know, and it is our pride to know, that man is by his

---

1 Sit igitur hoc ab initio persuasum civibus, dominos esse omnium rerum ac moderatores, deos; eaque, quæ gerantur, eorum geri vi, ditione, ac numine; eosdemque optime de genere hominum mereri; et qualis quisque sit, quid agat, quid in se admittat, qua mente, qua pietate colat religiones intueri; piorum et impiorum habere rationem. His enim rebus imbutæ mentes haud sane abhorrebunt ab utili et a vera sententia. Cic. de Legibus, l. 2.

constitution a religious animal; that atheism is against, not only our reason, but our instincts; and that it cannot prevail long. But if, in the moment of riot, and in a drunken delirium from the hot spirit drawn out of the alembic of hell, which in France is now so furiously boiling, we should uncover our nakedness, by throwing off that Christian religion which has hitherto been our boast and comfort, and one great source of civilization amongst us, and amongst many other nations, we are apprehensive (being well aware that the mind will not endure a void) that some uncouth, pernicious, and degrading superstition might take place of it.

For that reason, before we take from our establishment the natural, human means of estimation, and give it up to contempt, as you have done, and in doing it have incurred the penalties you well deserve to suffer, we desire that some other may be presented to us in the place of it. We shall then form our judgment.

On these ideas, instead of quarrelling with establishments, as some do, who have made a philosophy and a religion of their hostility to such institutions, we cleave closely to them. We are resolved to keep an established church, an established monarchy, an established aristocracy, and an established democracy, each in the degree it exists, and in no greater. I shall show you presently how much of each of these we possess.

It has been the misfortune (not, as these gentlemen think it, the glory) of this age, that everything is to be discussed, as if the constitution of our country were to be always a subject rather of altercation, than enjoyment. For this reason, as well as for the satisfaction of those among you (if any such you have among you) who may wish to profit of examples, I venture to trouble you with a few thoughts upon each of these establishments. I do not think they were unwise in ancient Rome, who, when they wished to new-model their laws, set commissioners to examine the best constituted republics within their reach.

First, I beg leave to speak of our church establishment, which is the first of our prejudices, not a prejudice destitute of reason, but involving in it profound and extensive wisdom. I speak of it first. It is first, and last, and midst in our minds. For, taking ground on that religious system, of which we are now in possession, we continue to act on the early received and uniformly continued sense of mankind. That sense not only, like a wise architect, hath built up the august fabric of states, but like a provident proprietor, to preserve the structure from profanation and ruin, as a sacred temple purged from all the impurities of fraud, and violence, and injustice, and tyranny, hath solemnly and for ever consecrated the commonwealth, and all that officiate in it. This consecration is made, that all who administer in the government of men, in which they stand in the person of God Himself, should have high and worthy notions of their function and destination; that their hope should be full of immortality; that they should not look to the paltry pelf of the moment, nor to the temporary and transient praise of the vulgar, but to a solid, permanent exercise, in the permanent part of their nature, and to a permanent fame and glory, in the example they leave as a rich inheritance to the world.

Such sublime principles ought to be infused into persons of exalted situations; and religious establishments provided, that may continually revive and enforce them. Every sort of moral, every sort of civil, every sort of politic institution, aiding the rational and natural ties that connect the human understanding and affections to the divine, are not more than necessary, in order to build up that wonderful structure, Man; whose prerogative it is, to be in a great degree a creature of his own making; and who, when made as he ought to be made, is destined to hold no trivial place in the creation. But whenever man is put over men, as the better nature ought ever to preside, in that case more particularly, he should as nearly as possible be approximated to his perfection.

The consecration of the state, by a state religious establishment, is necessary also to operate with a wholesome awe upon free citizens; because, in order to secure their freedom, they must enjoy some determinate portion of power. To them therefore a religion connected with the state, and with their duty towards it, becomes even more necessary than in such societies, where the people, by the terms of their subjection, are confined to private sentiments, and the management of their own family concerns. All persons possessing any portion of power ought to be strongly and awfully impressed with an idea that they act in trust : and that they are to account for their conduct in that trust to the one great Master, Author, and Founder of society.

This principle ought even to be more strongly impressed upon the minds of those who compose the collective sovereignty, than upon those of single princes. Without instruments, these princes can do nothing. Whoever uses instruments, in finding helps, finds also impediments. Their power is therefore by no means complete; nor are they safe in extreme abuse. Such persons, however elevated by flattery, arrogance, and self-opinion, must be sensible, that, whether covered or not by positive law, in some way or other they are accountable even here for the abuse of their trust. If they are not cut off by a rebellion of their people, they may be strangled by the very janissaries kept for their security against all other rebellion. Thus we have seen the king of France sold by his soldiers for an increase of pay. But where popular authority is absolute and unrestrained, the people have an infinitely greater, because a far better founded, confidence in their own power. They are themselves, in a great measure, their own instruments. They are nearer to their objects. Besides, they are less under responsibility to one of the greatest controlling powers on earth, the sense of fame and estimation. The share of infamy, that is likely to fall to the lot of each individual in public acts, is small indeed; the operation of opinion being in the inverse ratio to the number of those who abuse power. Their own approbation of their own acts has to them the appearance of a public judgment in their favour. A perfect democracy is therefore the most shameless thing in the world. As it is the most shameless, it is also the most fearless. No man apprehends in his person that he can be made subject to punishment. Certainly the people at large never ought : for as all punishments are for example towards the conservation of the people at large, the people at large can never become the subject of punishment by any human hand.[1] It is therefore of infinite importance that they should not be suffered to imagine that their will, any more than that of kings, is the standard

[1] Quicquid multis peccatur inultum.

of right and wrong. They ought to be persuaded that they are full as little entitled, and far less qualified with safety to themselves, to use any arbitrary power whatsoever; that therefore they are not, under a false show of liberty, but in truth, to exercise an unnatural, inverted domination, tyrannically to exact, from those who officiate in the state, not an entire devotion to their interest, which is their right, but an abject submission to their occasional will; extinguishing thereby, in all those who serve them, all moral principle, all sense of dignity, all use of judgment, and all consistency of character; whilst by the very same process they give themselves up a proper, a suitable, but a most contemptible prey to the servile ambition of popular sycophants, or courtly flatterers.

When the people have emptied themselves of all the lust of selfish will, which without religion it is utterly impossible they ever should, when they are conscious that they exercise, and exercise perhaps in a higher link of the order of delegation, the power, which to be legitimate must be according to that eternal, immutable law, in which will and reason are the same, they will be more careful how they place power in base and incapable hands. In their nomination to office, they will not appoint to the exercise of authority, as to a pitiful job, but as to a holy function; not according to their sordid, selfish interest, nor to their wanton caprice, nor to their arbitrary will; but they will confer that power (which any man may well tremble to give or to receive) on those only, in whom they may discern that predominant proportion of active virtue and wisdom, taken together and fitted to the charge, such, as in the great and inevitable mixed mass of human imperfections and infirmities, is to be found.

When they are habitually convinced that no evil can be acceptable, either in the act or the permission, to him whose essence is good, they will be better able to extirpate out of the minds of all magistrates, civil, ecclesiastical, or military, anything that bears the least resemblance to a proud and lawless domination.

But one of the first and most leading principles on which the commonwealth and the laws are consecrated, is lest the temporary possessors and life-renters in it, unmindful of what they have received from their ancestors, or of what is due to their posterity, should act as if they were the entire masters; that they should not think it among their rights to cut off the entail, or commit waste on the inheritance, by destroying at their pleasure the whole original fabric of their society; hazarding to leave to those who come after them a ruin instead of an habitation—and teaching these successors as little to respect their contrivances, as they had themselves respected the institutions of their forefathers. By this unprincipled facility of changing the state as often, and as much, and in as many ways, as there are floating fancies or fashions, the whole chain and continuity of the commonwealth would be broken. No one generation could link with the other. Men would become little better than the flies of a summer.

And first of all, the science of jurisprudence, the pride of the human intellect, which, with all its defects, redundancies, and errors, is the collected reason of ages, combining the principles of original justice with the infinite variety of human concerns, as a heap of old exploded errors, would be no longer studied. Personal self-sufficiency and arrogance (the certain attendants upon all those who have never experienced a wisdom greater than their own) would usurp the tribunal. Of course no certain laws, establishing invariable grounds of hope and fear, would keep the actions of men in a certain course, or direct them to a certain end. Nothing stable in the modes of holding property, or exercising function, could form a solid ground on which any parent could speculate in the education of his offspring, or in a choice for their future establishment in the world. No principles would be early worked into the habits. As soon as the most able instructor had completed his laborious course of institution, instead of sending forth his pupil, accomplished in a virtuous discipline, fitted to procure him attention and respect, in his place in society, he would find everything altered; and that he had turned out a poor creature to the contempt and derision of the world, ignorant of the true grounds of estimation. Who would insure a tender and delicate sense of honour to beat almost with the first pulses of the heart, when no man could know what would be the test of honour in a nation, continually varying the standard of its coin? No part of life would retain its acquisitions. Barbarism with regard to science and literature, unskilfulness with regard to arts and manufactures, would infallibly succeed to the want of a steady education and settled principle; and thus the commonwealth itself would, in a few generations, crumble away, be disconnected into the dust and powder of individuality, and at length dispersed to all the winds of heaven.

To avoid therefore the evils of inconstancy and versatility, ten thousand times worse than those of obstinacy and the blindest prejudice, we have consecrated the state, that no man should approach to look into its defects or corruptions but with due caution; that he should never dream of beginning its reformation by its subversion; that he should approach to the faults of the state as to the wounds of a father, with pious awe and trembling solicitude. By this wise prejudice we are taught to look with horror on those children of their country, who are prompt rashly to hack that aged parent in pieces, and put him into the kettle of magicians, in hopes that by their poisonous weeds, and wild incantations, they may regenerate the paternal constitution, and renovate their father's life.

Society is indeed a contract. Subordinate contracts for objects of mere occasional interest may be dissolved at pleasure—but the state ought not to be considered as nothing better than a partnership agreement in a trade of pepper and coffee, calico or tobacco, or some other such low concern, to be taken up for a little temporary interest, and to be dissolved by the fancy of the parties. It is to be looked on with other reverence; because it is not a partnership in things subservient only to the gross animal existence of a temporary and perishable nature. It is a partnership in all science; a partnership in all art; a partnership in every virtue, and in all perfection. As the ends of such a partnership cannot be obtained in many generations, it becomes a partnership not only between those who are living, but between those who are living, those who are dead, and those who are to be born. Each contract of each particular state is but a clause in the great primæval contract of eternal society, linking the lower with the higher natures, connecting the visible and invisible world, according to a fixed compact sanctioned by the inviolable oath which holds all physical and all moral natures, each in their appointed place. This law is not subject to the will of those, who by an obligation above them, and infinitely superior, are bound to submit their will to that law. The municipal corporations of that universal kingdom are not morally at liberty at their pleasure, and on their speculations of a contingent improvement, wholly to separate and tear asunder the bands of their subordinate community, and to dissolve it into an unsocial, uncivil, unconnected chaos of elementary principles. It is the first and supreme necessity only, a necessity that is not chosen, but chooses, a necessity paramount to deliberation, that admits no discussion, and demands no evidence, which alone can justify a resort to anarchy. This necessity is no exception to the rule; because this necessity itself is a part too of that moral and physical disposition of things, to which man must be obedient by consent or force : but if that which is only submission to necessity should be made the object of choice, the law is broken, nature is disobeyed, and the rebellious are outlawed, cast forth, and exiled, from this world of reason, and order, and peace, and virtue, and fruitful penitence, into the antagonist world of madness, discord, vice, confusion, and unavailing sorrow.

These, my dear Sir, are, were, and, I think, long will be, the sentiments of not the least learned and reflecting part of this kingdom. They, who are included in this description, form their opinions on such grounds as such persons ought to form them. The less inquiring receive them from an authority, which those whom Providence dooms to live on trust need not be ashamed to rely on. These two sorts of men move in the same direction, though in a different place. They both move with the order of the universe. They all know or feel this great ancient truth : "Quod illi principi et præpotenti Deo qui omnem hunc mundum regit, nihil eorum quæ quidem fiant in terris acceptius quam concilia et cœtus hominum jure sociati quæ civitates appellantur." They take this tenet of the head and heart, not from the great name which it immediately bears, nor from the greater from whence it is derived; but from that which alone can give true weight and sanction to any learned opinion, the common nature and common relation of men. Persuaded that all things ought to be done with reference, and referring all to the point of reference to which all should be directed, they think themselves bound, not only as individuals in the sanctuary of the heart, or as congregated in that personal capacity, to renew the memory of their high origin and caste; but also in their corporate character to perform their national homage to the institutor, and author, and protector of civil society; without which civil society man could not by any possibility arrive at the perfection of which his nature is capable, nor even make a remote and faint approach to it. They conceive that He who gave our nature to be perfected by our virtue, willed also the necessary means of its perfection.—He willed therefore the state—He willed its connexion with the source and original archetype of all perfection. They who are convinced of this His will, which is the law of laws, and the sovereign of sovereigns, cannot think it reprehensible that this our corporate fealty and homage, that this our recognition of a signiory paramount, I had almost said this oblation of the state itself, as a worthy offering on the high altar of universal praise, should be performed as all public, solemn acts are performed, in buildings, in music, in decoration, in speech, in the dignity of persons, according to the customs of mankind, taught by their nature; this is, with modest splendour and unassuming state, with mild majesty and sober pomp. For those purposes they think some part of the wealth of the country is as usefully employed as it can be in fomenting the luxury of individuals. It is the public ornament. It is the public consolation. It nourishes the public hope. The poorest man finds his own importance and dignity in it, whilst the wealth and pride of individuals at every moment makes the man of humble rank and fortune sensible of his inferiority, and degrades and vilifies his condition. It is for the man in humble life, and to raise his nature, and to put him in mind of a state in which the privileges of opulence will cease, when he will be equal by nature, and may be more than equal by virtue, that this portion of the general wealth of his country is employed and sanctified.

I assure you I do not aim at singularity. I give you opinions which have been accepted amongst us, from very early times to this moment, with a continued and general approbation, and which indeed are so worked into my mind, that I am unable to distinguish what I have learned from others from the results of my own meditation.

It is on some such principles that the majority of the people of England, far from thinking a religious national establishment unlawful, hardly think it lawful to be without one. In France you are wholly mistaken if you do not believe us above all other things attached to it, and beyond all other nations; and when this people has acted unwisely and unjustifiably in its favour (as in some instances they have done most certainly), in their very errors you will at least discover their zeal.

This principle runs through the whole system of their polity. They do not consider their church establishment as convenient, but as essential to their state; not as a thing heterogeneous and separable; something added for accommodation; what they may either keep or lay aside, according to their temporary ideas of convenience. They consider it as the foundation of their whole constitution, with which, and with every part of which, it holds an indissoluble union. Church and state are ideas inseparable in their minds, and scarcely is the one ever mentioned without mentioning the other.

Our education is so formed as to confirm and fix this impression. Our education is in a manner wholly in the hands of ecclesiastics, and in all stages from infancy to manhood. Even when our youth, leaving schools and universities, enter that most important period of life which begins to link experience and study together, and when with that view they visit other countries, instead of old domestics whom we have seen as governors to principal men from other parts, three-fourths of those who go abroad with our young nobility and gentlemen are ecclesiastics; not as austere masters, nor as mere followers; but as friends and companions of a graver character, and not seldom persons as well born as themselves. With them, as relations, they most constantly keep up a close connexion through life. By this connexion we conceive that we attach our gentlemen to the church; and we liberalize the church by an intercourse with the leading characters of the country.

So tenacious are we of the old ecclesiastical modes and fashions of institution, that very little alteration has been made in them since the fourteenth or fifteenth century : adhering in this particular, as in all things else, to our old settled maxim, never entirely nor at once to depart from antiquity. We found these old institutions, on the whole, favourable to morality and discipline; and we thought they were susceptible of amendment, without altering the ground. We thought that they were capable of receiving and meliorating, and above all of preserving, the accessions of science and literature, as the order of Providence should successively produce them. And after all, with this Gothic and monkish education (for such it is in the ground-work) we may put in our claim to as ample and as early a share in all the improvements in science, in arts, and in literature, which have illuminated and adorned the modern world, as any other nation in Europe : we think one main cause of this improvement was our not despising the patrimony of knowledge which was left us by our forefathers.

It is from our attachment to a church establishment, that the English nation did not think it wise to intrust that great, fundamental interest of the whole to what they trust no part of their civil or military public service, that is, to the unsteady and precarious contribution of individuals. They go further. They certainly never have suffered, and never will suffer, the fixed estate of the church to be converted into a pension, to depend on the treasury, and to be delayed, withheld, or perhaps to be extinguished, by fiscal difficulties : which difficulties may sometimes be pretended for political purposes, and are in fact often brought on by the extravagance, negligence, and rapacity of politicians. The people of England think that they have constitutional motives, as well as religious, against any project of turning their independent clergy into ecclesiastical pensioners of state. They tremble for their liberty, from the influence of a clergy dependent on the crown; they tremble for the public tranquillity from the disorders of a factious clergy, if it were made to depend upon any other than the crown. They therefore made their church, like their king and their nobility, independent.

From the united considerations of religion and constitutional policy, from their opinion of a duty to make sure provision for the consolation of the feeble and the instruction of the ignorant, they have incorporated and identified the estate of the church with the mass of *private property*, of which the state is not the proprietor, either for use or dominion, but the guardian only and the regulator. They have ordained that the provision of this establishment might be as stable as the earth on which it stands, and should not fluctuate with the Euripus of funds and actions.

The men of England, the men, I mean, of light and leading in England, whose wisdom (if they have any) is open and direct, would be ashamed, as of a silly, deceitful trick, to profess any religion in name, which, by their proceedings, they appear to contemn. If by their conduct (the only language that rarely lies) they seemed to regard the great ruling principle of the moral and the natural world, as a mere invention to keep the vulgar in obedience, they apprehend that by such a conduct they would defeat the politic purpose they have in view. They would find it difficult to make others believe in a system to which they manifestly give no credit themselves. The Christian statesmen of this land would indeed first provide for the *multitude;* because it is the *multitude;* and is therefore, as such, the first object in the ecclesiastical institution, and in all institutions. They have been taught, that the circumstance of the gospel's being preached to the poor, was one of the great tests of its true mission. They think, therefore, that those do not believe it, who do not take care it should be preached to the poor. But as they know that charity is not confined to any one description, but ought to apply itself to all men who have wants, they are not deprived of a due and anxious sensation of pity to the distresses of the miserable great. They are not repelled through a fastidious delicacy, at the stench of their arrogance and presumption, from a medicinal attention to their mental blotches and running sores. They are sensible, that religious instruction is of more consequence to them than to any others; from the greatness of the temptation to which they are exposed; from the important consequences that attend their faults; from the contagion of their ill example; from the necessity of bowing down the stubborn neck of their pride and ambition to the yoke of moderation and virtue; from a consideration of the fat stupidity and gross ignorance concerning what imports men most to know, which prevails at courts, and at the head of armies, and in senates, as much as at the loom and in the field.

The English people are satisfied, that to the great the consolations of religion are as necessary as its instructions. They too are among the unhappy. They feel personal pain, and domestic sorrow. In these they have no privilege, but are subject to pay their full contingent to the contributions levied on mortality. They want this sovereign balm under their gnawing cares and anxieties, which, being less conversant about the limited wants of animal life, range without limit, and are diversified by infinite combinations, in the wild and unbounded regions of imagination. Some charitable dole is wanting to these, our often very unhappy brethren, to fill the gloomy void that reigns in minds which have nothing on earth to hope or fear; something to relieve in the killing languor and over-laboured lassitude of those who have nothing to do; something to excite an appetite to existence in the palled satiety which attends on all pleasures which may be bought, where nature is not left to her own process, where even desire is anticipated, and therefore fruition defeated by meditated schemes and contrivances of delight; and no interval, no obstacle, is interposed between the wish and the accomplishment.

The people of England know how little influence the teachers of religion are likely to have with the wealthy and powerful of long standing, and how much less with the newly fortunate, if they appear in a manner no way assorted to those with whom they must associate, and over whom they must even exercise, in some cases, something like an authority. What must they think of that body of teachers, if they see it in no part above the establishment of their domestic servants? If the poverty were voluntary, there might be some difference. Strong instances of self-denial operate powerfully on our minds; and a man who has no wants has obtained great freedom, and firmness, and even dignity. But as the mass of any description of men are but men, and their poverty cannot be voluntary, that disrespect, which attends upon all lay poverty, will not depart from the ecclesiastical. Our provident constitution has therefore taken care that those who are to instruct presumptuous ignorance, those who are to be censors over insolent vice, should neither incur their contempt, nor live upon their alms; nor will it tempt the rich to a neglect of the true medicine of their minds. For these reasons, whilst we provide first for the poor, and with a parental solicitude, we have not relegated religion (like something we were ashamed to show) to obscure municipalities, or rustic villages. No! we will have her to exalt her mitred front in courts and parliaments. We will have her mixed throughout the whole mass of life, and blended with all the classes of society. The people of England will show to the haughty potentates of the world, and to their talking sophisters, that a free, a generous, an informed nation honours the high magistrates of its church; that it will not suffer the insolence of wealth and titles, or any other species of proud pretension, to look down with scorn upon what they look up to with reverence; nor presume to trample on that acquired personal nobility, which they intend always to be, and which often is, the fruit, not the reward (for what can be the reward?) of learning, piety, and virtue. They can see, without pain or grudging, an archbishop precede a duke. They can see a bishop of Durham, or a bishop of Winchester, in possession of ten thousand pounds a year; and cannot conceive why it is in worse hands than estates to the like amount in the hands of this earl, or that squire; although it may be true, that so many dogs and horses are not kept by the former, and fed with the victuals which ought to nourish the children of the people. It is true, the whole church revenue is not always employed, and to every shilling, in charity; nor perhaps ought it; but something is generally so employed. It is better to cherish virtue and humanity, by leaving much to free will, even with some loss to the object, than to attempt to make men mere machines and instruments of a political benevolence. The world on the whole will gain by a liberty, without which virtue cannot exist.

When once the commonwealth has established the estates of the church as property, it can, consistently, hear nothing of the more or the less. Too much and too little are treason against property. What evil can arise from the quantity in any hand, whilst the supreme authority has the full, sovereign superintendence over this, as over all property, to prevent every species of abuse; and, whenever it notably deviates, to give to it a direction agreeable to the purposes of its institution.

In England most of us conceive that it is envy and malignity towards those who are often the beginners of their own fortune, and not a love of the self-denial and mortification of the ancient church, that makes some look askance at the distinctions, and honours, and revenues, which, taken from no person, are set apart for virtue. The ears of the people of England are distinguishing. They hear these men speak broad. Their tongue betrays them. Their language is in the *patois* of fraud; in the cant and gibberish of hypocrisy. The people of England must think so, when these praters affect to carry back the clergy to that primitive, evangelic poverty, which, in the spirit, ought always to exist in them (and in us too, however we may like it), but in the thing must be varied, when the relation of that body to the state is altered; when manners, when modes of life, when indeed the whole order of human affairs, has undergone a total revolution. We shall believe those reformers then to be honest enthusiasts, not, as now we think them, cheats and deceivers, when we see them throwing their own goods into common, and submitting their own persons to the austere discipline of the early church.

With these ideas rooted in their minds, the Commons of Great Britain, in the national emergencies, will never seek their resource from the confiscation of the estates of the church and poor. Sacrilege and proscription are not among the ways and means of our committee of supply. The Jews in Change Alley have not yet dared to hint their hopes of a mortgage on the revenues belonging to the see of Canterbury. I am not afraid that I shall be disavowed, when I assure you, that there is not *one* public man in this kingdom, whom you would wish to quote, no not one, of any party or description, who does not reprobate the dishonest, perfidious, and cruel confiscation which the National Assembly has been compelled to make of that property, which it was their first duty to protect.

It is with the exultation of a little national pride I tell you, that those amongst us who have wished to pledge the societies of Paris in the cup of their abominations have been disappointed. The robbery of your church has proved a security to the possessions of ours. It has roused the people. They see with horror and alarm that enormous and shameless act of proscription. It has opened, and will more and more open, their eyes upon the selfish enlargement of mind, and the narrow liberality of sentiment, of insidious men, which, commencing in close hypocrisy and fraud, have ended in open violence and rapine. At home we behold similar beginnings. We are on our guard against similar conclusions.

I hope we shall never be so totally lost to all sense of the duties imposed upon us by the law of social union, as, upon any pretext of public service, to confiscate the goods of a single unoffending citizen. Who but a tyrant (a name expressive of everything which can vitiate and degrade human nature) could think of seizing on the property of men, unaccused, unheard, untried, by whole descriptions, by hundreds and thousands together? Who, that had not lost every trace of humanity, could think of casting down men of exalted rank and sacred function, some of them of an age to call at once for reverence and compassion, of casting them down from the highest situation in the commonwealth, wherein they were maintained by their own landed property, to a state of indigence, depression, and contempt?

The confiscators truly have made some allowance to their victims from the scraps and fragments of their own tables, from which they have been so harshly driven, and which have been so bountifully spread for a feast to the harpies of usury. But to drive men from independence to live on alms, is itself great cruelty. That which might be a tolerable condition to men in one state of life, and not habituated to other things, may, when all these circumstances are altered, be a dreadful revolution; and one to which a virtuous mind would feel pain in condemning any guilt, except that which would demand the life of the offender. But to many minds this punishment of *degradation* and *infamy* is worse than death. Undoubtedly it is an infinite aggravation of this cruel suffering, that the persons who were taught a double prejudice in favour of religion, by education, and by the place they held in the administration of its functions, are to receive the remnants of their property as alms from the profane and impious hands of those who had plundered them of all the rest; to receive (if they are at all to receive) not from the charitable contributions of the faithful, but from the insolent tenderness of known and avowed atheism, the maintenance of religion, measured out to them on the standard of the contempt in which it is held; and for the purpose of rendering those who receive the allowance vile and of no estimation in the eyes of mankind.

But this act of seizure of property, it seems, is a judgment in law, and not a confiscation. They have, it seems, found out in the academies of the *Palais Royal*, and the *Jacobins*, that certain men had no right to the possessions which they held under law, usage, the decisions of courts, and the accumulated prescription of a thousand years. They say that ecclesiastics are fictitious persons, creatures of the state, whom at pleasure they may destroy, and of course limit and modify in every particular; that the goods they possess are not properly theirs, but belong to the state which created the fiction; and we are therefore not to trouble ourselves with what they may suffer in their natural feelings and natural persons, on account of what is done towards them in this their constructive character. Of what import is it under what names you injure men, and deprive them of the just emoluments of a profession, in which they were not only permitted but encouraged by the state to engage; and upon the supposed certainty of which emoluments they had formed the plan of their lives, contracted debts, and led multitudes to an entire dependence upon them?

You do not imagine, Sir, that I am going to compliment this miserable distinction of persons with any long discussion. The arguments of tyranny are as contemptible as its force is dreadful. Had not your confiscators, by their early crimes, obtained a power which secures indemnity to all the crimes of which they have since been guilty, or that they can commit, it is not the syllogism of the logician, but the lash of the executioner, that would have refuted a sophistry which becomes an accomplice of theft and murder. The sophistic tyrants of Paris are loud in their declamations against the departed regal tyrants, who in former ages have vexed the world. They are thus bold, because they are safe from the dungeons and iron cages of their old masters. Shall we be more tender of the tyrants of our own time, when we see them acting worse tragedies under our eyes? shall we not use the same liberty that they do, when we can use it with the same safety? when to speak honest truth only requires a contempt of the opinions of those whose actions we abhor?

This outrage on all the rights of property was at first covered with what, on the system of their conduct, was the most astonishing of all pretexts—a regard to national faith. The enemies to property at first pretended a most tender, delicate, and scrupulous anxiety for keeping the king's engagements with the public creditor. These professors of the rights of men are so busy in teaching others, that they have not leisure to learn anything themselves; otherwise they would have known, that it is to the property of the citizen, and not to the demands of the creditor of the state, that the first and original faith of civil society is pledged. The claim of the citizen is prior in time, paramount in title, superior in equity. The fortunes of individuals, whether possessed by acquisition, or by descent, or in virtue of a participation in the goods of some community, were no part of the creditor's security, expressed or implied. They never so much as entered into his head when he made his bargain. He well knew that the public, whether represented by a monarch or by a senate, can pledge nothing but the public estate; and it can have no public estate, except in what it derives from a just and proportioned imposition upon the citizens at large. This was engaged, and nothing else could be engaged, to the public creditor. No man can mortgage his injustice as a pawn for his fidelity.

It is impossible to avoid some observation on the contradictions caused by the extreme rigour and the extreme laxity of this new public faith, which influenced in this transaction, and which influenced not according to the nature of the obligation, but to the description of the persons to whom it was engaged. No acts of the old government of the kings of France are held valid in the National Assembly, except his pecuniary engagements; acts of all others of the most ambiguous legality. The rest of the acts of that royal government are considered in so odious a light, that to have a claim under its authority is looked on as a sort of crime. A pension, given as a reward for service to the state, is surely as good a ground of property as any security for money advanced to the state. It is better; for money is paid, and well paid, to obtain that service. We have however seen multitudes of people under this description in France, who never had been deprived of their allowances by the most arbitrary ministers, in the most arbitrary times, by this assembly of the rights of men, robbed without mercy. They were told, in answer to their claim to the bread earned with their blood, that their services had not been rendered to the country that now exists.

This laxity of public faith is not confined to those unfortunate persons. The Assembly, with perfect consistency it must be owned, is engaged in a respectable deliberation how far it is bound by the treaties made with other nations under the former government, and their committee is to report which of them they ought to ratify, and which not. By this means they have put the external fidelity of this virgin state on a par with its internal.

It is not easy to conceive upon what rational principle the royal government should not, of the two, rather have possessed the power of rewarding service, and making treaties, in virtue of its prerogative, than that of pledging to creditors the revenue of the state, actual and possible. The treasure of the nation, of all things, has been the least allowed to the prerogative of the king of France, or to the prerogative of any king in Europe. To mortgage the public revenue implies the sovereign dominion, in the fullest sense, over the public purse. It goes far beyond the trust even of a temporary and occasional taxation. The acts however of that dangerous power (the distinctive mark of a boundless despotism) have been alone held sacred. Whence arose this preference given by a democratic assembly to a body of property deriving its title from the most critical and obnoxious of all the exertions of monarchical authority? Reason can furnish nothing to reconcile inconsistency; nor can partial favour be accounted for upon equitable principles. But the contradiction and partiality which admit no justification, are not the less without an adequate cause; and that cause I do not think it difficult to discover.

By the vast debt of France a great monied interest has insensibly grown up, and with it a great power. By the ancient usages which prevailed in that kingdom, the general circulation of property and in particular the mutual convertibility of land into money, and of money into land, had always been a matter of difficulty. Family settlements, rather more general and more strict than they are in England, the *jus retractus*, the great mass of landed property held by the crown, and, by a maxim of the French law, held unalienably, the vast estates of the ecclesiastic corporations,—all these had kept the landed and monied interests more separated in France, less miscible, and the owners of the two distinct species of property not so well disposed to each other as they are in this country.

The monied property was long looked on with rather an evil eye by the people. They saw it connected with their distresses, and aggravating them. It was no less envied by the old landed interests, partly for the same reasons that rendered it obnoxious to the people, but much more so as it eclipsed, by the splendour of an ostentatious luxury, the unendowed pedigrees and naked titles of several among the nobility. Even when the nobility, which represented the more permanent landed interest, united themselves by marriage (which sometimes was the case) with the other description, the wealth which saved the family from ruin, was supposed to contaminate and degrade it. Thus the enmities and heart-burnings of these parties were increased even by the usual means by which discord is made to cease and quarrels are turned into friendship. In the mean time, the pride of the wealthy men, not noble or newly noble, increased with its cause. They felt with resentment an inferiority, the grounds of which they did not acknowledge. There was no measure to which they were not willing to lend themselves, in order to be revenged of the outrages of this rival pride, and to exalt their wealth to what they considered as its natural rank and estimation. They struck at the nobility through the crown and the church. They attacked them particularly on the side on which they thought them the most vulnerable, that is, the possessions of the church, which, through the patronage of the crown, generally devolved upon the nobility. The bishoprics, and the great commendatory abbeys, were, with few exceptions, held by that order.

In this state of real, though not always perceived, warfare between the noble ancient landed interest and the new monied interest, the greatest because the most applicable strength was in the hands of the latter. The monied interest is in its nature more ready for any adventure; and its possessors more disposed to new enterprises of any kind. Being of a recent acquisition, it falls in more naturally with any novelties. It is therefore the kind of wealth which will be resorted to by all who wish for change.

Along with the monied interest, a new description of men had grown up, with whom that interest soon formed a close and marked union; I mean the political men of letters. Men of letters, fond of distinguishing themselves, are rarely averse to innovation. Since the decline of the life and greatness of Louis the Fourteenth, they were not so much cultivated either by him, or by the regent, or the successors to the crown; nor were they engaged to the court by favours and emoluments so systematically as during the splendid period of that ostentatious and not impolitic reign. What they lost in the old court protection, they endeavoured to make up by joining in a sort of incorporation of their own; to which the two academies of France, and afterwards the vast undertaking of the Encyclopædia, carried on by a society of these gentlemen, did not a little contribute.

The literary cabal had some years ago formed something like a regular plan for the destruction of the Christian religion. This object they pursued with a degree of zeal which hitherto had been discovered only in the propagators of some system of piety. They were possessed with a spirit of proselytism in the most fanatical degree; and from thence, by an easy progress, with the spirit of persecution according to their means.[1] What was not to be done towards their great end by any direct or immediate act, might be wrought by a longer process through the

[1] This (down to the end of the first sentence in the next paragraph) and some other parts here and there, were inserted, on his reading the manuscript, by my lost Son.

medium of opinion. To command that opinion, the first step is to establish a dominion over those who direct it. They contrived to possess themselves, with great method and perseverance, of all the avenues to literary fame. Many of them indeed stood high in the ranks of literature and science. The world had done them justice; and in favour of general talents forgave the evil tendency of their peculiar principles. This was true liberality; which they returned by endeavouring to confine the reputation of sense, learning, and taste to themselves or their followers. I will venture to say that this narrow, exclusive spirit has not been less prejudicial to literature and to taste, than to morals and true philosophy. These atheistical fathers have a bigotry of their own; and they have learnt to talk against monks with the spirit of a monk. But in some things they are men of the world. The resources of intrigue are called in to supply the defects of argument and wit. To this system of literary monopoly was joined an unremitting industry to blacken and discredit in every way, and by every means, all those who did not hold to their faction. To those who have observed the spirit of their conduct, it has long been clear that nothing was wanted but the power of carrying the intolerance of the tongue and of the pen into a persecution which would strike at property, liberty, and life.

The desultory and faint persecution carried on against them, more from compliance with form and decency, than with serious resentment, neither weakened their strength, nor relaxed their efforts. The issue of the whole was, that, what with opposition, and what with success, a violent and malignant zeal, of a kind hitherto unknown in the world, had taken an entire possession of their minds, and rendered their whole conversation, which otherwise would have been pleasing and instructive, perfectly disgusting. A spirit of cabal, intrigue, and proselytism, pervaded all their thoughts, words, and actions. And, as controversial zeal soon turns its thoughts on force, they began to insinuate themselves into a correspondence with foreign princes; in hopes, through their authority, which at first they flattered, they might bring about the changes they had in view. To them it was indifferent whether these changes were to be accomplished by the thunderbolt of despotism, or by the earthquake of popular commotion. The correspondence between this cabal and the late king of Prussia will throw no small light upon the spirit of all their proceedings.[1] For the same purpose for which they intrigued with princes, they cultivated, in a distinguished manner, the monied interest of France; and partly through the means furnished by those whose peculiar offices gave them the most extensive and certain means of communication, they carefully occupied all the avenues to opinion.

Writers, especially when they act in a body, and with one direction, have great influence on the public mind; the alliance, therefore, of these writers with the monied interest [2] had no small effect in removing the popular odium and envy which attended that species of wealth. These writers, like the propagators of all novelties, pretended to a great zeal for the poor, and the lower orders, whilst in their satires they rendered hateful, by every exaggeration, the faults of courts, of nobility, and of priesthood. They became a sort of demagogues. They served as a link to unite, in favour of one object, obnoxious wealth to restless and desperate poverty.

As these two kinds of men appear principal leaders in all the late transactions, their junction and politics will serve to account, not upon any principles of law or of policy, but as a *cause*, for the general fury with which all the landed property of ecclesiastical corporations has been attacked; and the great care which, contrary to their pretended principles, has been taken, of a monied interest originating from the authority of the crown. All the envy against wealth and power was artificially directed against other descriptions of riches. On what other principle than that which I have stated can we account for an appearance so extraordinary and unnatural as that of the ecclesiastical possessions, which had stood so many successions of ages and shocks of civil violences, and were girded at once by justice, and by prejudice, being applied to the payment of debts, comparatively recent, invidious, and contracted by a decried and subverted government?

[1] I do not choose to shock the feeling of the moral reader with any quotation of their vulgar, base, and profane language.
[2] Their connexion with Turgot and almost all the people of the finance.

Was the public estate a sufficient stake for the public debts? Assume that it was not, and that a loss *must* be incurred somewhere—When the only estate lawfully possessed, and which the contracting parties had in contemplation at the time in which their bargain was made, happens to fail, who according to the principles of natural and legal equity, ought to be the sufferer? Certainly it ought to be either the party who trusted, or the party who persuaded him to trust; or both; and not third parties who had no concern with the transaction. Upon any insolvency they ought to suffer who are weak enough to lend upon bad security, or they who fraudulently held out a security that was not valid. Laws are acquainted with no other rules of decision. But by the new institute of the rights of men, the only persons, who in equity ought to suffer, are the only persons who are to be saved harmless: those are to answer the debt who neither were lenders nor borrowers, mortgagers nor mortgagees.

What had the clergy to do with these transactions? What had they to do with any public engagement further than the extent of their own debt? To that, to be sure, their estates were bound to the last acre. Nothing can lead more to the true spirit of the Assembly, which fits for public confiscation, with its new equity, and its new morality, than an attention to their proceeding with regard to this debt of the clergy. The body of confiscators, true to that monied interest for which they were false to every other, have found the clergy competent to incur a legal debt. Of course they declared them legally entitled to the property which their power of incurring the debt and mortgaging the estate implied; recognizing the rights of those persecuted citizens, in the very act in which they were thus grossly violated.

If, as I said, any persons are to make good deficiencies to the public creditor, besides the public at large, they must be those who managed the agreement. Why therefore are not the estates of all the comptrollers-general confiscated?[1] Why not those of the long succession of ministers, financiers, and bankers who have been enriched whilst the nation was impoverished by their dealings and their counsels? Why is not the estate of M. Laborde

[1] All have been confiscated in their turn.

declared forfeited rather than of the archbishop of Paris, who has had nothing to do in the creation or in the jobbing of the public funds? Or, if you must confiscate old landed estates in favour of the money-jobbers, why is the penalty confined to one description? I do not know whether the expenses of the Duke de Choiseul have left anything of the infinite sums which he had derived from the bounty of his master, during the transactions of a reign which contributed largely by every species of prodigality in war and peace, to the present debt of France. If any such remains, why is not this confiscated? I remember to have been in Paris during the time of the old government. I was there just after the Duke d'Aiguillon had been snatched (as it was generally thought) from the block by the hand of a protecting despotism. He was a minister, and had some concern in the affairs of that prodigal period. Why do I not see his estate delivered up to the municipalities in which it is situated? The noble family of Noailles have long been servants (meritorious servants I admit) to the crown of France, and have had of course some share in its bounties. Why do I hear nothing of the application of their estates to the public debt? Why is the estate of the Duke de Rochefoucault more sacred than that of the Cardinal de Rochefoucault? The former is, I doubt not, a worthy person; and (if it were not a sort of profaneness to talk of the use, as affecting the title to property) he makes a good use of his revenues; but it is no disrespect to him to say, what authentic information well warrants me in saying, that the use made of a property equally valid, by his brother [1] the cardinal archbishop of Rouen, was far more laudable and far more public-spirited. Can one hear of the proscription of such persons, and the confiscation of their effects, without indignation and horror? He is not a man who does not feel such emotions on such occasions. He does not deserve the name of a free-man who will not express them.

Few barbarous conquerors have ever made so terrible a revolution in property. None of the heads of the Roman factions, when they established "*crudelem illam hastam*" in all their auctions of rapine, have ever set up to sale the

---

[1] Not his brother, nor any near relation; but this mistake does not affect the argument.

goods of the conquered citizen to such an enormous amount. It must be allowed in favour of those tyrants of antiquity, that what was done by them could hardly be said to be done in cold blood. Their passions were inflamed, their tempers soured, their understandings confused, with the spirit of revenge, with the innumerable reciprocated and recent inflictions and retaliations of blood and rapine. They were driven beyond all bounds of moderation by the apprehension of the return of power with the return of property, to the families of those they had injured beyond all hope of forgiveness.

These Roman confiscators, who were yet only in the elements of tyranny, and were not instructed in the rights of men to exercise all sorts of cruelties on each other without provocation, thought it necessary to spread a sort of colour over their injustice. They considered the vanquished party as composed of traitors who had borne arms, or otherwise had acted with hostility, against the commonwealth. They regarded them as persons who had forfeited their property by their crimes. With you, in your improved state of the human mind, there was no such formality. You seized upon five millions sterling of annual rent, and turned forty or fifty thousand human creatures out of their houses, because "such was your pleasure." The tyrant Harry the Eighth of England, as he was not better enlightened than the Roman Mariuses and Syllas, and had not studied in your new schools, did not know what an effectual instrument of despotism was to be found in that grand magazine of offensive weapons, the rights of men. When he resolved to rob the abbeys, as the club of the Jacobins have robbed all the ecclesiastics, he began by setting on foot a commission to examine into the crimes and abuses which prevailed in those communities. As it might be expected, his commission reported truths, exaggerations, and falsehoods. But truly or falsely, it reported abuses and offences. However, as abuses might be corrected, as every crime of persons does not infer a forfeiture with regard to communities, and as property, in that dark age, was not discovered to be a creature of prejudice, all those abuses (and there were enow of them) were hardly thought sufficient ground for such a confiscation as it was for his purpose to make. He therefore procured the formal surrender of these estates. All these operose proceedings were adopted by one of the most decided tyrants in the rolls of history, as necessary preliminaries, before he could venture, by bribing the members of his two servile houses with a share of the spoil, and holding out to them an eternal immunity from taxation, to demand a confirmation of his iniquitous proceedings by an act of parliament. Had fate reserved him to our times, four technical terms would have done his business, and saved him all this trouble; he needed nothing more than one short form of incantation—"*Philosophy, Light, Liberality, the Rights of Men.*"

I can say nothing in praise of those acts of tyranny, which no voice has hitherto ever commended under any of their false colours; yet in these false colours an homage was paid by despotism to justice. The power which was above all fear and all remorse was not set above all shame. Whilst shame keeps its watch, virtue is not wholly extinguished in the heart; nor will moderation be utterly exiled from the minds of tyrants.

I believe every honest man sympathizes in his reflections with our political poet on that occasion, and will pray to avert the omen whenever these acts of rapacious despotism present themselves to his view or his imagination:

> —"May no such storm
> Fall on our times, where ruin must reform.
> Tell me (my Muse) what monstrous dire offence,
> What crimes could any Christian king incense
> To such a rage? Was't luxury, or lust?
> Was *he* so temperate, so chaste, so just?
> Were these their crimes? they were his own much more,
> But wealth is crime enough to him that's poor." [1]

---

[1] The rest of the passage is this—

> "Who having spent the treasures of his crown,
> Condemns their luxury to feed his own.
> And yet this act, to varnish o'er the shame
> Of sacrilege, must bear devotion's name.
> No crime so bold, but would be understood
> A real, or at least a seeming good;
> Who fears not to do ill, yet fears the name,
> And, free from conscience, is a slave to fame.
> Thus he the church at once protects, and spoils;
> But princes' swords are sharper than their styles.
> And thus to th' ages past he makes amends,
> Their charity destroys, their faith defends.
> Then did religion in a lazy cell,
> In empty aery contemplation dwell;
> And, like the block, unmoved lay; but ours,
> As much too active, like the stork devours.

E 460

This same wealth, which is at all times treason and *lese nation* to indigent and rapacious despotism, under all modes of polity, was your temptation to violate property, law, and religion, united in one object. But was the state of France so wretched and undone, that no other resource but rapine remained to preserve its existence? On this point I wish to receive some information. When the states met, was the condition of the finances of France such, that, after economizing on principles of justice and mercy through all departments, no fair repartition of burthens upon all the orders could possibly restore them? If such an equal imposition would have been sufficient, you well know it might easily have been made. M. Necker, in the budget which he laid before the orders assembled at Versailles, made a detailed exposition of the state of the French nation.[1]

If we give credit to him, it was not necessary to have recourse to any new impositions whatsoever, to put the receipts of France on a balance with its expenses. He stated the permanent charges of all descriptions, including the interest of a new loan of four hundred millions, at 531,444,000 livres; the fixed revenue at 475,294,000, making the deficiency 56,150,000, or short of £2,200,000. But to balance it, he brought forward savings and improve-

---

Is there no temperate region can be known,
Betwixt their frigid and our torrid zone?
Could we not wake from that lethargic dream,
But to be restless in a worse extreme?
And for that lethargy was there no cure,
But to be cast into a calenture;
Can knowledge have no bound, but must advance
So far, to make us wish for ignorance?
And rather in the dark to grope our way,
Than, led by a false guide, to err by day?
Who sees these dismal heaps, but would demand,
What barbarous invader sacked the land?
But when he hears, no Goth, no Turk did bring
This desolation, but a Christian king;
When nothing, but the name of zeal, appears
'Twixt our best actions and the worst of theirs,
What does he think our sacrilege would spare,
When such th' effects of our devotion are?"

COOPER'S HILL, by Sir JOHN DENHAM.

[1] Rapport de Mons. le Directeur-Général des Finances, fait par ordre du Roi à Versailles. Mai 5, 1789.

ments of revenue (considered as entirely certain) to rather more than the amount of that deficiency; and he concludes with these emphatical words (p. 39), "Quel pays, Messieurs, que celui, où, *sans impôts* et avec de simples objets *inapperçus*, on peut faire disparoître un deficit qui a fait tant de bruit en Europe." As to the reimbursement, the sinking of debt, and the other great objects of public credit and political arrangement indicated in Mons. Necker's speech, no doubt could be entertained, but that a very moderate and proportioned assessment on the citizens without distinction would have provided for all of them to the fullest extent of their demand.

If this representation of Mons. Necker was false, then the Assembly are in the highest degree culpable for having forced the king to accept as his minister, and since the king's deposition, for having employed, as *their* minister, a man who had been capable of abusing so notoriously the confidence of his master and their own; in a matter too of the highest moment, and directly appertaining to his particular office. But if the representation was exact (as having always, along with you, conceived a high degree of respect for M. Necker, I make no doubt it was), then what can be said in favour of those, who, instead of moderate, reasonable, and general contribution, have in cold blood, and impelled by no necessity, had recourse to a partial and cruel confiscation?

Was that contribution refused on a pretext of privilege, either on the part of the clergy, or on that of the nobility? No, certainly. As to the clergy, they even ran before the wishes of the third order. Previous to the meeting of the states, they had in all their instructions expressly directed their deputies to renounce every immunity, which put them upon a footing distinct from the condition of their fellow-subjects. In this renunciation the clergy were even more explicit than the nobility.

But let us suppose that the deficiency had remained at the fifty-six millions (or £2,200,000 sterling), as at first stated by M. Necker. Let us allow that all the resources he opposed to that deficiency were impudent and groundless fictions; and that the Assembly (or their lords of articles [1] at the Jacobins) were from thence justified in

1 In the constitution of Scotland, during the Stuart reigns, a com-

laying the whole burthen of that deficiency on the clergy, —yet allowing all this, a necessity of £2,200,000 sterling will not support a confiscation to the amount of five millions. The imposition of £2,200,000 on the clergy, as partial, would have been oppressive and unjust, but it would not have been altogether ruinous to those on whom it was imposed; and therefore it would not have answered the real purpose of the managers.

Perhaps persons unacquainted with the state of France, on hearing the clergy and the noblesse were privileged in point of taxation, may be led to imagine, that, previous to the Revolution, these bodies had contributed nothing to the state. This is a great mistake. They certainly did not contribute equally with each other, nor either of them equally with the commons. They both however contributed largely. Neither nobility nor clergy enjoyed any exemption from the excise on consumable commodities, from duties of custom, or from any of the other numerous *indirect* impositions, which in France, as well as here, make so very large a proportion of all payments to the public. The noblesse paid the capitation. They paid also a land-tax, called the twentieth penny, to the height sometimes of three, sometimes of four, shillings in the pound; both of them *direct* impositions of no light nature, and no trivial produce. The clergy of the provinces annexed by conquest to France (which in extent make about an eighth part of the whole, but in wealth a much larger proportion), paid likewise to the capitation and the twentieth penny, at the rate paid by the nobility. The clergy in the old provinces did not pay the capitation; but they had redeemed themselves at the expense of about 24 millions, or a little more than a million sterling. They were exempted from the twentieths: but then they made free gifts; they contracted debts for the state; and they were subject to some other charges, the whole computed at about a thirteenth part of their clear income. They ought to have paid annually about forty thousand pounds more, to put them on a par with the contribution of the nobility.

When the terrors of this tremendous proscription hung over the clergy, they made an offer of a contribution,

mittee sat for preparing bills; and none could pass, but those previously approved by them. This committee was called lords of articles.

through the archbishop of Aix, which, for its extravagance, ought not to have been accepted. But it was evidently and obviously more advantageous to the public creditor, than anything which could rationally be promised by the confiscation. Why was it not accepted? The reason is plain—There was no desire that the church should be brought to serve the state. The service of the state was made a pretext to destroy the church. In their way to the destruction of the church they would not scruple to destroy their country : and they have destroyed it. One great end in the project would have been defeated, if the plan of extortion had been adopted in lieu of the scheme of confiscation. The new landed interest connected with the new republic, and connected with it for its very being, could not have been created. ·This was among the reasons why that extravagant ransom was not accepted.

The madness of the project of confiscation, on the plan that was first pretended, soon became apparent. To bring this unwieldy mass of landed property, enlarged by the confiscation of all the vast landed domain of the crown, at once into market, was obviously to defeat the profits proposed by the confiscation, by depreciating the value of those lands, and indeed of all the landed estates throughout France. Such a sudden diversion of all its circulating money from trade to land, must be an additional mischief. What step was taken? Did the Assembly, on becoming sensible of the inevitable ill effects of their projected sale, revert to the offers of the clergy? No distress could oblige them to travel in a course which was disgraced by any appearance of justice. Giving over all hopes from a general immediate sale, another project seems to have succeeded. They proposed to take stock in exchange for the church lands. In that project great difficulties arose in equalizing the objects to be exchanged. Other obstacles also presented themselves, which threw them back again upon some project of sale. The municipalities had taken an alarm. They would not hear of transferring the whole plunder of the kingdom to the stock-holders in Paris. Many of those municipalities had been (upon system) reduced to the most deplorable indigence. Money was nowhere to be seen. They were therefore led to the point that was so ardently desired. They panted for a currency of any kind which might revive their perishing industry. The municipalities were then to be admitted to a share in the spoil, which evidently rendered the first scheme (if ever it had been seriously entertained) altogether impracticable.   Public exigencies pressed upon all sides. The minister of finance reiterated his call for supply with a most urgent, anxious, and boding voice.   Thus pressed on all sides, instead of the first plan of converting their bankers into bishops and abbots, instead of paying the old debt, they contracted a new debt, at 3 per cent., creating a new paper currency, founded on an eventual sale of the church lands.   They issued this paper currency to satisfy in the first instance chiefly the demands made upon them by the *bank of discount*, the great machine, or paper-mill, of their fictitious•wealth.

The spoil of the church was now become the only resource of all their operations in finance, the vital principle of all their politics, the sole security for the existence of their power.   It was necessary by all, even the most violent means, to put every individual on the same bottom, and to bind the nation in one guilty interest to uphold this act, and the authority of those by whom it was done.   In order to force the most reluctant into a participation of their pillage, they rendered their paper circulation compulsory in all payments.   Those who consider the general tendency of their schemes to this one object as a centre, and a centre from which afterwards all their measures radiate, will not think that I dwell too long upon this part of the proceedings of the National Assembly.

To cut off all appearance of connexion between the crown and public justice, and to bring the whole under implicit obedience to the dictators in Paris, the old independent judicature of the parliaments, with all its merits, and all its faults, was wholly abolished.   Whilst the parliaments existed, it was evident that the people might some time or other come to resort to them, and rally under the standard of their ancient laws.   It became however a matter of consideration that the magistrates and officers, in the courts now abolished, *had purchased their places* at a very high rate, for which, as well as for the duty they performed, they received but a very low return of interest. Simple confiscation is a boon only for the clergy;—to the lawyers some appearances of equity are to be observed; and they are to receive compensation to an immense amount. Their compensation becomes part of the national debt, for the liquidation of which there is the one exhaustless fund. The lawyers are to obtain their compensation in the new church paper, which is to march with the new principles of judicature and legislature. The dismissed magistrates are to take their share of martyrdom with the ecclesiastics, or to receive their own property from such a fund, and in such a manner, as all those, who have been seasoned with the ancient principles of jurisprudence, and had been the sworn guardians of property, must look upon with horror. Even the clergy are to receive their miserable allowance out of the depreciated paper, which is stamped with the indelible character of sacrilege, and with the symbols of their own ruin, or they must starve. So violent an outrage upon credit, property, and liberty, as this compulsory paper currency, has seldom been exhibited by the alliance of bankruptcy and tyranny, at any time, or in any nation.

In the course of all these operations, at length comes out the grand *arcanum;*—that in reality, and in a fair sense, the lands of the church (so far as anything certain can be gathered from their proceedings) are not to be sold at all. By the late resolutions of the National Assembly, they are indeed to be delivered to the highest bidder. But it is to be observed, that *a certain portion only of the purchase money is to be laid down.* A period of twelve years is to be given for the payment of the rest. The philosophic purchasers are therefore, on payment of a sort of fine, to be put instantly into possession of the estate. It becomes in some respects a sort of gift to them; to be held on the feudal tenure of zeal to the new establishment. This project is evidently to let in a body of purchasers without money. The consequence will be, that these purchasers, or rather grantees, will pay, not only from the rents as they accrue, which might as well be received by the state, but from the spoil of the materials of buildings, from waste in woods, and from whatever money, by hands habituated to the gripings of usury, they can wring from the miserable peasant. He is to be delivered over to the mercenary and arbitrary discretion of men, who will be stimulated to every species of extortion by the growing demands on the growing profits of an estate held under the precarious settlement of a new political system.

When all the frauds, impostures, violences, rapines, burnings, murders, confiscations, compulsory paper currencies, and every description of tyranny and cruelty employed to bring about and to uphold this Revolution, have their natural effect, that is, to shock the moral sentiments of all virtuous and sober minds, the abettors of this philosophic system immediately strain their throats in a declamation against the old monarchial government of France. When they have rendered that deposed power sufficiently black, they then proceed in argument, as if all those who disapprove of their new abuses must of course be partisans of the old; that those who reprobate their crude and violent schemes of liberty ought to be treated as advocates for servitude. I admit that their necessities do compel them to this base and contemptible fraud. Nothing can reconcile men to their proceedings and projects, but the supposition that there is no third option between them and some tyranny as odious as can be furnished by the records of history, or by the invention of poets. This prattling of theirs hardly deserves the name of sophistry. It is nothing but plain impudence. Have these gentlemen never heard, in the whole circle of the worlds of theory and practice, of anything between the despotism of the monarch and the despotism of the multitude? Have they never heard of a monarchy directed by laws, controlled and balanced by the great hereditary wealth and hereditary dignity of a nation; and both again controlled by a judicious check from the reason and feeling of the people at large, acting by a suitable and permanent organ? Is it then impossible that a man may be found, who, without criminal ill intention, or pitiable absurdity, shall prefer such a mixed and tempered government to either of the extremes; and who may repute that nation to be destitute of all wisdom and of all virtue, which, having in its choice to obtain such a government with ease, *or rather to confirm it when actually possessed*, thought proper to commit a thousand crimes, and to subject their country to a thousand evils, in order to avoid it? Is it then a truth so universally acknowledged, that a pure democracy is the only tolerable form into which human society can be thrown, that a man is not permitted to hesitate about its merits, without the suspicion of being a friend to tyranny, that is, of being a foe to mankind?

I do not know under what description to class the present ruling authority in France. It affects to be a pure democracy, though I think it in a direct train of becoming shortly a mischievous and ignoble oligarchy. But for the present I admit it to be a contrivance of the nature and effect of what it pretends to. I reprobate no form of government merely upon abstract principles. There may be situations in which the purely democratic form will become necessary. There may be some (very few, and very particularly circumstanced) where it would be clearly desirable. This I do not take to be the case of France, or of any other great country. Until now, we have seen no examples of considerable democracies. The ancients were better acquainted with them. Not being wholly unread in the authors, who had seen the most of those constitutions, and who best understood them, I cannot help concurring with their opinion, that an absolute democracy, no more than absolute monarchy, is to be reckoned among the legitimate forms of government. They think it rather the corruption and degeneracy, than the sound constitution of a republic. If I recollect rightly, Aristotle observes, that a democracy has many striking points of resemblance with a tyranny.[1] Of this I am certain, that in a democracy, the majority of the citizens is capable of

---

[1] When I wrote this I quoted from memory, after many years had elapsed from my reading the passage. A learned friend has found it, and it is as follows :

Τὸ ἦθος τὸ αὐτὸ, καὶ ἄμφω δεσποτικὰ τῶν βελτιόνων, καὶ τὰ ψηφίσματα, ὥσπερ ἐκεῖ τὰ ἐπιτάγματα· καὶ ὁ δημαγωγὸς καὶ ὁ κόλαξ, οἱ αὐτοὶ καὶ ἀνάλογοι· καὶ μάλιστα ἑκάτεροι παρ' ἑκατέροις ἰσχύουσιν, οἱ μὲν κόλακες παρὰ τυράννοις, οἱ δὲ δημαγωγοὶ παρὰ τοῖς δήμοις τοῖς τοιούτοις.—

"The ethical character is the same ; both exercise despotism over the better class of citizens ; and decrees are in the one, what ordinances and arrêts are in the other : the demagogue too, and the court favourite, are not unfrequently the same identical men, and always bear a close analogy ; and these have the principal power, each in their respective forms of government, favourites with the absolute monarch, and demagogues with a people such as I have described." Arist. Politic. lib. iv. cap. 4.

*E 460

exercising the most cruel oppressions upon the minority, whenever strong divisions prevail in that kind of polity, as they often must; and that oppression of the minority will extend to far greater numbers, and will be carried on with much greater fury, than can almost ever be apprehended from the dominion of a single sceptre. In such a popular persecution, individual sufferers are in a much more deplorable condition than in any other. Under a cruel prince they have the balmy compassion of mankind to assuage the smart of their wounds; they have the plaudits of the people to animate their generous constancy under their sufferings: but those who are subjected to wrong under multitudes, are deprived of all external consolation. They seem deserted by mankind, overpowered by a conspiracy of their whole species.

But admitting democracy not to have that inevitable tendency to party tyranny, which I suppose it to have, and admitting it to possess as much good in it when unmixed, as I am sure it possesses when compounded with other forms; does monarchy, on its part, contain nothing at all to recommend it? I do not often quote Bolingbroke, nor have his works in general left any permanent impression on my mind. He is a presumptuous and a superficial writer. But he has one observation, which, in my opinion, is not without depth and solidity. He says, that he prefers a monarchy to other governments; because you can better ingraft any description of republic on a monarchy than anything of monarchy upon the republican forms. I think him perfectly in the right. The fact is so historically; and it agrees well with the speculation.

I know how easy a topic it is to dwell on the faults of departed greatness. By a revolution in the state, the fawning sycophant of yesterday is converted into the austere critic of the present hour. But steady, independent minds, when they have an object of so serious a concern to mankind as government under their contemplation, will disdain to assume the part of satirists and declaimers. They will judge of human institutions as they do of human characters. They will sort out the good from the evil, which is mixed in mortal institutions, as it is in mortal men.

Your government in France, though usually, and I think

justly, reputed the best of the unqualified or ill-qualified monarchies, was still full of abuses. These abuses accumulated in a length of time, as they must accumulate in every monarchy not under the constant inspection of a popular representative. I am no stranger to the faults and defects of the subverted government of France; and I think I am not inclined by nature or policy to make a panegyric upon anything which is a just and natural object of censure. But the question is not now of the vices of that monarchy, but of its existence. Is it then true, that the French government was such as to be incapable or undeserving of reform; so that it was of absolute necessity that the whole fabric should be at once pulled down, and the area cleared for the erection of a theoretic, experimental edifice in its place? All France was of a different opinion in the beginning of the year 1789. The instructions to the representatives to the states-general, from every district in that kingdom, were filled with projects for the reformation of that government, without the remotest suggestion of a design to destroy it. Had such a design been then even insinuated, I believe there would have been but one voice, and that voice for rejecting it with scorn and horror. Men have been sometimes led by degrees, sometimes hurried, into things of which, if they could have seen the whole together, they never would have permitted the most remote approach. When those instructions were given, there was no question but that abuses existed, and that they demanded a reform; nor is there now. In the interval between the instructions and the Revolution, things changed their shape; and, in consequence of that change, the true question at present is, Whether those who would have reformed, or those who have destroyed, are in the right?

To hear some men speak of the late monarchy of France you would imagine that they were talking of Persia bleeding under the ferocious sword of Tahmas Kouli Khân; or at least describing the barbarous anarchic despotism of Turkey, where the finest countries in the most genial climates in the world are wasted by peace more than any countries have been worried by war; where arts are unknown, where manufactures languish, where science is extinguished, where agriculture decays, where the human race itself melts away and perishes under the eye of the observer. Was this the case of France? I have no way of determining the question but by a reference to facts. Facts do not support this resemblance. Along with much evil, there is some good in monarchy itself; and some corrective to its evil from religion, from laws, from manners, from opinions, the French monarchy must have received; which rendered it (though by no means a free, and therefore by no means a good, constitution) a despotism rather in appearance than in reality.

Among the standards upon which the effects of government on any country are to be estimated, I must consider the state of its population as not the least certain. No country in which population flourishes, and is in progressive improvement, can be under a *very* mischievous government. About sixty years ago, the Intendants of the generalities of France made, with other matters, a report of the population of their several districts. I have not the books, which are very voluminous, by me, nor do I know where to procure them (I am obliged to speak by memory, and therefore the less positively), but I think the population of France was by them, even at that period, estimated at twenty-two millions of souls. At the end of the last century it had been generally calculated at eighteen. On either of these estimations, France was not ill peopled. M. Necker, who is an authority for his own time at least equal to the Intendants for theirs, reckons, and upon apparently sure principles, the people of France, in the year 1780, at twenty-four millions six hundred and seventy thousand. But was this the probable ultimate term under the old establishment? Dr. Price is of opinion, that the growth of population in France was by no means at its *acmé* in that year. I certainly defer to Dr. Price's authority a good deal more in these speculations, than I do in his general politics. This gentleman, taking ground on M. Necker's data, is very confident that since the period of that minister's calculation, the French population has increased rapidly; so rapidly, that in the year 1789 he will not consent to rate the people of that kingdom at a lower number than thirty millions. After abating much (and much I think ought to be abated) from the sanguine calculation of Dr. Price, I have no doubt that the population of France did increase considerably during this later period : but supposing that it increased to nothing more than will be sufficient to complete the twenty-four millions six hundred and seventy thousand to twenty-five millions, still a population of twenty-five millions, and that in an increasing progress, on a space of about twenty-seven thousand square leagues, is immense. It is, for instance, a good deal more than the proportionable population of this island, or even than that of England, the best peopled part of the United Kingdom.

It is not universally true, that France is a fertile country. Considerable tracts of it are barren, and labour under other natural disadvantages. In the portions of that territory where things are more favourable, as far as I am able to discover, the numbers of the people correspond to the indulgence of nature.[1] The Generality of Lisle (this I admit is the strongest example) upon an extent of four hundred and four leagues and a half, about ten years ago, contained seven hundred and thirty-four thousand six hundred souls, which is one thousand seven hundred and seventy-two inhabitants to each square league. The middle term for the rest of France is about nine hundred inhabitants to the same admeasurement.

I do not attribute this population to the deposed government; because I do not like to compliment the contrivances of men with what is due in a great degree to the bounty of Providence. But that decried government could not have obstructed, most probably it favoured, the operation of those causes (whatever they were), whether of nature in the soil, or habits of industry among the people, which has produced so large a number of the species throughout that whole kingdom, and exhibited in some particular places such prodigies of population. I never will suppose that fabric of a state to be the worst of all political institutions, which, by experience, is found to contain a principle favourable (however latent it may be) to the increase of mankind.

The wealth of a country is another, and no contemptible standard, by which we may judge whether, on the whole, a government be protecting or destructive. France far ex-

[1] De l'Administration des Finances de la France, par Mons. Necker, vol. i. p. 288.

ceeds England in the multitude of her people; but I apprehend that her comparative wealth is much inferior to ours; that it is not so equal in the distribution, nor so ready in the circulation. I believe the difference in the form of the two governments to be amongst the causes of this advantage on the side of England. I speak of England, not of the whole British dominions; which, if compared with those of France, will, in some degree, weaken the comparative rate of wealth upon our side. But that wealth, which will not endure a comparison with the riches of England, may constitute a very respectable degree of opulence. M. Necker's book, published in 1785,[1] contains an accurate and interesting collection of facts relative to public economy and to political arithmetic; and his speculations on the subject are in general wise and liberal. In that work he gives an idea of the state of France, very remote from the portrait of a country whose government was a perfect grievance, an absolute evil, admitting no cure but through the violent and uncertain remedy of a total revolution. He affirms, that from the year 1726 to the year 1784, there was coined at the mint of France, in the species of gold and silver, to the amount of about one hundred millions of pounds sterling.[2]

It is impossible that M. Necker should be mistaken in the amount of the bullion which has been coined in the mint. It is a matter of official record. The reasonings of this able financier, concerning the quantity of gold and silver which remained for circulation, when he wrote in 1785, that is, about four years before the deposition and imprisonment of the French king, are not of equal certainty; but they are laid on grounds so apparently solid, that it is not easy to refuse a considerable degree of assent to his calculation. He calculates the *numeraire*, or what we call *specie*, then actually existing in France, at about eighty-eight millions of the same English money. A great accumulation of wealth for one country, large as that country is! M. Necker was so far from considering this influx of wealth as likely to cease, when he wrote in 1785, that he presumes upon a future annual increase of two per cent. upon the money brought into France during the periods from which he computed.

[1] De l'Administration des Finances de la France, par Mons. Necker.
[2] Vol. iii. chap. 8 and chap 9.

Some adequate cause must have originally introduced all the money coined at its mint into that kingdom; and some cause as operative must have kept at home, or returned into its bosom, such a vast flood of treasure as M. Necker calculates to remain for domestic circulation. Suppose any reasonable deductions from M. Necker's computation, the remainder must still amount to an immense sum. Causes thus powerful to acquire, and to retain, cannot be found in discouraged industry, insecure property, and a positively destructive government. Indeed, when I consider the face of the kingdom of France; the multitude and opulence of her cities; the useful magnificence of her spacious high roads and bridges; the opportunity of her artificial canals and navigations opening the conveniences of maritime communication through a solid continent of so immense an extent; when I turn my eyes to the stupendous works of her ports and harbours, and to her whole naval apparatus, whether for war or trade; when I bring before my view the number of her fortifications, constructed with so bold and masterly a skill, and made and maintained at so prodigious a charge, presenting an armed front and impenetrable barrier to her enemies upon every side; when I recollect how very small a part of that extensive region is without cultivation, and to what complete perfection the culture of many of the best productions of the earth have been brought in France; when I reflect on the excellence of her manufactures and fabrics, second to none but ours, and in some particulars not second; when I contemplate the grand foundations of charity, public and private; when I survey the state of all the arts that beautify and polish life; when I reckon the men she has bred for extending her fame in war, her able statesmen, the multitude of her profound lawyers and theologians, her philosophers, her critics, her historians and antiquaries, her poets and her orators, sacred and profane; I behold in all this something which awes and commands the imagination, which checks the mind on the brink of precipitate and indiscriminate censure, and which demands that we should very seriously examine, what and how great are the latent vices that could authorize us at once to level so spacious a fabric with the ground. I do not recognize in this view of things, the despotism of Turkey. Nor do I discern the character of a government, that has been, on the whole, so oppressive, or so corrupt, or so negligent, as to be utterly unfit *for all reformation.* I must think such a government well deserved to have its excellencies heightened, its faults corrected, and its capacities improved into a British constitution.

Whoever has examined into the proceedings of that deposed government for several years back, cannot fail to have observed, amidst the inconstancy and fluctuation natural to courts, an earnest endeavour towards the prosperity and improvement of the country; he must admit, that it had long been employed, in some instances wholly to remove, in many considerably to correct, the abusive practices and usages that had prevailed in the state; and that even the unlimited power of the sovereign over the persons of his subjects, inconsistent, as undoubtedly it was, with law and liberty, had yet been every day growing more mitigated in the exercise. So far from refusing itself to reformation, that government was open, with a censurable degree of facility, to all sorts of projects and projectors on the subject. Rather too much countenance was given to the spirit of innovation, which soon was turned against those who fostered it, and ended in their ruin. It is but cold, and no very flattering, justice to that fallen monarchy, to say, that, for many years, it trespassed more by levity and want of judgment in several of its schemes, than from any defect in diligence or in public spirit. To compare the government of France for the last fifteen or sixteen years with wise and well-constituted establishments during that, or during any period, is not to act with fairness. But if in point of prodigality in the expenditure of money, or in point of rigour in the exercise of power, it be compared with any of the former reigns, I believe candid judges will give little credit to the good intentions of those who dwell perpetually on the donations to favourites, or on the expenses of the court, or on the horrors of the Bastile, in the reign of Louis the Sixteenth.[1]

Whether the system, if it deserves such a name, now built on the ruins of that ancient monarchy, will be able to

---

[1] The world is obliged to M. de Calonne for the pains he has taken to refute the scandalous exaggerations relative to some of the royal expenses, and to detect the fallacious account given of pensions, for the wicked purpose of provoking the populace to all sorts of crimes.

give a better account of the population and wealth of the country, which it has taken under its care, is a matter very doubtful. Instead of improving by the change, I apprehend that a long series of years must be told, before it can recover in any degree the effects of this philosophic revolution, and before the nation can be replaced on its former footing. If Dr. Price should think fit, a few years hence, to favour us with an estimate of the population of France, he will hardly be able to make up his tale of thirty millions of souls, as computed in 1789, or the Assembly's computation of twenty-six millions of that year; or even M. Necker's twenty-five millions in 1780. I hear that there are considerable emigrations from France; and that many, quitting that voluptuous climate, and that seductive *Circean* liberty, have taken refuge in the frozen regions, and under the British despotism, of Canada.

In the present disappearance of coin, no person could think it the same country, in which the present minister of the finances has been able to discover fourscore millions sterling in specie. From its general aspect one would conclude that it had been for some time past under the special direction of the learned academicians of Laputa and Balnibarbi.[1] Already the population of Paris has so declined, that M. Necker stated to the National Assembly the provision to be made for its subsistence at a fifth less than what had formerly been found requisite.[2] It is said (and I have never heard it contradicted) that a hundred thousand people are out of employment in that city, though it is become the seat of the imprisoned court and National Assembly. Nothing, I am credibly informed, can exceed the shocking and disgusting spectacle of mendicancy displayed in that capital. Indeed the votes of the National Assembly leave no doubt of the fact. They have lately appointed a standing committee of mendicancy. They are contriving at once a vigorous police on this subject, and, for the first time, the imposition of a tax to maintain the poor, for whose present relief great sums appear on the

[1] See Gulliver's Travels for the idea of countries governed by philosophers.

[2] M. de Calonne states the falling off of the population of Paris as far more considerable; and it may be so, since the period of M. Necker's calculation.

face of the public accounts of the year.[1]   In the meantime
the leaders of the legislative clubs and coffee-houses are
intoxicated with admiration at their own wisdom and
ability.   They speak with the most sovereign contempt of
the rest of the world.   They tell the people, to comfort
them in the rags with which they have clothed them, that
they are a nation of philosophers; and, sometimes, by all
the arts of quackish parade, by show, tumult, and bustle,
sometimes by the alarms of plots and invasions, they
attempt to drown the cries of indigence, and to divert the
eyes of the observer from the ruin and wretchedness of
the state.   A brave people will certainly prefer liberty
accompanied with a virtuous poverty to a depraved and
wealthy servitude.   But before the price of comfort and
opulence is paid, one ought to be pretty sure it is real
liberty which is purchased, and that she is to be purchased
at no other price.   I shall always, however, consider that
liberty as very equivocal in her appearance, which has not
wisdom and justice for her companions; and does not lead
prosperity and plenty in her train.

[1] Travaux de charité pour subvenir au manque de travail à Paris et dans les provinces	Livres	£	s.	d.
au manque de travail à Paris et dans les provinces	3,866,920 —	161,121	13	4
Destruction de vagabondage et de la mendicité	1,671,417 —	69,642	7	6
Primes pour l'importation de grains	5,671,907 —	236,329	9	2
Dépenses relatives aux subsistances, déduction fait des récouvrements qui ont eu lieu	39,871,790 —	1,661,324	11	8
Total Liv.	51,082,034 —	£2,128,418	1	8

When I sent this book to the press, I entertained some doubt concerning the nature and extent of the last article in the above accounts,
which is only under a general head, without any detail.   Since then
I have seen M. de Calonne's work.   I must think it a great loss to
me that I had not that advantage earlier.   M. de Calonne thinks
this article to be on account of general subsistence; but as he is not
able to comprehend how so great a loss as upwards of £1,661,000
sterling could be sustained on the difference between the price and the
sale of grain, he seems to attribute this enormous head of charge to
secret expenses of the Revolution.   I cannot say anything positively
on that subject.   The reader is capable of judging, by the aggregate
of these immense charges, on the state and condition of France; and
the system of public economy adopted in that nation.   These articles
of account produced no inquiry or discussion in the National Assembly.

The advocates for this Revolution, not satisfied with exaggerating the vices of their ancient government, strike at the fame of their country itself, by painting almost all that could have attracted the attention of strangers, I mean their nobility and their clergy, as objects of horror. If this were only a libel, there had not been much in it. But it has practical consequences. Had your nobility and gentry, who formed the great body of your landed men, and the whole of your military officers, resembled those of Germany, at the period when the Hanse-towns were necessitated to confederate against the nobles in defence of their property—had they been like the *Orsini* and *Vitelli* in Italy, who used to sally from their fortified dens to rob the trader and traveller—had they been such as the *Mamelukes* in Egypt, or the *Nayres* on the coast of Malabar, I do admit, that too critical an inquiry might not be advisable into the means of freeing the world from such a nuisance. The statues of Equity and Mercy might be veiled for a moment. The tenderest minds, confounded with the dreadful exigence in which morality submits to the suspension of its own rules in favour of its own principles, might turn aside whilst fraud and violence were accomplishing the destruction of a pretended nobility which disgraced, whilst it persecuted, human nature. The persons most abhorrent from blood, and treason, and arbitrary confiscation, might remain silent spectators of this civil war between the vices.

But did the privileged nobility who met under the king's precept at Versailles, in 1789, or their constituents, deserve to be looked on as the *Nayres* or *Mamelukes* of this age, or as the *Orsini* and *Vitelli* of ancient times? If I had then asked the question I should have passed for a madman. What have they since done that they were to be driven into exile, that their persons should be hunted about, mangled, and tortured, their families dispersed, their houses laid in ashes, and that their order should be abolished, and the memory of it, if possible, extinguished, by ordaining them to change the very names by which they were usually known? Read their instructions to their representatives. They breathe the spirit of liberty as warmly, and they recommend reformation as strongly, as any other order. Their privileges relative to contribution were voluntarily surrendered; as the king, from the beginning, surrendered all pretence to a right of taxation. Upon a free constitution there was but one opinion in France. The absolute monarchy was at an end. It breathed its last, without a groan, without struggle, without convulsion. All the struggle, all the dissension, arose afterwards upon the preference of a despotic democracy to a government of reciprocal control. The triumph of the victorious party was over the principles of a British constitution.

I have observed the affectation, which for many years past, has prevailed in Paris even to a degree perfectly childish, of idolizing the memory of your Henry the Fourth. If anything could put one out of humour with that ornament to the kingly character, it would be this overdone style of insidious panegyric. The persons who have worked this engine the most busily, are those who have ended their panegyrics in dethroning his successor and descendant; a man, as good-natured, at the least, as Henry the Fourth; altogether as fond of his people; and who has done infinitely more to correct the ancient vices of the state than that great monarch did, or we are sure he ever meant to do. Well it is for his panegyrists that they have not him to deal with. For Henry of Navarre was a resolute, active, and politic prince. He possessed indeed great humanity and mildness; but a humanity and mildness that never stood in the way of his interests. He never sought to be loved without putting himself first in a condition to be feared. He used soft language with determined conduct. He asserted and maintained his authority in the gross, and distributed his acts of concession only in the detail. He spent the income of his prerogative nobly; but he took care not to break in upon the capital; never abandoning for a moment any of the claims which he made under the fundamental laws, nor sparing to shed the blood of those who opposed him, often in the field, sometimes upon the scaffold. Because he knew how to make his virtues respected by the ungrateful, he has merited the praises of those, whom, if they had lived in his time, he would have shut up in the Bastile, and brought to punishment along with the regicides whom he hanged after he had famished Paris into a surrender.

If these panegyrists are in earnest in their admiration of Henry the Fourth, they must remember, that they cannot think more highly of him than he did of the noblesse of France; whose virtue, honour, courage, patriotism, and loyalty were his constant theme.

But the nobility of France are degenerated since the days of Henry the Fourth. This is possible. But it is more than I can believe to be true in any great degree. I do not pretend to know France as correctly as some others; but I have endeavoured through my whole life to make myself acquainted with human nature; otherwise I should be unfit to take even my humble part in the service of mankind. In that study I could not pass by a vast portion of our nature, as it appeared modified in a country but twenty-four miles from the shore of this island. On my best observation, compared with my best inquiries, I found your nobility for the greater part composed of men of high spirit, and of a delicate sense of honour, both with regard to themselves individually, and with regard to their whole corps, over whom they kept, beyond what is common in other countries, a censorial eye. They were tolerably well bred; very officious, humane, and hospitable; in their conversation frank and open; with a good military tone; and reasonably tinctured with literature, particularly of the authors in their own language. Many had pretensions far above this description. I speak of those who were generally met with.

As to their behaviour to the inferior classes, they appeared to me to comport themselves towards them with good-nature, and with something more nearly approaching to familiarity, than is generally practised with us in the intercourse between the higher and lower ranks of life. To strike any person, even in the most abject condition, was a thing in a manner unknown, and would be highly disgraceful. Instances of other ill-treatment of the humble part of the community were rare: and as to attacks made upon the property or the personal liberty of the commons, I never heard of any whatsoever from *them;* nor, whilst the laws were in vigour under the ancient government, would such tyranny in subjects have been permitted. As men of landed estates, I had no fault to find with their conduct, though much to reprehend, and much to wish changed, in many of the old tenures. Where the letting of their land was by rent, I could not discover that their agreements with their farmers were oppressive; nor when they were in partnership with the farmer, as often was the case, have I heard that they had taken the lion's share. The proportions seemed not inequitable. There might be exceptions; but certainly they were exceptions only. I have no reason to believe that in these respects the landed noblesse of France were worse than the landed gentry of this country; certainly in no respect more vexatious than the landholders, not noble, of their own nation. In cities the nobility had no manner of power; in the country very little. You know, Sir, that much of the civil government, and the police in the most essential parts, was not in the hands of that nobility which presents itself first to our consideration. The revenue, the system and collection of which were the most grievous parts of the French government, was not administered by the men of the sword; nor were they answerable for the vices of its principle, or the vexations, where any such existed, in its management.

Denying, as I am well warranted to do, that the nobility had any considerable share in the oppression of the people, in cases in which real oppression existed, I am ready to admit that they were not without considerable faults and errors. A foolish imitation of the worst part of the manners of England, which impaired their natural character, without substituting in its place what perhaps they meant to copy, has certainly rendered them worse than formerly they were. Habitual dissoluteness of manners continued beyond the pardonable period of life, was more common amongst them than it is with us; and it reigned with the less hope of remedy, though possibly with something of less mischief, by being covered with more exterior decorum. They countenanced too much that licentious philosophy which has helped to bring on their ruin. There was another error amongst them more fatal. Those of the commons, who approached to or exceeded many of the nobility in point of wealth, were not fully admitted to the rank and estimation which wealth, in reason and good policy, ought to bestow in every country; though I think not equally with that of other nobility. The two kinds of aristocracy were too punctiliously kept asunder; less so, however, than in Germany and some other nations.

This separation, as I have already taken the liberty of suggesting to you, I conceive to be one principal cause of the destruction of the old nobility. The military, particularly, was too exclusively reserved for men of family. But, after all, this was an error of opinion, which a conflicting opinion would have rectified. A permanent assembly, in which the commons had their share of power, would soon abolish whatever was too invidious and insulting in these distinctions; and even the faults in the morals of the nobility would have been probably corrected, by the greater varieties of occupation and pursuit to which a constitution by orders would have given rise.

All this violent cry against the nobility I take to be a mere work of art. To be honoured and even privileged by the laws, opinions, and inveterate usages of our country, growing out of the prejudice of ages, has nothing to provoke horror and indignation in any man. Even to be too tenacious of those privileges is not absolutely a crime. The strong struggle in every individual to preserve possession of what he has found to belong to him, and to distinguish him, is one of the securities against injustice and despotism implanted in our nature. It operates as an instinct to secure property, and to preserve communities in a settled state. What is there to shock in this? Nobility is a graceful ornament to the civil order. It is the Corinthian capital of polished society. *Omnes boni nobilitati semper favemus*, was the saying of a wise and good man. It is indeed one sign of a liberal and benevolent mind to incline to it with some sort of partial propensity. He feels no ennobling principle in his own heart, who wishes to level all the artificial institutions which have been adopted for giving a body to opinion, and permanence to fugitive esteem. It is a sour, malignant, envious disposition, without taste for the reality, or for any image or representation of virtue, that sees with joy the unmerited fall of what had long flourished in splendour and in honour. I do not like to see anything destroyed; any void produced in society; any ruin on the face of the land. It was therefore with no disappointment or dissatisfaction that my inquiries and observations did not present to me any incorrigible vices in the noblesse of France, or any abuse which could not be removed by a reform very short of abolition. Your noblesse did not deserve punishment : but to degrade is to punish.

It was with the same satisfaction I found that the result of my inquiry concerning your clergy was not dissimilar. It is no soothing news to my ears, that great bodies of men are incurably corrupt. It is not with much credulity I listen to any, when they speak evil of those whom they are going to plunder. I rather suspect that vices are feigned or exaggerated, when profit is looked for in their punishment. An enemy is a bad witness; a robber is a worse. Vices and abuses there were undoubtedly in that order, and must be. It was an old establishment, and not frequently revised. But I saw no crimes in the individuals that merited confiscation of their substance, nor those cruel insults and degradations, and that unnatural persecution, which have been substituted in the place of meliorating regulation.

If there had been any just cause for this new religious persecution, the atheistic libellers, who act as trumpeters to animate the populace to plunder, do not love any body so much as not to dwell with complacence on the vices of the existing clergy. This they have not done. They find themselves obliged to rake into the histories of former ages (which they have ransacked with a malignant and profligate industry) for every instance of oppression and persecution which has been made by that body or in its favour, in order to justify, upon very iniquitous, because very illogical, principles of retaliation, their own persecutions, and their own cruelties. After destroying all other genealogies and family distinctions, they invent a sort of pedigree of crimes. It is not very just to chastise men for the offences of their natural ancestors : but to take the fiction of ancestry in a corporate succession, as a ground for punishing men who have no relation to guilty acts, except in names and general descriptions, is a sort of refinement in injustice belonging to the philosophy of this enlightened age. The Assembly punishes men, many, if not most, of whom abhor the violent conduct of ecclesiastics in former times as much as their present persecutors can do, and who would be as loud and as strong in the expression of that sense, if they were not well aware of the purposes for which all this declamation is employed.

Corporate bodies are immortal for the good of the members, but not for their punishment. Nations themselves are such corporations. As well might we in England think of waging inexpiable war upon all Frenchmen for the evils which they have brought upon us in the several periods of our mutual hostilities. You might, on your part, think yourselves justified in falling upon all Englishmen on account of the unparalleled calamities brought on the people of France by the unjust invasions of our Henrys and our Edwards. Indeed we should be mutually justified in this exterminatory war upon each other, full as much as you are in the unprovoked persecution of your present countrymen, on account of the conduct of men of the same name in other times.

We do not draw the moral lessons we might from history. On the contrary, without care it may be used to vitiate our minds and to destroy our happiness. In history a great volume is unrolled for our instruction, drawing the materials of future wisdom from the past errors and infirmities of mankind. It may, in the perversion, serve for a magazine, furnishing offensive and defensive weapons for parties in church and state, and supplying the means of keeping alive, or reviving, dissensions and animosities, and adding fuel to civil fury. History consists, for the greater part, of the miseries brought upon the world by pride, ambition, avarice, revenge, lust, sedition, hypocrisy, ungoverned zeal, and all the train of disorderly appetites, which shake the public with the same

> "troublous storms that toss
> The private state, and render life unsweet."

These vices are the *causes* of those storms. Religion, morals, laws, prerogatives, privileges, liberties, rights of men, are the *pretexts*. The pretexts are always found in some specious appearance of a real good. You would not secure men from tyranny and sedition, by rooting out of the mind the principles to which these fraudulent pretexts apply? If you did, you would root out everything that is valuable in the human breast. As these are the pretexts, so the ordinary actors and instruments in great public evils are kings, priests, magistrates, senates, parliaments, national assemblies, judges, and captains. You would not cure the evil by resolving that there should be no more monarchs, nor ministers of state, nor of the gospel; no interpreters of law; no general officers; no public councils. You might change the names. The things in some shape must remain. A certain *quantum* of power must always exist in the community, in some hands, and under some appellation. Wise men will apply their remedies to vices, not to names; to the causes of evil which are permanent, not to the occasional organs by which they act, and the transitory modes in which they appear. Otherwise you will be wise historically, a fool in practice. Seldom have two ages the same fashion in their pretexts and the same modes of mischief. Wickedness is a little more inventive. Whilst you are discussing fashion, the fashion is gone by. The very same vice assumes a new body. The spirit transmigrates; and, far from losing its principle of life by the change of its appearance, it is renovated in its new organs with the fresh vigour of a juvenile activity. It walks abroad, it continues its ravages, whilst you are gibbeting the carcase, or demolishing the tomb. You are terrifying yourselves with ghosts and apparitions, whilst your house is the haunt of robbers. It is thus with all those, who, attending only to the shell and husk of history, think they are waging war with intolerance, pride, and cruelty, whilst, under colour of abhorring the ill principles of antiquated parties, they are authorizing and feeding the same odious vices in different factions, and perhaps in worse.

Your citizens of Paris formerly had lent themselves as the ready instruments to slaughter the followers of Calvin, at the infamous massacre of St. Bartholomew. What should we say to those who could think of retaliating on the Parisians of this day the abominations and horrors of that time? They are indeed brought to abhor *that* massacre. Ferocious as they are, it is not difficult to make them dislike it; because the politicians and fashionable teachers have no interest in giving their passions exactly the same direction. Still, however, they find it their interest to keep the same savage dispositions alive. It was but the other day that they caused this very massacre to be acted on the stage for the diversion of the descendants of those who committed it. In this tragic farce they produced the cardinal of Lorraine in his robes of function, ordering general slaughter. Was this spectacle intended to make the Parisians abhor persecution, and loathe the effusion of blood?—No; it was to teach them to persecute their own pastors; it was to excite them, by raising a disgust and horror of their clergy, to an alacrity in hunting down to destruction an order, which, if it ought to exist at all, ought to exist not only in safety, but in reverence. It was to stimulate their cannibal appetites (which one would think had been gorged sufficiently) by variety and seasoning; and to quicken them to an alertness in new murders and massacres, if it should suit the purpose of the Guises of the day. An Assembly, in which sat a multitude of priests and prelates, was obliged to suffer this indignity at its door. The author was not sent to the galleys, nor the players to the house of correction. Not long after this exhibition, those players came forward to the Assembly to claim the rites of that very religion which they had dared to expose, and to show their prostituted faces in the senate, whilst the archbishop of Paris, whose function was known to his people only by his prayers and benedictions, and his wealth only by his alms, is forced to abandon his house, and to fly from his flock (as from ravenous wolves), because, truly, in the sixteenth century, the cardinal of Lorraine was a rebel and a murderer.[1]

Such is the effect of the perversion of history, by those, who, for the same nefarious purposes, have perverted every other part of learning. But those who will stand upon that elevation of reason, which places centuries under our eye, and brings things to the true point of comparison, which obscures little names, and effaces the colours of little parties, and to which nothing can ascend but the spirit and moral quality of human actions, will say to the teachers of the Palais Royal,—The cardinal of Lorraine was the murderer of the sixteenth century, you have the glory of being the murderers in the eighteenth; and this is the only difference between you. But history in the

---

[1] This is on a supposition of the truth of this story, but he was not in France at the time. One name serves as well as another.

nineteenth century, better understood, and better employed, will, I trust, teach a civilized posterity to abhor the misdeeds of both these barbarous ages. It will teach future priests and magistrates not to retaliate upon the speculative and inactive atheists of future times, the enormities committed by the present practical zealots and furious fanatics of that wretched error, which, in its quiescent state, is more than punished, whenever it is embraced. It will teach posterity not to make war upon either religion or philosophy, for the abuse which the hypocrites of both have made of the two most valuable blessings conferred upon us by the bounty of the universal Patron, who in all things eminently favours and protects the race of man.

If your clergy, or any clergy, should show themselves vicious beyond the fair bounds allowed to human infirmity, and to those professional faults which can hardly be separated from professional virtues, though their vices never can countenance the exercise of oppression, I do admit, that they would naturally have the effect of abating very much of our indignation against the tyrants who exceed measure and justice in their punishment. I can allow in clergymen, through all their divisions, some tenaciousness of their own opinion, some overflowings of zeal for its propagation, some predilection to their own state and office, some attachment to the interest of their own corps, some preference to those who listen with docility to their doctrines, beyond those who scorn and deride them. I allow all this, because I am a man who has to deal with men, and who would not, through a violence of toleration, run into the greatest of all intolerance. I must bear with infirmities until they fester into crimes.

Undoubtedly, the natural progress of the passions, from frailty to vice, ought to be prevented by a watchful eye and a firm hand. But is it true that the body of your clergy had past those limits of a just allowance? From the general style of your late publications of all sorts, one would be led to believe that your clergy in France were a sort of monsters; a horrible composition of superstition, ignorance, sloth, fraud, avarice, and tyranny. But is this true? Is it true, that the lapse of time, the cessation of conflicting interests, the woeful experience of the evils resulting from party rage, have had no sort of influence gradually to meliorate their minds? Is it true, that the were daily renewing invasions on the civil power, troubling the domestic quiet of their country, and rendering the operations of its government feeble and precarious? Is it true, that the clergy of our times have pressed down the laity with an iron hand, and were, in all places, lighting up the fires of a savage persecution? Did they by every fraud endeavour to increase their estates? Did they use to exceed the due demands on estates that were their own? Or, rigidly screwing up right into wrong, did they convert a legal claim into a vexatious extortion? When not possessed of power, were they filled with the vices of those who envy it? Were they inflamed with a violent, litigious spirit of controversy? Goaded on with the ambition of intellectual sovereignty, were they ready to fly in the face of all magistracy, to fire churches, to massacre the priests of other descriptions, to pull down altars, and to make their way over the ruins of subverted governments to an empire of doctrine sometimes flattering, sometimes forcing, the consciences of men from the jurisdiction of public institutions into a submission to their personal authority, beginning with a claim of liberty, and ending with an abuse of power?

These, or some of these, were the vices objected, and not wholly without foundation, to several of the churchmen of former times, who belonged to the two great parties, which then divided and distracted Europe.

If there was in France, as in other countries there visibly is, a great abatement, rather than any increase of these vices, instead of loading the present clergy with the crimes of other men, and the odious character of other times, in common equity they ought to be praised, encouraged, and supported, in their departure from a spirit which disgraced their predecessors, and for having assumed a temper of mind and manners more suitable to their sacred function.

When my occasions took me into France, towards the close of the late reign, the clergy, under all their forms, engaged a considerable part of my curiosity. So far from finding (except from one set of men, not then very numerous, though very active) the complaints and discontents against that body, which some publications had given me reason to expect, I perceived little or no public or private uneasiness on their account. On further examination, I found the clergy, in general, persons of moderate minds and decorous manners; I include the seculars, and the regulars of both sexes. I had not the good fortune to know a great many of the parochial clergy : but in general I received a perfectly good account of their morals, and of their attention to their duties. With some of the higher clergy I had a personal acquaintance; and of the rest in that class, a very good means of information. They were, almost all of them, persons of noble birth. They resembled others of their own rank; and where there was any difference, it was in their favour. They were more fully educated than the military noblesse; so as by no means to disgrace their profession by ignorance, or by want of fitness for the exercise of their authority. They seemed to me, beyond the clerical character, liberal and open; with the hearts of gentlemen, and men of honour; neither insolent nor servile in their manners and conduct. They seemed to me rather a superior class; a set of men, amongst whom you would not be surprised to find a *Fénelon.* I saw among the clergy in Paris (many of the description are not to be met with anywhere) men of great learning and candour; and I had reason to believe, that this description was not confined to Paris. What I found in other places, I know was accidental; and therefore to be presumed a fair sample. I spent a few days in a provincial town, where, in the absence of the bishop, I passed my evenings with three clergymen, his vicars-general, persons who would have done honour to any church. They were all well informed; two of them of deep, general, and extensive erudition, ancient and modern, oriental and western; particularly in their own profession. They had a more extensive knowledge of our English divines than I expected; and they entered into the genius of those writers with a critical accuracy. One of these gentlemen is since dead, the Abbé *Morangis.* I pay this tribute, without reluctance, to the memory of that noble, reverend, learned, and excellent person; and I should do the same, with equal cheerfulness, to the merits of the others, who I believe are still living, if I did not fear to hurt those whom I am unable to serve.

Some of these ecclesiastics of rank are, by all titles, persons deserving of general respect. They are deserving of gratitude from me, and from many English. If this letter should ever come into their hands, I hope they will believe there are those of our nation who feel for their unmerited fall, and for the cruel confiscation of their fortunes, with no common sensibility. What I say of them is a testimony, as far as one feeble voice can go, which I owe to truth. Whenever the question of this unnatural persecution is concerned, I will pay it. No one shall prevent me from being just and grateful. The time is fitted for the duty; and it is particularly becoming to show our justice and gratitude, when those, who have deserved well of us and of mankind, are labouring under popular obloquy, and the persecutions of oppressive power.

You had before your Revolution about an hundred and twenty bishops. A few of them were men of eminent sanctity, and charity without limit. When we talk of the heroic, of course we talk of rare virtue. I believe the instances of eminent depravity may be as rare amongst them as those of transcendent goodness. Examples of avarice and of licentiousness may be picked out, I do not question it, by those who delight in the investigation which leads to such discoveries. A man as old as I am will not be astonished that several in every description do not lead that perfect life of self-denial, with regard to wealth or to pleasure, which is wished for by all, by some expected, but by none exacted with more rigour, than by those who are the most attentive to their own interests, or the most indulgent to their own passions. When I was in France, I am certain that the number of vicious prelates was not great. Certain individuals among them, not distinguishable for the regularity of their lives, made some amends for their want of the severe virtues, in their possession of the liberal; and were endowed with qualities which made them useful in the church and state. I am told, that, with few exceptions, Louis the Sixteenth had been more attentive to character, in his promotions to that rank, than his immediate predecessor; and I believe (as some spirit of reform has prevailed through the whole reign) that it may be true. But the present ruling power has shown a disposition only to plunder the church. It has punished *all* prelates; which is to favour the vicious, at least in point of reputation. It has made a degrading pensionary establishment, to which no man of liberal ideas or liberal condition will destine his children. It must settle into the lowest classes of the people. As with you the inferior clergy are not numerous enough for their duties; as these duties are, beyond measure, minute and toilsome, as you have left no middle classes of clergy at their ease, in future nothing of science or erudition can exist in the Gallican church. To complete the project, without the least attention to the rights of patrons, the Assembly has provided in future an elective clergy; an arrangement which will drive out of the clerical profession all men of sobriety; all who can pretend to independence in their function or their conduct; and which will throw the whole direction of the public mind into the hands of a set of licentious, bold, crafty, factious, flattering wretches, of such condition and such habits of life as will make their contemptible pensions (in comparison of which the stipend of an exciseman is lucrative and honourable) an object of low and illiberal intrigue. Those officers, whom they still call bishops, are to be elected to a provision comparatively mean, through the same arts (that is, electioneering arts), by men of all religious tenets that are known or can be invented. The new lawgivers have not ascertained anything whatsoever concerning their qualifications, relative either to doctrine or to morals; no more than they have done with regard to the subordinate clergy: nor does it appear but that both the higher and the lower may, at their discretion, practise or preach any mode of religion or irreligion that they please. I do not yet see what the jurisdiction of bishops over their subordinates is to be, or whether they are to have any jurisdiction at all.

In short, Sir, it seems to me, that this new ecclesiastical establishment is intended only to be temporary, and preparatory to the utter abolition, under any of its forms, of the Christian religion, whenever the minds of men are prepared for this last stroke against it, by the accomplishment of the plan for bringing its ministers into universal contempt. They who will not believe, that the philosophical fanatics, who guide in these matters, have long entertained such a design, are utterly ignorant of their character and proceedings. These enthusiasts do not scruple to avow their opinion, that a state can subsist without any religion better than with one; and that they are able to supply the place of any good which may be in it, by a project of their own—namely, by a sort of education they have imagined, founded in a knowledge of the physical wants of men; progressively carried to an enlightened self-interest, which, when well understood, they tell us, will identify with an interest more enlarged and public. The scheme of this education has been long known. Of late they distinguish it (as they have got an entirely new nomenclature of technical terms) by the name of a *Civic Education.*

I hope their partisans in England (to whom I rather attribute very inconsiderate conduct, than the ultimate object in this detestable design) will succeed neither in the pillage of the ecclesiastics, nor in the introduction of a principle of popular election to our bishoprics and parochial cures. This, in the present condition of the world, would be the last corruption of the church; the utter ruin of the clerical character; the most dangerous shock that the state ever received through a misunderstood arrangement of religion. I know well enough that the bishoprics and cures, under kingly and seignoral patronage, as now they are in England, and as they have been lately in France, are sometimes acquired by unworthy methods; but the other mode of ecclesiastical canvass subjects them infinitely more surely and more generally to all the evil arts of low ambition, which, operating on and through greater numbers, will produce mischief in proportion.

Those of you who have robbed the clergy think that they shall easily reconcile their conduct to all Protestant nations; because the clergy, whom they have thus plundered, degraded, and given over to mockery and scorn, are of the Roman Catholic, that is, of *their own* pretended persuasion. I have no doubt that some miserable bigots will be found here, as well as elsewhere, who hate sects and parties different from their own, more than they love the substance of religion; and who are more angry with those who differ from them in their particular plans and systems, than displeased with those who attack the foundation of our common hope. These men will write and speak on the subject in the manner that is to be expected from their temper and character. Burnet says, that, when he was in France, in the year 1683, "the method which carried over the men of the finest parts to Popery was this—they brought themselves to doubt of the whole Christian religion. When that was once done, it seemed a more indifferent thing of what side or form they continued outwardly." If this was then the ecclesiastical policy of France, it is what they have since but too much reason to repent of. They preferred atheism to a form of religion not agreeable to their ideas. They succeeded in destroying that form; and atheism has succeeded in destroying them. I can readily give credit to Burnet's story; because I have observed too much of a similar spirit (for a little of it is "much too much") amongst ourselves. The humour, however, is not general.

The teachers who reformed our religion in England bore no sort of resemblance to your present reforming doctors in Paris. Perhaps they were (like those whom they opposed) rather more than could be wished under the influence of a party spirit; but they were more sincere believers; men of the most fervent and exalted piety; ready to die (as some of them did die) like true heroes in defence of their particular ideas of Christianity; as they would with equal fortitude, and more cheerfully, for that stock of general truth, for the branches of which they contended with their blood. These men would have disavowed with horror those wretches who claimed a fellowship with them upon no other titles than those of their having pillaged the persons with whom they maintained controversies, and their having despised the common religion, for the purity of which they exerted themselves with a zeal, which unequivocally bespoke their highest reverence for the substance of that system which they wished to reform. Many of their descendants have retained the same zeal, but (as less engaged in conflict) with more moderation. They do not forget that justice and mercy are substantial parts of religion. Impious men do not recommend themselves to their communion by iniquity and cruelty towards any description of their fellow-creatures.

We hear these new teachers continually boasting of their spirit of toleration. That those persons should tolerate all opinions, who think none to be of estimation, is a matter of small merit. Equal neglect is not impartial kindness. The species of benevolence, which arises from contempt, is no true charity. There are in England abundance of men who tolerate in the true spirit of toleration. They think the dogmas of religion, though in different degrees, are all of moment: and that amongst them there is, as amongst all things of value, a just ground of preference. They favour, therefore, and they tolerate. They tolerate, not because they despise opinions, but because they respect justice. They would reverently and affectionately protect all religions, because they love and venerate the great principle upon which they all agree, and the great object to which they are all directed. They begin more and more plainly to discern, that we have all a common cause, as against a common enemy. They will not be so misled by the spirit of faction, as not to distinguish what is done in favour of their subdivision, from those acts of hostility, which, through some particular description, are aimed at the whole corps, in which they themselves, under another denomination, are included. It is impossible for me to say what may be the character of every description of men amongst us. But I speak for the greater part; and for them, I must tell you, that sacrilege is no part of their doctrine of good works; that, so far from calling you into their fellowship on such title, if your professors are admitted to their communion, they must carefully conceal their doctrine of the lawfulness of the proscription of innocent men; and that they must make restitution of all stolen goods whatsoever. Till then they are none of ours.

You may suppose that we do not approve your confiscation of the revenues of bishops, and deans, and chapters, and parochial clergy possessing independent estates arising from land, because we have the same sort of establishment in England. That objection, you will say, cannot hold as to the confiscation of the goods of monks and nuns, and the abolition of their order. It is true that this particular part of your general confiscation does not affect England, as a precedent in point: but the reason implies, and it goes a great way. The long parliament confiscated the lands of deans and chapters in England on the same ideas upon which your Assembly set to sale the lands of the monastic orders. But it is in the principle of injustice that the danger lies, and not in the description of persons on whom it is first exercised. I see, in a country very near us, a course of policy pursued, which sets justice, the common concern of mankind, at defiance. With the National Assembly of France, possession is nothing, law and usage are nothing. I see the National Assembly openly reprobate the doctrine of prescription, which, one of the greatest of their own lawyers [1] tells us, with great truth, is a part of the law of nature. He tells us, that the positive ascertainment of its limits, and its security from invasion, were among the causes for which civil society itself has been instituted. If prescription be once shaken, no species of property is secure, when it once becomes an object large enough to tempt the cupidity of indigent power. I see a practice perfectly correspondent to their contempt of this great fundamental part of natural law. I see the confiscators begin with bishops, and chapters, and monasteries; but I do not see them end there. I see the princes of the blood, who, by the oldest usages of that kingdom, held large landed estates (hardly with the compliment of a debate) deprived of their possessions, and, in lieu of their stable, independent property, reduced to the hope of some precarious, charitable pension, at the pleasure of an assembly, which of course will pay little regard to the rights of pensioners at pleasure, when it despises those of legal proprietors. Flushed with the insolence of their first inglorious victories, and pressed by the distresses caused by their lust of unhallowed lucre, disappointed but not discouraged, they have at length ventured completely to subvert all property of all descriptions throughout the extent of a great kingdom. They have compelled all men, in all transactions of commerce, in the disposal of lands, in civil dealing, and through the whole communion of life, to accept as perfect payment and good and lawful tender, the symbols of their speculations on a projected sale of their plunder. What vestiges of liberty or property have they left? The tenant-right of a cabbage-garden, a year's interest in a hovel, the good-will of an ale-house or a baker's shop, the very shadow of a constructive property, are more ceremoniously treated in our parliament, than with you the oldest and most valu-

---

[1] Domat.

able landed possessions, in the hands of the most respectable personages, or than the whole body of the monied and commercial interest of your country. We entertain a high opinion of the legislative authority; but we have never dreamt that parliaments had any right whatever to violate property, to overrule prescription, or to force a currency of their own fiction in the place of that which is real, and recognized by the law of nations. But you, who began with refusing to submit to the most moderate restraints, have ended by establishing an unheard-of despotism. I find the ground upon which your confiscators go is this; that indeed their proceedings could not be supported in a court of justice; but that the rules of prescription cannot bind a legislative assembly.[1] So that this legislative assembly of a free nation sits, not for the security, but for the destruction, of property, and not of property only, but of every rule and maxim which can give it stability, and of those instruments which can alone give it circulation.

When the Anabaptists of Münster, in the sixteenth century, had filled Germany with confusion, by their system of levelling, and their wild opinions concerning property, to what country in Europe did not the progress of their fury furnish just cause of alarm? Of all things, wisdom is the most terrified with epidemical fanaticism, because of all enemies it is that against which she is the least able to furnish any kind of resource. We cannot be ignorant of the spirit of atheistical fanaticism, that is inspired by a multitude of writings, dispersed with incredible assiduity and expense, and by sermons delivered in all the streets and places of public resort in Paris. These writings and sermons have filled the populace with a black and savage atrocity of mind, which supersedes in them the common feelings of nature, as well as all sentiments of morality and religion; insomuch that these wretches are induced to bear with a sullen patience the intolerable distresses brought upon them by the violent convulsions and permutations that have been made in property.[2] The spirit of proselyt-

---

[1] Speech of Mr. Camus, published by order of the National Assembly.

[2] Whether the following description is strictly true, I know not; but it is what the publishers would have pass for true in order to animate others. In a letter from Toul, given in one of their papers,

ism attends this spirit of fanaticism. They have societies to cabal and correspond at home and abroad for the propagation of their tenets. The republic of Berne, one of the happiest, the most prosperous, and the best governed countries upon earth, is one of the great objects, at the destruction of which they aim. I am told they have in some measure succeeded in sowing there the seeds of discontent. They are busy throughout Germany. Spain and Italy have not been untried. England is not left out of the comprehensive scheme of their malignant charity : and in England we find those who stretch out their arms to them, who recommend their example from more than one pulpit, and who choose in more than one periodical meeting, publicly to correspond with them, to applaud them, and to hold them up as objects for imitation ; who receive from them tokens of confraternity, and standards consecrated amidst their rights and mysteries ; [1] who suggest to them leagues of perpetual amity, at the very time when the power, to which our constitution has exclusively delegated the federative capacity of this kingdom, may find it expedient to make war upon them.

It is not the confiscation of our church property from this example in France that I dread, though I think this would be no trifling evil. The great source of my solici-

is the following passage concerning the poeple of that district : "Dans la Révolution actuelle, ils ont résisté à toutes les *séductions du bigotisme, aux persécutions, et aux tracasseries* des ennemis de la Révolution. *Oubliant leurs plus grands intérêts* pour rendre hommage aux vues d'ordre général qui ont déterminé l'Assemblée Nationale, ils voient, *sans se plaindre,* supprimer cette foule d'établissemens ecclésiastiques par lesquels *ils subsistoient ;* et même, en perdant leur siège épiscopal, la seule de toutes ces ressources qui pouvoit, ou plutôt *qui devoit, en toute équité,* leur être conservée ; condamnés *à la plus effrayante misère,* sans avoir *été ni pu être entendus, ils ne murmurent point,* ils restent fidèles aux principes du plus pur patriotisme ; ils sont encore prêts à *verser leur sang* pour le maintien de la Constitution, qui va réduire leur ville *à la plus déplorable nullité.*" These people are not supposed to have endured those sufferings and injustices in a struggle for liberty, for the same account states truly that they had been always free ; their patience in beggary and ruin, and their suffering, without remonstrance, the most flagrant and confessed injustice, if strictly true, can be nothing but the effect of this dire fanaticism. A great multitude all over France is in the same condition and the same temper.

[1] See the proceedings of the confederation at *Nantz.*

tude is, lest it should ever be considered in England as the policy of a state to seek a resource in confiscations of any kind; or that any one description of citizens should be brought to regard any of the others as their proper prey.[1] Nations are wading deeper and deeper into an ocean of boundless debt. Public debts, which at first were a security to governments, by interesting many in the public tranquillity, are likely in their excess to become the means of their subversion. If governments provide for these debts by heavy impositions, they perish by becoming odious to the people. If they do not provide for them they will be undone by the efforts of the most dangerous of all parties; I mean an extensive, discontented monied interest, injured and not destroyed. The men who compose this interest look for their security, in the first instance, to the fidelity of government; in the second, to its power. If they find the old governments effete, worn out, and with their springs relaxed, so as not to be of sufficient vigour for their purposes, they may seek new ones that shall be possessed of more energy; and this energy will be derived, not from an acquisition of resources, but from a contempt of justice. Revolutions are favourable to confiscation; and it is impossible to know under what obnoxious names the next confiscations will be authorized. I am sure that the principles predominant in France extend to very many persons, and descriptions of persons, in all countries who

---

[1] "Si plures sunt ii quibus improbe datum est, quam illi quibus injuste ademptum est, idcirco plus etiam valent? Non enim numero hæc judicantur sed pondere. Quam autem habet æquitatem, ut agrum multis annis, aut etiam sæculis ante possessum, qui nullum habuit habeat; qui autem habuit amittat? Ac, propter hoc injuriæ genus, Lacedæmonii Lysandrum Ephorum expulerunt: Agin regem (quod nunquam antea apud eos acciderat) necaverunt: exque eo tempore tantæ discordiæ secutæ sunt, ut et tyranni existerint, et optimates exterminarentur, et preclarissime constituta respublica dilaberetur. Nec vero solum ipsa cecidit, sed etiam reliquam Græciam evertit contagionibus malorum, quæ a Lacedæmoniis profectæ manarunt latius."—After speaking of the conduct of the model of true patriots, Aratus of Sicyon, which was in a very different spirit, he says, "Sic par est agere cum civibus; non ut bis jam vidimus, hastam in foro ponere et bona civium voci subjicere præconis. At ille Græcus (id quod fuit sapientis et præstantis viri) omnibus consulendum esse putavit: eaque est summa ratio et sapientia boni civis, commoda civium non divellere, sed omnes eadem æquitate continere."—Cic. Off. l. 2.

think their innoxious indolence their security. This kind of innocence in proprietors may be argued into inutility; and inutility into an unfitness for their estates. Many parts of Europe are in open disorder. In many others there is a hollow murmuring under ground; a confused movement is felt, that threatens a general earthquake in the political world. Already confederacies and correspondences of the most extraordinary nature are forming, in several countries.[1] In such a state of things we ought to hold ourselves upon our guard. In all mutations (if mutations must be) the circumstance which will serve most to blunt the edge of their mischief, and to promote what good may be in them, is, that they should find us with our minds tenacious of justice, and tender of property.

But it will be argued, that this confiscation in France ought not to alarm other nations. They say it is not made from wanton rapacity; that it is a great measure of national policy, adopted to remove an extensive, inveterate, superstitious mischief. It is with the greatest difficulty that I am able to separate policy from justice. Justice itself is the great standing policy of civil society; and any eminent departure from it, under any circumstances, lies under the suspicion of being no policy at all.

When men are encouraged to go into a certain mode of life by the existing laws, and protected in that mode as in a lawful occupation—when they have accommodated all their ideas and all their habits to it—when the law had long made their adherence to its rules a ground of reputation, and their departure from them a ground of disgrace and even of penalty—I am sure it is unjust in legislature, by an arbitrary act, to offer a sudden violence to their minds and their feelings; forcibly to degrade them from their state and condition, and to stigmatize with shame and infamy that character, and those customs, which before had been made the measure of their happiness and honour. If to this be added an expulsion from their habitations, and a confiscation of all their goods, I am not sagacious enough to discover how this despotic sport, made of the feelings, consciences, prejudices, and proper-

1 See two books intitled, Einige Originalschriften des Illuminatenordens—System und Folgen des Illuminatenordens. München, 1787.

ties of men, can be discriminated from the rankest tyranny.

If the injustice of the course pursued in France be clear, the policy of the measure, that is, the public benefit to be expected from it, ought to be at least as evident, and at least as important. To a man who acts under the influence of no passion, who has nothing in view in his projects but the public good, a great difference will immediately strike him between what policy would dictate on the original introduction of such institutions, and on a question of their total abolition, where they have cast their roots wide and deep, and where, by long habit, things more valuable than themselves are so adapted to them, and in a manner interwoven with them, that the one cannot be destroyed without notably impairing the other. He might be embarrassed if the case were really such as sophisters represent it in their paltry style of debating. But in this, as in most questions of state, there is a middle. There is something else than the mere alternative of absolute destruction, or unreformed existence. *Spartam nactus es; hanc exorna.* This is, in my opinion, a rule of profound sense, and ought never to depart from the mind of an honest reformer. I cannot conceive how any man can have brought himself to that pitch of presumption, to consider his country as nothing but *carte blanche*, upon which he may scribble whatever he pleases. A man full of warm, speculative benevolence may wish his society otherwise constituted than he finds it; but a good patriot, and a true politician, always considers how he shall make the most of the existing materials of his country. A disposition to preserve, and an ability to improve, taken together, would be my standard of a statesman. Everything else is vulgar in the conception, perilous in the execution.

There are moments in the fortune of states, when particular men are called to make improvements, by great mental exertion. In those moments, even when they seem to enjoy the confidence of their prince and country, and to be invested with full authority, they have not always apt instruments. A politician, to do great things, looks for a *power*, what our workmen call a *purchase*; and if he finds that power, in politics as in mechanics, he cannot be at a loss to apply it. In the monastic institutions, in my opinion, was found a great *power* for the mechanism of politic benevolence. There were revenues with a public direction; there were men wholly set apart and dedicated to public purposes, without any other than public ties and public principles; men without the possibility of converting the estate of the community into a private fortune; men denied to self-interests, whose avarice is for some community; men to whom personal poverty is honour, and implicit obedience stands in the place of freedom. In vain shall a man look to the possibility of making such things when he wants them. The winds blow as they list. These institutions are the products of enthusiasm; they are the instruments of wisdom. Wisdom cannot create materials; they are the gifts of nature or of chance; her pride is in the use. The perennial existence of bodies corporate and their fortunes are things particularly suited to a man who has long views; who meditates designs that require time in fashioning, and which propose duration when they are accomplished. He is not deserving to rank high, or even to be mentioned in the order of great statesmen, who, having obtained the command and direction of such a power as existed in the wealth, the discipline, and the habits of such corporations, as those which you have rashly destroyed, cannot find any way of converting it to the great and lasting benefit of his country. On the view of this subject, a thousand uses suggest themselves to a contriving mind. To destroy any power, growing wild from the rank productive force of the human mind, is almost tantamount, in the moral world, to the destruction of the apparently active properties of bodies in the material. It would be like the attempt to destroy (if it were in our competence to destroy) the expansive force of fixed air in nitre, or the power of steam, or of electricity, or of magnetism. These energies always existed in nature, and they were always discernible. They seemed, some of them unserviceable, some noxious, some no better than a sport to children; until contemplative ability, combining with practic skill, tamed their wild nature, subdued them to use, and rendered them at once the most powerful and the most tractable agents, in subservience to the great views and designs of men. Did fifty thousand persons, whose mental and whose bodily labour you might direct, and so many hundred thousand a year of a revenue, which was neither lazy nor superstitious, appear too big for your abilities to wield? Had you no way of using the men but by converting monks into pensioners? Had you no way of turning the revenue to account, but through the improvident resource of a spendthrift sale? If you were thus destitute of mental funds, the proceeding is in its natural course. Your politicians do not understand their trade; and therefore they sell their tools.

But the institutions savour of superstition in their very principle; and they nourish it by a permanent and standing influence. This I do not mean to dispute; but this ought not to hinder you from deriving from superstition itself any resources which may thence be furnished for the public advantage. You derive benefits from many dispositions and many passions of the human mind, which are of as doubtful a colour, in the moral eye, as superstition itself. It was your business to correct and mitigate everything which was noxious in this passion, as in all the passions. But is superstition the greatest of all possible vices? In its possible excess I think it becomes a very great evil. It is, however, a moral subject; and of course admits of all degrees and all modification. Superstition is the religion of feeble minds; and they must be tolerated in an intermixture of it, in some trifling or some enthusiastic shape or other, else you will deprive weak minds of a resource found necessary to the strongest. The body of all true religion consists, to be sure, in obedience to the will of the Sovereign of the world; in a confidence in his declarations; and in imitation of his perfections. The rest is our own. It may be prejudicial to the great end; it may be auxiliary. Wise men, who as such are not *admirers* (not admirers at least of the *Munera Terræ*), are not violently attached to these things, nor do they violently hate them. Wisdom is not the most severe corrector of folly. They are the rival follies, which mutually wage so unrelenting a war; and which make so cruel a use of their advantages, as they can happen to engage the immoderate vulgar, on the one side, or the other, in their quarrels. Prudence would be neuter; but if, in the contention between fond attachment and fierce antipathy concerning things in their nature not made to produce such heats, a prudent man were obliged to make a choice of what errors and excesses of enthusiasm he would condemn or bear, perhaps he would think the superstition which builds, to be more tolerable than that which demolishes—that which adorns a country, than that which deforms it—that which endows, than that which plunders—that which disposes to mistaken beneficence, than that which stimulates to real injustice—that which leads a man to refuse to himself lawful pleasures, than that which snatches from others the scanty subsistence of their self-denial. Such, I think, is very nearly the state of the question between the ancient founders of monkish superstition, and the superstition of the pretended philosophers of the hour.

For the present I postpone all consideration of the supposed public profit of the sale, which however I conceive to be perfectly delusive. I shall here only consider it as a transfer of property. On the policy of that transfer I shall trouble you with a few thoughts.

In every prosperous community something more is produced than goes to the immediate support of the producer. This surplus forms the income of the landed capitalist. It will be spent by a proprietor who does not labour. But this idleness is itself the spring of labour; this repose the spur to industry. The only concern of the state is, that the capital taken in rent from the land, should be returned again to the industry from whence it came; and that its expenditure should be with the least possible detriment to the morals of those who expend it, and to those of the people to whom it is returned.

In all the views of receipt, expenditure, and personal employment, a sober legislator would carefully compare the possessor whom he was recommended to expel, with the stranger who was proposed to fill his place. Before the inconveniences are incurred which *must* attend all violent revolutions in property through extensive confiscation, we ought to have some rational assurance that the purchasers of the confiscated property will be in a considerable degree more laborious, more virtuous, more sober, less disposed to extort an unreasonable proportion of the gains of the labourer, or to consume on themselves a larger share than is fit for the measure of an individual; or that they should be qualified to dispense the surplus in a more steady and equal mode, so as to answer the purposes of a politic expenditure, than the old possessors, call those possessors bishops, or canons, or commendatory abbots, or monks, or what you please. The monks are lazy. Be it so. Suppose them no otherwise employed than by singing in the choir. They are as usefully employed as those who neither sing nor say. As usefully even as those who sing upon the stage. They are as usefully employed as if they worked from dawn to dark in the innumerable servile, degrading, unseemly, unmanly, and often most unwholesome and pestiferous occupations, to which by the social economy so many wretches are inevitably doomed. If it were not generally pernicious to disturb the natural course of things, and to impede, in any degree, the great wheel of circulation which is turned by the strangely-directed labour of these unhappy people, I should be infinitely more inclined forcibly to rescue them from their miserable industry, than violently to disturb the tranquil repose of monastic quietude. Humanity, and perhaps policy, might better justify me in the one than in the other. It is a subject on which I have often reflected, and never reflected without feeling from it. I am sure that no consideration, except the necessity of submitting to the yoke of luxury, and the despotism of fancy, who in their own imperious way will distribute the surplus product of the soil, can justify the toleration of such trades and employments in a well-regulated state. But for this purpose of distribution, it seems to me, that the idle expenses of monks are quite as well directed as the idle expenses of us lay-loiterers.

When the advantages of the possession and of the project are on a par, there is no motive for a change. But in the present case, perhaps, they are not upon a par, and the difference is in favour of the possession. It does not appear to me, that the expenses of those whom you are going to expel, do in fact take a course so directly and so generally leading to vitiate and degrade and render miserable those through whom they pass, as the expenses of those favourites whom you are intruding into their houses. Why should the expenditure of a great landed property, which is a dispersion of the surplus product of the soil, appear intolerable to you or to me, when it takes its course through the accumulation of vast libraries, which are the history of the force and weakness of the human mind; through great collections of ancient records, medals, and coins, which attest and explain laws and customs; through paintings and statues, that, by imitating nature, seem to extend the limits of creation; through grand monuments of the dead, which continue the regards and connexions of life beyond the grave; through collections of the specimens of nature, which become a representative assembly of all the classes and families of the world, that by disposition facilitate, and, by exciting curiosity, open the avenues to science? If by great permanent establishments, all these objects of expense are better secured from the inconstant sport of personal caprice and personal extravagance, are they worse than if the same tastes prevailed in scattered individuals? Does not the sweat of the mason and carpenter, who toil in order to partake the sweat of the peasant, flow as pleasantly and as salubriously, in the construction and repair of the majestic edifices of religion, as in the painted booths and sordid sties of vice and luxury; as honourably and as profitably in repairing those sacred works, which grow hoary with innumerable years, as on the momentary receptacles of transient voluptuousness; in opera-houses, and brothels, and gaming-houses, and club-houses, and obelisks in the Champ de Mars? Is the surplus product of the olive and the vine worse employed in the frugal sustenance of persons, whom the fictions of a pious imagination raise to dignity by construing in the service of God, than in pampering the innumerable multitude of those who are degraded by being made useless domestics, subservient to the pride of man? Are the decorations of temples an expenditure less worthy a wise man, than ribbons, and laces, and national cockades, and petit maisons, and petit soupers, and all the innumerable fopperies and follies, in which opulence sports away the burthen of its superfluity?

We tolerate even these; not from love of them, but for fear of worse. We tolerate them, because property and liberty, to a degree, require that toleration. But why proscribe the other, and surely, in every point of view, the more laudable use of estates? Why, through the violation of all property, through an outrage upon every principle of liberty, forcibly carry them from the better to the worse?

This comparison between the new individuals and the old corps is made upon a supposition that no reform could be made in the latter. But, in a question of reformation, I always consider corporate bodies, whether sole or consisting of many, to be much more susceptible of a public direction by the power of the state, in the use of their property, and in the regulation of modes and habits of life in their members, than private citizens ever can be, or perhaps ought to be : and this seems to me a very material consideration for those who undertake anything which merits the name of a politic enterprise.—So far as to the estates of monasteries.

With regard to the estates possessed by bishops and canons, and commendatory abbots, I cannot find out for what reason some landed estates may not be held otherwise than by inheritance. Can any philosophic spoiler undertake to demonstrate the positive or the comparative evil of having a certain, and that too a large, portion of landed property, passing in succession through persons whose title to it is, always in theory, and often in fact, an eminent degree of piety, morals, and learning; a property, which, by its destination, in their turn, and on the score of merit, gives to the noblest families renovation and support, to the lowest the means of dignity and elevation; a property, the tenure of which is the performance of some duty (whatever value you may choose to set upon that duty), and the character of whose proprietors demands, at least, an exterior decorum, and gravity of manners; who are to exercise a generous but temperate hospitality; part of whose income they are to consider as a trust for charity; and who, even when they fail in their trust, when they slide from their character, and degenerate into a mere common secular nobleman or gentleman, are in no respect worse than those who may succeed them in their forfeited possessions? Is it better that estates should be held by those who have no duty, than by those who have one?— by those whose character and destination point to virtues, than by those who have no rule and direction in the expenditure of their estates but their own will and appetite? Nor are these estates held altogether in the character or with the evils supposed inherent in mortmain. They pass from hand to hand with a more rapid circulation than any other. No excess is good; and therefore too great a proportion of landed property may be held officially for life : but it does not seem to me of material injury to any commonwealth, that there should exist some estates that have a chance of being acquired by other means than the previous acquisition of money.

[PART II]

THIS letter is grown to a great length, though it is indeed short with regard to the infinite extent of the subject. Various avocations have from time to time called my mind from the subject. I was not sorry to give myself leisure to observe whether, in the proceedings of the National Assembly, I might not find reasons to change or to qualify some of my first sentiments. Everything has confirmed me more strongly in my first opinions. It was my original purpose to take a view of the principles of the National Assembly with regard to the great and fundamental establishments; and to compare the whole of what you have substituted in the place of what you have destroyed, with the several members of our British constitution. But this plan is of a greater extent than at first I computed, and I find that you have little desire to take the advantage of any examples. At present I must content myself with some remarks upon your establishments; reserving for another time what I proposed to say concerning the spirit of our British monarchy, aristocracy, and democracy, as practically they exist.

I have taken a view of what has been done by the governing power in France. I have certainly spoken of it with freedom. Those whose principle it is to despise the ancient, permanent sense of mankind, and to set up a scheme of society on new principles, must naturally expect that such of us, who think better of the judgment of the human race than of theirs, should consider both them and their devices, as men and schemes upon their trial. They must take it for granted that we attend much to their reason, but not at all to their authority. They have not one of the great influencing prejudices of mankind in their favour. They avow their hostility to opinion. Of course they must expect no support from that influence, which, with every other authority, they have deposed from the seat of its jurisdiction.

I can never consider this Assembly as anything else than a voluntary association of men, who have availed themselves of circumstances to seize upon the power of the state. They have not the sanction and authority of the character under which they first met. They have assumed another of a very different nature; and have completely altered and inverted all the relations in which they originally stood. They do not hold the authority they exercise under any constitutional law of the state. They have departed from the instructions of the people by whom they were sent; which instructions, as the Assembly did not act in virtue of any ancient usage or settled law, were the sole source of their authority. The most considerable of their acts have not been done by great majorities; and in this sort of near divisions, which carry only the constructive authority of the whole, strangers will consider reasons as well as resolutions.

If they had set up this new, experimental government, as a necessary substitute for an expelled tyranny, mankind would anticipate the time of prescription, which, through long usage, mellows into legality governments that were violent in their commencement. All those who have affections which lead them to the conservation of civil order would recognise, even in its cradle, the child as legitimate, which has been produced from those principles of cogent expediency to which all just governments owe their birth, and on which they justify their continuance. But they will be late and reluctant in giving any sort of countenance to the operations of a power, which has derived its birth from no law and no necessity; but which on the contrary has had its origin in those vices and sinister practices by which the social union is often disturbed and sometimes destroyed. This Assembly has hardly a year's prescription. We have their own word for it that they have made a revolution. To make a revolution is a measure which, *prima fronte*, requires an apology. To make a revolution is to subvert the ancient state of our country; and no common reasons are called for to justify so violent a proceeding. The sense of mankind authorizes us to examine into the mode of acquiring new power, and to criticise on the use that is made of it, with less awe and reverence than that which is usually conceded to a settled and recognised authority.

In obtaining and securing their power, the Assembly proceeds upon principles the most opposite to those which appear to direct them in the use of it. An observation on this difference will let us into the true spirit of their conduct. Everything which they have done, or continue to do, in order to obtain and keep their power, is by the most common arts. They proceed exactly as their ancestors of ambition have done before them. Trace them through all their artifices, frauds, and violences, you can find nothing at all that is new. They follow precedents and examples with the punctilious exactness of a pleader. They never depart an iota from the authentic formulas of tyranny and usurpation. But in all the regulations relative to the public good, the spirit has been the very reverse of this. There they commit the whole to the mercy of untried speculations; they abandon the dearest interests of the public to those loose theories, to which none of them would choose to trust the slightest of his private concerns. They make this difference, because in their desire of obtaining and securing power they are thoroughly in earnest; there they travel in the beaten road. The public interests, because about them they have no real solicitude, they abandon wholly to chance: I say to chance, because their schemes have nothing in experience to prove their tendency beneficial.

We must always see with a pity not unmixed with respect, the errors of those who are timid and doubtful of themselves with regard to points wherein the happiness of mankind is concerned. But in these gentlemen there is nothing of the tender, parental solicitude, which fears to cut up the infant for the sake of an experiment. In the vastness of their promises, and the confidence of their predictions, they far outdo all the boasting of empirics. The arrogance of their pretensions in a manner provokes and challenges us to an inquiry into their foundation.

I am convinced that there are men of considerable parts among the popular leaders in the National Assembly. Some of them display eloquence in their speeches and their writings. This cannot be without powerful and cultivated talents. But eloquence may exist without a proportionable degree of wisdom. When I speak of ability, I am obliged to distinguish. What they have done towards the support of their system bespeaks no ordinary men. In the system itself, taken as the scheme of a republic constructed for procuring the prosperity and security of the citizen, and for promoting the strength and grandeur of the state, I confess myself unable to find out anything which displays, in a single instance, the work of a comprehensive and disposing mind, or even the provisions of a vulgar prudence. Their purpose everywhere seems to have been to evade and slip aside from *difficulty*. This it has been the glory of the great masters in all the arts to confront, and to overcome; and when they had overcome the first difficulty, to turn it into an instrument for new conquests over new difficulties; thus to enable them to extend the empire of their science; and even to push forward, beyond the reach of their original thoughts, the landmarks of the human understanding itself. Difficulty is a severe instructor, set over us by the supreme ordinance of a parental Guardian and Legislator, who knows us better than we know ourselves, as he loves us better too. *Pater ipse colendi haud facilem esse viam voluit.* He that wrestles with us strengthens our nerves, and sharpens our skill. Our antagonist is our helper. This amicable conflict with difficulty obliges us to an intimate acquaintance with our object, and compels us to consider it in all its relations. It will not suffer us to be superficial. It is the want of nerves of understanding for such a task, it is the degenerate fondness for tricking short-cuts, and little fallacious facilities, that has in so many parts of the world created governments with arbitrary powers. They have created the late arbitrary monarchy of France. They have created the arbitrary republic of Paris. With them defects in wisdom are to be supplied by the plenitude of force. They get nothing by it. Commencing their labours on a principle of sloth, they have the common fortune of slothful men. The difficulties, which they rather had eluded than escaped, meet them again in their course; they multiply and thicken on them; they are involved, through a labyrinth of confused detail, in an industry without limit, and without direction; and, in conclusion, the whole of their work becomes feeble, vicious, and insecure.

It is this inability to wrestle with difficulty which has obliged the arbitrary Assembly of France to commence their schemes of reform with abolition and total destruction.[1] But is it in destroying and pulling down that skill is displayed? Your mob can do this as well at least as your assemblies. The shallowest understanding, the rudest hand, is more than equal to that task. Rage and phrensy will pull down more in half an hour, than prudence, deliberation, and foresight can build up in a hundred years. The errors and defects of old establishments are visible and palpable. It calls for little ability to point them out; and where absolute power is given, it requires but a word wholly to abolish the vice and the establishment together. The same lazy but restless disposition, which loves sloth and hates quiet, directs the politicians, when they come to work for supplying the place of what they have destroyed. To make everything the reverse of what they have seen is quite as easy as to destroy. No difficulties occur in what has never been tried. Criticism is almost baffled in discovering the defects of what has not existed; and eager enthusiasm and cheating hope have all the wide field of imagination, in which they may expatiate with little or no opposition.

At once to preserve and to reform is quite another thing. When the useful parts of an old establishment are kept, and what is superadded is to be fitted to what is retained, a vigorous mind, steady, persevering attention, various

[1] A leading member of the Assembly, M. Rabaud de St. Etienne, has expressed the principle of all their proceedings as clearly as possible—Nothing can be more simple : "*Tous les établissemens en France couronnent le malheur du peuple: pour le rendre heureux il faut le rénouveler; changer ses idées; changer ses loix; changer ses mœurs; . . . changer les hommes; changer les choses; changer les mots . . . tout détruire; oui, tout détruire; puisque tout est à recréer.*" This gentleman was chosen president in an assembly not sitting at the *Quinze-vingt*, or the *Petits Maisons*; and composed of persons giving themselves out to be rational beings; but neither his ideas, language, or conduct, differ in the smallest degree from the discourses, opinions, and actions of those within and without the Assembly, who direct the operations of the machine now at work in France.

powers of comparison and combination, and the resources of an understanding fruitful in expedients, are to be exercised; they are to be exercised in a continued conflict with the combined force of opposite vices, with the obstinacy that rejects all improvement, and the levity that is fatigued and disgusted with everything of which it is in possession. But you may object—"A process of this kind is slow. It is not fit for an assembly, which glories in performing in a few months the work of ages. Such a mode of reforming, possibly, might take up many years." Without question it might; and it ought. It is one of the excellencies of a method in which time is amongst the assistants, that its operation is slow, and in some cases almost imperceptible. If circumspection and caution are a part of wisdom, when we work only upon inanimate matter, surely they become a part of duty too, when the subject of our demolition and construction is not brick and timber, but sentient beings, by the sudden alteration of whose state, condition, and habits, multitudes may be rendered miserable. But it seems as if it were the prevalent opinion in Paris, that an unfeeling heart, and an undoubting confidence, are the sole qualifications for a perfect legislator. Far different are my ideas of that high office. The true lawgiver ought to have a heart full of sensibility. He ought to love and respect his kind, and to fear himself. It may be allowed to his temperament to catch his ultimate object with an intuitive glance; but his movements towards it ought to be deliberate. Political arrangement, as it is a work for social ends, is to be only wrought by social means. There mind must conspire with mind. Time is required to produce that union of minds which alone can produce all the good we aim at. Our patience will achieve more than our force. If I might venture to appeal to what is so much out of fashion in Paris, I mean to experience, I should tell you, that in my course I have known, and, according to my measure, have co-operated with great men; and I have never yet seen any plan which has not been mended by the observations of those who were much inferior in understanding to the person who took the lead in the business. By a slow but well-sustained progress, the effect of each step is watched; the good or ill success of the first gives light to us in the second; and so, from light to light, we are conducted with safety through the whole series. We see that the parts or the system do not clash. The evils latent in the most promising contrivances are provided for as they arise. One advantage is as little as possible sacrificed to another. We compensate, we reconcile, we balance. We are enabled to unite into a consistent whole the various anomalies and contending principles that are found in the minds and affairs of men. From hence arises, not an excellence in simplicity, but one far superior, an excellence in composition. Where the great interests of mankind are concerned through a long succession of generations, that succession ought to be admitted into some share in the councils which are so deeply to affect them. If justice requires this, the work itself requires the aid of more minds than one age can furnish. It is from this view of things that the best legislators have been often satisfied with the establishment of some sure, solid, and ruling principle in government; a power like that which some of the philosophers have called a plastic nature; and having fixed the principle, they have left it afterwards to its own operation.

To proceed in this manner, that is, to proceed with a presiding principle, and a prolific energy, is with me the criterion of profound wisdom. What your politicians think the marks of a bold, hardy genius, are only proofs of a deplorable want of ability. By their violent haste and their defiance of the process of nature, they are delivered over blindly to every projector and adventurer, to every alchymist and empiric. They despair of turning to account anything that is common. Diet is nothing in their system of remedy. The worst of it is, that this their despair of curing common distempers by regular methods, arises not only from defect of comprehension, but, I fear, from some malignity of disposition. Your legislators seem to have taken their opinions of all professions, ranks, and offices, from the declamations and buffooneries of satirists; who would themselves be astonished if they were held to the letter of their own descriptions. By listening only to these, your leaders regard all things only on the side of their vices and faults, and view those vices and faults under every colour of exaggeration. It is undoubtedly true, though it may seem paradoxical; but in general, those who are habitually employed in finding and displaying faults, are unqualified for the work of reformation : because their minds are not only unfurnished with patterns of the fair and good, but by habit they come to take no delight in the contemplation of those things. By hating vices too much, they come to love men too little. It is therefore not wonderful, that they should be indisposed and unable to serve them. From hence arises the complexional disposition of some of your guides to pull everything in pieces. At this malicious game they display the whole of their *quadrimanous* activity. As to the rest, the paradoxes of eloquent writers, brought forth purely as a sport of fancy, to try their talents, to rouse attention and excite surprise, are taken up by these gentlemen, not in the spirit of the original authors, as means of cultivating their taste and improving their style. These paradoxes become with them serious grounds of action, upon which they proceed in regulating the most important concerns of the state. Cicero ludicrously describes Cato as endeavouring to act, in the commonwealth, upon the school paradoxes, which exercised the wits of the junior students in the Stoic philosophy. If this was true of Cato, these gentlemen copy after him in the manner of some persons who lived about his time—*pede nudo Catonem*. Mr. Hume told me that he had from Rousseau himself the secrets of his principles of composition. That acute though eccentric observer had perceived, that to strike and interest the public, the marvellous must be produced; that the marvellous of the heathen mythology had long since lost its effects; that giants, magicians, fairies, and heroes of romance which succeeded, had exhausted the portion of credulity which belonged to their age; that now nothing was left to the writer but that species of the marvellous which might still be produced, and with as great an effect as ever, though in another way; that is, the marvellous in life, in manners, in characters, and in extraordinary situations, giving rise to new and unlooked-for strokes in politics and morals. I believe, that were Rousseau alive, and in one of his lucid intervals, he would be shocked at the practical phrensy of his scholars, who in their paradoxes are servile imitators, and even in their incredulity discover an implicit faith.

Men who undertake considerable things, even in a regular way, ought to give us ground to presume ability. But the physician of the state, who, not satisfied with the cure of distempers, undertakes to regenerate constitutions, ought to show uncommon powers. Some very unusual appearances of wisdom ought to display themselves on the face of the designs of those, who appeal to no practice, and who copy after no model. Has any such been manifested? I shall take a view (it shall for the subject be a very short one) of what the Assembly has done, with regard, first, to the constitution of the legislature; in the next place, to that of the executive power; then to that of the judicature; afterwards to the model of the army; and conclude with the system of finance; to see whether we can discover in any part of their schemes the portentous ability, which may justify these bold undertakers in the superiority which they assume over mankind.

It is in the model of the sovereign and presiding part of this new republic, that we should expect their grand display. Here they were to prove their title to their proud demands. For the plan itself at large, and for the reasons on which it is grounded, I refer to the journals of the Assembly of the 29th of September, 1789, and to the subsequent proceedings which have made any alterations in the plan. So far as in a matter somewhat confused I can see light, the system remains substantially as it has been originally framed. My few remarks will be such as regard its spirit, its tendency, and its fitness for framing a popular commonwealth, which they profess theirs to be, suited to the ends for which any commonwealth, and particularly such a commonwealth, is made. At the same time, I mean to consider its consistency with itself and its own principles.

Old establishments are tried by their effects. If the people are happy, united, wealthy, and powerful, we presume the rest. We conclude that to be good from whence good is derived. In old establishments various correctives have been found for their aberrations from theory. Indeed they are the results of various necessities and expediences. They are not often constructed after any theory; theories are rather drawn from them. In them we often see the end best obtained, where the means seem not perfectly reconcilable to what we may fancy was the original scheme. The means taught by experience may be better suited to political ends than those contrived in the original project. They again react upon the primitive constitution, and sometimes improve the design itself, from which they seem to have departed. I think all this might be curiously exemplified in the British Constitution. At worst, the errors and deviations of every kind in reckoning are found and computed, and the ship proceeds in her course. This is the case of old establishments; but in a new and merely theoretic system, it is expected that every contrivance shall appear, on the face of it, to answer its ends; especially where the projectors are no way embarrassed with an endeavour to accommodate the new building to an old one, either in the walls or on the foundations.

The French builders, clearing away as mere rubbish whatever they found, and, like their ornamental gardeners, forming everything into an exact level, propose to rest the whole local and general legislature on three bases of three different kinds; one geometrical, one arithmetical, and the third financial; the first of which they call the *basis of territory;* the second, the *basis of population;* and the third, the *basis of contribution.* For the accomplishment of the first of these purposes, they divide the area of their country into eighty-three pieces, regularly square, of eighteen leagues by eighteen. These large divisions are called *Departments.* These they portion, proceeding by square measurement, into seventeen hundred and twenty districts, called *Communes.* These again they subdivide, still proceeding by square measurement, into smaller districts called *Cantons,* making in all 6400.

At first view this geometrical basis of theirs presents not much to admire or to blame. It calls for no great legislative talents. Nothing more than an accurate land surveyor, with his chain, sight, and theodolite, is requisite for such a plan as this. In the old divisions of the country, various accidents at various times, and the ebb and flow of various properties and jurisdictions, settled their bounds. These bounds were not made upon any fixed system undoubtedly. They were subject to some inconveniences: but they were inconveniences for which use had found remedies, and habit had supplied accommodation and patience.   In this new pavement of square within square, and this organization, and semi-organization, made on the system of Empedocles and Buffon, and not upon any politic principle, it is impossible that innumerable local inconveniences, to which men are not habituated, must not arise.   But these I pass over, because it requires an accurate knowledge of the country, which I do not possess, to specify them.

When these state surveyors came to take a view of their work of measurement, they soon found, that in politics the most fallacious of all things was geometrical demonstration.   They had then recourse to another basis (or rather buttress) to support the building, which tottered on that false foundation.   It was evident, that the goodness of the soil, the number of the people, their wealth, and the largeness of their contribution, made such infinite variations between square and square, as to render mensuration a ridiculous standard of power in the commonwealth, and equality in geometry the most unequal of all measures in the distribution of men.   However, they could not give it up.   But dividing their political and civil representation into three parts, they allotted one of those parts to the square measurement, without a single fact or calculation to ascertain whether this territorial proportion of representation was fairly assigned, and ought upon any principle really to be a third.   Having, however, given to geometry this portion (of a third for her dower) out of compliment, I suppose, to that sublime science, they left the other two to be scuffled for between the other parts, population and contribution.

When they came to provide for population, they were not able to proceed quite so smoothly as they had done in the field of their geometry.   Here their arithmetic came to bear upon their juridical metaphysics.   Had they stuck to their metaphysic principles, the arithmetical process would be simple indeed.   Men, with them, are strictly equal, and are entitled to equal rights in their own government.   Each head, on this system, would have its vote, and every man would vote directly for the person who was to represent him in the legislature.   "But soft—by regular degrees, not yet."   This metaphysic principle, to which law, custom, usage, policy, reason, were to yield, is to yield itself

to their pleasure. There must be many degrees, and some
stages, before the representative can come in contact with
his constituent. Indeed, as we shall soon see, these two
persons are to have no sort of communion with each other.
First, the voters in the *Canton*, who compose what they
call *primary assemblies*, are to have a *qualification*. What!
a qualification on the indefeasible rights of men? Yes;
but it shall be a very small qualification. Our injustice
shall be very little oppressive; only the local valuation of
three days' labour paid to the public. Why, this is not
much, I readily admit, for anything but the utter subversion of your equalising principle. As a qualification it
might as well be let alone; for it answers no one purpose
for which qualifications are established; and, on your ideas,
it excludes from a vote the man of all others whose natural
equality stands the most in need of protection and defence:
I mean the man who has nothing else but his natural
equality to guard him. You order him to buy the right,
which you before told him nature had given to him gratuitously at his birth, and of which no authority on earth could
lawfully deprive him. With regard to the person who
cannot come up to your market, a tyrannous aristocracy,
as against him, is established at the very outset, by you
who pretend to be its sworn foe.

The gradation proceeds. These primary assemblies of
the *Canton* elect deputies to the *Commune;* one for every
two hundred qualified inhabitants. Here is the first
medium put between the primary elector and the representative legislator; and here a new turnpike is fixed for
taxing the rights of men with a second qualification: for
none can be elected into the *Commune* who does not pay
the amount of ten days' labour. Nor have we yet done.
There is still to be another gradation.[1] These *Communes*, chosen by the *Canton*, choose to the *Department;*

---

1 The Assembly, in executing the plan of their committee, made
some alterations. They have struck out one stage in these gradations; this removes a part of the objection; but the main objection,
namely, that in their scheme the first constituent voter has no connexion with the representative legislator, remains in all its force.
There are other alterations, some possibly for the better, some certainly for the worse; but to the author the merit or demerit of these
smaller alterations appears to be of no moment where the scheme
itself is fundamentally vicious and absurd.

and the deputies of the *Department* choose their deputies to the *National Assembly*. Here is a third barrier of a senseless qualification. Every deputy to the National Assembly must pay, in direct contribution, to the value of a *mark of silver*. Of all these qualifying barriers we must think alike; that they are impotent to secure independence; strong only to destroy the rights of men.

In all this process, which in its fundamental elements affects to consider only *population* upon a principle of natural right, there is a manifest attention to *property;* which, however just and reasonable on other schemes, is on theirs perfectly unsupportable.

When they come to their third basis, that of *Contribution*, we find that they have more completely lost sight of their rights of men. This last basis rests *entirely* on property. A principle totally different from the equality of men, and utterly irreconcilable to it, is thereby admitted; but no sooner is this principle admitted, than (as usual) it is subverted; and it is not subverted (as we shall presently see) to approximate the inequality of riches to the level of nature. The additional share in the third portion of representation (a portion reserved exclusively for the higher contribution) is made to regard the *district* only, and not the individuals in it who pay. It is easy to perceive, by the course of their reasonings, how much they were embarrassed by their contradictory ideas of the rights of men and the privileges of riches. The committee of constitution do as good as admit that they are wholly irreconcilable. "The relation with regard to the contributions, is without doubt *null* (say they) when the question is on the balance of the political rights as between individual and individual; without which *personal equality would be destroyed*, and *an aristocracy of the rich* would be established. But this inconvenience entirely disappears when the proportional relation of the contribution is only considered in the *great masses*, and is solely between province and province; it serves in that case only to form a just reciprocal proportion between the cities, without affecting the personal rights of the citizens."

Here the principle of *contribution*, as taken between man and man, is reprobated as *null*, and destructive to equality : and as pernicious too; because it leads to the establishment of an *aristocracy of the rich*. However, it must not be abandoned. And the way of getting rid of the difficulty is to establish the inequality as between department and department, leaving all the individuals in each department upon an exact par. Observe, that this parity between individuals had been before destroyed, when the qualifications within the departments were settled; nor does it seem a matter of great importance whether the equality of men be injured by masses or individually. An individual is not of the same importance in a mass represented by a few, as in a mass represented by many. It would be too much to tell a man jealous of his equality, that the elector has the same franchise who votes for three members as he who votes for ten.

Now take it in the other point of view, and let us suppose their principle of representation according to contribution, that is, according to riches, to be well imagined, and to be a necessary basis for their republic. In this their third basis they assume, that riches ought to be respected, and that justice and policy require that they should entitle men, in some mode or other, to a larger share in the administration of public affairs; it is now to be seen how the Assembly provides for the pre-eminence, or even for the security, of the rich, by conferring, in virtue of their opulence, that larger measure of power to their district which is denied to them personally. I readily admit (indeed I should lay it down as a fundamental principle) that in a republican government, which has a democratic basis, the rich do require an additional security above what is necessary to them in monarchies. They are subject to envy, and through envy to oppression. On the present scheme it is impossible to divine what advantage they derive from the aristocratic preference upon which the unequal representation of the masses is founded. The rich cannot feel it, either as a support to dignity, or as security to fortune: for the aristocratic mass is generated from purely democratic principles; and the preference given to it in the general representation has no sort of reference to, or connexion with, the persons, upon account of whose property this superiority of the mass is established. If the contrivers of this scheme meant any sort of favour to the rich, in consequence of their contribution, they ought to have conferred the privilege either on the individual rich, or on some class formed of rich persons (as historians represent Servius Tullius to have done in the early constitution of Rome); because the contest between the rich and the poor is not a struggle between corporation and corporation, but a contest between men and men; a competition not between districts, but between descriptions. It would answer its purpose better if the scheme were inverted; that the votes of the masses were rendered equal; and that the votes within each mass were proportioned to property.

Let us suppose one man in a district (it is an easy supposition) to contribute as much as an hundred of his neighbours. Against these he has but one vote. If there were but one representative for the mass, his poor neighbours would outvote him by an hundred to one for that single representative. Bad enough. But amends are to be made him. How? The district, in virtue of his wealth, is to choose, say ten members instead of one: that is to say, by paying a very large contribution he has the happiness of being outvoted, an hundred to one, by the poor for ten representatives, instead of being outvoted exactly in the same proportion for a single member. In truth, instead of benefitting by this superior quantity of representation, the rich man is subjected to an additional hardship. The increase of representation within his province sets up nine persons more, and as many more than nine as there may be democratic candidates, to cabal and intrigue, and to flatter the people at his expense and to his oppression. An interest is by this means held out to multitudes of the inferior sort, in obtaining a salary of eighteen livres a day (to them a vast object), besides the pleasure of a residence in Paris, and their share in the government of the kingdom. The more the objects of ambition are multiplied and become democratic, just in that proportion the rich are endangered.

Thus it must fare between the poor and the rich in the province deemed aristocratic, which in its internal relation is the very reverse of that character. In its external relation, that is, its relation to the other provinces, I cannot see how the unequal representation, which is given to masses on account of wealth, becomes the means of preserving the equipoise and the tranquillity of the common-

wealth. For if it be one of the objects to secure the weak
from being crushed by the strong (as in all society undoubtedly it is), how are the smaller and poorer of these
masses to be saved from the tyranny of the more wealthy?
Is it by adding to the wealthy further and more systematical
means of oppressing them? When we come to a balance
of representation between corporate bodies, provincial
interests, emulations, and jealousies are full as likely to
arise among them as among individuals; and their divisions are likely to produce a much hotter spirit of dissension, and something leading much more nearly to a war.

I see that these aristocratic masses are made upon what
is called the principle of direct contribution. Nothing can
be a more unequal standard than this. The indirect contribution, that which arises from duties on consumption,
is in truth a better standard, and follows and discovers
wealth more naturally than this of direct contribution. It
is difficult indeed to fix a standard of local preference on
account of the one, or of the other, or of both, because
some provinces may pay the more of either or of both,
on account of causes not intrinsic, but originating from
those very districts over whom they have obtained a
preference in consequence of their ostensible contribution.
If the masses were independent, sovereign bodies, who
were to provide for a federative treasury by distinct con-
tingents, and that the revenue had not (as it has) many
impositions running through the whole, which affect men
individually, and not corporately, and which, by their
nature, confound all territorial limits, something might be
said for the basis of contribution as founded on masses.
But of all things, this representation, to be measured by
contribution, is the most difficult to settle upon principles
of equity in a country, which considers its districts as
members of a whole. For a great city, such as Bordeaux,
or Paris, appears to pay a vast body of duties, almost out
of all assignable proportion to other places, and its mass
is considered accordingly. But are these cities the true
contributors in that proportion? No. The consumers of
the commodities imported into Bordeaux, who are scattered through all France, pay the import duties of
Bordeaux. The produce of the vintage in Guienne and
Languedoc give to that city the means of its contribution

growing out of an export commerce. The land-holders who spend their estates in Paris, and are thereby the creators of that city, contribute for Paris from the provinces out of which their revenues arise. Very nearly the same arguments will apply to the representative share given on account of *direct* contribution : because the direct contribution must be assessed on wealth real or presumed ; and that local wealth will itself arise from causes not local, and which therefore in equity ought not to produce a local preference.

It is very remarkable, that in this fundamental regulation, which settles the representation of the mass upon the direct contribution, they have not yet settled how that direct contribution shall be laid, and how apportioned. Perhaps there is some latent policy towards the continuance of the present Assembly in this strange procedure. However, until they do this, they can have no certain constitution. It must depend at last upon the system of taxation, and must vary with every variation in that system. As they have contrived matters, their taxation does not so much depend on their constitution, as their constitution on their taxation. This must introduce great confusion among the masses ; as the variable qualification for votes within the district must, if ever real contested elections take place, cause infinite internal controversies.

To compare together the three bases, not on their political reason, but on the ideas on which the Assembly works, and to try its consistency with itself, we cannot avoid observing, that the principle which the committee call the basis of *population*, does not begin to operate from the same point with the two other principles called the bases of *territory* and of *contribution*, which are both of an aristocratic nature. The consequence is, that, where all three begin to operate together, there is the most absurd inequality produced by the operation of the former on the two latter principles. Every canton contains four square leagues, and is estimated to contain, on the average, 4000 inhabitants, or 680 voters in the *primary assemblies*, which vary in numbers with the population of the canton, and send *one deputy* to the *commune* for every 200 voters. *Nine cantons* make a *commune*.

Now let us take *a canton* containing *a sea-port town of trade*, or *a great manufacturing town*. Let us suppose the population of this canton to be 12,700 inhabitants, or 2193 voters, forming *three primary assemblies*, and sending *ten deputies* to the *commune*.

Oppose to this *one* canton, *two* others of the remaining eight in the same commune. These we may suppose to have their fair population of 4000 inhabitants and 680 voters each, or 8000 inhabitants and 1360 voters, both together. These will form only *two primary assemblies*, and send only *six* deputies to the *commune*.

When the assembly of the *commune* comes to vote on the *basis of territory*, which principle is first admitted to operate in that assembly, the *single canton*, which has *half* the territory of the *other two*, will have *ten* voices to *six* in the election of *three deputies* to the assembly of the department, chosen on the express ground of a representation of territory. This inequality, striking as it is, will be yet highly aggravated, if we suppose, as we fairly may, the *several* other cantons of the *commune* to fall proportionably short of the average population, as much as the *principal canton* exceeds it.

Now as to *the basis of contribution*, which also is a principle admitted first to operate in the assembly of the *commune*. Let us again take *one* canton, such as is stated above. If the whole of the direct contributions paid by a great trading or manufacturing town be divided equally among the inhabitants, each individual will be found to pay much more than an individual living in the country according to the same average. The whole paid by the inhabitants of the former will be more than the whole paid by the inhabitants of the latter—we may fairly assume one-third more. Then the 12,700 inhabitants, or 2193 voters of the canton, will pay as much as 19,050 inhabitants, or 3289 voters of the *other cantons*, which are nearly the estimated proportion of inhabitants and voters of *five* other cantons. Now the 2193 voters will, as I before said, send only *ten* deputies to the Assembly; the 3289 voters will send *sixteen*. Thus, for an *equal* share in the contribution of the whole *commune*, there will be a difference of *sixteen* voices to *ten* in voting for deputies to be chosen on the principle of representing the general contribution of the whole *commune*.

By the same mode of computation we shall find 15,875

inhabitants, or 2741 voters of the *other* cantons, who pay *one-sixth* LESS to the contribution of the whole *commune* will have *three* voices MORE than the 12,700 inhabitants, or 2193 voters of the *one* canton.

Such is the fantastical and unjust inequality between mass and mass, in this curious repartition of the rights of representation arising out of *territory* and *contribution*. The qualifications which these confer are in truth negative qualifications, that give a right in an inverse proportion to the possession of them.

In this whole contrivance of the three bases, consider it in any light you please, I do not see a variety of objects reconciled in one consistent whole, but several contradictory principles reluctantly and irreconcilably brought and held together by your philosophers, like wild beasts shut up in a cage, to claw and bite each other to their mutual destruction.

I am afraid I have gone too far into their way of considering the formation of a constitution. They have much, but bad, metaphysics; much, but bad, geometry; much, but false, proportionate arithmetic; but if it were all as exact as metaphysics, geometry, and arithmetic ought to be, and if their schemes were perfectly consistent in all their parts, it would make only a more fair and sightly vision. It is remarkable, that, in a great arrangement of mankind, not one reference whatsoever is to be found to anything moral or anything politic; nothing that relates to the concerns, the actions, the passions, the interests of men. *Hominem non sapiunt.*

You see I only consider this constitution as electoral, and leading by steps to the National Assembly. I do not enter into the internal government of the departments, and their genealogy through the communes and cantons. These local governments are, in the original plan, to be as nearly as possible composed in the same manner and on the same principles with the elective assemblies. They are each of them bodies perfectly compact and rounded in themselves.

You cannot but perceive in this scheme, that it has a direct and immediate tendency to sever France into a variety of republics, and to render them totally independent of each other without any direct constitutional means of coherence, connexion, or subordination, except what may be derived from their acquiescence in the determination of the general congress of the ambassadors from each independent republic. Such in reality is the National Assembly, and such governments I admit do exist in the world, though in forms infinitely more suitable to the local and habitual circumstances of their people. But such associations, rather than bodies politic, have generally been the effect of necessity, not choice; and I believe the present French power is the very first body of citizens, who, having obtained full authority to do with their country what they pleased, have chosen to dissever it in this barbarous manner.

It is impossible not to observe, that, in the spirit of this geometrical distribution, and arithmetical arrangement, these pretended citizens treat France exactly like a country of conquest. Acting as conquerors, they have imitated the policy of the harshest of that harsh race. The policy of such barbarous victors, who contemn a subdued people, and insult their feelings, has ever been, as much as in them lay, to destroy all vestiges of the ancient country, in religion, in polity, in laws, and in manners; to confound all territorial limits; to produce a general poverty; to put up their properties to auction; to crush their princes, nobles, and pontiffs; to lay low everything which had lifted its head above the level, or which could serve to combine or rally, in their distresses, the disbanded people, under the standard of old opinion. They have made France free in the manner in which those sincere friends to the rights of mankind, the Romans, freed Greece, Macedon, and other nations. They destroyed the bonds of their union, under colour of providing for the independence of each of their cities.

When the members who compose these new bodies of cantons, communes, and departments, arrangements purposely produced through the medium of confusion, begin to act, they will find themselves in a great measure strangers to one another. The electors and elected throughout, especially in the rural *cantons*, will be frequently without any civil habitudes or connexions, or any of that natural discipline which is the soul of a true republic. Magistrates and collectors of revenue are now no longer acquainted with their districts, bishops with their dioceses, or curates with their parishes. These new colonies of the rights of men bear a strong resemblance to that sort of military colonies which Tacitus has observed upon in the declining policy of Rome. In better and wiser days (whatever course they took with foreign nations) they were careful to make the elements of methodical subordination and settlement to be coeval; and even to lay the foundations of civil discipline in the military.[1] But, when all the good arts had fallen into ruin, they proceeded, as your Assembly does, upon the equality of men, and with as little judgment, and as little care for those things which make a republic tolerable or durable. But in this, as well as almost every instance, your new commonwealth is born, and bred, and fed, in those corruptions which mark degenerated and worn-out republics. Your child comes into the world with the symptoms of death; the *facies Hippocratica* forms the character of its physiognomy, and the prognostic of its fate.

The legislators who framed the ancient republics knew that their business was too arduous to be accomplished with no better apparatus than the metaphysics of an undergraduate, and the mathematics and arithmetic of an exciseman. They had to do with men, and they were obliged to study human nature. They had to do with citizens, and they were obliged to study the effects of those habits which are communicated by the circumstances of civil life. They were sensible that the operation of this second nature on the first produced a new combination; and thence arose many diversities amongst men, according to their birth, their education, their professions, the periods of their lives, their residence in towns or in the country, their several ways of acquiring and of fixing property, and according to the quality of the property itself, all which rendered them as it were so many different species of animals. From hence they thought themselves obliged to dispose their

---

[1] Non, ut olim, universæ legiones deducebantur cum tribunis, et centurionibus, et sui cujusque ordinis militibus, ut consensu et caritate rempublicam afficerent; sed ignoti inter se, diversis manipulis, sine rectore, sine affectibus mutuis, quasi ex alio genere mortalium, repente in unum collecti, numerus magis quam colonia. Tac. Annal. l. 14, sect. 27. All this will be still more applicable to the unconnected, rotatory, biennial national assemblies, in this absurd and senseless constitution.

citizens into such classes, and to place them in such situations in the state, as their peculiar habits might qualify them to fill, and to allot to them such appropriated privileges as might secure to them what their specific occasions required, and which might furnish to each description such force as might protect it in the conflict caused by the diversity of interests, that must exist, and must contend, in all complex society : for the legislator would have been ashamed, that the coarse husbandman should well know how to assort and to use his sheep, horses, and oxen, and should have enough of common sense, not to abstract and equalize them all into animals, without providing for each kind an appropriate food, care, and employment ; whilst he, the economist, disposer, and shepherd of his own kindred, subliming himself into an airy metaphysician, was resolved to know nothing of his flocks but as men in general. It is for this reason that Montesquieu observed very justly, that in their classification of the citizens, the great legislators of antiquity made the greatest display of their powers, and even soared above themselves. It is here that your modern legislators have gone deep into the negative series, and sunk even below their own nothing. As the first sort of legislators attended to the different kinds of citizens, and combined them into one commonwealth, the others, the metaphysical and alchemistical legislators, have taken the direct contrary course. They have attempted to confound all sorts of citizens, as well as they could, into one homogeneous mass ; and then they divided this their amalgama into a number of incoherent republics. They reduce men to loose counters, merely for the sake of simple telling, and not to figures whose power is to arise from their place in the table. The elements of their own metaphysics might have taught them better lessons. The troll of their categorical table might have informed them that there was something else in the intellectual world besides *substance* and *quantity*. They might learn from the catechism of metaphysics that there were eight heads more,[1] in every complex deliberation, which they have never thought of ; though these, of all the ten, are the subjects on which the skill of man can operate anything at all.

[1] Qualitas, Relatio, Actio, Passio, Ubi, Quando, Situs, Habitus.

So far from this able disposition of some of the old republican legislators, which follows with a solicitous accuracy the moral conditions and propensities of men, they have levelled and crushed together all the orders which they found, even under the coarse unartificial arrangement of the monarchy, in which mode of government the classing of the citizens is not of so much importance as in a republic. It is true, however, that every such classification, if properly ordered, is good in all forms of government; and composes a strong barrier against the excesses of despotism, as well as it is the necessary means of giving effect and permanence to a republic. For want of something of this kind, if the present project of a republic should fail, all securities to a moderated freedom fail along with it; all the indirect restraints which mitigate despotism are removed; insomuch that if monarchy should ever again obtain an entire ascendency in France, under this or under any other dynasty, it will probably be, if not voluntarily tempered, at setting out, by the wise and virtuous counsels of the prince, the most completely arbitrary power that has ever appeared on earth. This is to play a most desperate game.

The confusion which attends on all such proceedings, they even declare to be one of their objects, and they hope to secure their constitution by a terror of a return of those evils which attended their making it. "By this," say they, "its destruction will become difficult to authority, which cannot break it up without the entire disorganization of the whole state." They presume, that if this authority should ever come to the same degree of power that they have acquired, it would make a more moderate and chastised use of it, and would piously tremble entirely to disorganize the state in the savage manner that they have done. They expect, from the virtues of returning despotism, the security which is to be enjoyed by the offspring of their popular vices.

I wish, Sir, that you and my readers would give an attentive perusal to the work of M. de Calonne, on this subject. It is indeed not only an eloquent, but an able and instructive, performance. I confine myself to what he says relative to the constitution of the new state, and to the condition of the revenue. As to the disputes of this minister with his rivals, I do not wish to pronounce upon them. As little do I mean to hazard any opinion concerning his ways and means, financial or political, for taking his country out of its present disgraceful and deplorable situation of servitude, anarchy, bankruptcy, and beggary. I cannot speculate quite so sanguinely as he does : but he is a Frenchman, and has a closer duty relative to those objects, and better means of judging of them, than I can have. I wish that the formal avowal which he refers to, made by one of the principal leaders in the Assembly, concerning the tendency of their scheme to bring France not only from a monarchy to a republic, but from a republic to a mere confederacy, may be very particularly attended to. It adds new force to my observations : and indeed M. de Calonne's work supplies my deficiencies by many new and striking arguments on most of the subjects of this letter.[1]

It is this resolution, to break their country into separate republics, which has driven them into the greatest number of their difficulties and contradictions. If it were not for this, all the questions of exact equality, and these balances, never to be settled, of individual rights, population, and contribution, would be wholly useless. The representation, though derived from parts, would be a duty which equally regarded the whole. Each deputy to the Assembly would be the representative of France, and of all its descriptions, of the many and of the few, of the rich and of the poor, of the great districts and of the small. All these districts would themselves be subordinate to some standing authority, existing independently of them, an authority in which their representation, and everything that belongs to it, originated, and to which it was pointed. This standing, unalterable, fundamental government would make, and it is the only thing which could make, that territory truly and properly a whole. With us, when we elect popular representatives, we send them to a council, in which each man individually is a subject, and submitted to a government complete in all its ordinary functions. With you the elective Assembly is the sovereign, and the sole sovereign : all the members are therefore integral parts of this sole sovereignty. But with us it

[1] See l'Etat de la France, p. 363.

is totally different. With us the representative, separated from the other parts, can have no action and no existence. The government is the point of reference of the several members and districts of our representation. This is the centre of our unity. This government of reference is a trustee for the *whole*, and not for the parts. So is the other branch of our public council, I mean the House of Lords. With us the king and the lords are several and joint securities for the equality of each district, each province, each city. When did you hear in Great Britain of any province suffering from the inequality of its representation; what district from having no representation at all? Not only our monarchy and our peerage secure the equality on which our unity depends, but it is the spirit of the House of Commons itself. The very inequality of representation, which is so foolishly complained of, is perhaps the very thing which prevents us from thinking or acting as members for districts. Cornwall elects as many members as all Scotland. But is Cornwall better taken care of than Scotland? Few trouble their heads about any of your bases, out of some giddy clubs. Most of those who wish for any change, upon any plausible grounds, desire it on different ideas.

Your new constitution is the very reverse of ours in its principle; and I am astonished how any persons could dream of holding out anything done in it, as an example for Great Britain. With you there is little, or rather no, connexion between the last representative and the first constituent. The member who goes to the National Assembly is not chosen by the people, nor accountable to them. There are three elections before he is chosen : two sets of magistracy intervene between him and the primary assembly, so as to render him, as I have said, an ambassador of a state, and not the representative of the people within a state. By this the whole spirit of the election is changed; nor can any corrective, which your constitution-mongers have devised, render him anything else than what he is. The very attempt to do it would inevitably introduce a confusion, if possible, more horrid than the present. There is no way to make a connection between the original constituent and the representative, but by the circuitous means which may lead the candidate to apply in the first instance to the primary electors, in order that by their authoritative instructions (and something more perhaps) these primary electors may force the two succeeding bodies of electors to make a choice agreeable to their wishes. But this would plainly subvert the whole scheme. It would be to plunge them back into that tumult and confusion of popular election, which, by their interposed gradation of elections, they mean to avoid, and at length to risk the whole fortune of the state with those who have the least knowledge of it, and the least interest in it. This is a perpetual dilemma, into which they are thrown by the vicious, weak, and contradictory principles they have chosen. Unless the people break up and level this gradation, it is plain that they do not at all substantially elect to the Assembly; indeed they elect as little in appearance as reality.

What is it we all seek for in an election? To answer its real purposes, you must first possess the means of knowing the fitness of your man; and then you must retain some hold upon him by personal obligation or dependence. For what end are these primary electors complimented, or rather mocked, with a choice? They can never know anything of the qualities of him that is to serve them, nor has he any obligation whatsoever to them. Of all the powers unfit to be delegated by those who have any real means of judging, that most peculiarly unfit is what relates to a *personal* choice. In case of abuse, that body of primary electors never can call the representative to an account for his conduct. He is too far removed from them in the chain of representation. If he acts improperly at the end of his two years' lease, it does not concern him for two years more. By the new French constitution the best and the wisest representatives go equally with the worst into this *Limbus Patrum*. Their bottoms are supposed foul, and they must go into dock to be refitted. Every man who has served in an assembly is ineligible for two years after. Just as these magistrates begin to learn their trade, like chimney-sweepers, they are disqualified for exercising it. Superficial, new, petulant acquisition, and interrupted, dronish, broken, ill recollection, is to be the destined character of all your future governors. Your constitution has too much of jealousy to have much of sense in it. You consider the breach of trust in the representative so principally, that you do not at all regard the question of his fitness to execute it.

This purgatory interval is not unfavourable to a faithless representative, who may be as good a canvasser as he was a bad governor. In this time he may cabal himself into a superiority over the wisest and most virtuous. As, in the end, all the members of this elective constitution are equally fugitive, and exist only for the election, they may be no longer the same persons who had chosen him, to whom he is to be responsible when he solicits for a renewal of his trust. To call all the secondary electors of the *Commune* to account, is ridiculous, impracticable, and unjust; they may themselves have been deceived in their choice, as the third set of electors, those of the *Department,* may be in theirs. In your elections responsibility cannot exist.

Finding no sort of principle of coherence with each other in the nature and constitution of the several new republics of France, I considered what coment the legislators had provided for them from any extraneous materials. Their confederations, their *spectacles,* their civic feasts, and their enthusiasm, I take no notice of; they are nothing but mere tricks; but tracing their policy through their actions, I think I can distinguish the arrangements by which they propose to hold these republics together. The first is the *confiscation,* with the compulsory paper currency annexed to it; the second is the supreme power of the city of Paris; the third is the general army of the state. Of this last I shall reserve what I have to say, until I come to consider the army as a head by itself.

As to the operation of the first (the confiscation and paper currency) merely as a cement, I cannot deny that these, the one depending on the other, may for some time compose some sort of cement, if their madness and folly in the management, and in the tempering of the parts together, does not produce a repulsion in the very outset. But allowing to the scheme some coherence and some duration, it appears to me, that if, after a while, the confiscation should not be found sufficient to support the paper coinage (as I am morally certain it will not), then, instead of cementing, it will add infinitely to the dissociation, distraction, and confusion of these confederate republics, both with relation to each other, and to the several parts within themselves. But if the confiscation should so far succeed as to sink the paper currency, the cement is gone with the circulation. In the mean time its binding force will be very uncertain, and it will straiten or relax with every variation in the credit of the paper.

One thing only is certain in this scheme, which is an effect seemingly collateral, but direct, I have no doubt, in the minds of those who conduct this business, that is, its effect in producing an *Oligarchy* in every one of the republics. A paper circulation, not founded on any real money deposited or engaged for, amounting already to four-and-forty millions of English money, and this currency by force substituted in the place of the coin of the kingdom, becoming thereby the substance of its revenue, as well as the medium of all its commercial and civil intercourse, must put the whole of what power, authority, and influence is left, in any form whatsoever it may assume, into the hands of the managers and conductors of this circulation.

In England we feel the influence of the bank; though it is only the centre of a voluntary dealing. He knows little indeed of the influence of money upon mankind, who does not see the force of the management of a monied concern, which is so much more extensive, and in its nature so much more depending on the managers, than any of ours. But this is not merely a money concern. There is another member in the system inseparably connected with this money management. It consists in the means of drawing out at discretion portions of the confiscated lands for sale; and carrying on a process of continual transmutation of paper into land, and land into paper. When we follow this process in its effects, we may conceive something of the intensity of the force with which this system must operate. By this means the spirit of money-jobbing and speculation goes into the mass of land itself, and incorporates with it. By this kind of operation that species of property becomes (as it were) volatilized; it assumes an unnatural and monstrous activity, and thereby throws into the hands of the several managers, principal and subordinate, Parisian and provincial, all the representative of money, and perhaps a full tenth part of all the land in France, which has now acquired the worst and most pernicious part of the evil of a paper circulation, the greatest possible uncertainty in its value. They have reversed the Latonian kindness to the landed property of Delos. They have sent theirs to be blown about, like the light fragments of a wreck, *oras et littora circum.*

The new dealers, being all habitually adventurers, and without any fixed habits or local predilections, will purchase to job out again, as the market of paper, or of money, or of land, shall present an advantage. For though a holy bishop thinks that agriculture will derive great advantages from the "*enlightened*" usurers who are to purchase the church confiscations, I, who am not a good, but an old farmer, with great humility beg leave to tell his late lordship, that usury is not a tutor of agriculture; and if the word "enlightened" be understood according to the new dictionary, as it always is in your new schools, I cannot conceive how a man's not believing in God can teach him to cultivate the earth with the least of any additional skill or encouragement. "*Diis immortalibus sero,*" said an old Roman, when he held one handle of the plough, whilst Death held the other. Though you were to join in the commission all the directors of the two academies to the directors of the *Caisse d'Escompte*, one old, experienced peasant is worth them all. I have got more information upon a curious and interesting branch of husbandry, in one short conversation with an old Carthusian monk, than I have derived from all the Bank directors that I have ever conversed with. However, there is no cause for apprehension from the meddling of money-dealers with rural economy. These gentlemen are too wise in their generation. At first, perhaps, their tender and susceptible imaginations may be captivated with the innocent and unprofitable delights of a pastoral life; but in a little time they will find that agriculture is a trade much more laborious, and much less lucrative, than that which they had left. After making its panegyric, they will turn their backs on it like their great precursor and prototype. They may, like him, begin by singing "*Beatus ille*"—but what will be the end?

> *Hæc ubi locutus fœnerator Alphius,*
> *Jam jam futurus rusticus*
> *Omnem redegit idibus pecuniam;*
> *Quærit calendis ponere.*

They will cultivate the *Caisse d'Église*, under the sacred auspices of this prelate, with much more profit than its vineyards and its corn-fields. They will employ their talents according to their habits and their interests. They will not follow the plough whilst they can direct treasuries, and govern provinces.

Your legislators, in everything new, are the very first who have founded a commonwealth upon gaming, and infused this spirit into it as its vital breath. The great object in these politics is to metamorphose France from a great kingdom into one great play-table; to turn its inhabitants into a nation of gamesters; to make speculation as extensive as life; to mix it with all its concerns; and to divert the whole of the hopes and fears of the people from their usual channels into the impulses, passions, and superstitions of those who live on chances. They loudly proclaim their opinion, that this their present system of a republic cannot possibly exist without this kind of gaming fund; and that the very thread of its life is spun out of the staple of these speculations. The old gaming in funds was mischievous enough undoubtedly; but it was so only to individuals. Even when it had its greatest extent, in the Mississippi and South Sea, it affected but few, comparatively; where it extends farther, as in lotteries, the spirit has but a single object. But where the law, which in most circumstances forbids, and in none countenances, gaming, is itself debauched, so as to reverse its nature and policy, and expressly to force the subject to this destructive table, by bringing the spirit and symbols of gaming into the minutest matters, and engaging everybody in it, and in everything, a more dreadful epidemic distemper of that kind is spread than yet has appeared in the world. With you a man can neither earn nor buy his dinner without a speculation. What he receives in the morning will not have the same value at night. What he is compelled to take as pay for an old debt will not be received as the same when he comes to pay a debt contracted by himself; nor will it be the same when by prompt payment he would avoid contracting any debt at all. Industry must wither away. Economy must be driven from your country. Careful provision will have no existence. Who will labour without knowing the amount of his pay? Who will study to increase what none can estimate? Who will accumulate, when he does not know the value of what he saves? If you abstract it from its uses in gaming, to accumulate your paper wealth, would be not the providence of a man, but the distempered instinct of a jackdaw.

The truly melancholy part of the policy of systematically making a nation of gamesters is this, that though all are forced to play, few can understand the game; and fewer still are in a condition to avail themselves of the knowledge. The many must be the dupes of the few who conduct the machine of these speculations. What effect it must have on the country people is visible. The townsman can calculate from day to day; not so the inhabitant of the country. When the peasant first brings his corn to market, the magistrate in the towns obliges him to take the assignat at par; when he goes to the shop with his money, he finds it seven per cent. the worse for crossing the way. This market he will not readily resort to again. The towns-people will be inflamed; they will force the country people to bring their corn. Resistance will begin, and the murders of Paris and St. Denis may be renewed through all France.

What signifies the empty compliment paid to the country, by giving it, perhaps, more than its share in the theory of your representation? Where have you placed the real power over monied and landed circulation? Where have you placed the means of raising and falling the value of every man's freehold? Those, whose operations can take from, or add ten per cent. to, the possessions of every man in France, must be the masters of every man in France. The whole of the power obtained by this revolution will settle in the towns among the burghers, and the monied directors who lead them. The landed gentleman, the yeoman, and the peasant, have, none of them, habits, or inclinations, or experience, which can lead them to any share in this the sole source of power and influence now left in France. The very nature of a country life, the very nature of landed property, in all the occupations, and all the pleasures they afford, render combination and arrangement (the sole way of procuring and exerting influence) in a manner impossible amongst country people. Combine them by all the art you can, and all the industry, they are always dissolving into individuality. Anything in the nature of incorporation is almost impracticable amongst them. Hope, fear, alarm, jealousy, the ephemerous tale that does its business and dies in a day, all these things, which are the reins and spurs by which leaders check or urge the minds of followers, are not easily employed, or hardly at all, amongst scattered people. They assemble, they arm, they act, with the utmost difficulty, and at the greatest charge. Their efforts, if ever they can be commenced, cannot be sustained. They cannot proceed systematically. If the country gentlemen attempt an influence through the mere income of their property, what is it to that of those who have ten times their income to sell, and who can ruin their property by bringing their plunder to meet it at market? If the landed man wishes to mortgage, he falls the value of his land, and raises the value of assignats. He augments the power of his enemy by the very means he must take to contend with him. The country gentleman therefore, the officer by sea and land, the man of liberal views and habits, attached to no profession, will be as completely excluded from the government of his country as if he were legislatively proscribed. It is obvious, that in the towns, all the things which conspire against the country gentleman combine in favour of the money manager and director. In towns combination is natural. The habits of burghers, their occupations, their diversion, their business, their idleness, continually bring them into mutual contact. Their virtues and their vices are sociable; they are always in garrison; and they come embodied and half disciplined into the hands of those who mean to form them for civil or military action.

All these considerations leave no doubt on my mind, that, if this monster of a constitution can continue, France will be wholly governed by the agitators in corporations, by societies in the towns formed of directors of assignats, and trustees for the sale of church lands, attorneys, agents, money-jobbers, speculators, and adventurers, composing an ignoble oligarchy, founded on the destruction of the crown, the church, the nobility, and the people. Here end all the deceitful dreams and visions of the equality and rights of men. In "the Serbonian bog" of this base oligarchy they are all absorbed, sunk, and lost for ever.

Though human eyes cannot trace them, one would be tempted to think some great offences in France must cry to heaven, which has thought fit to punish it with a subjection to a vile and inglorious domination, in which no comfort or compensation is to be found in any even of those false splendours, which, playing about other tyrannies, prevent mankind from feeling themselves dishonoured even whilst they are oppressed. I must confess I am touched with a sorrow, mixed with some indignation, at the conduct of a few men, once of great rank, and still of great character, who, deluded with specious names, have engaged in a business too deep for the line of their understanding to fathom; who have lent their fair reputation, and the authority of their high-sounding names, to the designs of men with whom they could not be acquainted; and have thereby made their very virtues operate to the ruin of their country.

So far as to the first cementing principle.

The second material of cement for their new republic is the superiority of the city of Paris: and this I admit is strongly connected with the other cementing principle of paper circulation and confiscation. It is in this part of the project we must look for the cause of the destruction of all the old bounds of provinces and jurisdictions, ecclesiastical and secular, and the dissolution of all ancient combinations of things, as well as the formation of so many small unconnected republics. The power of the city of Paris is evidently one great spring of all their politics. It is through the power of Paris, now become the centre and focus of jobbing, that the leaders of this faction direct, or rather command, the whole legislative and the whole executive government. Everything therefore must be done which can confirm the authority of that city over the other republics. Paris is compact; she has an enormous strength, wholly disproportioned to the force of any of the square republics; and this strength is collected and condensed within a narrow compass. Paris has a natural and easy connexion of its parts, which will not be affected by any scheme of a geometrical constitution, nor does it much signify whether its proportion of representation be more or less, since it has the whole draft of fishes in its drag-net. The other divisions of the kingdom being hackled and torn to pieces, and separated from all their habitual means, and even principles of union, cannot, for some time at least, confederate against her. Nothing was to be left in all the subordinate members, but weakness, disconnexion, and confusion. To confirm this part of the plan, the Assembly has lately come to a resolution, that no two of their republics shall have the same commander-in-chief.

To a person who takes a view of the whole, the strength of Paris, thus formed, will appear a system of general weakness. It is boasted that the geometrical policy has been adopted, that all local ideas should be sunk, and that the people should no longer be Gascons, Picards, Bretons, Normans; but Frenchmen, with one country, one heart, and one Assembly. But instead of being all Frenchmen, the greater likelihood is, that the inhabitants of that region will shortly have no country. No man ever was attached by a sense of pride, partiality, or real affection, to a description of square measurement. He never will glory in belonging to the Chequer No. 71, or to any other badge-ticket. We begin our public affections in our families. No cold relation is a zealous citizen. We pass on to our neighbourhoods, and our habitual provincial connexions. These are inns and resting-places. Such divisions of our country as have been formed by habit, and not by a sudden jerk of authority, were so many little images of the great country in which the heart found something which it could fill. The love to the whole is not extinguished by this subordinate partiality. Perhaps it is a sort of elemental training to those higher and more large regards, by which alone men come to be affected, as with their own concern, in the prosperity of a kingdom so extensive as that of France. In that general territory itself, as in the old name of provinces, the citizens are interested from old prejudices and unreasoned habits, and not on account of the geometric properties of its figure. The power and pre-eminence of Paris does certainly press down, and hold these republics together as long as it lasts. But, for the reasons I have already given you, I think it cannot last very long.

Passing from the civil creating and the civil cementing

principles of this constitution, to the National Assembly, which is to appear and act as sovereign, we see a body in its constitution with every possible power, and no possible external control. We see a body without fundamental laws, without established maxims, without respected rules of proceeding, which nothing can keep firm to any system whatsoever. Their idea of their powers is always taken at the utmost stretch of legislative competency, and their examples for common cases from the exceptions of the most urgent necessity. The future is to be in most respects like the present Assembly; but, by the mode of the new elections and the tendency of the new circulations, it will be purged of the small degree of internal control existing in a minority chosen originally from various interests, and preserving something of their spirit. If possible, the next Assembly must be worse than the present. The present, by destroying and altering everything, will leave to their successors apparently nothing popular to do. They will be roused by emulation and example to enterprises the boldest and the most absurd. To suppose such an Assembly sitting in perfect quietude is ridiculous.

Your all-sufficient legislators, in their hurry to do everything at once, have forgot one thing that seems essential, and which I believe never has been before, in the theory or the practice, omitted by any projector of a republic. They have forgot to constitute a *senate*, or something of that nature and character. Never, before this time, was heard of a body politic composed of one legislative and active assembly, and its executive officers, without such a council; without something to which foreign states might connect themselves; something to which, in the ordinary detail of government, the people could look up; something which might give a bias, and steadiness, and preserve something like consistency in the proceedings of state. Such a body kings generally have as a council. A monarchy may exist without it; but it seems to be in the very essence of a republican government. It holds a sort of middle place between the supreme power exercised by the people, or immediately delegated from them, and the mere executive. Of this there are no traces in your constitution; and, in providing nothing of this kind, your

Solons and Numas have, as much as in anything else, discovered a sovereign incapacity.

Let us now turn our eyes to what they have done towards the formation of an executive power. For this they have chosen a degraded king. This their first executive officer is to be a machine, without any sort of deliberative discretion in any one act of his function. At best he is but a channel to convey to the National Assembly such matter as it may import that body to know. If he had been made the exclusive channel, the power would not have been without its importance; though infinitely perilous to those who would choose to exercise it. But public intelligence and statement of facts may pass to the Assembly with equal authenticity, through any other conveyance. As to the means, therefore, of giving a direction to measures by the statement of an authorized reporter, this office of intelligence is as nothing.

To consider the French scheme of an executive officer, in its two natural divisions of civil and political.—In the first it must be observed, that, according to the new constitution, the higher parts of judicature, in either of its lines, are not in the king. The king of France is not the fountain of justice. The judges, neither the original nor the appellate, are of his nomination. He neither proposes the candidates, nor has a negative on the choice. He is not even the public prosecutor. He serves only as a notary to authenticate the choice made of the judges in the several districts. By his officers he is to execute their sentence. When we look into the true nature of his authority, he appears to be nothing more than a chief of bumbailiffs, serjeants at mace, catchpoles, jailers, and hangmen. It is impossible to place anything called royalty in a more degrading point of view. A thousand times better had it been for the dignity of this unhappy prince, that he had nothing at all to do with the administration of justice, deprived as he is of all that is venerable, and all that is consolatory, in that function, without power of originating any process; without a power of suspension, mitigation, or pardon. Everything in justice that is vile and odious is thrown upon him. It was not for nothing that the Assembly has been at such pains to remove the stigma from certain offices, when they are resolved to place the person who had lately been their king in a situation but one degree above the executioner, and in an office nearly of the same quality. It is not in nature, that, situated as the king of the French now is, he can respect himself, or can be respected by others.

View this new executive officer on the side of his political capacity, as he acts under the orders of the National Assembly. To execute laws is a royal office; to execute orders is not to be a king. However, a political executive magistracy, though merely such, is a great trust. It is a trust indeed that has much depending upon its faithful and diligent performance, both in the person presiding in it and in all its subordinates. Means of performing this duty ought to be given by regulation; and dispositions towards it ought to be infused by the circumstances attendant on the trust. It ought to be environed with dignity, authority, and consideration, and it ought to lead to glory. The office of execution is an office of exertion. It is not from impotence we are to expect the tasks of power. What sort of person is a king to command executory service, who has no means whatsoever to reward it? Not in a permanent office; not in a grant of land; no, not in a pension of fifty pounds a year; not in the vainest and most trivial title. In France the king is no more the fountain of honour than he is the fountain of justice. All rewards, all distinctions, are in other hands. Those who serve the king can be actuated by no natural motive but fear; by a fear of everything except their master. His functions of internal coercion are as odious as those which he exercises in the department of justice. If relief is to be given to any municipality, the Assembly gives it. If troops are to be sent to reduce them to obedience to the Assembly, the king is to execute the order; and upon every occasion he is to be spattered over with the blood of his people. He has no negative; yet his name and authority is used to enforce every harsh decree. Nay, he must concur in the butchery of those who shall attempt to free him from his imprisonment, or show the slightest attachment to his person or to his ancient authority.

Executive magistracy ought to be constituted in such a manner, that those who compose it should be disposed to love and to venerate those whom they are bound to obey. A purposed neglect, or, what is worse, a literal but perverse and malignant obedience, must be the ruin of the wisest counsels. In vain will the law attempt to anticipate or to follow such studied neglects and fraudulent attentions. To make them act zealously is not in the competence of law. Kings, even such as are truly kings, may and ought to bear the freedom of subjects that are obnoxious to them. They may too, without derogating from themselves, bear even the authority of such persons, if it promotes their service. Louis the Thirteenth mortally hated the Cardinal de Richelieu; but his support of that minister against his rivals was the source of all the glory of his reign, and the solid foundation of his throne itself. Louis the Fourteenth, when come to the throne, did not love the Cardinal Mazarin; but for his interests he preserved him in power. When old, he detested Louvois; but for years, whilst he faithfully served his greatness, he endured his person. When George the Second took Mr. Pitt, who certainly was not agreeable to him, into his councils, he did nothing which could humble a wise sovereign. But these ministers, who were chosen by affairs, not by affections, acted in the name of, and in trust for, kings; and not as their avowed, constitutional, and ostensible masters. I think it impossible that any king, when he has recovered his first terrors, can cordially infuse vivacity and vigour into measures which he knows to be dictated by those, who, he must be persuaded, are in the highest degree ill affected to his person. Will any ministers, who serve such a king (or whatever he may be called) with but a decent appearance of respect, cordially obey the orders of those whom but the other day in his name they had committed to the Bastile? will they obey the orders of those whom, whilst they were exercising despotic justice upon them, they conceived they were treating with lenity; and from whom, in a prison, they thought they had provided an asylum? If you expect such obedience, amongst your other innovations and regenerations, you ought to make a revolution in nature, and provide a new constitution for the human mind. Otherwise, your supreme government cannot harmonize with its executory system. There are cases in which we cannot take up with names and abstractions. You may call half-a-dozen leading individuals, whom we have reason to fear and hate, the nation. It makes no other difference, than to make us fear and hate them the more. If it had been thought justifiable and expedient to make such a revolution by such means, and through such persons, as you have made yours, it would have been more wise to have completed the business of the fifth and sixth of October. The new executive officer would then owe his situation to those who are his creators as well as his masters; and he might be bound in interest, in the society of crime, and (if in crimes there could be virtues) in gratitude, to serve those who had promoted him to a place of great lucre and great sensual indulgence; and of something more: for more he must have received from those who certainly would not have limited an aggrandized creature, as they have done a submitting antagonist.

A king circumstanced as the present, if he is totally stupified by his misfortunes, so as to think it not the necessity, but the premium and privilege, of life, to eat and sleep, without any regard to glory, can never be fit for the office. If he feels as men commonly feel, he must be sensible, that an office so circumstanced is one in which he can obtain no fame or reputation. He has no generous interest that can excite him to action. At best, his conduct will be passive and defensive. To inferior people such an office might be matter of honour. But to be raised to it, and to descend to it, are different things, and suggest different sentiments. Does he *really* name the ministers? They will have a sympathy with him. Are they forced upon him? The whole business between them and the nominal king will be mutual counteraction. In all other countries, the office of ministers of state is of the highest dignity. In France it is full of peril, and incapable of glory. Rivals, however, they will have in their nothingness, whilst shallow ambition exists in the world, or the desire of a miserable salary is an incentive to short-sighted avarice. Those competitors of the ministers are enabled by your constitution to attack them in their vital parts, whilst they have not the means of repelling their charges in any other than the degrading character of culprits. The ministers of state in France are the only persons in that country who are incapable of a share in the national councils. What ministers! What councils! What a nation!—But they are responsible. It is a poor service that is to be had from responsibility. The elevation of mind to be derived from fear will never make a nation glorious. Responsibility prevents crimes. It makes all attempts against the laws dangerous. But for a principle of active and zealous service, none but idiots could think of it. Is the conduct of a war to be trusted to a man who may abhor its principle; who, in every step he may take to render it successful, confirms the power of those by whom he is oppressed? Will foreign states seriously treat with him who has no prerogative of peace or war; no, not so much as in a single vote by himself or his ministers, or by any one whom he can possibly influence? A state of contempt is not a state for a prince: better get rid of him at once.

I know it will be said that these humours in the court and executive government will continue only through this generation; and that the king has been brought to declare the dauphin shall be educated in a conformity to his situation. If he is made to conform to his situation, he will have no education at all. His training must be worse even than that of an arbitrary monarch. If he reads—whether he reads or not, some good or evil genius will tell him his ancestors were kings. Thenceforward his object must be to assert himself, and to avenge his parents. This you will say is not his duty. That may be; but it is nature; and whilst you pique nature against you, you do unwisely to trust to duty. In this futile scheme of polity, the state nurses in its bosom, for the present, a source of weakness, perplexity, counteraction, inefficiency, and decay; and it prepares the means of its final ruin. In short, I see nothing in the executive force (I cannot call it authority) that has even an appearance of vigour, or that has the smallest degree of just correspondence or symmetry, or amicable relation with the supreme power, either as it now exists, or as it is planned for the future government.

You have settled, by an economy as perverted as the policy, two [1] establishments of government; one real, one

---

[1] In reality three, to reckon the provincial republican establishments.

fictitious. Both maintained at a vast expense; but the
fictitious at, I think, the greatest. Such a machine as the
latter is not worth the grease of its wheels. The expense
is exorbitant; and neither the show nor the use deserve
the tenth part of the charge. Oh! but I don't do justice
to the talents of the legislators: I don't allow, as I ought
to do, for necessity. Their scheme of executive force was
not their choice. This pageant must be kept. The people
would not consent to part with it. Right; I understand
you. You do, in spite of your grand theories, to which
you would have heaven and earth to bend, you do know
how to conform yourselves to the nature and circumstances
of things. But when you were obliged to conform thus
far to circumstances, you ought to have carried your submission farther, and to have made, what you were obliged
to take, a proper instrument, and useful to its end. That
was in your power. For instance, among many others, it
was in your power to leave to your king the right of peace
and war. What! to leave to the executive magistrate the
most dangerous of all prerogatives? I know none more
dangerous; nor any one more necessary to be so trusted.
I do not say that this prerogative ought to be trusted to
your king, unless he enjoyed other auxiliary trusts along
with it, which he does not now hold. But, if he did
possess them, hazardous as they are undoubtedly, advantages would arise from such a constitution, more than
compensating the risk. There is no other way of keeping
the several potentates of Europe from intriguing distinctly
and personally with the members of your Assembly, from
intermeddling in all your concerns, and fomenting, in the
heart of your country, the most pernicious of all factions;
factions in the interest and under the direction of foreign
powers. From that worst of evils, thank God, we are still
free. Your skill, if you had any, would be well employed
to find out indirect corrections and controls upon this
perilous trust. If you did not like those which in England we have chosen, your leaders might have exerted their
abilities in contriving better. If it were necessary to
exemplify the consequences of such an executive government as yours, in the management of great affairs, I
should refer you to the late reports of M. de Montmorin
to the National Assembly, and all the other proceedings
relative to the differences between Great Britain and Spain.

It would be treating your understanding with disrespect to point them out to you.

I hear that the persons who are called ministers have signified an intention of resigning their places. I am rather astonished that they have not resigned long since. For the universe I would not have stood in the situation in which they have been for this last twelvemonth. They wished well, I take it for granted, to the Revolution. Let this fact be as it may, they could not, placed as they were upon an eminence, though an eminence of humiliation, but be the first to see collectively, and to feel each in his own department, the evils which have been produced by that Revolution. In every step which they took, or forbore to take, they must have felt the degraded situation of their country, and their utter incapacity of serving it. They are in a species of subordinate servitude, in which no men before them were ever seen. Without confidence from their sovereign, on whom they were forced, or from the Assembly who forced them upon him, all the noble functions of their office are executed by committees of the Assembly, without any regard whatsoever to their personal or their official authority. They are to execute, without power; they are to be responsible, without discretion; they are to deliberate, without choice. In their puzzled situation, under two sovereigns, over neither of whom they have any influence, they must act in such a manner as (in effect, whatever they may intend) sometimes to betray the one, sometimes the other, and always to betray themselves. Such has been their situation; such must be the situation of those who succeed them. I have much respect, and many good wishes, for M. Necker. I am obliged to him for attentions. I thought when his enemies had driven him from Versailles, that his exile was a subject of most serious congratulation—*sed multæ urbes et publica vota vicerunt.* He is now sitting on the ruins of the finances, and of the monarchy of France.

A great deal more might be observed on the strange constitution of the executory part of the new government; but fatigue must give bounds to the discussion of subjects, which in themselves have hardly any limits.

As little genius and talent am I able to perceive in the plan of judicature formed by the National Assembly.

According to their invariable course, the framers of your constitution have begun with the utter abolition of the parliaments. These venerable bodies, like the rest of the old government, stood in need of reform, even though there should be no change made in the monarchy. They required several more alterations to adapt them to the system of a free constitution. But they had particulars in their constitution, and those not a few which deserved approbation from the wise. They possessed one fundamental excellence; they were independent. The most doubtful circumstance attendant on their office, that of its being vendible, contributed, however, to this independency of character. They held for life. Indeed they may be said to have held by inheritance. Appointed by the monarch, they were considered as nearly out of his power. The most determined exertions of that authority against them only showed their radical independence. They composed permanent bodies politic, constituted to resist arbitrary innovation; and from that corporate constitution, and from most of their forms, they were well calculated to afford both certainty and stability to the laws. They had been a safe asylum to secure these laws, in all the revolutions of humour and opinion. They had saved that sacred deposit of the country during the reigns of arbitrary princes, and the struggles of arbitrary factions. They kept alive the memory and record of the constitution. They were the great security to private property; which might be said (when personal liberty had no existence) to be, in fact, as well guarded in France as in any other country. Whatever is supreme in a state, ought to have, as much as possible, its judicial authority so constituted as not only not to depend upon it, but in some sort to balance it. It ought to give a security to its justice against its power. It ought to make its judicature, as it were, something exterior to the state.

These parliaments had furnished, not the best certainly, but some considerable corrective to the excesses and vices of the monarchy. Such an independent judicature was ten times more necessary when a democracy became the absolute power of the country. In that constitution, elective, temporary, local judges, such as you have contrived, exercising their dependent functions in a narrow society, must be the worst of all tribunals. In them it will be vain to look for any appearance of justice towards strangers, towards the obnoxious rich, towards the minority of routed parties, towards all those who in the election have supported unsuccessful candidates. It will be impossible to keep the new tribunals clear of the worst spirit of faction. All contrivances by ballot we know experimentally to be vain and childish to prevent a discovery of inclinations. Where they may the best answer the purposes of concealment, they answer to produce suspicion, and this is a still more mischievous cause of partiality.

If the parliaments had been preserved, instead of being dissolved at so ruinous a change to the nation, they might have served in this new commonwealth, perhaps not precisely the same (I do not mean an exact parallel), but nearly the same, purposes as the court and senate of Areopagus did in Athens; that is, as one of the balances and correctives to the evils of a light and unjust democracy. Every one knows that this tribunal was the great stay of that state; every one knows with what care it was upheld, and with what a religious awe it was consecrated. The parliaments were not wholly free from faction, I admit; but this evil was exterior and accidental, and not so much the vice of their constitution itself, as it must be in your new contrivance of sexennial elective judicatories. Several English commend the abolition of the old tribunals, as supposing that they determined everything by bribery and corruption. But they have stood the test of monarchic and republican scrutiny. The court was well disposed to prove corruption on those bodies when they were dissolved in 1771. Those who have again dissolved them would have done the same if they could, but both inquisitions having failed, I conclude, that gross pecuniary corruption must have been rather rare amongst them.

It would have been prudent, along with the parliaments, to preserve their ancient power of registering, and of remonstrating at least, upon all the decrees of the National Assembly, as they did upon those which passed in the time of the monarchy. It would be a means of squaring the occasional decrees of a democracy to some principles of general jurisprudence. The vice of the ancient demo-

cracies, and one cause of their ruin, was, that they ruled,
as you do, by occasional decrees, *psephismata*. This practice soon broke in upon the tenor and consistency of the
laws; it abated the respect of the people towards them;
and totally destroyed them in the end.

Your vesting the power of remonstrance, which, in the
time of the monarchy, existed in the parliament of Paris,
in your principal executive officer, whom, in spite of common sense, you persevere in calling king, is the height of
absurdity. You ought never to suffer remonstrance from
him who is to execute. This is to understand neither
council nor execution; neither authority nor obedience.
The person whom you call king, ought not to have this
power, or he ought to have more.

Your present arrangement is strictly judicial. Instead
of imitating your monarchy, and seating your judges on
a bench of independence, your object is to reduce them
to the most blind obedience. As you have changed all
things, you have invented new principles of order. You
first appoint judges, who, I suppose, are to determine
according to law, and then you let them know, that, at
some time or other, you intend to give them some law by
which they are to determine. Any studies which they have
made (if any they have made) are to be useless to them.
But to supply these studies, they are to be sworn to obey
all the rules, orders, and instructions which from time to
time they are to receive from the National Assembly.
These if they submit to, they leave no ground of law to
the subject. They become complete and most dangerous
instruments in the hands of the governing power, which,
in the midst of a cause, or on the prospect of it, may
wholly change the rule of decision. If these orders of the
National Assembly come to be contrary to the will of the
people, who locally choose those judges, such confusion
must happen as is terrible to think of. For the judges
owe their places to the local authority; and the commands
they are sworn to obey come from those who have no share
in their appointment. In the meantime they have the
example of the court of *Chatelet* to encourage and guide
them in the exercise of their functions. That court is to
try criminals sent to it by the National Assembly, or
brought before it by other courses of delation. They sit

under a guard to save their own lives. They know not by what law they judge, nor under what authority they act, nor by what tenure they hold. It is thought that they are sometimes obliged to condemn at peril of their lives. This is not perhaps certain, nor can it be ascertained; but when they acquit, we know they have seen the persons whom they discharge, with perfect impunity to the actors, hanged at the door of their court.

The Assembly indeed promises that they will form a body of law, which shall be short, simple, clear, and so forth. That is, by their short laws, they will leave much to the discretion of the judge; whilst they have exploded the authority of all the learning which could make judicial discretion (a thing perilous at best) deserving the appellation of a *sound* discretion.

It is curious to observe, that the administrative bodies are carefully exempted from the jurisdiction of these new tribunals. That is, those persons are exempted from the power of the laws, who ought to be the most entirely submitted to them. Those who execute public pecuniary trusts, ought of all men to be the most strictly held to their duty. One would have thought that it must have been among your earliest cares, if you did not mean that those administrative bodies should be real, sovereign, independent states, to form an awful tribunal, like your late parliaments, or like our king's bench, where all corporate officers might obtain protection in the legal exercise of their functions, and would find coercion if they trespassed against their legal duty. But the cause of the exemption is plain. These administrative bodies are the great instruments of the present leaders in their progress through democracy to oligarchy. They must therefore be put above the law. It will be said, that the legal tribunals which you have made are unfit to coerce them. They are undoubtedly. They are unfit for any rational purpose. It will be said too, that the administrative bodies will be accountable to the general assembly. This I fear is talking without much consideration of the nature of that assembly, or of these corporations. However, to be subject to the pleasure of that assembly, is not to be subject to law either for protection or for constraint.

This establishment of judges as yet wants something to

its completion. It is to be crowned by a new tribunal.
This is to be a grand state judicature; and it is to judge
of crimes committed against the nation, that is, against
the power of the Assembly. It seems as if they had something in their view of the nature of the high court of
justice erected in England during the time of the great
usurpation. As they have not yet finished this part of the
scheme, it is impossible to form a right judgment upon it.
However, if great care is not taken to form it in a spirit
very different from that which has guided them in their
proceedings relative to state offences, this tribunal, subservient to their inquisition, the *committee of research*,
will extinguish the last sparks of liberty in France, and
settle the most dreadful and arbitrary tyranny ever known
in any nation. If they wish to give to this tribunal any
appearance of liberty and justice, they must not evoke
from or send to it the causes relative to their own members,
at their pleasure. They must also remove the seat of that
tribunal out of the republic of Paris.[1]

Has more wisdom been displayed in the constitution of
your army than what is discoverable in your plan of judicature? The able arrangement of this part is the more difficult, and requires the greater skill and attention, not only
as a great concern in itself, but as it is the third cementing
principle in the new body of republics, which you call the
French nation. Truly it is not easy to divine what that
army may become at last. You have voted a very large
one, and on good appointments, at least fully equal to
your apparent means of payment. But what is the
principle of its discipline? or whom is it to obey? You
have got the wolf by the ears, and I wish you joy of the
happy position in which you have chosen to place yourselves, and in which you are well circumstanced for a
free deliberation, relatively to that army, or to anything
else.

The minister and secretary of state for the war department is M. de la Tour du Pin. This gentleman, like his
colleagues in administration, is a most zealous assertor
of the Revolution, and a sanguine admirer of the new con-

[1] For further elucidations upon the subject of all these judicatures,
and of the committee of research, see M. de Calonne's work.

stitution, which originated in that event. His statement of facts, relative to the military of France, is important, not only from his official and personal authority, but because it displays very clearly the actual condition of the army in France, and because it throws light on the principles upon which the Assembly proceeds, in the administration of this critical object. It may enable us to form some judgment, how far it may be expedient in this country to imitate the martial policy of France.

M. de la Tour du Pin, on the fourth of last June, comes to give an account of the state of his department, as it exists under the auspices of the National Assembly. No man knows it so well; no man can express it better. Addressing himself to the National Assembly, he says, "His Majesty has *this day* sent me to apprize you of the multiplied disorders of which *every day* he receives the most distressing intelligence. The army (le corps militaire) threatens to fall into the most turbulent anarchy. Entire regiments have dared to violate at once the respect due to the laws, to the king, to the order established by your decrees, and to the oaths which they have taken with the most awful solemnity. Compelled by my duty to give you information of these excesses, my heart bleeds when I consider who they are that have committed them. Those, against whom it is not in my power to withhold the most grievous complaints, are a part of that very soldiery which to this day have been so full of honour and loyalty, and with whom, for fifty years, I have lived the comrade and the friend.

"What incomprehensible spirit of delirium and delusion has all at once led them astray? Whilst you are indefatigable in establishing uniformity in the empire, and moulding the whole into one coherent and consistent body; whilst the French are taught by you, at once the respect which the laws owe to the rights of man, and that which the citizens owe to the laws, the administration of the army presents nothing but disturbance and confusion. I see in more than one corps the bonds of discipline relaxed or broken; the most unheard-of pretensions avowed directly and without any disguise; the ordinances without force; the chiefs without authority; the military chest and the colours carried off; the authority of the king himself [*risum teneatis?*] proudly defied; the officers despised, degraded, threatened, driven away, and some of them prisoners in the midst of their corps, dragging on a precarious life in the bosom of disgust and humiliation. To fill up the measure of all these horrors, the commandants of places have had their throats cut, under the eyes, and almost in the arms, of their own soldiers.

"These evils are great; but they are not the worst consequences which may be produced by such military insurrections. Sooner or later they may menace the nation itself. *The nature of things requires* that the army should never act but as *an instrument.* The moment that, erecting itself into a deliberative body, it shall act according to its own resolutions, the *government, be it what it may, will immediately degenerate into a military democracy;* a species of political monster, which has always ended by devouring those who have produced it.

"After all this, who must not be alarmed at the irregular consultations, and turbulent committees, formed in some regiments by the common soldiers and non-commissioned officers, without the knowledge, or even in contempt of the authority, of their superiors; although the presence and concurrence of those superiors could give no authority to such monstrous democratic assemblies [comices]."

It is not necessary to add much to this finished picture: finished as far as its canvas admits; but as I apprehend, not taking in the whole of the nature and complexity of the disorders of this military democracy, which, the minister at war truly and wisely observes, wherever it exists, must be the true constitution of the state, by whatever formal appellation it may pass. For, though he informs the Assembly that the more considerable part of the army have not cast off their obedience, but are still attached to their duty, yet those travellers, who have seen the corps whose conduct is the best, rather observe in them the absence of mutiny, than the existence of discipline.

I cannot help pausing here for a moment, to reflect upon the expressions of surprise which this minister has let fall, relative to the excesses he relates. To him the departure of the troops from their ancient principles of loyalty and honour seems quite inconceivable. Surely those to whom he addresses himself know the causes of it but too well.

They know the doctrines which they have preached, the decrees which they have passed, the practices which they have countenanced. The soldiers remember the 6th of October. They recollect the French guards. They have not forgotten the taking of the king's castles in Paris and Marseilles. That the governors in both places were murdered with impunity, is a fact that has not passed out of their minds. They do not abandon the principles laid down so ostentatiously and laboriously of the equality of men. They cannot shut their eyes to the degradation of the whole noblesse of France, and the suppression of the very idea of a gentleman. The total abolition of titles and distinctions is not lost upon them. But M. de la Tour du Pin is astonished at their disloyalty, when the doctors of the Assembly have taught them at the same time the respect due to laws. It is easy to judge which of the two sorts of lessons men with arms in their hands are likely to learn. As to the authority of the king, we may collect from the minister himself (if any argument on that head were not quite superfluous) that it is not of more consideration with these troops, than it is with everybody else. "The king," says he, "has over and over again repeated his orders to put a stop to these excesses : but, in so terrible a crisis, *your* [the Assembly's] concurrence is become indispensably necessary to prevent the evils which menace the state. *You* unite to the force of the legislative power *that of opinion* still more important." To be sure the army can have no opinion of the power or authority of the king. Perhaps the soldier has by this time learned, that the Assembly itself does not enjoy a much greater degree of liberty than that royal figure.

It is now to be seen what has been proposed in this exigency, one of the greatest that can happen in a state. The minister requests the Assembly to array itself in all its terrors, and to call forth all its majesty. He desires that the grave and severe principles announced by them may give vigour to the king's proclamation. After this we should have looked for courts civil and martial; breaking of some corps, decimating of others, and all the terrible means which necessity has employed in such cases to arrest the progress of the most terrible of all evils; particularly, one might expect, that a serious inquiry would be made into the murder of commandants in the view of their soldiers. Not one word of all this, or of anything like it. After they had been told that the soldiery trampled upon the decrees of the Assembly promulgated by the king, the Assembly pass new decrees; and they authorize the king to make new proclamations. After the secretary at war had stated that the regiments had paid no regard to oaths *prêtés avec la plus imposante solemnité* —they propose—what? More oaths. They renew decrees and proclamations as they experience their insufficiency, and they multiply oaths in proportion as they weaken, in the minds of men, the sanctions of religion. I hope that handy abridgments of the excellent sermons of Voltaire, d'Alembert, Diderot, and Helvetius, on the Immortality of the Soul, on a particular superintending Providence, and on a Future State of Rewards and Punishments, are sent down to the soldiers along with their civic oaths. Of this I have no doubt; as I understand that a certain description of reading makes no inconsiderable part of their military exercises, and that they are full as well supplied with the ammunition of pamphlets as of cartridges.

To prevent the mischiefs arising from conspiracies, irregular consultations, seditious committees, and monstrous democratic assemblies ["comitia, comices"] of the soldiers, and all the disorders arising from idleness, luxury, dissipation, and insubordination, I believe the most astonishing means have been used that ever occurred to men, even in all the inventions of this prolific age. It is no less than this :—The king has promulgated in circular letters to all the regiments his direct authority and encouragement, that the several corps should join themselves with the clubs and confederations in the several municipalities, and mix with them in their feasts and civic entertainments ! This jolly discipline, it seems, is to soften the ferocity of their minds ; to reconcile them to their bottle companions of other descriptions ; and to merge particular conspiracies in more general associations.[1] That this remedy would be pleasing to the soldiers,

[1] Comme sa Majesté y a reconnu, non une système d'associations particulières, mais une réunion de volontés de tous les François pour la liberté et la prosperité communes, ainsi pour le maintien de l'ordre publique ; il a pensé qu'il convenoit que chaque régiment prît part à

as they are described by M. de la Tour du Pin, I can readily believe; and that, however mutinous otherwise, they will dutifully submit themselves to *these* royal proclamations. But I should question whether all this civic swearing, clubbing, and feasting, would dispose them, more than at present they are disposed, to an obedience to their officers; or teach them better to submit to the austere rules of military discipline. It will make them admirable citizens after the French mode, but not quite so good soldiers after any mode. A doubt might well arise, whether the conversations at these good tables would fit them a great deal the better for the character of *mere instruments*, which this veteran officer and statesman justly observes the nature of things always requires an army to be.

Concerning the likelihood of this improvement in discipline, by the free conversation of the soldiers with municipal festive societies, which is thus officially encouraged by royal authority and sanction, we may judge by the state of the municipalities themselves, furnished to us by the war minister in this very speech. He conceives good hopes of the success of his endeavours towards restoring order *for the present* from the good disposition of certain regiments; but he finds something cloudy with regard to the future. As to preventing the return of confusion, "for this, the administration (says he) cannot be answerable to you, as long as they see the muncipalities arrogate to themselves an authority over the troops, which your institutions have reserved wholly to the monarch. You have fixed the limits of the military authority and the municipal authority. You have bounded the action, which you have permitted to the latter over the former, to the right of requisition; but never did the letter or the spirit of your decrees authorize the commons in these municipalities to break the officers, to try them, to give orders to the soldiers, to drive them from the posts committed to their guard, to stop them in their marches ordered by the king, or, in a word, to enslave the troops to

ces fêtes civiques pour multiplier les rapports et reserrer les liens d'union entre les citoyens et les troupes.—Lest I should not be credited, I insert the words, authorizing the troops to feast with the popular confederacies.

the caprice of each of the cities, or even market towns, through which they are to pass."

Such is the character and disposition of the municipal society which is to reclaim the soldiery, to bring them back to the true principles of military subordination, and to render them machines in the hands of the supreme power of the country! Such are the distempers of the French troops! Such is their cure! As the army is, so is the navy. The municipalities supersede the orders of the Assembly, and the seamen in their turn supersede the orders of the municipalities. From my heart I pity the condition of a respectable servant of the public, like this war minister, obliged in his old age to pledge the Assembly in their civic cups, and to enter with a hoary head into all the fantastic vagaries of these juvenile politicians. Such schemes are not like propositions coming from a man of fifty years' wear and tear amongst mankind. They seem rather such as ought to be expected from those grand compounders in politics, who shorten the road to their degrees in the state; and have a certain inward fanatical assurance and illumination upon all subjects; upon the credit of which one of their doctors has thought fit, with great applause, and greater success, to caution the Assembly not to attend to old men, or to any persons who valued themselves upon their experience. I suppose all the ministers of state must qualify, and take this test; wholly abjuring the errors and heresies of experience and observation. Every man has his own relish. But I think if I could not attain to the wisdom, I would at least preserve something of the stiff and peremptory dignity of age. These gentlemen deal in regeneration: but at any price I should hardly yield my rigid fibres to be regenerated by them; nor begin, in my grand climacteric, to squall in their new accents, or to stammer, in my second cradle, the elemental sounds of their barbarous metaphysics.[1] *Si isti mihi largiantur ut repuerascam, et in eorum cunis vagiam, valde recusem!*

The imbecility of any part of the puerile and pedantic system, which they call a constitution, cannot be laid open without discovering the utter insufficiency and mischief of

[1] This war minister has since quitted the school, and resigned his office.

every other part with which it comes in contact, or that bears any the remotest relation to it. You cannot propose a remedy for the incompetence of the crown, without displaying the debility of the Assembly. You cannot deliberate on the confusion of the army of the state, without disclosing the worse disorders of the armed municipalities. The military lays open the civil, and the civil betrays the military, anarchy. I wish everybody carefully to peruse the eloquent speech (such it is) of Mons. de la Tour du Pin. He attributes the salvation of the municipalities to the good behaviour of some of the troops. These troops are to preserve the well-disposed part of those municipalities, which is confessed to be the weakest, from the pillage of the worst disposed, which is the strongest. But the municipalities affect a sovereignty, and will command those troops which are necessary for their protection. Indeed they must command them or court them. The municipalities, by the necessity of their situation, and by the republican powers they have obtained, must, with relation to the military, be the masters, or the servants, or the confederates, or each successively; or they must make a jumble of all together, according to circumstances. What government is there to coerce the army but the municipality, or the municipality but the army? To preserve concord where authority is extinguished, at the hazard of all consequences, the Assembly attempts to cure the distempers by the distempers themselves; and they hope to preserve themselves from a purely military democracy, by giving it a debauched interest in the municipal.

If the soldiers once come to mix for any time in the municipal clubs, cabals, and confederacies, an elective attraction will draw them to the lowest and most desperate part. With them will be their habits, affections, and sympathies. The military conspiracies, which are to be remedied by civic confederacies; the rebellious municipalities, which are to be rendered obedient by furnishing them with the means of seducing the very armies of the state that are to keep them in order; all these chimeras of a monstrous and portentous policy must aggravate the confusions from which they have arisen. There must be blood. The want of common judgment manifested in the construc-

tion of all their descriptions of forces, and in all their kinds
of civil and judicial authorities, will make it flow.   Disorders may be quieted in one time and in one part.   They
will break out in others; because the evil is radical and
intrinsic.   All these schemes of mixing mutinous soldiers
with seditious citizens must weaken still more and more
the military connexion of soldiers with their officers, as
well as add military and mutinous audacity to turbulent
artificers and peasants.   To secure a real army, the officer
should be first and last in the eye of the soldier; first and
last in his attention, observance, and esteem.   Officers it
seems there are to be, whose chief qualification must be
temper and patience.   They are to manage their troops
by electioneering arts.   They must bear themselves as
candidates, not as commanders.   But as by such means
power may be occasionally in their hands, the authority
by which they are to be nominated becomes of high
importance.

What you may do finally does not appear; nor is it of
much moment, whilst the strange and contradictory relation between your army and all the parts of your republic,
as well as the puzzled relation of those parts to each other
and to the whole, remain as they are.   You seem to have
given the provisional nomination of the officers, in the
first instance, to the king, with a reserve of approbation
by the National Assembly.   Men who have an interest
to pursue are extremely sagacious in discovering the true
seat of power.   They must soon perceive that those, who
can negative indefinitely, in reality appoint.   The officers
must therefore look to their intrigues in that Assembly,
as the sole, certain road to promotion.   Still, however,
by your new constitution they must begin their solicitation
at court.   This double negotiation for military rank seems
to me a contrivance as well adapted, as if it were studied
for no other end, to promote faction in the Assembly
itself, relative to this vast military patronage; and then
to poison the corps of officers with factions of a nature
still more dangerous to the safety of government, upon any
bottom on which it can be placed, and destructive in the
end to the efficiency of the army itself.   Those officers,
who lose the promotions intended for them by the crown,
must become of a faction opposite to that of the Assembly

which has rejected their claims, and must nourish discontents in the heart of the army against the ruling powers. Those officers, on the other hand, who, by carrying their point through an interest in the Assembly, feel themselves to be at best only second in the good-will of the crown, though first in that of the Assembly, must slight an authority which would not advance and could not retard their promotion. If to avoid these evils you will have no other rule for command or promotion than seniority, you will have an army of formality; at the same time it will become more independent, and more of a military republic. Not they, but the king is the machine. A king is not to be deposed by halves. If he is not everything in the command of an army, he is nothing. What is the effect of a power placed nominally at the head of the army, who to that army is no object of gratitude, or of fear? Such a cipher is not fit for the administration of an object, of all things the most delicate, the supreme command of military men. They must be constrained (and their inclinations lead them to what their necessities require) by a real, vigorous, effective, decided, personal authority. The authority of the Assembly itself suffers by passing through such a debilitating channel as they have chosen. The army will not long look to an assembly acting through the organ of false show, and palpable imposition. They will not seriously yield obedience to a prisoner. They will either despise a pageant, or they will pity a captive king. This relation of your army to the crown will, if I am not greatly mistaken, become a serious dilemma in your politics.

It is besides to be considered, whether an assembly like yours, even supposing that it was in possession of another sort of organ through which its orders were to pass, is fit for promoting the obedience and discipline of an army. It is known, that armies have hitherto yielded a very precarious and uncertain obedience to any senate, or popular authority; and they will least of all yield it to an assembly which is only to have a continuance of two years. The officers must totally lose the characteristic disposition of military men, if they see with perfect submission and due admiration, the dominion of pleaders; especially when they find that they have a new court to pay to an endless succession of those pleaders; whose military policy, and the genius of whose command (if they should have any), must be as uncertain as their duration is transient. In the weakness of one kind of authority, and in the fluctuation of all, the officers of an army will remain for some time mutinous and full of faction, until some popular general, who understands the art of conciliating the soldiery, and who possesses the true spirit of command, shall draw the eyes of all men upon himself. Armies will obey him on his personal account. There is no other way of securing military obedience in this state of things. But the moment in which that event shall happen, the person who really commands the army is your master; the master (that is little) of your king, the master of your assembly, the master of your whole republic.

How came the Assembly by their present power over the army? Chiefly, to be sure, by debauching the soldiers from their officers. They have begun by a most terrible operation. They have touched the central point, about which the particles that compose armies are at repose. They have destroyed the principle of obedience in the great, essential, critical link between the officer and the soldier, just where the chain of military subordination commences and on which the whole of that system depends. The soldier is told he is a citizen, and has the rights of man and citizen. The right of a man, he is told, is to be his own governor, and to be ruled only by those to whom he delegates that self-government. It is very natural he should think that he ought most of all to have his choice where he is to yield the greatest degree of obedience. He will therefore, in all probability, systematically do, what he does at present occasionally; that is, he will exercise at least a negative in the choice of his officers. At present the officers are known at best to be only permissive, and on their good behaviour. In fact, there have been many instances in which they have been cashiered by their corps. Here is a second negative on the choice of the king; a negative as effectual at least as the other of the Assembly. The soldiers know already that it has been a question, not ill received in the National Assembly, whether they ought not to have the direct choice of their officers, or some proportion of them? When such matters are in deliberation it is no extravagant supposition that they will incline to the opinion most favourable to their pretensions. They will not bear to be deemed the army of an imprisoned king, whilst another army in the same country, with whom too they are to feast and confederate, is to be considered as the free army of a free constitution. They will cast their eyes on the other and more permanent army; I mean the municipal. That corps, they well know, does actually elect its own officers. They may not be able to discern the ground of distinction on which they are not to elect a Marquis de la Fayette (or what is his new name?) of their own. If this election of a commander-in-chief be a part of the rights of men, why not of theirs? They see elective justices of peace, elective judges, elective curates, elective bishops, elective municipalities, and elective commanders of the Parisian army. Why should they alone be excluded? Are the brave troops of France the only men in that nation who are not the fit judges of military merit, and of the qualifications necessary for a commander-in-chief? Are they paid by the state, and do they therefore lose the rights of men? They are a part of that nation themselves, and contribute to that pay. And is not the king, is not the National Assembly, and are not all who elect the National Assembly, likewise paid? Instead of seeing all these forfeit their rights by their receiving a salary, they perceive that in all these cases a salary is given for the exercise of those rights. All your resolutions, all your proceedings, all your debates, all the works of your doctors in religion and politics, have industriously been put into their hands; and you expect that they will apply to their own case just as much of your doctrines and examples as suits your pleasure.

Everything depends upon the army in such a government as yours; for you have industriously destroyed all the opinions, and prejudices, and, as far as in you lay, all the instincts which support government. Therefore the moment any difference arises between your National Assembly and any part of the nation, you must have recourse to force. Nothing else is left to you; or rather you have left nothing else to yourselves. You see, by the report of your war minister, that the distribution of the army is in a great measure made with a view of internal

coercion.[1] You must rule by an army; and you have infused into that army by which you rule, as well as into
the whole body of the nation, principles which after a time
must disable you in the use you resolve to make of it.
The king is to call out troops to act against his people,
when the world has been told, and the assertion is still
ringing in our ears, that troops ought not to fire on
citizens.   The colonies assert to themselves an independent constitution and a free trade.   They must be constrained by troops.   In what chapter of your code of the
rights of men are they able to read, that it is a part of the
rights of men to have their commerce monopolized and
restrained for the benefit of others?   As the colonists rise
on you, the negroes rise on them.   Troops again—
Massacre, torture, hanging!   These are your rights of
men!   These are the fruits of metaphysic declarations
wantonly made, and shamefully retracted!   It was but
the other day, that the farmers of land in one of your
provinces refused to pay some sort of rents to the lord of
the soil.   In consequence of this, you decree, that the
country people shall pay all rents and dues, except those
which as grievances you have abolished; and if they refuse,
then you order the king to march troops against them.
You lay down metaphysic propositions which infer
universal consequences, and then you attempt to limit
logic by despotism.   The leaders of the present system tell
them of their rights, as men, to take fortresses, to murder
guards, to seize on kings without the least appearance of
authority even from the Assembly, whilst, as the sovereign
legislative body, that Assembly was sitting in the name
of the nation—and yet these leaders presume to order out
the troops which have acted in these very disorders, to
coerce those who shall judge on the principles, and follow
the examples, which have been guaranteed by their own
approbation.
   The leaders teach the people to abhor and reject all
feodality as the barbarism of tyranny, and they tell them
afterwards how much of that barbarous tyranny they are
to bear with patience.   As they are prodigal of light with
regard to grievances, so the people find them sparing in

   [1] Courier François, 30th July, 1790. Assemblée Nationale,
Numéro 210.

the extreme with regard to redress. They know that not only certain quit-rents and personal duties, which you have permitted them to redeem (but have furnished no money for the redemption), are as nothing to those burthens for which you have made no provision at all. They know, that almost the whole system of landed property in its origin is feudal; that it is the distribution of the possessions of the original proprietors, made by a barbarous conqueror to his barbarous instruments; and that the most grievous effects of the conquest are the land rents of every kind, as without question they are.

The peasants, in all probability, are the descendants of these ancient proprietors, Romans or Gauls. But if they fail, in any degree, in the titles which they make on the principles of antiquaries and lawyers, they retreat into the citadel of the rights of men. There they find that men are equal; and the earth, the kind and equal mother of all, ought not to be monopolized to foster the pride and luxury of any men, who by nature are no better than themselves, and who, if they do not labour for their bread, are worse. They find, that by the laws of nature the occupant and subduer of the soil is the true proprietor; that there is no prescription against nature; and that the agreements (where any there are) which have been made with the landlords, during the time of slavery, are only the effect of duresse and force; and that when the people re-entered into the rights of men, those agreements were made as void, as everything else which had been settled under the prevalence of the old feudal and aristocratic tyranny. They will tell you that they see no difference between an idler with a hat and a national cockade, and an idler in a cowl, or in a rochet. If you ground the title to rents on succession and prescription, they tell you from the speech of M. Camus, published by the National Assembly for their information, that things ill begun cannot avail themselves of prescription; that the title of these lords was vicious in its origin; and that force is at least as bad as fraud. As to the title by succession, they will tell you, that the succession of those who have cultivated the soil is the true pedigree of property, and not rotten parchments and silly substitutions; that the lords have enjoyed their usurpation too long; and that if they allow to these lay monks any charitable pension, they ought to be thankful to the bounty of the true proprietor, who is so generous towards a false claimant to his goods.

When the peasants give you back that coin of sophistic reason, on which you have set your image and superscription, you cry it down as base money, and tell them you will pay for the future with French guards, and dragoons, and hussars. You hold up, to chastise them, the second-hand authority of a king, who is only the instrument of destroying, without any power of protecting either the people or his own person. Through him it seems you will make yourselves obeyed. They answer, You have taught us that there are no gentlemen; and which of your principles teach us to bow to kings whom we have not elected? We know, without your teaching, that lands were given for the support of feudal dignities, feudal titles, and feudal offices. When you took down the cause as a grievance, why should the more grievous effect remain? As there are now no hereditary honours, and no distinguished families, why are we taxed to maintain what you tell us ought not to exist? You have sent down our old aristocratic landlords in no other character, and with no other title, but that of exactors under your authority. Have you endeavoured to make these your rent-gatherers respectable to us? No. You have sent them to us with their arms reversed, their shields broken, their impresses defaced; and so displumed, degraded, and metamorphosed, such unfeathered two-legged things, that we no longer know them. They are strangers to us. They do not even go by the names of our ancient lords. Physically they may be the same men; though we are not quite sure of that, on your new philosophic doctrines of personal identity. In all other respects they are totally changed. We do not see why we have not as good a right to refuse them their rents, as you have to abrogate all their honours, titles, and distinctions. This we have never commissioned you to do; and it is one instance, among many indeed, of your assumption of undelegated power. We see the burghers of Paris, through their clubs, their mobs, and their national guards, directing you at their pleasure, and giving that as law to you, which, under your authority, is transmitted as law to us. Through you, these burghers dispose of the lives and fortunes of us all. Why should not you attend as much to the desires of the laborious husbandman with regard to our rent, by which we are affected in the most serious manner, as you do to the demands of these insolent burghers, relative to distinctions and titles of honour, by which neither they nor we are affected at all? But we find you pay more regard to their fancies than to our necessities. Is it among the rights of man to pay tribute to his equals? Before this measure of yours, we might have thought we were not perfectly equal. We might have entertained some old, habitual, unmeaning prepossession in favour of those landlords; but we cannot conceive with what other view than that of destroying all respect to them, you could have made the law that degrades them. You have forbidden us to treat them with any of the old formalities of respect, and now you send troops to sabre and to bayonet us, into a submission to fear and force, which you did not suffer us to yield to the mild authority of opinion.

The ground of some of these arguments is horrid and ridiculous to all rational ears; but to the politicians of metaphysics who have opened schools for sophistry, and made establishments for anarchy, it is solid and conclusive. It is obvious, that on a mere consideration of the right, the leaders in the Assembly would not in the least have scrupled to abrogate the rents along with the titles and family ensigns. It would be only to follow up the principle of their reasonings, and to complete the analogy of their conduct. But they had newly possessed themselves of a great body of landed property by confiscation. They had this commodity at market; and the market would have been wholly destroyed, if they were to permit the husbandmen to riot in the speculations with which they so freely intoxicated themselves. The only security which property enjoys in any one of its descriptions, is from the interests of their rapacity with regard to some other. They have left nothing but their own arbitrary pleasure to determine what property is to be protected and what subverted.

Neither have they left any principle by which any of their municipalities can be bound to obedience; or even conscientiously obliged not to separate from the whole to become independent, or to connect itself with some other state. The people of Lyons, it seems, have refused lately to pay taxes. Why should they not? What lawful authority is there left to exact them? The king imposed some of them. The old states, methodized by orders, settled the more ancient. They may say to the Assembly, Who are you, that are not our kings, nor the states we have elected, nor sit on the principles on which we have elected you? And who are we, that when we see the *gabelles*, which you have ordered to be paid, wholly shaken off, when we see the act of disobedience afterwards ratified by yourselves, who are we, that we are not to judge what taxes we ought or ought not to pay, and who are not to avail ourselves of the same powers, the validity of which you have approved in others? To this the answer is, We will send troops. The last reason of kings is always the first with your Assembly. This military aid may serve for a time, whilst the impression of the increase of pay remains and the vanity of being umpires in all disputes is flattered. But this weapon will snap short, unfaithful to the hand that employs it. The Assembly keep a school, where, systematically, and with unremitting perseverance, they teach principles, and form regulations, destructive to all spirit of subordination, civil and military—and then they expect that they shall hold in obedience an anarchic people by an anarchic army.

The municipal army which, according to their new policy, is to balance this national army, if considered in itself only, is of a constitution much more simple, and in every respect less exceptionable. It is a mere democratic body, unconnected with the crown or the kingdom; armed, and trained, and officered at the pleasure of the districts to which the corps severally belong; and the personal service of the individuals, who compose it, or the fine in lieu of personal service, are directed by the same authority.[1] Nothing is more uniform. If, however, con-

---

[1] I see by M. Necker's account, that the national guards of Paris have received, over and above the money levied within their own city, about £145,000 sterling out of the public treasures. Whether this be an actual payment for the nine months of their existence, or an estimate of their yearly charge, I do not clearly perceive. It is of no great importance, as certainly they may take whatever they please.

sidered in any relation to the crown, to the National Assembly, to the public tribunals, or to the other army, or considered in a view to any coherence or connexion between its parts, it seems a monster, and can hardly fail to terminate its perplexed movements in some great national calamity. It is a worse preservative of a general constitution, than the systasis of Crete, or the confederation of Poland, or any other ill-devised corrective which has yet been imagined, in the necessities produced by an ill-constructed system of government.

Having concluded my few remarks on the constitution of the supreme power, the executive, the judicature, the military, and on the reciprocal relation of all these establishments, I shall say something of the ability showed by your legislators with regard to the revenue.

In their proceedings relative to this object, if possible, still fewer traces appear of political judgment or financial resource. When the states met, it seemed to be the great object to improve the system of revenue, to enlarge its collection, to cleanse it of oppression and vexation, and to establish it on the most solid footing. Great were the expectations entertained on that head throughout Europe. It was by this grand arrangement that France was to stand or fall; and this became, in my opinion, very properly, the test by which the skill and patriotism of those who ruled in that Assembly would be tried. The revenue of the state is the state. In effect all depends upon it, whether for support or for reformation. The dignity of every occupation wholly depends upon the quantity and the kind of virtue that may be exerted in it. As all great qualities of the mind which operate in public, and are not merely suffering and passive, require force for their display, I had almost said for their unequivocal existence, the revenue, which is the spring of all power, becomes in its administration the sphere of every active virtue. Public virtue, being of a nature magnificent and splendid, instituted for great things, and conversant about great concerns, requires abundant scope and room, and cannot spread and grow under confinement, and in circumstances straitened, narrow, and sordid. Through the revenue alone the body politic can act in its true genius and character, and therefore it will display just as much of its collective virtue, and as much of that virtue which may characterize those who move it, and are, as it were, its life and guiding principle, as it is possessed of a just revenue. For from hence not only magnanimity, and liberality, and beneficence, and fortitude, and providence, and the tutelary protection of all good arts, derive their food, and the growth of their organs, but continence, and self-denial, and labour, and vigilance, and frugality, and whatever else there is in which the mind shows itself above the appetite, are nowhere more in their proper element than in the provision and distribution of the public wealth. It is therefore not without reason that the science of speculative and practical finance, which must take to its aid so many auxiliary branches of knowledge, stands high in the estimation not only of the ordinary sort, but of the wisest and best men; and as this science has grown with the progress of its object, the prosperity and improvement of nations has generally increased with the increase of their revenues; and they will both continue to grow and flourish, as long as the balance between what is left to strengthen the efforts of individuals, and what is collected for the common efforts of the state, bear to each other a due reciprocal proportion, and are kept in a close correspondence and communication. And perhaps it may be owing to the greatness of revenues, and to the urgency of state necessities, that old abuses in the constitution of finances are discovered, and their true nature and rational theory comes to be more perfectly understood; insomuch, that a smaller revenue might have been more distressing in one period than a far greater is found to be in another; the proportionate wealth even remaining the same. In this state of things, the French Assembly found something in their revenues to preserve, to secure, and wisely to administer, as well as to abrogate and alter. Though their proud assumption might justify the severest tests, yet in trying their abilities on their financial proceedings, I would only consider what is the plain, obvious duty of a common finance minister, and try them upon that, and not upon models of ideal perfection.

The objects of a financier are, then, to secure an ample revenue; to impose it with judgment and equally; to employ it economically; and, when necessity obliges him to make use of credit, to secure its foundations in that instance, and for ever, by the clearness and candour of his proceedings, the exactness of his calculations, and the solidity of his funds. On these heads we may take a short and distinct view of the merits and abilities of those in the National Assembly, who have taken to themselves the management of this arduous concern. Far from any increase of revenue in their hands, I find, by a report of M. Vernier, from the committee of finances, of the second of August last, that the amount of the national revenue, as compared with its produce before the Revolution, was diminished by the sum of two hundred millions, or *eight millions sterling* of the annual income—considerably more than one-third of the whole !

If this be the result of great ability, never surely was ability displayed in a more distinguished manner, or with so powerful an effect. No common folly, no vulgar incapacity, no ordinary official negligence, even no official crime, no corruption, no peculation, hardly any direct hostility which we have seen in the modern world, could in so short a time have made so complete an overthrow of the finances, and with them, of the strength of a great kingdom.—*Cedo qui vestram rempublicam tantam amisistis tam cito?*

The sophisters and declaimers, as soon as the Assembly met, began with decrying the ancient constitution of the revenue in many of its most essential branches, such as the public monopoly of salt. They charged it, as truly as unwisely, with being ill-contrived, oppressive, and partial. This representation they were not satisfied to make use of in speeches preliminary to some plan of reform; they declared it in a solemn resolution or public sentence, as it were judicially, passed upon it; and this they dispersed throughout the nation. At the time they passed the decree, with the same gravity they ordered the same absurd, oppressive, and partial tax to be paid, until they could find a revenue to replace it. The consequence was inevitable. The provinces which had been always exempted from this salt monopoly, some of whom were charged with other contributions, perhaps equivalent, were totally disinclined to bear any part of the burthen, which by an equal distribution was to redeem the others. As to the Assembly, occupied as it was with the declaration and violation of the rights of men, and with their arrangements for general confusion, it had neither leisure nor capacity to contrive, nor authority to enforce, any plan of any kind relative to the replacing the tax or equalizing it, or compensating the provinces, or for conducting their minds to any scheme of accommodation with the other districts which were to be relieved.

The people of the salt provinces, impatient under taxes, damned by the authority which had directed their payment, very soon found their patience exhausted. They thought themselves as skilful in demolishing as the Assembly could be. They relieved themselves by throwing off the whole burthen. Animated by this example, each district, or part of a district, judging of its own grievance by its own feeling, and of its remedy by its own opinion, did as it pleased with other taxes.

We are next to see how they have conducted themselves in contriving equal impositions, proportioned to the means of the citizens, and the least likely to lean heavy on the active capital employed in the generation of that private wealth, from whence the public fortune must be derived. By suffering the several districts, and several of the individuals in each district, to judge of what part of the old revenue they might withhold, instead of better principles of equality, a new inequality was introduced of the most oppressive kind. Payments were regulated by dispositions. The parts of the kingdom which were the most submissive, the most orderly, or the most affectionate to the commonwealth, bore the whole burthen of the state. Nothing turns out to be so oppressive and unjust as a feeble government. To fill up all the deficiencies in the old impositions, and the new deficiencies of every kind which were to be expected, what remained to a state without authority? The National Assembly called for a voluntary benevolence; for a fourth part of the income of all the citizens, to be estimated on the honour of those who were to pay. They obtained something more than could be rationally calculated, but what was far indeed from answerable to their real necessities, and much less to their fond expectations. Rational people could have hoped for little from this their tax in the disguise of a benevolence; a tax weak, ineffective, and unequal; a tax by which luxury, avarice, and selfishness were screened, and the load thrown upon productive capital, upon integrity, generosity, and public spirit—a tax of regulation upon virtue. At length the mask is thrown off, and they are now trying means (with little success) of exacting their benevolence by force.

This benevolence, the rickety offspring of weakness, was to be supported by another resource, the twin brother of the same prolific imbecility. The patriotic donations were to make good the failure of the patriotic contribution. John Doe was to become security for Richard Roe. By this scheme they took things of much price from the giver, comparatively of small value to the receiver; they ruined several trades; they pillaged the crown of its ornaments, the churches of their plate, and the people of their personal decorations. The invention of these juvenile pretenders to liberty was in reality nothing more than a servile imitation of one of the poorest resources of doting despotism. They took an old huge full-bottomed periwig out of the wardrobe of the antiquated frippery of Louis the Fourteenth, to cover the premature baldness of the National Assembly. They produced this old-fashioned formal folly, though it had been so abundantly exposed in the Memoirs of the Duke de St. Simon, if to reasonable men it had wanted any arguments to display its mischief and insufficiency. A device of the same kind was tried in my memory by Louis the Fifteenth, but it answered at no time. However, the necessities of ruinous wars were some excuse for desperate projects. The deliberations of calamity are rarely wise. But here was a season for disposition and providence. It was in a time of profound peace, then enjoyed for five years, and promising a much longer continuance, that they had recourse to this desperate trifling. They were sure to lose more reputation by sporting, in their serious situation, with these toys and playthings of finance, which have filled half their journals, than could possibly be compensated by the poor temporary supply which they afforded. It seemed as if those who adopted such projects were wholly ignorant of their circumstances, or wholly unequal to their necessities.

Whatever virtue may be in these devices, it is obvious that neither the patriotic gifts, nor the patriotic contribution, can ever be resorted to again. The resources of public folly are soon exhausted. The whole indeed of their scheme of revenue is to make, by any artifice, an appearance of a full reservoir for the hour, whilst at the same time they cut off the springs and living fountains of perennial supply. The account not long since furnished by M. Necker was meant, without question, to be favourable. He gives a flattering view of the means of getting through the year; but he expresses, as it is natural he should, some apprehension for that which was to succeed. On this last prognostic, instead of entering into the grounds of this apprehension, in order, by a proper foresight, to prevent the prognosticated evil, M. Necker receives a sort of friendly reprimand from the president of the Assembly.

As to their other schemes of taxation, it is impossible to say anything of them with certainty; because they have not yet had their operation: but nobody is so sanguine as to imagine they will fill up any perceptible part of the wide gaping breach which their incapacity has made in their revenues. At present the state of their treasury sinks every day more and more in cash, and swells more and more in fictitious representation. When so little within or without is now found but paper, the representative not of opulence but of want, the creature not of credit but of power, they imagine that our flourishing state in England is owing to that bank-paper, and not the bank-paper to the flourishing condition of our commerce, to the solidity of our credit, and to the total exclusion of all idea of power from any part of the transaction. They forget that, in England, not one shilling of paper-money of any description is received but of choice; that the whole has had its origin in cash actually deposited; and that it is convertible at pleasure, in an instant, and without the smallest loss, into cash again. Our paper is of value in commerce, because in law it is of none. It is powerful on 'Change, because in Westminster Hall it is impotent. In payment of a debt of twenty shillings, a creditor may refuse all the paper of the bank of England. Nor is there amongst us a single public security, of any quality or nature whatsoever, that is enforced by authority.

In fact it might be easily shown, that our paper wealth, instead of lessening the real coin, has a tendency to increase it; instead of being a substitute for money, it only facilitates its entry, its exit, and its circulation; that it is the symbol of prosperity, and not the badge of distress. Never was a scarcity of cash, and an exuberance of paper, a subject of complaint in this nation.

Well! but a lessening of prodigal expenses, and the economy which has been introduced by the virtuous and sapient Assembly, make amends for the losses sustained in the receipt of revenue. In this at least they have fulfilled the duty of a financier.—Have those, who say so, looked at the expenses of the National Assembly itself? of the municipalities? of the city of Paris? of the increased pay of the two armies? of the new police? of the new judicatures? Have they even carefully compared the present pension list with the former? These politicians have been cruel, not economical. Comparing the expenses of the former prodigal government and its relation to the then revenues with the expenses of this new system as opposed to the state of its new treasury, I believe the present will be found beyond all comparison more chargeable.[1]

It remains only to consider the proofs of financial ability, furnished by the present French managers when they are to raise supplies on credit. Here I am a little at a stand; for credit, properly speaking, they have none. The credit of the ancient government was not indeed the best; but they could always, on some terms, command money, not

---

[1] The reader will observe, that I have but lightly touched (my plan demanded nothing more) on the condition of the French finances, as connected with the demands upon them. If I had intended to do otherwise, the materials in my hands for such a task are not altogether perfect. On this subject I refer the reader to M. de Calonne's work; and the tremendous display that he has made of the havoc and devastation in the public estate, and in all the affairs of France, caused by the presumptuous good intentions of ignorance and incapacity. Such effects those causes will always produce. Looking over that account with a pretty strict eye, and, with perhaps too much rigour, deducting everything which may be placed to the account of a financier out of place, who might be supposed by his enemies desirous of making the most of his cause, I believe it will be found, that a more salutary lesson of caution against the daring spirit of innovators, than what has been supplied at the expense of France, never was at any time furnished to mankind.

only at home, but from most of the countries of Europe where a surplus capital was accumulated; and the credit of that government was improving daily. The establishment of a system of liberty would of course be supposed to give it new strength: and so it would actually have done, if a system of liberty had been established. What offers has their government of pretended liberty had from Holland, from Hamburgh, from Switzerland, from Genoa, from England, for a dealing in their paper? Why should these nations of commerce and economy enter into any pecuniary dealings with a people, who attempt to reverse the very nature of things; amongst whom they see the debtor prescribing at the point of the bayonet, the medium of his solvency to the creditor; discharging one of his engagements with another; turning his very penury into his resource; and paying his interest with his rags?

Their fanatical confidence in the omnipotence of church plunder has induced these philosophers to overlook all care of the public estate, just as the dream of the philosopher's stone induces dupes, under the more plausible delusion of the hermetic art, to neglect all rational means of improving their fortunes. With these philosophic financiers, this universal medicine made of church mummy is to cure all the evils of the state. These gentlemen perhaps do not believe a great deal in the miracles of piety; but it cannot be questioned, that they have an undoubting faith in the prodigies of sacrilege. Is there a debt which presses them?—Issue *assignats*. Are compensations to be made, or a maintenance decreed to those whom they have robbed of their freehold in their office, or expelled from their profession?—*Assignats*. Is a fleet to be fitted out? *Assignats*. If sixteen millions sterling of these *assignats*, forced on the people, leave the wants of the state as urgent as ever—issue, says one, thirty millions sterling of *assignats*—says another, issue fourscore millions more of *assignats*. The only difference among their financial factions is on the greater or the lesser quantity of *assignats* to be imposed on the public sufferance. They are all professors of *assignats*. Even those, whose natural good sense and knowledge of commerce, not obliterated by philosophy, furnish decisive arguments against this delusion, conclude their arguments, by proposing the emission of *assignats*. I suppose they must talk of *assignats*, as no other language would be understood. All experience of their inefficacy does not in the least discourage them. Are the old *assignats* depreciated at market?—What is the remedy? Issue new *assignats.*—*Mais si maladia, opiniatria, non vult se garire, quid illi facere? assignare—postea assignare; ensuita assignare.* The word is a trifle altered. The Latin of your present doctors may be better than that of your old comedy; their wisdom and the variety of their resources are the same. They have not more notes in their song than the cuckoo; though, far from the softness of that harbinger of summer and plenty, their voice is as harsh and as ominous as that of the raven.

Who but the most desperate adventurers in philosophy and finance could at all have thought of destroying the settled revenue of the state, the sole security for the public credit, in the hope of rebuilding it with the materials of confiscated property? If, however, an excessive zeal for the state should have let a pious and venerable prelate (by anticipation a father of the church [1]) to pillage his own order, and, for the good of the church and people, to take upon himself the place of grand financier of confiscation, and comptroller-general of sacrilege, he and his coadjutors were, in my opinion, bound to show, by their subsequent conduct, that they knew something of the office they assumed. When they had resolved to appropriate to the *Fisc*, a certain portion of the landed property of their conquered country, it was their business to render their bank a real fund of credit, as far as such a bank was capable of becoming so.

To establish a current circulating credit upon any *Landbank*, under any circumstances whatsoever, has hitherto proved difficult at the very least. The attempt has commonly ended in bankruptcy. But when the Assembly were led, through a contempt of moral, to a defiance of economical, principles, it might at least have been expected, that nothing would be omitted on their part to lessen this difficulty, to prevent any aggravation of this bankruptcy. It might be expected, that, to render your *Land-bank* tolerable, every means would be adopted that could display openness and candour in the statement of the security;

[1] La Bruyère of Bossuet.

everything which could aid the recovery of the demand. To take things in their most favourable point of view, your condition was that of a man of a large landed estate, which he wished to dispose of for the discharge of a debt, and the supply of certain services. Not being able instantly to sell, you wished to mortgage. What would a man of fair intentions, and a commonly clear understanding, do in such circumstances? Ought he not first to ascertain the gross value of the estate; the charges of its management and disposition; the encumbrances perpetual and temporary of all kinds that affect it; then, striking a net surplus, to calculate the just value of the security? When that surplus (the only security to the creditor) had been clearly ascertained, and properly vested in the hands of trustees; then he would indicate the parcels to be sold, and the time and conditions of sale; after this, he would admit the public creditor, if he chose it, to subscribe his stock into this new fund; or he might receive proposals for an *assignat* from those who would advance money to purchase this species of security.

This would be to proceed like men of business, methodically and rationally; and on the only principles of public and private credit that have an existence. The dealer would then know exactly what he purchased, and the only doubt which could hang upon his mind would be, the dread of the resumption of the spoil, which one day might be made (perhaps with an addition of punishment) from the sacrilegious gripe of those execrable wretches who could become purchasers at the auction of their innocent fellow-citizens.

An open and exact statement of the clear value of the property, and of the time, the circumstances, and the place of sale, were all necessary, to efface as much as possible the stigma that has hitherto been branded on every kind of Land-bank. It became necessary on another principle, that is, on account of a pledge of faith previously given on that subject, that their future fidelity in a slippery concern might be established by their adherence to their first engagement. When they had finally determined on a state resource from church booty, they came, on the 14th of April, 1790, to a solemn resolution on the subject; and pledged themselves to their country, "that in the statement of the public charges for each year, there should be brought to account a sum sufficient for defraying the expenses of the R. C. A. religion, the support of the ministers at the altars, the relief of the poor, the pensions to the ecclesiastics, secular as well as regular, of the one and of the other sex, *in order that the estates and goods which are at the disposal of the nation may be disengaged of all charges, and employed by the representatives, or the legislative body, to the great and most pressing exigences of the state.*" They further engaged, on the same day, that the sum necessary for the year 1791 should be forthwith determined.

In this resolution they admit it their duty to show distinctly the expense of the above objects, which, by other resolutions, they had before engaged should be first in the order of provision. They admit that they ought to show the estate clear and disengaged of all charges, and that they should show it immediately. Have they done this immediately, or at any time? Have they ever furnished a rent-roll of the immovable estates, or given in an inventory of the movable effects, which they confiscate to their assignats? In what manner they can fulfil their engagements of holding out to public service, "an estate disengaged of all charges," without authenticating the value of the estate, or the quantum of the charges, I leave it to their English admirers to explain. Instantly upon this assurance, and previously to any one step towards making it good, they issue, on the credit of so handsome a declaration, sixteen millions sterling of their paper. This was manly. Who, after this masterly stroke, can doubt of their abilities in finance?—But then, before any other emission of these financial *indulgences*, they took care at least to make good their original promise!—If such estimate, either of the value of the estate or the amount of the encumbrances, has been made, it has escaped me. I never heard of it.

At length they have spoken out, and they have made a full discovery of their abominable fraud, in holding out the church lands as a security for any debts, or any service whatsoever. They rob only to enable them to cheat; but in a very short time they defeat the ends both of the robbery and the fraud, by making out accounts for other purposes, which blow up their whole apparatus of force and of deception. I am obliged to M. de Calonne for his reference to the document which proves this extraordinary fact; it had by some means escaped me. Indeed it was not necessary to make out my assertion as to the breach of faith on the declaration of the 14th of April, 1790. By a report of their committee it now appears, that the charge of keeping up the reduced ecclesiastical establishments, and other expenses attendant on religion, and maintaining the religious of both sexes, retained or pensioned, and the other concomitant expenses of the same nature, which they have brought upon themselves by this convulsion in property, exceeds the income of the estates acquired by it in the enormous sum of two millions sterling annually; besides a debt of seven millions and upwards. These are the calculating powers of imposture! This is the finance of philosophy! This is the result of all the delusions held out to engage a miserable people in rebellion, murder, and sacrilege, and to make them prompt and zealous instruments in the ruin of their country! Never did a state, in any case, enrich itself by the confiscations of the citizens. This new experiment has succeeded like all the rest. Every honest mind, every true lover of liberty and humanity, must rejoice to find that injustice is not always good policy, nor rapine the high road to riches. I subjoin with pleasure, in a note, the able and spirited observations of M. de Calonne on this subject.[1]

[1] "Ce n'est point à l'assemblée entière que je m'adresse ici ; je ne parle qu'à ceux qui l'égarent, en lui cachant sous des gazes séduisantes le but où ils l'entraînent. C'est à eux que je dis ; votre objet, vous n'en disconviendrez pas, c'est d'ôter tout espoir au clergé, et de consommer sa ruine ; c'est-là, en ne vous soupçonnant d'aucune combinaison de cupidité, d'aucun regard sur le jeu des effets publics, c'est-là ce qu'on doit croire que vous avez en vue dans la terrible opération que vous proposez ; c'est ce qui doit en être le fruit. Mais le peuple que vous y intéressez, quel avantage peut-il y trouver ? En vous servant sans cesse de lui, que faites vous pour lui ? Rien, absolument rien ; et, au contraire, vous faites ce qui ne conduit qu'à l'accabler de nouvelles charges. Vous avez rejeté, à son préjudice, une offre de 400 millions, dont l'acceptation pouvoit devenir un moyen de soulagement en sa faveur ; et à cette ressource, aussi profitable que légitime, vous avez substitué une injustice ruineuse, qui, de votre propre aveu, charge le trésor public, et par conséquent le peuple, d'un surcroît de dépense annuelle de 50 millions au moins et d'un remboursement de 150 millions.

In order to persuade the world of the bottomless
resource of ecclesiastical confiscation, the Assembly have
proceeded to other confiscations of estates in offices, which
could not be done with any common colour without being
compensated out of this grand confiscation of landed property. They have thrown upon this fund, which was to
show a surplus disengaged of all charges, a new charge;
namely, the compensation to the whole body of the disbanded judicature; and of all suppressed offices and
estates; a charge which I cannot ascertain, but which unquestionably amounts to many French millions. Another
of the new charges is an annuity of four hundred and
eighty thousand pounds sterling, to be paid (if they choose
to keep faith) by daily payments, for the interest of the
first *assignats*. Have they ever given themselves the
trouble to state fairly the expense of the management of
the church lands in the hands of the municipalities, to
whose care, skill, and diligence, and that of their legion
of unknown underagents, they have chosen to commit
the charge of the forfeited estates, and the consequence of
which had been so ably pointed out by the bishop of Nancy?

But it is unnecessary to dwell on these obvious heads of
encumbrance. Have they made out any clear state of the
grand encumbrance of all, I mean the whole of the general
and municipal establishments of all sorts, and compared it
with the regular income by revenue? Every deficiency in
these becomes a charge on the confiscated estate, before
the creditor can plant his cabbages on an acre of church
property. There is no other prop than this confiscation to
keep the whole state from tumbling to the ground. In
this situation they have purposely covered all, that they
ought industriously to have cleared, with a thick fog;
and then, blindfold themselves, like bulls that shut their
eyes when they push, they drive, by the point of the
bayonets, their slaves, blindfolded indeed no worse than
their lords, to take their fictions for currencies, and to
swallow down paper pills by thirty-four millions sterling at

"Malheureux peuple ! voilà ce que vous vaut en dernier résultat
l'expropriation de l'Eglise, et la dureté des décrets taxateurs du traite-
ment des ministres d'une religion bienfaisante ; et désormais ils seront
à votre charge : leurs charités soulageoient les pauvres ; et vous allez
être imposés pour subvenir à leur entretien ! "—*De l'État de la
France*, p. 81. See also p. 92, and the following pages.

a dose. Then they proudly lay in their claim to a future credit, on failure of all their past engagements, and at a time when (if in such a matter anything can be clear) it is clear that the surplus estates will never answer even the first of their mortgages, I mean that of the four hundred millions (or sixteen millions sterling) of *assignats*. In all this procedure I can discern neither the solid sense of plain dealing, nor the subtle dexterity of ingenious fraud. The objections within the Assembly to pulling up the flood-gates for this inundation of fraud are unanswered; but they are thoroughly refuted by a hundred thousand financiers in the street. These are the numbers by which the meta-physic arithmeticians compute. These are the grand calculations on which a philosophical public credit is founded in France. They cannot raise supplies; but they can raise mobs. Let them rejoice in the applauses of the club at Dundee, for their wisdom and patriotism in having thus applied the plunder of the citizens to the service of the state. I hear of no address upon this subject from the directors of the bank of England; though their appro-bation would be of a *little* more weight in the scale of credit than that of the club at Dundee. But, to do justice to the club, I believe the gentlemen who compose it to be wiser than they appear; that they will be less liberal of their money than of their addresses; and that they would not give a dog's-ear of their most rumpled and ragged Scotch paper for twenty of your fairest *assignats*.

Early in this year the Assembly issued paper to the amount of sixteen millions sterling: what must have been the state into which the Assembly has brought your affairs, that the relief afforded by so vast a supply has been hardly perceptible? This paper also felt an almost immediate depreciation of five per cent., which in a little time came to about seven. The effect of these *assignats* on the receipt of the revenue is remarkable. M. Necker found that the collectors of the revenue, who received in coin, paid the treasury in *assignats*. The collectors made seven per cent. by thus receiving in money, and accounting in depreciated paper. It was not very difficult to foresee, that this must be inevitable. It was, however, not the less embarrassing. M. Necker was obliged (I believe, for a considerable part, in the market of London) to buy gold and silver for the mint, which amounted to about twelve thousand pounds above the value of the commodity gained. That minister was of opinion, that, whatever their secret nutritive virtue might be, the state could not live upon *assignats* alone; that some real silver was necessary, particularly for the satisfaction of those who, having iron in their hands, were not likely to distinguish themselves for patience, when they should perceive that, whilst an increase of pay was held out to them in real money, it was again to be fraudulently drawn back by depreciated paper. The minister, in this very natural distress, applied to the Assembly, that they should order the collectors to pay in specie what in specie they had received. It could not escape him, that if the treasury paid three per cent. for the use of a currency, which should be returned seven per cent. worse than the minister issued it, such a dealing could not very greatly tend to enrich the public. The Assembly took no notice of his recommendation. They were in this dilemma—If they continued to receive the *assignats*, cash must become an alien to their treasury : if the treasury should refuse those paper *amulets*, or should discountenance them in any degree, they must destroy the credit of their sole resource. They seem then to have made their option; and to have given some sort of credit to their paper by taking it themselves; at the same time in their speeches they made a sort of swaggering declaration, something, I rather think, above legislative competence; that is, that there is no difference in value between metallic money and their *assignats*. This was a good, stout, proof article of faith, pronounced under an anathema, by the venerable fathers of this philosophic synod. *Credat* who will—certainly not *Judæus Apella.*

A noble indignation rises in the minds of your popular leaders, on hearing the magic lantern in their show of finance compared to the fraudulent exhibitions of Mr. Law. They cannot bear to hear the sands of his Mississippi compared with the rock of the church, on which they build their system. Pray let them suppress this glorious spirit, until they show to the world what piece of solid ground there is for their *assignats*, which they have not preoccupied by other charges. They do injustice to that great, mother fraud, to compare it with their degenerate imitation. It is not true that Law built solely on a speculation concerning the Mississippi. He added the East India trade; he added the African trade; he added the farms of all the farmed revenue of France. All these together unquestionably could not support the structure which the public enthusiasm, not he, chose to build upon these bases. But these were, however, in comparison, generous delusions. They supposed, and they aimed at, an increase of the commerce of France. They opened to it the whole range of the two hemispheres. They did not think of feeding France from its own substance. A grand imagination found in this flight of commerce something to captivate. It was wherewithal to dazzle the eye of an eagle. It was not made to entice the smell of a mole, nuzzling and burying himself in his mother earth, as yours is. Men were not then quite shrunk from their natural dimensions by a degrading and sordid philosophy, and fitted for low and vulgar deceptions. Above all, remember, that, in imposing on the imagination, the then managers of the system made a compliment to the freedom of men. In their fraud there was no mixture of force. This was reserved to our time, to quench the little glimmerings of reason which might break in upon the solid darkness of this enlightened age.

On recollection, I have said nothing of a scheme of finance which may be urged in favour of the abilities of these gentlemen, and which has been introduced with great pomp, though not yet finally adopted, in the National Assembly. It comes with something solid in aid of the credit of the paper circulation; and much has been said of its utility and its elegance. I mean the project for coining into money the bells of the suppressed churches. This is their alchymy. There are some follies which baffle argument; which go beyond ridicule; and which incite no feeling in us but disgust; and therefore I say no more upon it.

It is as little worth remarking any further upon all their drawing and re-drawing, on their circulation for putting off the evil day, on the play between the treasury and the *Caisse d'Escompte*, and on all these old, exploded contrivances of mercantile fraud, now exalted into policy of state. The revenue will not be trifled with. The prattling about the rights of men will not be accepted in payment for a biscuit or a pound of gunpowder. Here then the metaphysicians descend from their airy speculations, and faithfully follow examples. What examples? The examples of bankrupts. But defeated, baffled, disgraced, when their breath, their strength, their inventions, their fancies desert them, their confidence still maintains its ground. In the manifest failure of their abilities, they take credit for their benevolence. When the revenue disappears in their hands, they have the presumption, in some of their late proceedings, to value *themselves* on the relief given to the people. They did not relieve the people. If they entertained such intentions, why did they order the obnoxious taxes to be paid? The people relieved themselves in spite of the Assembly.

But waiving all discussion on the parties who may claim the merit of this fallacious relief, has there been, in effect, any relief to the people in any form? Mr. Bailly, one of the grand agents of paper circulation, lets you into the nature of this relief. His speech to the National Assembly contained a high and laboured panegyric on the inhabitants of Paris, for the constancy and unbroken resolution with which they have borne their distress and misery. A fine picture of public felicity! What! great courage and unconquerable firmness of mind to endure benefits, and sustain redress? One would think from the speech of this learned lord mayor, that the Parisians, for this twelve-month past, had been suffering the straits of some dreadful blockade; that Henry the Fourth had been stopping up the avenues to their supply, and Sully thundering with his ordnance at the gates of Paris; when in reality they are besieged by no other enemies than their own madness and folly, their own credulity and perverseness. But Mr. Bailly will sooner thaw the eternal ice of his Atlantic regions, than restore the central heat to Paris, whilst it remains "smitten with the cold, dry, petrific mace" of a false and unfeeling philosophy. Some time after this speech, that is, on the thirteenth of last August, the same magistrate, giving an account of his government at the bar of the same Assembly, expresses himself as follows: "In the month of July, 1789" [the period of everlasting commemoration], "the finances of the city of Paris were *yet* in good order; the expenditure was counterbalanced by the receipt, and she had at that time a million" [forty thousand pounds sterling] "in bank. The expenses which she has been constrained to incur, *subsequent to the Revolution*, amount to 2,500,000 livres. From these expenses, and the great falling off in the product of *the free gifts*, not only a momentary, but a *total*, want of money has taken place." This is the Paris, upon whose nourishment, in the course of the last year, such immense sums, drawn from the vitals of all France, have been expended. As long as Paris stands in the place of ancient Rome, so long she will be maintained by the subject provinces. It is an evil inevitably attendant on the dominion of sovereign democratic republics. As it happened in Rome, it may survive that republican domination which gave rise to it. In that case despotism itself must submit to the vices of popularity. Rome, under her emperors, united the evils of both systems; and this unnatural combination was one great cause of her ruin.

To tell the people that they are relieved by the dilapidation of their public estate, is a cruel and insolent imposition. Statesmen, before they valued themselves on the relief given to the people by the destruction of their revenue, ought first to have carefully attended to the solution of this problem :—Whether it be more advantageous to the people to pay considerably, and to gain in proportion ; or to gain little or nothing, and to be disburthened of all contribution? My mind is made up to decide in favour of the first proposition. Experience is with me and, I believe, the best opinions also. To keep a balance between the power of acquisition on the part of the subject and the demands he is to answer on the part of the state is the fundamental part of the skill of a true politician. The means of acquisition are prior in time and in arrangement. Good order is the foundation of all good things. To be enabled to acquire, the people, without being servile must be tractable and obedient. The magistrate must have his reverence, the laws their authority. The body of the people must not find the principles of natural subordination by art rooted out of their minds. They must respect that property of which they cannot partake. The must labour to obtain what by labour can be obtained; and when they find, as they commonly do, the success dispro-portioned to the endeavour, they must be taught their consolation in the final proportions of eternal justice. Of this consolation whoever deprives them, deadens their industry, and strikes at the root of all acquisition as of all conservation. He that does this is the cruel oppressor, the merciless enemy of the poor and wretched; at the same time that by his wicked speculations he exposes the fruits of successful industry, and the accumulations of fortune, to the plunder of the negligent, the disappointed, and the unprosperous.

Too many of the financiers by profession are apt to see nothing in revenue but banks, and circulations, and annui-ties on lives, and tontines, and perpetual rents, and all the small wares of the shop. In a settled order of the state, these things are not to be slighted, nor is the skill in them to be held of trivial estimation. They are good, but then only good, when they assume the effects of that settled order, and are built upon it. But when men think that these beggarly contrivances may supply a resource for the evils which result from breaking up the foundations of public order, and from causing or suffering the principles of property to be subverted, they will, in the ruin of their country, leave a melancholy and lasting monument of the effect of preposterous politics, and presumptuous, short-sighted, narrow-minded wisdom.

The effects of the incapacity shown by the popular leaders in all the great members of the commonwealth are to be covered with the "all-atoning name" of liberty. In some people I see great liberty indeed; in many, if not in the most, an oppressive, degrading servitude. But what is liberty without wisdom, and without virtue? It is the greatest of all possible evils; for it is folly, vice, and mad-ness, without tuition or restraint. Those who know what virtuous liberty is, cannot bear to see it disgraced by incapable heads, on account of their having high-sounding words in their mouths. Grand, swelling sentiments of liberty I am sure I do not despise. They warm the heart; they enlarge and liberalize our minds; they animate our courage in a time of conflict. Old as I am, I read the fine raptures of Lucan and Corneille with pleasure.

Neither do I wholly condemn the little arts and devices of popularity. They facilitate the carrying of many points of moment; they keep the people together; they refresh the mind in its exertions; and they diffuse occasional gaiety over the severe brow of moral freedom. Every politician ought to sacrifice to the graces; and to join compliance with reason. But in such an undertaking as that in France, all these subsidiary sentiments and artifices are of little avail. To make a government requires no great prudence. Settle the seat of power; teach obedience: and the work is done. To give freedom is still more easy. It is not necessary to guide; it only requires to let go the rein. But to form a *free government;* that is, to temper together these opposite elements of liberty and restraint in one consistent work, requires much thought, deep reflection, a sagacious, powerful, and combining mind. This I do not find in those who take the lead in the National Assembly. Perhaps they are not so miserably deficient as they appear. I rather believe it. It would put them below the common level of human understanding. But when the leaders choose to make themselves bidders at an auction of popularity, their talents, in the construction of the state, will be of no service. They will become flatterers instead of legislators; the instruments, not the guides, of the people. If any of them should happen to propose a scheme of liberty, soberly limited, and defined with proper qualifications, he will be immediately outbid by his competitors, who will produce something more splendidly popular. Suspicions will be raised of his fidelity to his cause. Moderation will be stigmatized as the virtue of cowards; and compromise as the prudence of traitors; until, in hopes of preserving the credit which may enable him to temper, and moderate, on some occasions, the popular leader is obliged to become active in propagating doctrines, and establishing powers, that will afterwards defeat any sober purpose at which he ultimately might have aimed.

But am I so unreasonable as to see nothing at all that deserves commendation in the indefatigable labours of this Assembly? I do not deny that, among an infinite number of acts of violence and folly, some good may have been done. They who destroy everything certainly will remove some grievance. They who make everything new, have a chance that they may establish something beneficial. To give them credit for what they have done in virtue of the authority they have usurped, or which can excuse them in the crimes by which that authority has been acquired, it must appear, that the same things could not have been accomplished without producing such a revolution. Most assuredly they might; because almost every one of the regulations made by them, which is not very equivocal, was either in the cession of the king, voluntarily made at the meeting of the states, or in the concurrent instructions to the orders. Some usages have been abolished on just grounds; but they were such, that if they had stood as they were to all eternity, they would little detract from the happiness and prosperity of any state. The improvements of the National Assembly are superficial, their errors fundamental.

Whatever they are, I wish my countrymen rather to recommend to our neighbours the example of the British constitution, than to take models from them for the improvement of our own. In the former they have got an invaluable treasure. They are not, I think, without some causes of apprehension and complaint; but these they do not owe to their constitution, but to their own conduct. I think our happy situation owing to our constitution; but owing to the whole of it, and not to any part singly; owing in a great measure to what we have left standing in our several reviews and reformations, as well as to what we have altered or superadded. Our people will find employment enough for a truly patriotic, free, and independent spirit, in guarding what they possess from violation. I would not exclude alteration neither; but even when I changed, it should be to preserve. I should be led to my remedy by a great grievance. In what I did, I should follow the example of our ancestors. I would make the reparation as nearly as possible in the style of the building. A politic caution, a guarded circumspection, a moral rather than a complexional timidity, were among the ruling principles of our forefathers in their most decided conduct. Not being illuminated with the light of which the gentlemen of France tell us they have got so abundant a share, they acted under a strong impression of the ignorance and fallibility of mankind. He that had made them thus fallible, rewarded them for having in their conduct attended to their nature. Let us imitate their caution, if we wish to deserve their fortune, or to retain their bequests. Let us add, if we please, but let us preserve what they have left; and standing on the firm ground of the British constitution, let us be satisfied to admire, rather than attempt to follow in their desperate flights, the aëronauts of France.

I have told you candidly my sentiments. I think they are not likely to alter yours. I do not know that they ought. You are young; you cannot guide, but must follow the fortune of your country. But hereafter they may be of some use to you, in some future form which your commonwealth may take. In the present it can hardly remain; but before its final settlement it may be obliged to pass, as one of our poets says, "through great varieties of untried being," and in all its transmigrations to be purified by fire and blood.

I have little to recommend my opinions but long observation and much impartiality. They come from one who has been no tool of power, no flatterer of greatness; and who in his last acts does not wish to belie the tenor of his life. They come from one, almost the whole of whose public exertion has been a struggle for the liberty of others; from one in whose breast no anger durable or vehement has ever been kindled, but by what he considered as tyranny; and who snatches from his share in the endeavours which are used by good men to discredit opulent oppression, the hours he has employed on your affairs; and who in so doing persuades himself he has not departed from his usual office: they come from one who desires honours, distinctions, and emoluments but little; and who expects them not at all; who has no contempt for fame, and no fear of obloquy; who shuns contention, though he will hazard an opinion: from one who wishes to preserve consistency, but who would preserve consistency by varying his means to secure the unity of his end; and, when the equipoise of the vessel in which he sails may be endangered by overloading it upon one side, is desirous of carrying the small weight of his reasons to that which may preserve its equipoise.

A LETTER FROM MR. BURKE

TO A

MEMBER OF THE NATIONAL ASSEMBLY

IN ANSWER

TO SOME OBJECTIONS TO HIS BOOK

ON

FRENCH AFFAIRS

1791

Sir,

I HAD the honour to receive your letter of the 17th of November last; in which, with some exceptions, you are pleased to consider favourably the letter I have written on the affairs of France. I shall ever accept any mark of approbation attended with instruction with more pleasure than general and unqualified praises. The latter can serve only to flatter our vanity; the former, whilst it encourages us to proceed, may help to improve us in our progress.

Some of the errors you point out to me in my printed letter are really such. One only I find to be material. It is corrected in the edition which I take the liberty of sending to you. As to the cavils which may be made on some part of my remarks, with regard to the *gradations* in your new constitution, you observe justly that they do not affect the substance of my objections. Whether there be a round more or less in the ladder of representation, by which your workmen ascend from their parochial tyranny to their federal anarchy, when the whole scale is false, appears to me of little or no importance.

I published my thoughts on that constitution, that my countrymen might be enabled to estimate the wisdom of the plans which were held out to their imitation. I conceived that the true character of those plans would be best collected from the committee appointed to prepare them. I thought that the scheme of their building would be better comprehended in the design of the architects than in the execution of the masons. It was not worth my reader's while to occupy himself with the alterations by which bungling practice corrects absurd theory. Such an investigation would be endless : because every day's past experience of impracticability has driven, and every day's future experience will drive, those men to new devices as exceptionable as the old ; and which are no otherwise worthy of observation than as they give a daily proof of the delusion of their promises, and the falsehood of their professions. Had I followed all these changes, my letter would have been only a gazette of their wanderings ; a journal of their march from error to error, through a dry, dreary desert, unguided by the lights of heaven, or by the contrivance which wisdom has invented to supply their place.

I am unalterably persuaded that the attempt to oppress, degrade, impoverish, confiscate and extinguish the original gentlemen and landed property of a whole nation, cannot be justified under any form it may assume. I am satisfied beyond a doubt that the project of turning a great empire into a vestry, or into a collection of vestries, and of governing it in the spirit of a parochial administration, is senseless and absurd, in any mode, or with any qualifications. I can never be convinced that the scheme of placing the highest powers of the state in churchwardens and constables, and other such officers, guided by the prudence of litigious attorneys, and Jew brokers, and set in action by shameless women of the lowest condition, by keepers of hotels, taverns and brothels, by pert apprentices, by clerks, shop-boys, hair-dressers, fiddlers, and dancers on the stage, (who, in such a commonwealth as yours, will in future overbear, as already they have overborne, the sober incapacity of dull, uninstructed men, of useful but laborious occupations,) can never be put into any shape, that must not be both disgraceful and destructive. The whole of this project, even if it were what it pretends to be, and was not, in reality, the dominion, through that disgraceful medium, of half a dozen, or perhaps fewer, intriguing politicians, in so mean, so low-minded, so stupid a contrivance, in point of wisdom as well as so perfectly detestable for its wickedness, that I must always consider the correctives, which might make it in any degree practicable, to be so many new objections to it.

In that wretched state of things, some are afraid that the authors of your miseries may be led to precipitate their further designs, by the hints they may receive from the very arguments used to expose the absurdity of their system, to mark the incongruity of its parts, and its inconsistency with their own principles; and that your masters may be led to render their schemes more consistent, by rendering them more mischievous. Excuse the liberty which your indulgence authorizes me to take, when I observe to you, that such apprehensions as these would prevent all exertion of our faculties in this great cause of mankind.

A rash recourse to *force* is not to be justified in a state of real weakness. Such attempts bring on disgrace; and, in their failure, discountenance and discourage more rational endeavours. But *reason* is to be hazarded, though it may be perverted by craft and sophistry; for reason can suffer no loss nor shame, nor can it impede any useful plan of future policy. In the unavoidable uncertainty, as to the effect, which attends on every measure of human prudence, nothing seems a surer antidote to the poison of fraud than its detection. It is true the fraud may be swallowed after this discovery; and perhaps even swallowed the more greedily for being a detected fraud. Men sometimes make a point of honour not to be disabused; and they had rather fall into a hundred errors than confess one. But after all,—when neither our principles nor our dispositions nor, perhaps, our talents, enable us to encounter delusion with delusion, we must use our best reason to those that ought to be reasonable creatures, and to take our chance for the event. We cannot act on these anomalies in the minds of men. I do not conceive that the persons who have contrived these things can be made much the better or the worse for anything which can be said to them. *They* are reason proof. Here and there, some men, who were at first carried away by wild, good intentions may be led, when their first fervours are abated, to join in a sober survey of the schemes into which they had been deluded. To those only (and I am sorry to say they are not likely to make a large description) we apply with any hope. I may speak it upon an assurance almost approaching to absolute knowledge that nothing has been done that has not been contrived from the beginning, even before the states had assembled. *Nulla nova mihi res inopinave surgit.* They are the same men and the same designs that they were from the first, though varied in their appearance. It was the very same animal that at first crawled about in the shape of a caterpillar, that you now see rise into the air and expand his wings to the sun.

Proceeding therefore, as we are obliged to proceed, that is upon an hypothesis that we address rational men, can false political principles be more effectually exposed, than by demonstrating that they lead to consequences directly inconsistent with, and subversive of, the arrangements grounded upon them? If this kind of demonstration is not permitted, the process of reasoning called *deductio ad absurdum,* which even the severity of geometry does not reject, could not be employed at all in legislative discussions. One of our strongest weapons against folly acting with authority would be lost.

You know, sir, that even the virtuous efforts of your patriots to prevent the ruin of your country have had this very turn given to them. It has been said here, and in France too, that the reigning usurpers would not have carried their tyranny to such destructive lengths, if they had not been stimulated and provoked to it by the acrimony of your opposition. There is a dilemma to which every opposition to successful iniquity must, in the nature of things, be liable. If you lie still, you are considered as an accomplice in the measures in which you silently acquiesce. If you resist, you are accused of provoking irritable power to new excesses. The conduct of a losing party never appears right: at least it never can possess the only infallible criterion of wisdom to vulgar judgments—success.

The indulgence of a sort of undefined hope, an obscure confidence, that some lurking remains of virtue, some degree of shame, might exist in the breasts of the oppressors of France, has been among the causes which have helped to bring on the common ruin of king and people. There is no safety for honest men, but by believing all possible evil of evil men, and by acting with promptitude, decision, and steadiness on that belief. I well remember, at every epocha of this wonderful history, in every scene of this tragic business, that when your sophistic usurpers were laying down mischievous principles, and even applying them in direct resolutions, it was the fashion to say that they never intended to execute those declarations in their rigour. This made men careless in their opposition, and remiss in early precaution. By holding out this fallacious hope, the impostors deluded sometimes one description of men, and sometimes another, so that no means of resistance were provided against them, when they came to execute in cruelty what they had planned in fraud.

There are cases in which a man would be ashamed not to have been imposed on. There is a confidence necessary to human intercourse, and without which men are often more injured by their own suspicions than they would be by the perfidy of others. But when men whom we *know* to be wicked impose upon us, we are something worse than dupes. When we know them, their fair pretences become new motives for distrust. There is one case indeed, in which it would be madness not to give the fullest credit to the most deceitful of men, that is, when they make declarations of hostility against us.

I find that some persons entertain other hopes, which I confess appear more specious than those by which at first so many were deluded and disarmed. They flatter themselves that the extreme misery brought upon the people by their folly will at last open the eyes of the multitude, if not of their leaders. Much the contrary, I fear. As to the leaders in this system of imposture,— you know that cheats and deceivers never can repent. The fraudulent have no resource but in fraud. They have no other goods in their magazine. They have no virtue or wisdom in their minds, to which, in a disappointment concerning the profitable effects of fraud and cunning, they can retreat. The wearing out of an old serves only to put them upon the invention of a new delusion. Unluckily too, the credulity of dupes is as inexhaustible as the invention of knaves. They never give people possession; but they always keep them in hope. Your state doctors do not so much as pretend that any good whatsoever has hitherto been derived from their operations, or that the public has prospered in any one instance, under their management. The nation is sick, very sick, by their medicines. But the *charlatan* tells them that what is passed cannot be helped;—they have taken the draught, and they must wait its operation with patience;—that the first effects indeed are unpleasant, but that the very sickness is a proof that the dose is of no sluggish operation;—that sickness is inevitable in all constitutional revolutions;—that the body must pass through pain to ease;—that the prescriber is not an empiric who proceeds by vulgar experience, but one who grounds his practice [1] on the sure rules of art, which cannot possibly fail. You have read, sir, the last manifesto, or mountebank's bill, of the National Assembly. You see their presumption in their promises is not lessened by all their failures in the performance. Compare this last address of the assembly and the present state of your affairs with the early engagements of that body; engagements which, not content with declaring, they solemnly deposed upon oath; swearing lustily, that if they were supported they would make their country glorious and happy; and then judge whether those who can write such things, or those who can bear to read them, are of *themselves* to be brought to any reasonable course of thought or action.

As to the people at large, when once these miserable sheep have broken the fold, and have got themselves loose, not from the restraint, but from the protection of all the principles of natural authority and legitimate

---

[1] It is said in the last quackish address of the National Assembly to the people of France, that they have not formed their arrangements upon vulgar practice; but on a theory which cannot fail; or something to that effect.

subordination, they become the natural prey of impostors. When they have once tasted of the flattery of knaves, they can no longer endure reason, which appears to them only in the form of censure and reproach. Great distress has never hitherto taught, and whilst the world lasts it never will teach, wise lessons to any part of mankind. Men are as much blinded by the extremes of misery as by the extremes of prosperity. Desperate situations produce desperate councils and desperate measures. The people of France, almost generally, have been taught to look for other resources than those which can be derived from order, frugality, and industry. They are generally armed; and they are made to expect much from the use of arms. *Nihil non arrogant armis*. Besides this, the retrograde order of society has something flattering to the dispositions of mankind. The life of adventurers, gamesters, gipsies, beggars, and robbers is not unpleasant. It requires restraint to keep men from falling into that habit. The shifting tides of fear and hope, the flight and the pursuit, the peril and escape, the alternate famine and feasts of the savage and the thief, after a time, render all course of slow, steady, progressive, unvaried occupation, and the prospect only of a limited mediocrity at the end of long labour, to the last degree tame, languid, and insipid. Those who have been once intoxicated with power, and have derived any kind of emolument from it, even though but for one year, never can willingly abandon it. They may be distressed in the midst of all their power; but they will never look to anything but power for their relief. When did distress ever oblige a prince to abdicate his authority? And what effect will it have upon those who are made to believe themselves a people of princes?

The more active and stirring part of the lower orders having got government and the distribution of plunder into their hands, they will use its resources in each municipality to form a body of adherents. These rulers and their adherents will be strong enough to overpower the discontents of those who have not been able to assert their share of the spoil. The unfortunate adventurers in the cheating lottery of plunder will probably be the least sagacious, or the most inactive and irresolute of the gang. If, on disappointment, they should dare to stir, they will soon be suppressed as rebels and mutineers by their brother rebels. Scantily fed for a while with the offal of plunder, they will drop off by degrees; they will be driven out of sight and out of thought; and they will be left to perish obscurely, like rats, in holes and corners.

From the forced repentance of invalid mutineers and disbanded thieves, you can hope for no resource. Government itself, which ought to constrain the more bold and dexterous of these robbers, is their accomplice. Its arms, its treasures, its all are in their hands. Judicature, which above all things should awe them, is their creature and their instrument. Nothing seems to me to render your internal situation more desperate than this one circumstance of the state of your judicature. Many days are not passed since we have seen a set of men brought forth by your rulers for a most critical function. Your rulers brought forth a set of men, steaming from the sweat and drudgery, and all black with the smoke and soot of the forge of confiscation and robbery—*ardentis massæ fuligine lippos*, a set of men brought forth from the trade of hammering arms of proof, offensive and defensive, in aid of the enterprises, and for the subsequent protection of housebreakers, murderers, traitors, and malefactors; men, who had their minds seasoned with theories perfectly conformable to their practice, and who had always laughed at possession and prescription, and defied all the fundamental maxims of jurisprudence. To the horror and stupefaction of all the honest part of this nation, and indeed of all nations who are spectators, we have seen, on the credit of those very practices and principles, and to carry them further into effect, these very men placed on the sacred seat of justice in the capital city of your late kingdom. We see that in future you are to be destroyed with more form and regularity. This is not peace; it is only the introduction of a sort of discipline in their hostility. Their tyranny is complete in their justice; and their lanterne is not half so dreadful as their court.

One would think that out of common decency they would have given you men who had not been in the habit of trampling upon law and justice in the assembly, neutral men, or men apparently neutral, for judges who are to dispose of your lives and fortunes.

Cromwell, when he attempted to legalize his power, and to settle his conquered country in a state of order, did not look for dispensers of justice in the instruments of his usurpation. Quite the contrary. He sought out, with great solicitude and selection, and even from the party most opposite to his designs, men of weight and decorum of character; men unstained with the violence of the times, and with hands not fouled with confiscation and sacrilege: for he chose an *Hale* for his chief justice, though he absolutely refused to take his civic oaths, or to make any acknowledgment whatsoever of the legality of his government. Cromwell told this great lawyer that since he did not approve his title, all he required of him was to administer, in a manner agreeable to his pure sentiments and unspotted character, that justice without which human society cannot subsist: that it was not his particular government, but civil order itself, which, as a judge, he wished him to support. Cromwell knew how to separate the institutions expedient to his usurpation from the administration of the public justice of his country. For Cromwell was a man in whom ambition had not wholly suppressed, but only suspended the sentiments of religion, and the love (as far as it could consist with his designs) of fair and honourable reputation. Accordingly, we are indebted to this act of his for the preservation of our laws, which some senseless assertors of the rights of men were then on the point of entirely erasing, as relics of feudality and barbarism. Besides, he gave in the appointment of that man, to that age and to all posterity the most brilliant example of sincere and fervent piety, exact justice, and profound jurisprudence.[1] But these are not the things in which your philosophic usurpers choose to follow Cromwell.

One would think that after an honest and necessary revolution (if they had a mind that theirs should pass for such) your masters would have imitated the virtuous policy of those who have been at the head of revolutions of that glorious character. Burnet tells us, that nothing tended to reconcile the English nation to the government

[1] See Burnet's Life of Hale.

of King William so much as the care he took to fill the vacant bishoprics with men who had attracted the public esteem by their learning, eloquence, and piety, and, above all, by their known moderation in the state. With you, in your purifying revolution, whom have you chosen to regulate the church? Mr. Mirabeau is a fine speaker —and a fine writer,—and a fine—a very fine man; but really nothing gave more surprise to everybody here, than to find him the supreme head of your ecclesiastical affairs. The rest is of course. Your assembly addresses a manifesto to France, in which they tell the people, with an insulting irony, that they have brought the church to its primitive condition. In one respect their declaration is undoubtedly true; for they have brought it to a state of poverty and persecution. What can be hoped for after this? Have not men, (if they deserve the name,) under this new hope and head of the church, been made bishops for no other merit than having acted as instruments of atheists; for no other merit than having thrown the children's bread to dogs; and, in order to gorge the whole gang of usurers, pedlers, and itinerant Jew-discounters at the corners of streets, starved the poor of their Christian flocks, and their own brother pastors? Have not such men been made bishops to administer in temples, in which (if the patriotic donations have not already stripped them of their vessels) the churchwardens ought to take security for the altar plate, and not so much as to trust the chalice in their sacrilegious hands, so long as Jews have assignats on ecclesiastical plunder, to exchange for the silver stolen from churches?

I am told, that the very sons of such Jew-jobbers have been made bishops; persons not to be suspected of any sort of *Christian* superstition, fit colleagues to the holy prelate of Autun, and bred at the feet of that Gamaliel. We know who it was that drove the money-changers out of the temple. We see, too, who it is that brings them in again. We have in London very respectable persons of the Jewish nation, whom we will keep; but we have of the same tribe others of a very different description,— house-breakers, and receivers of stolen goods, and forgers of paper currency, more than we can conveniently hang. These we can spare to France, to fill the new episcopal thrones : men well versed in swearing; and who will scruple no oath which the fertile genius of any of your reformers can devise.

In matters so ridiculous, it is hard to be grave. On a view of their consequences, it is almost inhuman to treat them lightly. To what a state of savage, stupid, servile insensibility must your people be reduced, who can endure such proceedings in their church, their state, and their judicature, even for a moment ! But the deluded people of France are like other madmen, who, to a miracle, bear hunger, and thirst, and cold, and confinement, and the chains and lash of their keeper, whilst all the while they support themselves by the imagination that they are generals of armies, prophets, kings, and emperors. As to a change of mind in these men, who consider infamy as honour, degradation as preferment, bondage to low tyrants as liberty, and the practical scorn and contumely of their upstart masters as marks of respect and homage, I look upon it as absolutely impracticable. These madmen, to be cured, must first, like other madmen, be subdued. The sound part of the community, which I believe to be large, but by no means the largest part, has been taken by surprise, and is disjointed, terrified, and disarmed. That sound part of the community must first be put into a better condition, before it can do anything in the way of deliberation or persuasion. This must be an act of power, as well as of wisdom; of power, in the hands of firm, determined patriots, who can distinguish the misled from traitors, who will regulate the state (if such should be their fortune) with a discriminating, manly, and provident mercy; men who are purged of the surfeit and indigestion of systems, if ever they have been admitted into the habit of their minds; men who will lay the foundation of a real reform, in effacing every vestige of that philosophy which pretends to have made discoveries in the *terra australis* of morality; men who will fix the state upon these bases of morals and politics, which are our old and immemorial and, I hope, will be our eternal possession.

This power, to such men, must come from *without*. It may be given to you in pity; for surely no nation ever called so pathetically on the compassion of all its neighbours. It may be given by those neighbours on motives of safety to themselves. Never shall I think any country in Europe to be secure, whilst there is established, in the very centre of it, a state (if so it may be called) founded on principles of anarchy, and which is, in reality, a college of armed fanatics, for the propagation of the principles of assassination, robbery, rebellion, fraud, faction, oppression, and impiety. *Mahomet,* hid, as for a time he was, in the bottom of the sands of Arabia, had his spirit and character been discovered, would have been an object of precaution to provident minds. What if he had erected his fanatic standard for the destruction of the Christian religion in *luce Asiæ,* in the midst of the then noon-day splendour of the then civilized world? The princes of Europe, in the beginning of this century, did well not to suffer the monarchy of France to swallow up the others. They ought not now, in my opinion, to suffer all the monarchies and commonwealths to be swallowed up in the gulf of this polluted anarchy. They may be tolerably safe at present, because the comparative power of France for the present is little. But times and occasions make dangers. Intestine troubles may rise in other countries. There is a power always on the watch, qualified and disposed to profit of every conjuncture, to establish its own principles and modes of mischief, wherever it can hope for success. What mercy would these usurpers have on other sovereigns, and on other nations, when they treat their own king with such unparalleled indignities, and so cruelly oppress their own countrymen?

The King of Prussia, in concurrence with us, nobly interfered to save Holland from confusion. The same power, joined with the rescued Holland and with Great Britain, has put the emperor in the possession of the Netherlands; and secured, under that prince, from all arbitrary innovation, the ancient, hereditary constitution of those provinces. The chamber of Wetzlar has restored the Bishop of Liége, unjustly dispossessed by the rebellion of his subjects. The King of Prussia was bound by no treaty, nor alliance of blood, nor had any particular reason for thinking the emperor's government would be more mischievous or more oppressive to human nature than that of the Turk; yet on mere motives of policy that prince has interposed with the threat of all his force, to snatch even the Turk from the pounces of the imperial eagle. If this is done in favour of a barbarous nation, with a barbarous neglect of police, fatal to the human race, in favour of a nation, by principle in eternal enmity with the Christian name; a nation which will not so much as give the salutation of peace (Salam) to any of us; nor make any pact with any Christian nation beyond a truce;—if this be done in favour of the Turk, shall it be thought either impolitic, or unjust, or uncharitable, to employ the same power to rescue from captivity a virtuous monarch (by the courtesy of Europe considered as Most Christian), who, after an intermission of one hundred and seventy-five years, had called together the states of his kingdom to reform abuses, to establish a free government, and to strengthen his throne; a monarch, who, at the very outset, without force, even without solicitation, had given to his people such a Magna Charta of privileges as never was given by any king to any subjects?—Is it to be tamely borne by kings who love their subjects, or by subjects who love their kings, that this monarch, in the midst of these gracious acts, was insolently and cruelly torn from his palace, by a gang of traitors and assassins, and kept in close prison to this very hour, whilst his royal name and sacred character were used for the total ruin of those whom the laws had appointed him to protect?

The only offence of this unhappy monarch towards his people was his attempt, under a monarchy, to give them a free constitution. For this, by an example hitherto unheard-of in the world, he has been deposed. It might well disgrace sovereigns to take part with a deposed tyrant. It would suppose in them a vicious sympathy. But not to make a common cause with a just prince, dethroned by traitors and rebels, who proscribe, plunder, confiscate, and in every way cruelly oppress their fellow-citizens, in my opinion is to forget what is due to the honour and to the rights of all virtuous and legal government.

I think the King of France to be as much an object both of policy and compassion as the Grand Seignior or his states. I do not conceive that the total annihilation of France (if that could be effected) is a desirable thing to Europe; or even to this its rival nation. Provident patriots did not think it good for Rome that even Carthage should be quite destroyed; and he was a wise Greek, wise for the general Grecian interests, as well as a brave Lacedemonian enemy and generous conqueror, who did not wish, by the destruction of Athens, to pluck out the other eye of Greece.

However, sir, what I have here said of the interference of foreign princes is only the opinion of a private individual; who is neither the representative of any state, nor the organ of any party; but who thinks himself bound to express his own sentiments with freedom and energy in a crisis of such importance to the whole human race.

I am not apprehensive that in speaking freely on the subject of the King and Queen of France, I shall accelerate (as you fear) the execution of traitorous designs against them. You are of opinion, sir, that the usurpers may, and that they will, gladly lay hold of any pretext to throw off the very name of a king:—assuredly I do not wish ill to your king; but better for him not to live (he does not reign) than to live the passive instrument of tyranny and usurpation.

I certainly mean to show, to the best of my power, that the existence of such an executive officer, in such a system of republic as theirs, is absurd in the highest degree. But in demonstrating this—to *them*, at least, I can have made no discovery. They only held out the royal name to catch those Frenchmen to whom the name of king is still venerable. They calculate the duration of that sentiment; and when they find it nearly expiring, they will not trouble themselves with excuses for extinguishing the name, as they have the thing. They used it as a sort of navel-string to nourish their unnatural offspring from the bowels of royalty itself. Now that the monster can purvey for its own subsistence, it will only carry the mark about it, as a token of its having torn the womb it came from. Tyrants seldom want pretexts. Fraud is the ready minister of injustice; and whilst the currency of false pretence and sophistic reasoning was expedient to their designs, they were under no necessity of drawing upon me to furnish them with that coin. But pretexts and sophisms have had their day, and have done their work. The usurpation no longer seeks plausibility. It trusts to power.

Nothing that I can say, or that you can say, will hasten them, by a single hour, in the execution of a design which they have long since entertained. In spite of their solemn declarations, their soothing addresses, and the multiplied oaths which they have taken and forced others to take, they will assassinate the king when his name will no longer be necessary to their designs; but not a moment sooner. They will probably first assassinate the queen, whenever the renewed menace of such an assassination loses its effect upon the anxious mind of an affectionate husband. At present, the advantage which they derive from the daily threats against her life is her only security for preserving it. They keep their sovereign alive for the purpose of exhibiting him, like some wild beast at a fair; as if they had a Bajazet in a cage. They choose to make monarchy contemptible by exposing it to derision in the person of the most benevolent of their kings.

In my opinion their insolence appears more odious even than their crimes. The horrors of the 5th and 6th of October were less detestable than the festival of the 14th of July There are situations (God forbid I should think that of the 5th and 6th of October one of them) in which the best men may be confounded with the worst, and in the darkness and confusion, in the press and medley of such extremities, it may not be so easy to discriminate the one from the other. The necessities created, even by ill designs, have their excuse. They may be forgotten by others, when the guilty themselves do not choose to cherish their recollection, and by ruminating their offences, nourish themselves through the example of their past, to the perpetration of future crimes. It is in the relaxation of security, it is in the expansion of prosperity, it is in the hour of dilatation of the heart, and of its softening into festivity and pleasure, that the real character of men is discerned. If there is any good in them, it appears then or never. Even wolves and tigers, when gorged with their prey, are safe and gentle. It is at such times that noble minds give all the reins to their good nature. They indulge their genius even to intemperance, in kindness to the afflicted, in generosity to the conquered; forbearing insults, forgiving injuries, overpaying benefits. Full of dignity themselves, they respect dignity in all, but they feel it sacred in the unhappy. But it is then, and basking in the sunshine of unmerited fortune, that low, sordid, ungenerous, and reptile souls swell with their hoarded poisons; it is then that they display their odious splendour, and shine out in full lustre of their native villany and baseness. It is in that season that no man of sense or honour can be mistaken for one of them. It was in such a season, for them of political ease and security, though their people were but just emerged from actual famine, and were ready to be plunged into the gulf of penury and beggary, that your philosophic lords chose, with an ostentatious pomp and luxury, to feast an incredible number of idle and thoughtless people, collected, with art and pains, from all quarters of the world. They constructed a vast amphitheatre in which they raised a species of pillory.[1] On this pillory they set their lawful king and queen, with an insulting figure over their heads. There they exposed these objects of pity and respect to all good minds to the derision of an unthinking and unprincipled multitude, degenerated even from the versatile tenderness which marks the irregular and capricious feelings of the populace. That their cruel insult might have nothing wanting to complete it, they chose the anniversary of that day in which they exposed the life of their prince to the most imminent dangers, and the vilest indignities, just following the instant when the assassins, whom they had hired without owning, first openly took up arms against their king, corrupted his guards, surprised his castle, butchered some of the poor invalids of his garrison, murdered his governor, and, like wild beasts, tore to pieces the chief magistrate of his capital city, on account of his fidelity to his service.

Till the justice of the world is awakened, such as these will go on, without admonition, and without provocation, to every extremity. Those who have made the exhibition of the 14th of July are capable of every evil. They do not commit crimes for their designs; but they form designs that they may commit crimes. It is not

---

[1] The pillory (carcan) in England is generally made very high, like that raised for exposing the King of France.

their necessity, but their nature, which impels them. They are modern philosophers; which when you say of them you express everything that is ignoble, savage, and hard-hearted.

Besides the sure tokens which are given by the spirit of their particular arrangements, there are some characteristic lineaments in the general policy of your tumultuous despotism, which, in my opinion, indicate, beyond a doubt, that no revolution whatsoever *in their disposition* is to be expected. I mean their scheme of educating the rising generation, the principles which they intend to instil, and the sympathies which they wish to form in the mind at the season in which it is the most susceptible. Instead of forming their young minds to that docility, to that modesty, which are the grace and charm of youth, to an admiration of famous examples, and to an averseness to anything which approaches to pride, petulance, and self-conceit, (distempers to which that time of life is of itself sufficiently liable,) they artificially foment these evil dispositions, and even form them into springs of action. Nothing ought to be more weighed than the nature of books recommended by public authority. So recommended, they soon form the character of the age. Uncertain indeed is the efficacy, limited indeed is the extent, of a virtuous institution. But if education takes in *vice* as any part of its system, there is no doubt but that it will operate with abundant energy, and to an extent indefinite. The magistrate, who in favour of freedom thinks himself obliged to suffer all sorts of publications, is under a stricter duty than any other well to consider what sort of writers he shall authorize, and shall recommend by the strongest of all sanctions, that is, by public honours and rewards. He ought to be cautioned how he recommends authors of mixed or ambiguous morality. He ought to be fearful of putting into the hands of youth writers indulgent to the peculiarities of their own complexion, lest they should teach the humours of the professor, rather than the principles of the science. He ought, above all, to be cautious in recommending any writer who has carried marks of a deranged understanding; for where there is no sound reason there can be no real virtue; and madness is ever vicious and malignant.

The assembly proceeds on maxims the very reverse of these. The assembly recommends to its youth a study of the bold experimenters in morality. Everybody knows that there is a great dispute amongst their leaders, which of them is the best resemblance of Rousseau. In truth, they all resemble him. His blood they transfuse into their minds and into their manners. Him they study; him they meditate; him they turn over in all the time they can spare from the laborious mischief of the day, or the debauches of the night. Rousseau is their canon of holy writ; in his life he is their canon of *Polycletus;* he is their standard figure of perfection. To this man and this writer, as a pattern to authors and to Frenchmen, the foundries of Paris are now running for statues, with the kettles of their poor and the bells of their churches. If an author had written like a great genius on geometry, though his practical and speculative morals were vicious in the extreme, it might appear, that in voting the statue, they honoured only the geometrician. But Rousseau is a moralist, or he is nothing. It is impossible, therefore, putting the circumstances together, to mistake their design in choosing the author with whom they have begun to recommend a course of studies.

Their great problem is to find a substitute for all the principles which hitherto have been employed to regulate the human will and action. They find dispositions in the mind of such force and quality as may fit men, far better than the old morality, for the purposes of such a state as theirs, and may go much further in supporting their power, and destroying their enemies. They have therefore chosen a selfish, flattering, seductive, ostentatious vice, in the place of plain duty. True the basis of the Christian system, humility, is the low, but deep and firm foundation of all real virtue. But this, as very painful in the practice, and little imposing in the appearance, they have totally discarded. Their object is to merge all natural and all social sentiment in inordinate vanity. In a small degree, and conversant in little things, vanity is of little moment. When full grown, it is the worst of vices, and the occasional mimic of them all. It makes the whole man false. It leaves nothing sincere or trustworthy about him. His best qualities are poisoned and perverted by it, and operate exactly as the worst. When your lords had many writers as immoral as the object of their statue (such as Voltaire and others) they chose Rousseau; because in him that peculiar vice, which they wished to erect into ruling virtue, was by far the most conspicuous.

We have had the great professor and founder of *the philosophy of vanity* in England. As I had good opportunities of knowing his proceedings almost from day to day, he left no doubt on my mind that he entertained no principle either to influence his heart, or to guide his understanding but *vanity*. With this vice he was possessed to a degree little short of madness. It is from the same deranged, eccentric vanity, that this, the insane *Socrates* of the National Assembly, was impelled to publish a mad confession of his mad faults, and to attempt a new sort of glory from bringing hardily to light the obscure and vulgar vices, which we know may sometimes be blended with eminent talents. He has not observed on the nature of vanity who does not know that it is omnivorous; that it has no choice in its food; that it is fond to talk even of its own faults and vices, as what will excite surprise and draw attention, and what will pass at worst for openness and candour.

It was this abuse and perversion, which vanity makes even of hypocrisy, that has driven Rousseau to record a life not so much as chequered, or spotted here and there, with virtues, or even distinguished by a single good action. It is such a life he chooses to offer to the attention of mankind. It is such a life that, with a wild defiance, he flings in the face of his Creator, whom he acknowledges only to brave. Your assembly, knowing how much more powerful example is found than precept, has chosen this man (by his own account without a single virtue) for a model. To him they erect their first statue. From him they commence their series of honours and distinctions.

It is that new invented virtue, which your masters canonize, that led their moral hero constantly to exhaust the stores of his powerful rhetoric in the expression of universal benevolence; whilst his heart was incapable of harbouring one spark of common parental affection. Benevolence to the whole species, and want of feeling for every individual with whom the professors come in contact, form the character of the new philosophy. Setting up for an unsocial independence, this their hero of vanity refuses the just price of common labour, as well as the tribute which opulence owes to genius, and which, when paid, honours the giver and the receiver; and then he pleads his beggary as an excuse for his crimes. He melts with tenderness for those only who touch him by the remotest relation, and then, without one natural pang, casts away, as a sort of offal and excrement, the spawn of his disgustful amours, and sends his children to the hospital of foundlings. The bear loves, licks, and forms her young; but bears are not philosophers. Vanity, however, finds its account in reversing the train of our natural feelings. Thousands admire the sentimental writer; the affectionate father is hardly known in his parish.

Under this philosophic instructor in the *ethics of vanity,* they have attempted in France a regeneration of the moral constitution of man. Statesmen, like your present rulers, exist by everything which is spurious, fictitious, and false; by everything which takes the man from his house, and sets him on a stage; which makes him up an artificial creature, with painted, theatric sentiments, fit to be seen by the glare of candlelight, and formed to be contemplated at a due distance. Vanity is too apt to prevail in all of us, and in all countries. To the improvement of Frenchmen it seems not absolutely necessary that it should be taught upon system. But it is plain that the present rebellion was its legitimate offspring, and it is piously fed by that rebellion with a daily dole.

If the system of instruction recommended by the assembly be false and theatric, it is because their system of government is of the same character. To that, and to that alone, it is strictly conformable. To understand either, we must connect the morals with the politics of the legislators. Your practical philosophers, systematic in everything, have wisely begun at the source. As the relation between parents and children is the first amongst the elements of vulgar, natural morality;[1] they erect statues

---

[1] Filiola tua te delectari lætor et probari tibi φυσικὴν esse τὴν πρὸς τὰ τέκνα: etenim, si hæc non est, nulla potest homini esse ad hominem naturæ adjunctio: qua sublata vitæ societas tollitur. Valete Patron (Rousseau) et tui condiscipuli! (L'Assemblée Nationale.)—Cic. Ep. ad Atticum.

to a wild, ferocious, low-minded, hard-hearted father, of fine general feelings : a lover of his kind, but a hater of his kindred. Your masters reject the duties of his vulgar relation, as contrary to liberty; as not founded in the social compact; and not binding according to the rights of men; because the relation is not, of course, the result of *free election;* never so on the side of the children, not always on the part of the parents.

The next relation which they regenerate by their statues to Rousseau is that which is next in sanctity to that of a father. They differ from those old-fashioned thinkers, who considered pedagogues as sober and venerable characters, and allied to the parental. The moralists of the dark times, *preceptorem sancti voluere parentis esse loco.* In this age of light, they teach the people that preceptors ought to be in the place of gallants. They systematically corrupt a very corruptible race (for some time a growing nuisance amongst you), a set of pert, petulant literators, to whom instead of their proper, but severe unostentatious duties, they assign the brilliant part of men of wit and pleasure, of gay, young, military sparks, and danglers at toilets. They call on the rising generation in France to take a sympathy in the adventures and fortunes, and they endeavour to engage their sensibility on the side of pedagogues who betray the most awful family trusts, and vitiate their female pupils. They teach the people that the debauchers of virgins, almost in the arms of their parents, may be safe inmates in their houses, and even fit guardians of the honour of those husbands who succeed legally to the office which the young literators had pre-occupied, without asking leave of law or conscience.

Thus they dispose of all the family relations of parents and children, husbands and wives. Through this same instructor, by whom they corrupt the morals, they corrupt the taste. Taste and elegance, though they are reckoned only among the smaller and secondary morals, yet are of no mean importance in the regulation of life. A moral taste is not of force to turn vice into virtue; but it recommends virtue with something like the blandishments of pleasure ; and it infinitely abates the evils of vice. Rousseau, a writer of great force and vivacity, is totally destitute of taste in any sense of the word. Your masters, who are his scholars, conceive that all refinement has an aristocratic character. The last age had exhausted all its powers in giving a grace and nobleness to our mutual appetites, and in raising them into a higher class and order than seemed justly to belong to them. Through Rousseau, your masters are resolved to destroy these aristocratic prejudices. The passion called love has so general and powerful an influence; it makes so much of the entertainment, and indeed so much of the occupation of that part of life which decides the character for ever, that the mode and the principles on which it engages the sympathy, and strikes the imagination, become of the utmost importance to the morals and manners of every society. Your rulers are well aware of this; and in their system of changing your manners to accommodate them to their politics, they found nothing so convenient as Rousseau. Through him they teach men to love after the fashion of philosophers; that is, they teach to men, to Frenchmen, a love without gallantry; a love without anything of that fine flower of youthfulness and gentility, which places it, if not among the virtues, among the ornaments of life. Instead of this passion, naturally allied to grace and manners, they infuse into their youth an unfashioned, indelicate, sour, gloomy, ferocious medley of pedantry and lewdness; of metaphysical speculations blended with the coarsest sensuality. Such is the general morality of the passions to be found in their famous philosopher, in his famous work of philosophic gallantry the *Nouvelle Éloise.*

When the fence from the gallantry of preceptors is broken down, and your families are no longer protected by decent pride, and salutary domestic prejudice, there is but one step to a frightful corruption. The rulers in the National Assembly are in good hopes that the females of the first families in France may become an easy prey to dancing-masters, fiddlers, pattern-drawers, friseurs, and valets de chambre, and other active citizens of that description, who having the entry into your houses, and being half domesticated by their situation, may be blended with you by regular and irregular relations. By a law they have made these people their equals. By adopting the sentiments of Rousseau they have made them your rivals. In this manner these great legislators complete their plan of levelling, and establish their rights of men on a sure foundation.

I am certain that the writings of Rousseau lead directly to this kind of shameful evil. I have often wondered how he comes to be so much more admired and followed on the Continent than he is here. Perhaps a secret charm in the language may have its share in this extraordinary difference. We certainly perceive, and to a degree we feel, in this writer, a style glowing, animated, enthusiastic; at the same time that we find it lax, diffuse, and not in the best taste of composition; all the members of the piece being pretty equally laboured and expanded, without any due selection or subordination of parts. He is generally too much on the stretch, and his manner has little variety. We cannot rest upon any of his works, though they contain observations which occasionally discover a considerable insight into human nature. But his doctrines, on the whole, are so inapplicable to real life and manners, that we never dream of drawing from them any rule for laws or conduct, or for fortifying or illustrating anything by a reference to his opinions. They have with us the fate of older paradoxes,

Cum ventum ad *verum* est *sensus moresque* repugnant,
Atque ipsa utilitas justi prope mater et æqui.

Perhaps bold speculations are more acceptable because more new to you than to us, who have been long since satiated with them. We continue, as in the two last ages, to read, more generally than I believe is now done on the Continent, the authors of sound antiquity. These occupy our minds. They give us another taste and turn; and will not suffer us to be more than transiently amused with paradoxical morality. It is not that I consider this writer as wholly destitute of just notions. Amongst his irregularities, it must be reckoned that he is sometimes moral, and moral in a very sublime strain. But the *general spirit and tendency* of his works is mischievous; and the more mischievous for this mixture: for perfect depravity of sentiment is not reconcilable with eloquence; and the mind (though corruptible, not complexionally vicious) would reject, and throw off with disgust, a lesson of pure and unmixed evil. These writers make even virtue a pander to vice.

However, I less consider the author than the system of the assembly in perverting morality through his means. This I confess makes me nearly despair of any attempt upon the minds of their followers, through reason, honour, or conscience. The great object of your tyrants is to destroy the gentlemen of France; and for that purpose they destroy, to the best of their power, all the effect of those relations which may render considerable men powerful or even safe. To destroy that order, they vitiate the whole community. That no means may exist of confederating against their tyranny, by the false sympathies of the *Nouvelle Éloise* they endeavour to subvert those principles of domestic trust and fidelity, which form the discipline of social life. They propagate principles by which every servant may think it, if not his duty, at least his privilege to betray his master. By these principles every considerable father of a family loses the sanctuary of his house. *Debet sua cuique domus esse perfugium tutissimum,* says the law, which your legislators have taken so much pains first to decry, then to repeal. They destroy all the tranquillity and security of domestic life; turning the asylum of the house into a gloomy prison, where the father of the family must drag out a miserable existence, endangered in proportion to the apparent means of his safety; where he is worse than solitary in a crowd of domestics, and more apprehensive from his servants and inmates, than from the hired, bloodthirsty mob without doors, who are ready to pull him to the lanterne.

It is thus, and for the same end, that they endeavour to destroy that tribunal of conscience which exists independently of edicts and decrees. Your despots govern by terror. They know that he who fears God fears nothing else : and therefore they eradicate from the mind, through their Voltaire, their Helvetius, and the rest of that infamous gang, that only sort of fear which generates true courage. Their object is, that their fellow-citizens may be under the dominion of no awe, but that of their committee of research, and of their lanterne.

Having found the advantage of assassination in the formation of their tyranny, it is the grand resource in which they trust for the support of it. Whoever opposes any of their proceedings, or is suspected of a design to oppose them, is to answer it with his life, or the lives of his wife and children. This infamous, cruel, and cowardly practice of assassination they have the impudence to call *merciful*. They boast that they operated their usurpation rather by terror than by force; and that a few seasonable murders have prevented the bloodshed of many battles. There is no doubt they will extend these acts of mercy whenever they see an occasion. Dreadful, however, will be the consequences of their attempt to avoid the evils of war by the merciful policy of murder. If, by effectual punishment of the guilty, they do not wholly disavow that practice, and the threat of it too, as any part of their policy; if ever a foreign prince enters into France, he must enter it as into a country of assassins. The mode of civilized war will not be practised; nor are the French who act on the present system entitled to expect it. They, whose known policy is to assassinate every citizen whom they suspect to be discontented by their tyranny, and to corrupt the soldiery of every open enemy, must look for no modified hostility. All war, which is not battle, will be military execution. This will beget acts of retaliation from you; and every retaliation will beget a new revenge. The hell-hounds of war, on all sides, will be uncoupled and unmuzzled. The new school of murder and barbarism, set up in Paris, having destroyed (so far as in it lies) all the other manners and principles which have hitherto civilized Europe, will destroy also the mode of civilized war which, more than anything else, has distinguished the Christian world. Such is the approaching golden age, which the Virgil [1] of your assembly has sung to his Pollios!

In such a situation of your political, your civil, and your social morals and manners, how can you be hurt by the freedom of any discussion? Caution is for those who have something to lose. What I have said, to justify myself in not apprehending any ill consequence from a free discussion of the absurd consequences which flow from the relation of the lawful king to the usurped constitution, will apply to my vindication with regard to the exposure I have made of the state of the army under the same sophistic

[1] Mirabeau's speech concerning universal peace.

usurpation. The present tyrants want no arguments to prove, what they must daily feel, that no good army can exist on their principles. They are in no want of a monitor to suggest to them the policy of getting rid of the army, as well as of the king, whenever they are in a condition to effect that measure. What hopes may be entertained of your army for the restoration of your liberties, I know not. At present, yielding obedience to the pretended orders of a king, who, they are perfectly apprized, has no will, and who never can issue a mandate which is not intended, in the first operation, or in its certain consequences, for his own destruction, your army seems to make one of the principal links in the chain of that servitude of anarchy, by which a cruel usurpation holds an undone people at once in bondage and confusion.

You ask me what I think of the conduct of General Monk. How this affects your case I cannot tell. I doubt whether you possess, in France, any persons of a capacity to serve the French monarchy in the same manner in which Monk served the monarchy of England. The army which Monk commanded had been formed by Cromwell to a perfection of discipline which perhaps has never been exceeded. That army was besides of an excellent composition. The soldiers were men of extraordinary piety after their mode, of the greatest regularity, and even severity of manners; brave in the field, but modest, quiet, and orderly in their quarters; men who abhorred the idea of assassinating their officers or any other persons; and who (they at least who served in this island) were firmly attached to those generals by whom they were well treated and ably commanded. Such an army, once gained, might be depended on. I doubt much, if you could now find a Monk, whether a Monk could find in France such an army.

I certainly agree with you that in all probability we owe our whole constitution to the restoration of the English monarchy. The state of things from which Monk relieved England was however by no means, at that time, so deplorable in any sense as yours is now, and under the present sway is likely to continue. Cromwell had delivered England from anarchy. His government, though military and despotic, had been regular and orderly. Under the iron, and under the yoke, the soil yielded its produce.

After his death the evils of anarchy were rather dreaded than felt. Every man was yet safe in his house and in his property. But it must be admitted that Monk freed this nation from great and just apprehensions both of future anarchy and of probable tyranny in some form or other. The king whom he gave us was indeed the very reverse of your benignant sovereign, who, in reward for his attempt to bestow liberty on his subjects, languishes himself in prison. The person given to us by Monk was a man without any sense of his duty as a prince; without any regard to the dignity of his crown; without any love to his people; dissolute, false, venal, and destitute of any positive good quality whatsoever, except a pleasant temper and the manners of a gentleman. Yet the restoration of our monarchy, even in the person of such a prince, was everything to us; for without monarchy in England, most certainly we never can enjoy either peace or liberty. It was under this conviction that the very first regular step, which we took on the Revolution of 1688, was to fill the throne with a real king; and even before it could be done in due form, the chiefs of the nation did not attempt themselves to exercise authority so much as by *interim*. They instantly requested the Prince of Orange to take the government on himself. The throne was not effectively vacant for an hour.

Your fundamental laws, as well as ours, suppose a monarchy. Your zeal, sir, in standing so firmly for it as you have done, shows not only a sacred respect for your honour and fidelity, but a well informed attachment to the real welfare and true liberties of your country. I have expressed myself ill, if I have given you cause to imagine that I prefer the conduct of those who have retired from this warfare to your behaviour, who, with a courage and constancy almost supernatural, have struggled against tyranny, and kept the field to the last. You see I have corrected the exceptionable part in the edition which I now send you. Indeed, in such terrible extremities as yours, it is not easy to say, in a political view, what line of conduct is the most advisable. In that state of things, I cannot bring myself severely to condemn persons who are wholly unable to bear so much as the sight of those men in the throne of legislation, who are only fit to be the objects of criminal justice. If fatigue, if disgust, if unsurmountable nausea drive them away from such spectacles, *ubi miseriarum pars non minima erat, videre et aspici,* I cannot blame them. He must have a heart of adamant who could hear a set of traitors puffed up with unexpected and undeserved power, obtained by an ignoble, unmanly, and perfidious rebellion, treating their honest fellow-citizens as *rebels,* because they refused to bind themselves, through their conscience, against the dictates of conscience itself, and had declined to swear an active compliance with their own ruin. How could a man of common flesh and blood endure that those, who but the other day had skulked unobserved in their antechambers, scornfully insulting men, illustrious in their rank, sacred in their function, and venerable in their character, now in decline of life, and swimming on the wrecks of their fortunes, that those miscreants should tell such men scornfully and outrageously, after they had robbed them of all their property, that it is more than enough if they are allowed what will keep them from absolute famine, and that for the rest, they must let their grey hairs fall over the plough, to make out a scanty subsistence, with the labour of their hands! Last, and worst, who could endure to hear this unnatural, insolent, and savage despotism called liberty? If, at this distance, sitting quietly by my fire, I cannot read their decrees and speeches without indignation, shall I condemn those who have fled from the actual sight and hearing of all these horrors? No, no! mankind has no title to demand that we should be slaves to their guilt and insolence; or that we should serve them in spite of themselves. Minds, sore with the poignant sense of insulted virtue, filled with high disdain against the pride of triumphant baseness, often have it not in their choice to stand their ground. Their complexion (which might defy the rack) cannot go through such a trial. Something very high must fortify men to that proof. But when I am driven to comparison, surely I cannot hesitate for a moment to prefer to such men as are common those heroes, who, in the midst of despair, perform all the tasks of hope; who subdue their feelings to their duties; who, in the cause of humanity, liberty, and honour, abandon all the satisfactions of life, and every day incur a fresh risk of life itself. Do me the justice to believe that I never can prefer any fastidious virtue (virtue still) to the unconquered perseverance, to the affectionate patience of those who watch day and night, by the bed-side of their delirious country, who, for their love to that dear and venerable name, bear all the disgusts, and all the buffets they receive from their frantic mother. Sir, I do look on you as true martyrs; I regard you as soldiers who act far more in the spirit of our Commander-in-chief, and the Captain of our salvation, than those who have left you; though I must first bolt myself very thoroughly, and know that I could do better, before I can censure them. I assure you, sir, that, when I consider your unconquerable fidelity to your sovereign and to your country; the courage, fortitude, magnanimity, and long suffering of yourself, and the Abbé Maury, and of Mr. Cazales, and of many worthy persons of all orders, in your assembly, I forget, in the lustre of these great qualities, that on your side has been displayed an eloquence so rational, manly, and convincing, that no time or country, perhaps, has ever excelled. But your talents disappear in my admiration of your virtues.

As to Mr. Mounier and Mr. Lally, I have always wished to do justice to their parts and their eloquence, and the general purity of their motives. Indeed I saw very well from the beginning, the mischiefs which, with all these talents and good intentions, they would do their country, through their confidence in systems. But their distemper was an epidemic malady. They were young and inexperienced; and when will young and inexperienced men learn caution and distrust of themselves? And when will men, young or old, if suddenly raised to far higher power than that which absolute kings and emperors commonly enjoy, learn anything like moderation? Monarchs, in general, respect some settled order of things, which they find it difficult to move from its basis, and to which they are obliged to conform, even when there are no positive limitations to their power. These gentlemen conceived that they were chosen to new-model the state, and even the whole order of society itself. No wonder that *they* entertained dangerous visions, when the king's ministers, trustees for the sacred deposit of the monarchy, were so infected with the contagion of project and system (I can hardly think

it black premeditated treachery) that they publicly advertised for plans and schemes of government, as if they
were to provide for the rebuilding of a hospital that had
been burned down. What was this, but to unchain the
fury of rash speculation amongst a people of itself but too
apt to be guided by a heated imagination and a wild spirit
of adventure?

The fault of Mr. Mounier and Mr. Lally was very great;
but it was very general. If those gentlemen stopped when
they came to the brink of the gulf of guilt and public
misery, that yawned before them in the abyss of these dark
and bottomless speculations, I forgive their first error; in
that they were involved with many. Their repentance was
their own.

They who consider Mounier and Lally as deserters, must
regard themselves as murderers and as traitors; for from
what else than murder and treason did they desert? For
my part, I honour them for not having carried mistake
into crime. If, indeed, I thought they were not cured by
experience; that they were not made sensible that those
who would reform a state ought to assume some actual
constitution of government which is to be reformed; if
they are not at length satisfied that it is become a necessary
preliminary to liberty in France, to commence by the re-
establishment of order and property of *every* kind, and,
through the re-establishment of their monarchy, of every
one of the old habitual distinctions and classes of the state;
if they do not see that these classes are not to be confounded in order to be afterwards revived and separated; if
they are not convinced that the scheme of parochial and
club governments takes up the state at the wrong end, and
is a low and senseless contrivance (as making the sole constitution of a supreme power), I should then allow that
their early rashness ought to be remembered to the last
moment of their lives.

You gently reprehend me, because, in holding out the
picture of your disastrous situation, I suggest no plan for
a remedy. Alas! sir, the proposition of plans, without an
attention to circumstances, is the very cause of all your
misfortunes; and never shall you find me aggravating, by
the infusion of any speculations of mine, the evils which
have arisen from the speculations of others. Your malady,

in this respect, is a disorder of repletion. You seem to think that my keeping back my poor ideas may arise from an indifference to the welfare of a foreign, and, sometimes, a hostile nation. No, sir, I faithfully assure you, my reserve is owing to no such causes. Is this letter, swelled to a second book, a mark of national antipathy, or even of national indifference? I should act altogether in the spirit of the same caution in a similar state of our own domestic affairs. If I were to venture any advice in any case it would be my best. The sacred duty of an adviser (one of the most inviolable that exists) would lead me, towards a real enemy, to act as if my best friend were the party concerned. But I dare not risk a speculation with no better view of your affairs than at present I can command; my caution is not from disregard, but from solicitude for your welfare. It is suggested solely from my dread of becoming the author of inconsiderate counsel.

It is not that, as this strange series of actions has passed before my eyes, I have not indulged my mind in a great variety of political speculations concerning them. But compelled by no such positive duty as does not permit me to evade an opinion : called upon by no ruling power, without authority as I am and without confidence, I should ill answer my own ideas of what would become myself, or what would be serviceable to others, if I were, as a volunteer, to obtrude any project of mine upon a nation, to whose circumstances I could not be sure it might be applicable.

Permit me to say that, if I were as confident, as I ought to be diffident in my own loose, general ideas, I never should venture to broach them, if but at twenty leagues' distance from the centre of your affairs. I must see with my own eyes, I must, in a manner, touch with my own hands, not only the fixed, but the momentary circumstances, before I could venture to suggest any political project whatsoever. I must know the power and disposition to accept, to execute, to persevere. I must see all the aids and all the obstacles. I must see the means of correcting the plan, where correctives would be wanted. I must see the things; I must see the men. Without a concurrence and adaptation of these to the design, the very best speculative projects might become not only useless but mischievous. Plans must be made for men. We cannot think of making men, and binding nature to our designs. People at a distance must judge ill of men. They do not always answer to their reputation when you approach them. Nay, the perspective varies, and shows them quite otherwise than you thought them. At a distance, if we judge uncertainly of men, we must judge worse of *opportunities,* which continually vary their shapes and colours, and pass away like clouds. The eastern politicians never do anything without the opinion of the astrologers on the *fortunate moment.* They are in the right if they can do no better; for the opinion of fortune is something towards commanding it. Statesmen of a more judicious prescience look for the fortunate moment too; but they seek it, not in the conjunctions and oppositions of planets, but in the conjunctions and oppositions of men and things. These form their almanac.

To illustrate the mischief of a wise plan, without any attention to means and circumstances, it is not necessary to go farther than to your recent history. In the condition in which France was found three years ago, what better system could be proposed, what less, even savouring of wild theory, what fitter to provide for all the exigencies whilst it reformed all the abuses of government, than the convention of the states-general? I think nothing better could be imagined. But I have censured, and do still presume to censure your parliament of Paris for not having suggested to the king, that this proper measure was of all measures the most critical and arduous; one in which the utmost circumspection and the greatest number of precautions were the most absolutely necessary. The very confession that a government wants either amendment in its conformation, or relief to great distress, causes it to lose half its reputation, and as great a proportion of its strength as depends upon that reputation. It was therefore necessary, first to put government out of danger, whilst at its own desire it suffered such an operation, as a general reform at the hands of those who were much more filled with a sense of the disease, than provided with rational means of a cure.

It may be said that this care, and these precautions, were more naturally the duty of the king's ministers, than that of the parliament. They were so; but every man must answer in his estimation for the advice he gives, when he puts the conduct of his measure into hands who he does not know will execute his plans according to his ideas. Three or four ministers were not to be trusted with the being of the French monarchy of all the orders, and of all the distinctions, and all the property of the kingdom. What must be the prudence of those who could think, in the then known temper of the people of Paris, of assembling the states at a place situated as Versailles?

The parliament of Paris did worse than to inspire this blind confidence into the king. For, as if names were things, they took no notice of (indeed they rather countenanced) the deviations which were manifest in the execution, from the true ancient principles of the plan which they recommended. These deviations (as guardians of the ancient laws, usages, and constitution of the kingdom) the parliament of Paris ought not to have suffered, without the strongest remonstrances to the throne. It ought to have sounded the alarm to the whole nation, as it had often done on things of infinitely less importance. Under pretence of resuscitating the ancient constitution, the parliament saw one of the strongest acts of innovation, and the most leading in its consequences, carried into effect before their eyes; and an innovation through the medium of despotism; that is, they suffered the king's ministers to new-model the whole representation of the *tiers état,* and, in a great measure, that of the clergy too, and to destroy the ancient proportions of the orders. These changes, unquestionably, the king had no right to make; and here the parliaments failed in their duty, and, along with their country, have perished by this failure.

What a number of faults have led to this multitude of misfortunes, and almost all from this one source,—that of considering certain general maxims, without attending to circumstances, to times, to places, to conjunctures, and to actors; if we do not attend scrupulously to all these, the medicine of to-day becomes the poison of to-morrow. If any measure was in the abstract better than another, it was to call the states—*ea visa salus morientibus una.*— Certainly it had the appearance.—But see the consequences of not attending to critical moments, of not regarding the symptoms which discriminate diseases, and which distinguish constitutions, complexions, and humours :

> Mox erat hoc ipsum exitio; furiisque refecti,
> Ardebant; ipsique suos, jam morte sub ægra,
> Discissos nudis laniabant dentibus artus.

Thus the potion which was given to strengthen the constitution, to heal divisions, and to compose the minds of men, became the source of debility, frenzy, discord, and utter dissolution.

In this, perhaps, I have answered, I think, another of your questions—Whether the British constitution is adapted to your circumstances? When I praised the British constitution, and wished it to be well studied, I did not mean that its exterior form and positive arrangement should become a model for you, or for any people servilely to copy. I meant to recommend the *principles* from which it has grown, and the policy on which it has been progressively improved out of elements common to you and to us. I am sure it is no visionary theory of mine. It is not an advice that subjects you to the hazard of any experiment. I believed the ancient principles to be wise in all cases of a large empire that would be free. I thought you possessed our principles in your old forms, in as great a perfection as we did originally. If your states agreed (as I think they did) with your circumstances, they were best for you. As you had a constitution formed upon principles similar to ours, my idea was that you might have improved them as we have done, conforming them to the state and exigencies of the times, and the condition of property in your country; having the conservation of that property, and the substantial basis of your monarchy, as principal objects in all your reforms.

I do not advise a House of Lords to you. Your ancient course by representatives of the noblesse (in your circumstances) appears to me rather a better institution. I know that, with you, a set of men of rank have betrayed their constituents, their honour, their trust, their king, and their country, and levelled themselves with their footmen, that through this degradation they might afterwards put themselves above their natural equals. Some of these persons have entertained a project that, in reward of this their black perfidy and corruption, they may be chosen to give rise to a new order, and to establish themselves into a House of Lords. Do you think that, under the name of a British constitution, I mean to recommend to you such lords, made of such kind of stuff? I do not, however, include in this description all of those who are fond of this scheme.

If you were now to form such a House of Peers, it would bear, in my opinion, but little resemblance to ours in its origin, character, or the purposes which it might answer, at the same time that it would destroy your true natural nobility; but if you are not in a condition to frame a House of Lords, still less are you capable, in my opinion, of framing anything which virtually and substantially could be answerable (for the purposes of a stable, regular government) to our House of Commons. That House is, within itself, a much more subtle and artificial combination of parts and powers, than people are generally aware of. What knits it to the other members of the constitution; what fits it to be at once the great support, and the great control of government; what makes it of such admirable service to that monarchy which, if it limits, it secures and strengthens, would require a long discourse, belonging to the leisure of a contemplative man, not to one whose duty it is to join in communicating practically to the people the blessings of such a constitution.

Your *tiers état* was not in effect and substance a House of Commons. You stood in absolute need of something else to supply the manifest defects in such a body as your *tiers état*. On a sober and dispassionate view of your old constitution, as connected with all the present circumstances, I was fully persuaded, that the crown, standing as things have stood (and are likely to stand, if you are to have any monarchy at all) was and is incapable, alone and by itself, of holding a just balance between the two orders, and at the same time of effecting the interior and exterior purposes of a protecting government. I, whose leading principle it is, in a reformation of the state, to make use of existing materials, am of opinion that the representation of the clergy, as a separate order, was an institution which touched all the orders more nearly than any of them touched the other; that it was well fitted to connect them, and to hold a place in any wise, monarchical commonwealth. If I refer you to your original constitution, and think it, as I do, substantially a good one, I do not amuse you in this, more than in other things, with any inventions of mine. A certain intemperance of intellect is the disease of the time, and the source of all its other diseases. I will keep myself as untainted by it as I can. Your architects build without a foundation. I would readily lend a helping hand to any superstructure, when once this is effectually secured—but first I would say δός που στῶ.

You think, sir, and you might think rightly, upon the first view of the theory, that to provide for the exigencies of an empire, so situated and so related as that of France, its king ought to be invested with powers very much superior to those which the King of England possesses under the letter of our constitution. Every degree of power necessary to the state, and not destructive to the rational and moral freedom of individuals, to that personal liberty, and personal security, which contribute so much to the vigour, the prosperity, the happiness, and the dignity of a nation—every degree of power which does not suppose the total absence of all control, and all responsibility on the part of ministers,—a king of France, in common sense, ought to possess. But whether the exact measure of authority, assigned by the letter of the law to the King of Great Britain, can answer to the exterior or interior purposes of the French monarchy, is a point which I cannot venture to judge upon. Here, both in the power given, and its limitations, we have always cautiously felt our way. The parts of our constitution have gradually, and almost insensibly, in a long course of time, accommodated themselves to each other, and to their common, as well as to their separate purposes. But this adaptation of contending parts, as it has not been in ours, so it can never be in yours, or in any country, the effect of a single instantaneous regulation, and no sound heads could ever think of doing it in that manner.

I believe, sir, that many on the Continent altogether mistake the condition of a king of Great Britain. He is a real king and not an executive officer. If he will not trouble himself with contemptible details, nor wish to degrade himself by becoming a party in little squabbles, I am far from sure that a king of Great Britain, in whatever concerns him as a king, or indeed as a rational man, who combines his public interest with his personal satisfaction, does not possess a more real, solid, extensive power, than the King of France was possessed of before this miserable revolution. The direct power of the King of England is considerable. His indirect, and far more certain power, is great indeed. He stands in need of nothing towards dignity; of nothing towards splendour; of nothing towards authority; of nothing at all towards consideration abroad. When was it that a king of England wanted wherewithal to make him respected, courted, or perhaps even feared in every state of Europe?

I am constantly of opinion that your states, in three orders, on the footing on which they stood in 1614, were capable of being brought into a proper and harmonious combination with royal authority. This constitution by estates, was the natural and only just representation of France. It grew out of the habitual conditions, relations, and reciprocal claims of men. It grew out of the circumstances of the country, and out of the state of property. The wretched scheme of your present masters is not to fit the constitution to the people, but wholly to destroy conditions, to dissolve relations, to change the state of the nation, and to subvert property, in order to fit their country to their theory of a constitution.

Until you make out practically that great work, a combination of opposing forces, "a work of labour long, and endless praise," the utmost caution ought to have been used in the reduction of the royal power, which alone was capable of holding together the comparatively heterogeneous mass of your states. But, at this day, all these considerations are unseasonable. To what end should we discuss the limitations of royal power? Your king is in prison. Why speculate on the measure and standard of liberty? I doubt much, very much, indeed, whether France is at all ripe for liberty on any standard. Men are qualified for civil liberty in exact proportion to their disposition to put moral chains upon their own appetites; in proportion as their love of justice is above their rapacity; in proportion as their soundness and sobriety of understanding is above their vanity and presumption; in proportion as they are more disposed to listen to the counsels of the wise and good, in preference to the flattery of knaves. Society cannot exist unless a controlling power upon will and appetite be placed somewhere, and the less of it there is within, the more there must be without. It is ordained in the eternal constitution of things, that men of intemperate minds cannot be free. Their passions forge their fetters.

This sentence the prevalent part of your countrymen execute on themselves. They possessed not long since, what was next to freedom, a mild paternal monarchy. They despised it for its weakness. They were offered a well-poised, free constitution. It did not suit their taste nor their temper. They carved for themselves; they flew out, murdered, robbed, and rebelled. They have succeeded, and put over their country an insolent tyranny made up of cruel and inexorable masters, and that too of a description hitherto not known in the world. The powers and policies by which they have succeeded are not those of great statesmen, or great military commanders, but the practices of incendiaries, assassins, housebreakers, robbers, spreaders of false news, forgers of false orders from authority, and other delinquencies, of which ordinary justice takes cognizance. Accordingly the spirit of their rule is exactly correspondent to the means by which they obtained it. They act more in the manner of thieves who have got possession of a house, than of conquerors who have subdued a nation.

Opposed to these, in appearance, but in appearance only, is another band, who call themselves the *moderate*. These, if I conceive rightly of their conduct, are a set of men who approve heartily of the whole new constitution, but wish to lay heavily on the most atrocious of those crimes, by which this fine constitution of theirs has been obtained. They are a sort of people who affect to proceed as if they thought that men may deceive without fraud, rob without injustice, and overturn everything without violence. They are men who would usurp the government of their country with decency and moderation. In fact, they are nothing more or better, than men engaged in desperate designs, with feeble minds. They are not honest; they are only ineffectual and unsystematic in their iniquity. They are persons who want not the dispositions, but the energy and vigour, that is necessary for great evil machinations. They find that in such designs they fall at best into a secondary rank, and others take the place and lead in usurpation, which they are not qualified to obtain or to hold. They envy to their companions the natural fruit of their crimes; they join to run them down with the hue and cry of mankind, which pursues their common offences; and then hope to mount into their places on the credit of the sobriety with which they show themselves disposed to carry on what may seem most plausible in the mischievous projects they pursue in common. But these men are naturally despised by those who have heads to know, and hearts that are able to go through the necessary demands of bold wicked enterprises. They are naturally classed below the latter description, and will only be used by them as inferior instruments. They will be only the Fairfaxes of your Cromwells. If they mean honestly, why do they not strengthen the arms of honest men, to support their ancient, legal, wise, and free government, given to them in the spring of 1788, against the inventions of craft, and the theories of ignorance and folly? If they do not, they must continue the scorn of both parties; sometimes the tool, sometimes the incumbrance of that whose views they approve, whose conduct they decry. These people are only made to be the sport of tyrants. They never can obtain or communicate freedom.

You ask me, too, whether we have a committee of research. No, sir,—God forbid! It is the necessary instrument of tyranny and usurpation; and, therefore, I do not wonder that it has had an early establishment under your present lords. We do not want it.

Excuse my length. I have been somewhat occupied since I was honoured with your letter; and I should not have been able to answer it at all, but for the holidays, which have given me means of enjoying the leisure of the country. I am called to duties which I am neither able nor willing to evade. I must soon return to my old conflict with the corruptions and oppressions which have prevailed in our eastern dominions. I must turn myself wholly from those of France.

In England we *cannot* work so hard as Frenchmen. Frequent relaxation is necessary to us. You are naturally more intense in your application. I did not know this part of your national character, until I went into France in 1773. At present, this your disposition to labour is rather increased than lessened. In your assembly you do not allow yourselves a recess even on Sundays. We have two days in the week, besides the festivals; and besides five or six months of the summer and autumn. This continued, unremitted effort of the members of your assembly, I take to be one among the causes of the mischief they have done. They who always labour can have no true judgment. You never give yourselves time to cool. You can never survey, from its proper point of sight, the work you have finished, before you decree its final execution. You can never plan the future by the past. You never go into the country, soberly and dispassionately to observe the effect of your measures on their objects. You cannot feel distinctly how far the people are rendered better and improved, or more miserable and depraved, by what you have done. You cannot see with your own eyes the sufferings and afflictions you cause. You know them but at a distance, on the statements of those who always flatter the reigning power, and who, amidst their representations of the grievances, inflame your minds against those who are oppressed. These are amongst the effects of unremitted labour, when men exhaust their attention, burn out their candles, and are left in the dark.—*Malo meorum negligentiam, quam istorum obscuram diligentiam.*

I have the honour, &c.

(Signed)   EDMUND BURKE.

Beaconsfield, January 19, 1791.

THOUGHTS

ON

FRENCH AFFAIRS

ETC., ETC.

WRITTEN IN DECEMBER

1791

IN all our transactions with France, and at all periods, we have treated with that state on the footing of a monarchy. Monarchy was considered in all the external relations of that kingdom with every power in Europe as its legal and constitutional government, and that in which alone its federal capacity was vested.

It is not yet a year since Monsieur de Montmorin formally, and with as little respect as can be imagined to the king, and to all crowned heads, announced a total revolution in that country. He has informed the British ministry, that its frame of government is wholly altered; that he is one of the ministers of the new system; and, in effect, that the king is no longer his master (nor does he even call him such) but the "*first of the ministers*," in the new system.

The second notification was that of the king's acceptance of the new constitution; accompanied with fanfaronades in the modern style of the French bureaus; things which have much more the air and character of the saucy declamations of their clubs, than the tone of regular office.

It has not been very usual to notify to foreign courts anything concerning the internal arrangements of any state. In the present case, the circumstances of these two notifications, with the observations with which they are attended, does not leave it in the choice of the sovereigns of Christendom to appear ignorant either of this French revolution, or (what is more important) of its principles.

We know that, very soon after this manifesto of Monsieur de Montmorin, the King of France, in whose name it was made, found himself obliged to fly, with his whole family; leaving behind him a declaration, in which he disavows and annuls that constitution, as having been the effect of force on his person and usurpation on his authority. It is equally notorious that this unfortunate prince was, with many circumstances of insult and outrage, brought back prisoner, by a deputation of the pretended National Assembly, and afterwards suspended by their authority, from his government. Under equally notorious constraint, and under menaces of total deposition, he has been compelled to accept what they call a constitution, and to agree to whatever else the usurped power, which holds him in confinement, thinks proper to impose.

His next brother, who had fled with him, and his third brother, who had fled before him, all the princes of his blood who remained faithful to him, and the flower of his magistracy, his clergy, and his nobility, continue in foreign countries, protesting against all acts done by him in his present situation, on the grounds upon which he had himself protested against them at the time of his flight; with this addition, that they deny his very competence, (as on good grounds they may,) to abrogate the royalty, or the ancient constitutional orders of the kingdom. In this protest they are joined by three hundred of the late assembly itself, and, in effect, by a great part of the French nation. The new government (so far as the people dare to disclose their sentiments) is disdained, I am persuaded, by the greater number; who, as M. de la Fayette complains, and as the truth is, have declined to take any share in the new elections to the National Assembly, either as candidates or electors.

In this state of things (that is, in the case of a *divided* kingdom) [1] by the law of nations, Great Britain, like every other power, is free to take any part she pleases. She may decline, with more or less formality, according to her discretion, to acknowledge this new system; or she may recognize it as a government *de facto,* setting aside all discussion of its original legality, and considering the

[1] See Vattel, b. ii. c. 4, sect. 56, and b. iii. c. 18. sect. 296.

ancient monarchy as at an end. The law of nations leaves our court open to its choice. We have no direction but what is found in the well understood policy of the king and kingdom.

This declaration of a *new species* of government, on new principles (such it professes itself to be), is a real crisis in the politics of Europe. The conduct, which prudence ought to dictate to Great Britain, will not depend (as hitherto our connexion or quarrel with other states has for some time depended) upon merely *external* relations; but in a great measure also upon the system which we may think it right to adopt for the internal government of our own country.

If it be our policy to assimilate our government to that of France, we ought to prepare for this change, by encouraging the schemes of authority established there. We ought to wink at the captivity and deposition of a prince, with whom, if not in close alliance, we were in friendship. We ought to fall in with the ideas of Mons. Montmorin's circular manifesto; and to do business of course with the functionaries who act under the new power, by which that king, to whom his majesty's minister has been sent to reside, has been deposed and imprisoned. On that idea we ought also to withhold all sorts of direct or indirect countenance from those who are treating in Germany for the re-establishment of the French monarchy and of the ancient orders of that state. This conduct is suitable to this policy.

The question is, whether this policy be suitable to the interests of the crown and subjects of Great Britain. Let us, therefore, a little consider the true nature and probable effects of the revolution which, in such a very unusual manner, has been twice diplomatically announced to his majesty.

There have been many internal revolutions in the government of countries, both as to persons and forms, in which the neighbouring states have had little or no concern. Whatever the government might be with respect to those persons and those forms, the stationary interests of the nation concerned have most commonly influenced the new governments in the same manner in which they influenced the old; and the revolution, turning on matter of local grievance, or of local accommodation, did not extend beyond its territory.

The present revolution in France seems to me to be quite of another character and description; and to bear little resemblance or analogy to any of those which have been brought about in Europe, upon principles merely political. *It is a revolution of doctrine and theoretic dogma.* It has a much greater resemblance to those changes which have been made upon religious grounds in which a spirit of proselytism makes an essential part.

The last revolution of doctrine and theory which has happened in Europe is the Reformation. It is not for my purpose to take any notice here of the merits of that revolution, but to state one only of its effects.

That effect was *to introduce other interests into all countries than those which arose from their locality and natural circumstances.* The principle of the Reformation was such as, by its essence, could not be local or confined to the country in which it had its origin. For instance, the doctrine of "justification by faith or by works," which was the original basis of the Reformation, could not have one of its alternatives true as to Germany, and false as to every other country. Neither are questions of theoretic truth and falsehood governed by circumstances any more than by places. On that occasion, therefore, the spirit of proselytism expanded itself with great elasticity upon all sides: and great divisions were everywhere the result.

These divisions, however, in appearance merely dogmatic, soon became mixed with the political; and their effects were rendered much more intense from this combination. Europe was for a long time divided into two great factions, under the name of Catholic and Protestant, which not only often alienated state from state, but also divided almost every state within itself. The warm parties in each state were more affectionately attached to those of their own doctrinal interest in some other country, than to their fellow-citizens, or to their natural government, when they or either of them happened to be of a different persuasion. These factions, wherever they prevailed, if they did not absolutely destroy, at least weakened and distracted the locality of patriotism. The public affections came to have other motives and other ties.

It would be to repeat the history of the two last centuries to exemplify the effects of this revolution.

Although the principles to which it gave rise did not operate with a perfect regularity and constancy, they never wholly ceased to operate. Few wars were made, and few treaties were entered into, in which they did not come in for some part. They gave a colour, a character, and direction, to all the politics of Europe.

These principles of internal as well as external division and coalition are but just now extinguished. But they, who will examine into the true character and genius of some late events, must be satisfied that other sources of faction, combining parties among the inhabitants of different countries into one connexion, are opened, and that from these sources are likely to arise effects full as important as those which had formerly arisen from the jarring interests of the religious sects. The intention of the several actors in the change in France is not a matter of doubt. It is very openly professed.

In the modern world, before this time, there has been no instance of this spirit of general political faction, separated from religion, pervading several countries, and forming a principle of union between the partisans in each. But the thing is not less in human nature. The ancient world has furnished a strong and striking instance of such a ground for faction, full as powerful and full as mischievous as our spirit of religious system had ever been ; exciting in all the states of Greece (European and Asiatic) the most violent animosities, and the most cruel and bloody persecutions and proscriptions. These ancient factions in each commonwealth of Greece connected themselves with those of the same description in some other states ; and secret cabals and public alliances were carried on and made, not upon a conformity of general political interests, but for the support and aggrandizement of the two leading states which headed the aristocratic and democratic factions. For, as in latter times, the King of Spain was at the head of a Catholic, and the King of Sweden of a Protestant interest, (France, though Catholic, acting subordinately to the latter,) in the like manner the Lacedemonians were everywhere at the head of the aristocratic interests, and the Athenians of the democratic. The two leading powers kept alive a constant cabal and conspiracy in every state, and the political dogmas concerning the constitution of a republic were the great instruments by which these leading states chose to aggrandize themselves. Their choice was not unwise; because the interest in opinions (merely as opinions, and without any experimental reference to their effects) when once they take strong hold of the mind, become the most operative of all interests, and indeed very often supersede every other.

I might further exemplify the possibility of a political sentiment running through various states, and combining factions in them, from the history of the middle ages in the Guelfs and Ghibellines. These were political factions originally in favour of the emperor and the pope, with no mixture of religious dogmas : or if anything religiously doctrinal they had in them originally, it very soon disappeared; as their first political objects disappeared also, though the spirit remained. They became no more than names to distinguish factions : but they were not the less powerful in their operation, when they had no direct point of doctrine, eithei religious or civil, to assert. For a long time, however, those factions gave no small degree of influence to the foreign chiefs in every commonwealth in which they existed. I do not mean to pursue further the track of these parties. I allude to this part of history only, as it furnishes an instance of that species of faction which broke the locality of public affections, and united descriptions of citizens more with strangers than with their countrymen of different opinions.

The political dogma, which, upon the new French system is to unite the factions of different nations, is this, "That the majority, told by the head, of the taxable people in every country, is the perpetual, natural, unceasing, indefeasible sovereign; that this majority is perfectly master of the form, as well as the administration, of the state, and that the magistrates, under whatever names they are called, are only functionaries to obey the orders (general as laws or particular as decrees) which that majority may make; that this is the only natural government; that all others are tyranny and usurpation."

In order to reduce this dogma into practice, the republicans in France, and their associates in other countries, make it always their business, and often their public profession, to destroy all traces of ancient establishments, and to form a new commonwealth in each country, upon the basis of the French *Rights of Men*. On the principle of these rights, they mean to institute in every country, and, as it were, the germ of the whole, parochial governments, for the purpose of what they call equal representation. From them is to grow, by some media, a general council and representative of all the parochial governments. In that representative is to be vested the whole national power; totally abolishing hereditary name and office, levelling all conditions of men (except where money *must* make a difference), breaking all connexion between territory and dignity, and abolishing every species of nobility, gentry, and church establishments; all their priests, and all their magistrates, being only creatures of election, and pensioners at will.

Knowing how opposite a permanent landed interest is to that scheme, they have resolved, and it is the great drift of their regulations, to reduce that description of men to a mere peasantry for the sustenance of the towns, and to place the true effective government in cities, among the tradesmen, bankers, and voluntary clubs of bold, presuming young persons; advocates, attorneys, notaries, managers of newspapers, and those cabals of literary men, called academies. Their republic is to have a first functionary, (as they call him,) under the name of king, or not, as they think fit. This officer, when such an officer is permitted, is, however, neither in fact nor name, to be considered a sovereign, nor the people as his subjects. The very use of these appellations is offensive to their ears.

This system, as it has first been realized, dogmatically, as well as practically, in France, makes France the natural head of all factions formed on a similar principle, wherever they may prevail, as much as Athens was the head and settled ally of all democratic factions, wherever they existed. The other system has no head.

This system has very many partisans in every country in Europe, but particularly in England, where they are already formed into a body, comprehending most of the dissenters of the three leading denominations; to these are readily aggregated all who are dissenters in character, temper, and disposition, though not belonging to any of their congregations—that is, all the restless people who resemble them, of all ranks and all parties—Whigs, and even Tories—the whole race of half-bred speculators;—all the Atheists, Deists, and Socinians;—all those who hate the clergy, and envy the nobility;—a good many among the monied people;—the East Indians almost to a man, who cannot bear to find that their present importance does not bear a proportion to their wealth. These latter have united themselves into one great, and, in my opinion, formidable club,[1] which, though now quiet, may be brought into action with considerable unanimity and force.

Formerly few, except the ambitious great, or the desperate and indigent, were to be feared as instruments in revolutions. What has happened in France teaches us, with many other things, that there are more causes than have commonly been taken into our consideration, by which government may be subverted. The monied men, merchants, principal tradesmen, and men of letters (hitherto generally thought the peaceable and even timid part of society), are the chief actors in the French revolution. But the fact is, that as money increases and circulates, and as the circulation of news, in politics and letters, becomes more and more diffused, the persons who diffuse this money, and this intelligence, become more and more important. This was not long undiscovered. Views of ambition were in France, for the first time, presented to these classes of men. Objects in the state, in the army, in the system of civil offices of every kind. Their eyes were dazzled with this new prospect. They were, as it were, electrified and made to lose the natural spirit of their situation. A bribe, great without example in the history of the world, was held out to them—the whole government of a very large kingdom.

There are several who are persuaded that the same thing cannot happen in England, because here (they say) the occupations of merchants, tradesmen, and manufacturers,

[1] Originally called the Bengal Club; but since opened to persons from the other presidencies, for the purpose of consolidating the whole Indian interest.

are not held as degrading situations. I once thought that the low estimation in which commerce was held in France might be reckoned among the causes of the late revolution; and I am still of opinion, that the exclusive spirit of the French nobility did irritate the wealthy of other classes. But I found long since, that persons in trade and business were by no means despised in France in the manner I had been taught to believe. As to men of letters, they were so far from being despised or neglected, that there was no country, perhaps, in the universe, in which they were so highly esteemed, courted, caressed, and even feared: tradesmen naturally were not so much sought in society (as not furnishing so largely to the fund of conversation as they do to the revenues of the state), but the latter description got forward every day. M. Bailly, who made himself the popular mayor on the rebellion of the Bastile, and is a principal actor in the revolt, before the change possessed a pension or office under the crown of six hundred pounds English a year; for that country, no contemptible provision: and this he obtained solely as a man of letters, and on no other title. As to the monied men—whilst the monarchy continued, there is no doubt, that merely as such, they did not enjoy the *privileges* of nobility; but nobility was of so easy an acquisition, that it was the fault or neglect of all of that description, who did not obtain its privileges, for their lives at least, in virtue of office. It attached under the royal government to an innumerable multitude of places, real and nominal, that were vendible; and such nobility were as capable of everything as their degree of influence or interest could make them, that is, as nobility of no considerable rank or consequence. M. Necker, so far from being a French gentleman, was not so much as a Frenchman born, and yet we all know the rank in which he stood on the day of the meeting of the states.

As to the mere matter of estimation of the mercantile or any other class, this is regulated by opinion and prejudice. In England, a security against the envy of men in these classes is not so very complete as we may imagine. We must not impose upon ourselves. What institutions and manners together had done in France, manners alone do here. It is the natural operation of things where there exists a crown, a court, splendid orders of knighthood, and an hereditary nobility;—where there exists a fixed, permanent, landed gentry, continued in greatness and opulence by the law of primogeniture, and by a protection given to family settlements;—where there exists a standing army and navy;—where there exists a church establishment, which bestows on learning and parts an interest combined with that of religion and the state;—in a country where such things exist, wealth, new in its acquisition, and precarious in its duration, can never rank first, or even near the first; though wealth has its natural weight further than as it is balanced and even preponderated amongst us as amongst other nations, by artificial institutions and opinions growing out of them. At no period in the history of England have so few peers been taken out of trade or from families newly created by commerce. In no period has so small a number of noble families entered into the counting-house. I can call to mind but one in all England, and his is of near fifty years' standing. Be that as it may, it appears plain to me, from my best observation, that envy and ambition may, by art, management, and disposition, be as much excited amongst these descriptions of men in England, as in any other country; and that they are just as capable of acting a part in any great change.

What direction the French spirit of proselytism is likely to take, and in what order it is likely to prevail in the several parts of Europe, it is not easy to determine.

The seeds are sown almost everywhere, chiefly by newspaper circulations, infinitely more efficacious and extensive than ever they were. And they are a more important instrument than generally is imagined. They are a part of the reading of all, they are the whole of the reading of the far greater number. There are thirty of them in Paris alone. The language diffuses them more widely than the English, though the English too are much read. The writers of these papers, indeed, for the greater part, are either unknown or in contempt, but they are like a battery in which the stroke of any one ball produces no great effect, but the amount of continual repetition is decisive. Let us only suffer any person to tell us his story, morning and evening, but for one twelvemonth, and he will become our master.

All those countries in which several states are comprehended under some general geographical description, and loosely united by some federal constitution; countries of which the members are small, and greatly diversified in their forms of government, and in the titles by which they are held—these countries, as it might be well expected, are the principal objects of their hopes and machinations. Of these, the chief are Germany and Switzerland: after them, Italy has its place, as in circumstances somewhat similar.

As to Germany, (in which, from their relation to the emperor, I comprehended the Belgic provinces,) it appears to me to be from several circumstances, internal and external, in a very critical situation, and the laws and liberties of the empire are by no means secure from the contagion of the French doctrines, and the effect of French intrigues; or from the use which two of the greater German powers may make of a general derangement, to the general detriment. I do not say that the French do not mean to bestow on these German states liberties, and laws too, after their mode; but those are not what have hitherto been understood as the laws and liberties of the empire. These exist and have always existed under the principles of feudal tenure and succession, under imperial constitutions, grants and concessions of sovereigns, family compacts, and public treaties, made under the sanction, and some of them guaranteed by the sovereign powers of other nations, and particularly the old government of France, the author and natural support of the treaty of Westphalia.

In short, the Germanic body is a vast mass of heterogeneous states, held together by that heterogeneous body of old principles, which formed the public law positive and doctrinal. The modern laws and liberties, which the new power in France proposes to introduce into Germany, and to support with all its force, of intrigue and of arms, is of a very different nature, utterly irreconcilable with the first, and indeed fundamentally the reverse of it: I mean the *rights and liberties of the man,* the *droit de l'homme.* That this doctrine has made an amazing progress in Germany there cannot be a shadow of doubt. They are infected by it along the whole course of the Rhine, the Maese, the Moselle, and in the greater part of Suabia and Franconia. It is particularly prevalent amongst all the

lower people, churchmen, and laity, in the dominions of
the ecclesiastical electors. It is not easy to find or to conceive governments more mild and indulgent than these
church sovereignties; but good government is as nothing
when the rights of man take possession of the mind.
Indeed, the loose rein held over the people in these
provinces must be considered as one cause of the facility
with which they lend themselves to any schemes of innovation, by inducing them to think lightly of their governments, and to judge of grievances, not by feeling, but by
imagination.

It is in these electorates that the first impressions of
France are likely to be made, and if they succeed, it is
over with the Germanic body as it stands at present. A
great revolution is preparing in Germany; and a revolution, in my opinion, likely to be more decisive upon the
general fate of nations than that of France itself; other
than as in France is to be found the first source of all the
principles which are in any way likely to distinguish the
troubles and convulsions of our age. If Europe does not
conceive the independence, and the equilibrium of the
empire to be in the very essence of the system of balanced
power in Europe, and if the scheme of public law, or mass
of laws, upon which that independence and equilibrium
are founded, be of no leading consequence as they are
preserved or destroyed, all the politics of Europe for more
than two centuries have been miserably erroneous.

If the two great leading powers of Germany do not
regard this danger (as apparently they do not) in the light
in which it presents itself so naturally, it is because they
are powers too great to have a social interest. That sort
of interest belongs only to those whose state of weakness
or mediocrity is such as to give them greater cause of
apprehension from what may destroy them, than of hope
from any thing by which they may be aggrandized.

As long as those two princes are at variance, so long
the liberties of Germany are safe. But, if ever they
should so far understand one another, as to be persuaded
that they have a more direct and more certainly defined
interest in a proportioned, mutual aggrandizement, than
in a reciprocal reduction, that is, if they come to think
that they are more likely to be enriched by a division of

spoil, than to be rendered secure by keeping to the old policy of preventing others from being spoiled by either of them, from that moment the liberties of Germany are no more.

That a junction of two in such a scheme is neither impossible nor improbable, is evident from the partition of Poland in 1773, which was effected by such a junction as made the interposition of other nations to prevent it, not easy. Their circumstances at that time hindered any other three states, or indeed any two, from taking measures in common to prevent it, though France was at that time an existing power, and had not yet learned to act upon a system of politics of her own invention. The geographical position of Poland was a great obstacle to any movements of France in opposition to this, at that time, unparalleled league. To my certain knowledge, if Great Britain had at that time been willing to concur in preventing the execution of a project so dangerous in the example, even exhausted as France then was by the preceding war, and under a lazy and unenterprisng prince, she would have at every risk taken an active part in this business. But a languor with regard to so remote an interest, and the principles and passions which were then strongly at work at home, were the causes why Great Britain would not give France any encouragement in such an enterprise. At that time, however, and with regard to that object, in my opinion, Great Britain and France had a common interest.

But the position of Germany is not like that of Poland, with regard to France, either for good or for evil. If a conjunction between Prussia and the emperor should be formed for the purpose of secularizing and rendering hereditary the ecclesiastical electorates and the bishopric of Munster, for settling two of them on the children of the emperor, and uniting Cologne and Munster to the dominions of the King of Prussia on the Rhine, or if any other project of mutual aggrandizement should be in prospect, and that, to facilitate such a scheme, the modern French should be permitted and encouraged to shake the internal and external security of these ecclesiastical electorates, Great Britain is so situated, that she could not with any effect set herself in opposition to such a design.

Her principal arm, her marine, could here be of no sort of use.

France, the author of the treaty of Westphalia, is the natural guardian of the independence and balance of Germany. Great Britain (to say nothing of the king's concern as one of that august body) has a serious interest in preserving it; but, except through the power of France, *acting upon the common old principles of state policy,* in the case we have supposed, she has no sort of means of supporting that interest. It is always the interest of Great Britain that the power of France should be kept within the bounds of moderation. It is not her interest that that power should be wholly annihilated in the system of Europe. Though at one time through France the independence of Europe was endangered, it is, and ever was, through her alone that the common liberty of Germany can be secured against the single or the combined ambition of any other power. In truth, within this century the aggrandizement of other sovereign houses has been such that there has been a great change in the whole state of Europe; and other nations as well as France may become objects of jealousy and apprehension.

In this state of things, a new principle of alliances and wars is opened. The treaty of Westphalia is, with France, an antiquated fable. The rights and liberties she was bound to maintain are now a system of wrong and tyranny which she is bound to destroy. Her good and ill dispositions are shown by the same means. *To communicate peaceably* the rights of men is the true mode of her showing her *friendship;* to force sovereigns to *submit* to those rights is her mode of *hostility.* So that either as friend or foe her whole scheme has been, and is, to throw the empire into confusion; and those statesmen, who follow the old routine of politics, may see, in this general confusion, and in the danger of the *lesser* princes, an occasion, as protectors or enemies, of connecting their territories to one or the other of the *two great* German powers. They do not take into consideration that the means which they encourage, as leading to the event they desire, will with certainty not only ravage and destroy the empire, but, if they should for a moment seem to aggrandize the two great houses, will also establish principles, and confirm tempers amongst the people, which will preclude the two sovereigns from the possibility of holding what they acquire, or even the dominions which they have inherited. It is on the side of the ecclesiastical electorates that the dykes, raised to support the German liberty, first will give way.

The French have begun their general operations by seizing upon those territories of the pope, the situation of which was the most inviting to the enterprise. Their method of doing it was by exciting sedition and spreading massacre and desolation through these unfortunate places, and then, under an idea of kindness and protection, bringing forward an antiquated title of the crown of France, and annexing Avignon and the two cities of the Comtat, with their territory, to the French republic. They have made an attempt on Geneva, in which they very narrowly failed of success. It is known that they hold out from time to time the idea of uniting all the other provinces of which Gaul was anciently composed, including Savoy on the other side, and on this side bounding themselves by the Rhine.

As to Switzerland, it is a country whose long union, rather than its possible division, is the matter of wonder. Here I know they entertain very sanguine hopes. The aggregation to France of the democratic Swiss republics appears to them to be a work half done by their very form; and it might seem to them rather an increase of importance to these little commonwealths, than a derogation from their independency, or a change in the manner of their government. Upon any quarrel amongst the cantons, nothing is more likely than such an event. As to the aristocratic republics, the general clamour and hatred which the French excite against the very name, (and with more facility and success than against monarchs,) and the utter impossibility of their government making any sort of resistance against an insurrection, where they have no troops, and the people are all armed and trained, render their hopes, in that quarter, far indeed from unfounded. It is certain that the republic of Berne thinks itself obliged to a vigilance next to hostile, and to imprison or expel all the French whom it finds in its territories. But, indeed, those aristocracies, which comprehend whatever is considerable, wealthy, and valuable, in Switzerland, do now so wholly depend upon opinion, and the humour of their multitude, that the lightest puff of wind is sufficient to blow them down. If France, under its ancient regimen, and upon the ancient principles of policy, was the support of the Germanic constitution, it was much more so of that of Switzerland, which almost from the very origin of that confederacy rested upon the closeness of its connexion with France, on which the Swiss Cantons wholly reposed themselves for the preservation of the parts of their body in their respective rights and permanent forms, as well as for the maintenance of all in their general independency.

Switzerland and Germany are the first objects of the new French politicians. When I contemplate what they have done at home, which is, in effect, little less than an amazing conquest wrought by a change of opinion, in a great part (to be sure far from altogether) very sudden, I cannot help letting my thoughts run along with their designs, and, without attending to geographical order, considering the other states of Europe so far as they may be any way affected by this astonishing revolution. If early steps are not taken in some way or other to prevent the spreading of this influence, I scarcely think any of them perfectly secure.

Italy is divided, as Germany and Switzerland are, into many smaller states, and with some considerable diversity as to forms of government; but as these divisions and varieties in Italy are not so considerable, so neither do I think the danger altogether so imminent there as in Germany and Switzerland. Savoy I know that the French consider as in a very hopeful way, and I believe not at all without reason. They view it as an old member of the kingdom of France which may be easily re-united in the manner, and on the principles of the re-union of Avignon. This country communicates with Piedmont; and, as the King of Sardinia's dominions were long the key of Italy, and as such long regarded by France, whilst France acted on her old maxims, and with views on Italy; so, in this new French Empire of sedition, if once she gets that key into her hands, she can easily lay open the barrier which hinders the entrance of her present politics into that inviting region. Milan, I am sure, nourishes great disquiets— and, if Milan should stir, no part of Lombardy is secure to the present possessors—whether the Venetian or the Austrian. Genoa is closely connected with France.

The first prince of the house of Bourbon has been obliged to give himself up entirely to the new system, and to pretend even to propagate it with all zeal; at least that club of intriguers who assemble at the Feuillans, and whose cabinet meets at Madame de Stael's, and makes and directs all the ministers, is the real executive government of France. The emperor is perfectly in concert, and they will not long suffer any prince of the house of Bourbon to keep by force the French emissaries out of their dominions; nor whilst France has a commerce with them, especially through Marseilles (the hottest focus of sedition in France), will it be long possible to prevent the intercourse or the effects.

Naples has an old, inveterate disposition to republicanism, and (however for some time past quiet) is as liable to explosion as its own Vesuvius. Sicily, I think, has these dispositions in full as strong a degree. In neither of these countries exists anything which very well deserves the name of government or exact police.

In the States of the Church, notwithstanding their strictness in banishing the French out of that country, they are not wanting the seeds of a revolution. The spirit of nepotism prevails there nearly as strong as ever. Every pope of course is to give origin or restoration to a great family, by the means of large donations. The foreign revenues have long been gradually on the decline, and seem now in a manner dried up. To supply this defect the resource of vexatious and impolitic jobbing at home, if anything, is rather increased than lessened. Various well intended but ill understood practices, some of them existing, in their spirit at least, from the time of the old Roman empire, still prevail; and that government is as blindly attached to old, abusive customs, as others are wildly disposed to all sorts of innovations and experiments. These abuses were less felt whilst the pontificate drew riches from abroad, which in some measure counterbalanced the evils of their remiss and jobbish government at home. But now it can subsist only on the resources of domestic management; and abuses in that management of course will be more intimately and more severely felt.

In the midst of the apparently torpid languor of the ecclesiastical state, those who have had opportunity of a near observation have seen a little rippling in that smooth water, which indicates something alive under it. There is, in the ecclesiastical state, a personage who seems capable of acting (but with more force and steadiness) the part of the tribune Rienzi. The people, once inflamed, will not be destitute of a leader. They have such an one already in the Cardinal or Archbishop *Buon Campagna*. He is, of all men, if I am not ill informed, the most turbulent, seditious, intriguing, bold, and desperate. He is not at all made for a Roman of the present day. I think he lately held the first office of their state, that of great chamberlain, which is equivalent to high treasurer. At present he is out of employment, and in disgrace. If he should be elected pope, or even come to have any weight with a new pope, he will infallibly conjure up a democratic spirit in that country. He may indeed be able to effect it without these advantages. The next interregnum will probably show more of him. There may be others of the same character, who have not come to my knowledge. This much is certain, that the Roman people, if once the blind reverence they bear to the sanctity of the pope, which is their only bridle, should relax, are naturally turbulent, ferocious, and headlong, whilst the police is defective, and the government feeble and resourceless beyond all imagination.

As to Spain, it is a nerveless country. It does not possess the use, it only suffers the abuse, of a nobility. For some time, and even before the settlement of the Bourbon dynasty, that body has been systematically lowered, and rendered incapable by exclusion, and for incapacity excluded from affairs. In this circle the body is in a manner annihilated,—and so little means have they of any weighty exertion either to control or to support the crown, that if they at all interfere, it is only by abetting desperate and mobbish insurrections, like that at Madrid, which drove Squillace from his place. Florida Blanca is a creature of office, and has little connexion and no sympathy with that body.

As to the clergy, they are the only thing in Spain that looks like an independent order, and they are kept in some respect by the Inquisition, the sole but unhappy resource of public tranquillity and order now remaining in Spain. As in Venice, it is become mostly an engine of state, which indeed to a degree it has always been in Spain. It wars no longer with Jews and heretics; it has no such war to carry on. Its great object is to keep atheistic and republican doctrines from making their way in that kingdom. No French book upon any subject can enter there which does not contain such matter. In Spain, the clergy are of moment from their influence, but at the same time with the envy and jealousy that attend great riches and power. Though the crown has by management with the pope got a very great share of the ecclesiastical revenues into its own hands, much still remains to them. There will always be about that court those who look out to a farther division of the church property as a resource, and to be obtained by shorter methods, than those of negotiations with the clergy and their chief. But at present I think it likely that they will stop, lest the business should be taken out of their hands : and lest that body, in which remains the only life that exists in Spain, and is not a fever, may with their property lose all the influence necessary to preserve the monarchy, or, being poor and desperate, may employ whatever influence remains to them as active agents in its destruction.

The Castilians have still remaining a good deal of their old character, their *gravidad, lealdad,* and *il timor de Dios ;* but that character neither is, nor ever was, exactly true, except of the Castilians only. The several kingdoms, which compose Spain, have, perhaps, some features which run through the whole; but they are in many particulars as different as nations who go by different names : the Catalans, for instance, and the Arragonians too, in a great measure have the spirit of the Miquelets, and much more of republicanism than of an attachment to royalty. They are more in the way of trade and intercourse with France; and, upon the least internal movement, will disclose and probably let loose a spirit that may throw the whole Spanish monarchy into convulsions.

It is a melancholy reflection that the spirit of melioration which has been going on in that part of Europe, more or less during this century, and the various schemes very lately on foot for further advancement, are all put a stop to at once.

Reformation certainly is nearly connected with innovation —and, where that latter comes in for too large a share, those who undertake to improve their country may risk their own safety. In times where the correction, which includes the confession, of an abuse, is turned to criminate the authority which has long suffered it, rather than to honour those who would amend it, (which is the spirit of this malignant French distemper,) every step out of the common course becomes critical, and renders it a task full of peril for princes of moderate talents to engage in great undertakings. At present the only safety of Spain is the old national hatred to the French. How far that can be depended upon, if any great ferments should be excited, it is impossible to say.

As to Portugal, she is out of the high road of these politics—I shall, therefore, not divert my thoughts that way; but return again to the North of Europe, which at present seems the part most interested, and there it appears to me that the French speculation on the northern countries may be valued in the following, or some such manner.

Denmark and Norway do not appear to furnish any of the materials of a democratic revolution, or the dispositions to it. Denmark can only be *consequentially* affected by anything done in France; but of Sweden I think quite otherwise. The present power in Sweden is too new a system and too green, and too sore, from its late revolution, to be considered as perfectly assured. The king, by his astonishing activity, his boldness, his decision, his ready versatility, and by rousing and employing the old military spirit of Sweden, keeps up the top with continual agitation and lashing. The moment it ceases to spin, the royalty is a dead bit of box. Whenever Sweden is quiet externally for some time, there is great danger that all the republican elements she contains will be animated by the new French spirit, and of this I believe the king is very sensible.

The Russian Government is of all others the most liable to be subverted by military seditions, by court conspiracies, and sometimes by headlong rebellions of the people, such as the turbinating movement of Pugatchef. It is not quite so probable that in any of these changes the spirit of system may mingle in the manner it has done in France. The Muscovites are no great speculators—but I should not much rely on their uninquisitive disposition, if any of their ordinary motives to sedition should arise. The little catechism of the rights of men is soon learned; and the inferences are in the passions.

Poland, from one cause or other, is always unquiet. The new constitution only serves to supply that restless people with new means, at least new modes of cherishing their turbulent disposition. The bottom of the character is the same. It is a great question, whether the joining that crown with the electorate of Saxony will contribute most to strengthen the royal authority of Poland, or to shake the ducal in Saxony. The elector is a Catholic; the people of Saxony are, six-sevenths at the very least, Protestants. He *must* continue a Catholic, according to the Polish law, if he accepts that crown. The pride of the Saxons, formerly flattered by having a crown in the house of their prince, though an honour which cost them dear; the German probity, fidelity and loyalty; the weight of the constitution of the empire under the treaty of Westphalia; the good temper and good nature of the princes of the house of Saxony; had formerly removed from the people all apprehension with regard to their religion, and kept them perfectly quiet, obedient, and even affectionate. The seven years' war made some change in the minds of the Saxons. They did not, I believe, regret the loss of what might be considered almost as the succession to the crown of Poland, the possession of which, by annexing them to a foreign interest, had often obliged them to act an arduous part, towards the support of which that foreign interest afforded no proportionable strength. In this very delicate situation of their political interests, the speculations of the French and German *economists,* and the cabals, and the secret, as well as public doctrines of the *illuminatenorden* and *free masons,* have made a considerable progress in that country; and a turbulent spirit under colour of religion, but in reality arising from the French rights of man, has already shown itself, and is ready on every occasion to blaze out.

The present elector is a prince of a safe and quiet temper, of great prudence, and goodness. He knows that, in the actual state of things, not the power and respect belonging to sovereigns, but their very existence depends on a reasonable frugality. It is very certain that not one sovereign in Europe can either promise for the continuance of his authority in a state of indigence and insolvency, or dares to venture on a new imposition to relieve himself. Without abandoning wholly the ancient magnificence of his court, the elector has conducted his affairs with infinitely more economy than any of his predecessors, so as to restore his finances beyond what was thought possible from the state in which the seven years' war had left Saxony. Saxony, during the whole of that dreadful period, having been in the hands of an exasperated enemy, rigorous by resentment, by nature and by necessity, was obliged to bear in a manner the whole burden of the war; in the intervals when their allies prevailed, the inhabitants of that country were not better treated.

The moderation and prudence of the present elector, in my opinion, rather perhaps respites the troubles than secures the peace of the electorate. The offer of the succession to the crown of Poland is truly critical, whether he accepts, or whether he declines it. If the states will consent to his acceptance, it will add to the difficulties, already great, of his situation between the King of Prussia and the emperor. But these thoughts lead me too far, when I mean to speak only of the interior condition of these princes. It has always, however, some necessary connexion with their foreign politics.

With regard to Holland, and the ruling party there, I do not think it at all tainted, or likely to be so, except by fear; or that it is likely to be misled, unless indirectly and circuitously. But the predominant party in Holland is not Holland. The suppressed faction, though suppressed, exists. Under the ashes, the embers of the late commotions are still warm. The anti-Orange party has from the day of its origin been French, though alienated in some degree for some time, through the pride and folly of Louis XIV. It will ever hanker after a French connexion; and now that the internal government in France has been assimilated in so considerable a degree to that which the immoderate republicans began so very lately to introduce into Holland, their connexion, as still more natural, will be more desired. I do not well understand the present exterior politics of the stadtholder, nor the treaty into which the newspapers say he has entered for the States with the emperor. But the emperor's own politics with regard to the Netherlands seem to me to be exactly calculated to answer the purpose of the French revolutionists. He endeavours to crush the aristocratic party—and to nourish one in avowed connexion with the most furious democratists in France.

These provinces in which the French game is so well played, they consider as part of the old French empire : certainly they were amongst the oldest parts of it. These they think very well situated, as their party is well disposed to a re-union. As to the greater nations, they do not aim at making a direct conquest of them, but by disturbing them through a propagation of their principles, they hope to weaken, as they will weaken them, and to keep them in perpetual alarm and agitation, and thus render all their efforts against them utterly impracticable, whilst they extend the dominion of their sovereign anarchy on all sides.

As to England, there may be some apprehension from vicinity, from constant communication, and from the very name of liberty, which, as it ought to be very dear to us, in its worst abuses carries something seductive. It is the abuse of the first and best of the objects which we cherish. I know that many, who sufficiently dislike the system of France, have yet no apprehension of its prevalence here. I say nothing to the ground of this security in the attachment of the people to their constitution, and their satisfaction in the discreet portion of liberty which it measures out to them. Upon this I have said all I have to say, in the appeal I have published. That security is something, and not inconsiderable. But if a storm arises I should not much rely upon it.

There are other views of things which may be used to give us a perfect (though in my opinion a delusive) assurance of our own security. The first of these is from the weakness and rickety nature of the new system in the place of its first formation. It is thought that the monster of a commonwealth cannot possibly live—that at any rate the ill contrivance of their fabric will make it fall in pieces of itself—that the assembly must be bankrupt, and that this bankruptcy will totally destroy that system, from the contagion of which apprehensions are entertained.

For my part I have long thought that one great cause of the stability of this wretched scheme of things in France was an opinion that it could not stand; and, therefore, that all external measures to destroy it were wholly useless.

As to the bankruptcy, that event has happened long ago, as much as it is ever likely to happen. As soon as a nation compels a creditor to take paper currency in discharge of his debt, there is a bankruptcy. The compulsory paper has in some degree answered; not because there was a surplus from church lands, but because faith has not been kept with the clergy. As to the holders of the old funds, to them the payments will be dilatory, but they will be made, and whatever may be the discount on paper, whilst paper is taken, paper will be issued.

As to the rest, they have shot out three branches of revenue to supply all those which they have destroyed, that is, *the Universal Register of all Transactions,* the heavy and universal *Stamp Duty,* and the new *Territorial Impost,* levied chiefly on the reduced estates of the gentlemen. These branches of the revenue, especially as they take assignats in payment, answer their purpose in a considerable degree, and keep up the credit of their paper; for as they receive it in their treasury, it is in reality funded upon all their taxes and future resources of all kinds, as well as upon the church estates. As this paper is become in a manner the only visible maintenance of the whole people, the dread of a bankruptcy is more apparently connected with the delay of a counter-revolution, than with the duration of this republic; because the interest of the new republic manifestly leans upon it; and, in my opinion, the counter-revolution cannot exist along with it. The above three projects ruined some ministers under the old government, merely for having conceived them. They are the salvation of the present rulers.

As the assembly has laid a most unsparing and cruel hand on all men who have lived by the bounty, the justice, or the abuses of the old government, they have lessened many expenses. The royal establishment, though excessively and ridiculously great for *their* scheme of things, is reduced at least one-half; the estates of the king's brothers, which under the ancient government had been in truth royal revenues, go to the general stock of the confiscation; and as to the crown lands, though, under the monarchy, they never yielded two hundred and fifty thousand a year, by many they are thought at least worth three times as much.

As to the ecclesiastical charge, whether as a compensation for losses, or a provision for religion, of which they made at first a great parade, and entered into a solemn engagement in favour of it, it was estimated at a much larger sum than they could expect from the church property, movable or immovable: they are completely bankrupt as to that article. It is just what they wish; and it is not productive of any serious inconvenience. The non-payment produces discontent and occasional sedition; but it is only by fits and spasms, and amongst the country people who are of no consequence. These seditions furnish new pretexts for non-payment to the church establishment, and help the assembly wholly to get rid of the clergy, and indeed of any form of religion, which is not only their real, but avowed object.

They are embarrassed indeed in the highest degree, but not wholly resourceless. They are without the species of money. Circulation of money is a great convenience, but a substitute for it may be found. Whilst the great objects of production and consumption, corn, cattle, wine, and the like, exist in a country, the means of giving them circulation, with more or less convenience, cannot be *wholly* wanting. The great confiscation of the church and of the crown lands, and of the appendages of the princes, for the purchase of all which their paper is always received at par, gives means of continually destroying and continually creating, and this perpetual destruction and renovation feeds the speculative market, and prevents, and will prevent, till that fund of confiscation begins to fail, a *total* depreciation.

But all consideration of public credit in France is of little avail at present. The action indeed of the monied interest was of absolute necessity at the beginning of this revolution; but the French republic can stand without any assistance from that description of men, which, as things are now circumstanced, rather stands in need of assistance itself from the power which alone substantially exists in France; I mean the several districts and municipal republics, and the several clubs which direct all their affairs and appoint all their magistrates. This is the power now paramount to everything, even to the Assembly itself called National, and that to which tribunals, priesthoods, laws, finances, and both descriptions of military power are wholly subservient, so far as the military power of either description yields obedience to any name of authority.

The world of contingency and political combination is much larger than we are apt to imagine. We never can say what may, or may not happen, without a view to all the actual circumstances. Experience, upon other data than those, is of all things the most delusive. Prudence in new cases can do nothing on grounds of retrospect. A constant vigilance and attention to the train of things as they successively emerge, and to act on what they direct, are the only sure courses. The physician that let blood, and by blood-letting cured one kind of plague, in the next added to its ravages. That power goes with property is not universally true, and the idea that the operation of it is certain and invariable may mislead us very fatally.

Whoever will take an accurate view of the state of those republics, and of the composition of the present assembly deputed by them (in which assembly there are not quite fifty persons possessed of an income amounting to 100*l.* sterling yearly), must discern clearly, *that the political and civil power of France is wholly separated from its property of every description;* and of course that neither the landed nor the monied interest possesses the smallest weight or consideration in the direction of any public concern. The whole kingdom is directed by the *refuse of its chicane,* with the aid of the bustling, presumptuous young clerks of counting-houses and shops, and some intermixture of young gentlemen of the same character in the several towns. The rich peasants are bribed with church lands; and the poorer of that description are, and can be, counted for nothing. They may rise in ferocious, ill-directed tumults—but they can only disgrace themselves and signalize the triumph of their adversaries.

The *truly* active citizens, that is, the above descriptions, are all concerned in intrigue respecting the various objects in their local or their general government. The rota, which the French have established for their National Assembly, holds out the highest objects of ambition to such vast multitudes as, in an unexampled measure, to widen the bottom of a new species of interest merely political, and wholly unconnected with birth or property. This scheme of a rota, though it enfeebles the state, considered as one solid body, and indeed wholly disables it from acting as such, gives a great, an equal, and a diffusive strength to the democratic scheme. Seven hundred and fifty people, every two years raised to the supreme power, has already produced at least fifteen hundred bold, acting politicians; a great number for even so great a country as France. These men never will quietly settle in ordinary occupations, nor submit to any scheme which must reduce them to an entirely private condition, or to the exercise of a steady, peaceful, but obscure and unimportant industry. Whilst they sit in the assembly they are denied offices of trust and profit—but their short duration makes this no restraint—during their probation and apprenticeship they are all salaried with an income to the greatest part of them immense; and, after they have passed the novitiate, those who take any sort of lead are placed in very lucrative offices, according to their influence and credit, or appoint those who divide their profits with them.

This supply of recruits to the corps of the highest civil ambition goes on with a regular progression. In very few years it must amount to many thousands. These, however, will be as nothing in comparison to the multitude of municipal officers, and officers of district and department, of all sorts, who have tasted of power and profit, and who hunger for the periodical return of the meal. To these needy agitators, the glory of the state, the general wealth and prosperity of the nation, and the rise or fall of public credit, are as dreams; nor have arguments deduced from these topics any sort of weight with them. The indifference with which the assembly regards the state of their colonies, the only valuable part of the French commerce, is a full proof how little they are likely to be affected by anything but the selfish game of their own ambition, now universally diffused.

It is true, amidst all these turbulent means of security to their system, very great discontents everywhere prevail. But they only produce misery to those who nurse them at home, or exile, beggary, and in the end confiscation, to those who are so impatient as to remove from them. Each municipal republic has a committee, or something in the nature of a *committee of research.* In these petty republics the tyranny is so near its object, that it becomes instantly acquainted with every act of every man. It stifles conspiracy in its very first movements. Their power is absolute and uncontrollable. No stand can be made against it. The republics are besides so disconnected, that very little intelligence of what happens in them is to be obtained, beyond their own bounds, except by the means of their clubs, who keep up a constant correspondence, and who give what colour they please to such facts as they choose to communicate out of the track of their correspondence. They all have some sort of communication, just as much or as little as they please, with the centre. By this confinement of all communication to the ruling faction, any combination, grounded on the abuses and discontents in one, scarcely can reach the other. There is not one man, in any one place, to head them. The old government had so much abstracted the nobility from the cultivation of provincial interest, that no man in France exists, whose power, credit, or consequence, extends to two districts, or who is capable of uniting them in any design, even if any man could assemble ten men together, without being sure of a speedy lodging in a prison. One must not judge of the state of France by what has been observed elsewhere. It does not in the least resemble any other country. Analogical reasoning from history or from recent experience in other places is wholly delusive.

In my opinion there never was seen so strong a government internally as that of the French municipalities. If ever any rebellion can arise against the present system, it must begin where the revolution which gave birth to it did, at the capital. Paris is the only place in which there is the least freedom of intercourse. But even there, so many servants as any man has, so many spies, and irreconcilable domestic enemies.

But that place being the chief seat of the power and intelligence of the ruling faction, and the place of occasional resort for their fiercest spirits, even there a revolution is not likely to have anything to feed it. The leaders of the aristocratic party have been drawn out of the kingdom by order of the princes, on the hopes held out by the emperor and the King of Prussia at Pilnitz; and as to the democratic factions in Paris, amongst them there are no leaders possessed of an influence for any other purpose but that of maintaining the present state of things. The moment they are seen to warp, they are reduced to nothing. They have no attached army—no party that is at all personal.

It is not to be imagined because a political system is, under certain aspects, very unwise in its contrivance, and very mischievous in its effects, that it therefore can have no long duration. Its very defects may tend to its stability, because they are agreeable to its nature. The very faults in the constitution of Poland made it last; the *veto* which destroyed all its energy preserved its life. What can be conceived so monstrous as the republic of Algiers? and that no less strange republic of the Mamelukes in Egypt? They are of the worst form imaginable, and exercised in the worst manner, yet they have existed as a nuisance on the earth for several hundred years.

From all these considerations, and many more that crowd upon me, three conclusions have long since arisen in my mind—

First, that no counter-revolution is to be expected in France, from internal causes solely.

Secondly, that the longer the present system exists, the greater will be its strength; the greater its power to destroy discontents at home, and to resist all foreign attempts in favour of these discontents.

Thirdly, that as long as it exists in France, it will be the interest of the managers there, and it is in the very essence of their plan, to disturb and distract all other governments, and their endless succession of restless politicians will continually stimulate them to new attempts.

Princes are generally sensible that this is their common

cause; and two of them have made a public declaration of their opinion to this effect. Against this common danger, some of them, such as the King of Spain, the King of Sardinia, and the republic of Berne, are very diligent in using defensive measures.

If they were to guard against an invasion from France, the merits of this plan of a merely defensive resistance might be supported by plausible topics; but as the attack does not operate against these countries externally, but by an internal corruption (a sort of dry rot); they, who pursue this merely defensive plan, against a danger which the plan itself supposes to be serious, cannot possibly escape it. For it is in the nature of all defensive measures to be sharp and vigorous under the impressions of the first alarm, and to relax by degrees; until at length the danger, by not operating instantly, comes to appear as a false alarm; so much so that the next menacing appearance will look less formidable, and will be less provided against. But to those who are on the offensive it is not necessary to be always alert. Possibly it is more their interest not to be so. For their unforeseen attacks contribute to their success.

In the meantime a system of French conspiracy is gaining ground in every country. This system happening to be founded on principles the most delusive indeed, but the most flattering to the natural propensities of the unthinking multitude, and to the speculations of all those who think, without thinking very profoundly, must daily extend its influence. A predominant inclination towards it appears in all those who have no religion, when otherwise their disposition leads them to be advocates even for despotism. Hence Hume, though I cannot say that he does not throw out some expressions of disapprobation on the proceedings of the levellers in the reign of Richard II., yet affirms that the doctrines of *John Ball* were "conformable to the ideas of primitive equality, *which are engraven in the hearts of all men.*"

Boldness formerly was not the character of Atheists as such. They were even of a character nearly the reverse; they were formerly like the old Epicureans, rather an unenterprising race. But of late they are grown active, designing, turbulent, and seditious. They are sworn enemies to kings, nobility, and priesthood. We have seen all the academicians at Paris, with Condorcet, the friend and correspondent of Priestley, at their head, the most furious of the extravagant republicans.

The late assembly, after the last captivity of the king, had actually chosen this Condorcet by a majority in the ballot, for preceptor to the dauphin, who was to be taken out of the hands and direction of his parents, and to be delivered over to this fanatic atheist, and furious demo-cratic republican. His untractability to these leaders, and his figure in the club of Jacobins, which at that time they wished to bring under, alone prevented that part of the arrangement, and others in the same style, from being carried into execution. Whilst he was candidate for this office he produced his title to it by promulgating the follow-ing ideas of the title of his royal pupil to the crown. In a paper written by him, and published with his name, against the re-establishment, even of the appearance of monarchy under any qualifications, he says : "Jusqu'à ce moment ils [l'Assemblée Nationale] n'ont rien préjugé encore. En se réservant de nommer un gouverneur au dauphin, ils n'ont pas prononcé *que cet enfant dût regner;* mais seulement qu'il *étoit possible* que la constitution l'y destinât; ils ont voulu que l'éducation, effaçant tout ce que *les prestiges du trône* ont pu lui inspirer de préjugés sur les droits pré-tendus de sa naissance, qu'elle lui fît connoître de bonne heure, et *l'égalité naturelle des hommes, et la souveraineté du peuple;* qu'elle lui apprît à ne pas oublier que c'est du *peuple* qu'il tiendra le tître de roi, et que *le peuple n'a pas même le droit de renoncer à celui de l'en dépouiller.*

"Ils ont voulu que cette éducation le rendît également digne par ses lumières, et ses vertus, de recevoir *avec resignation* le fardeau dangereux d'une couronne, ou de la *déposer avec joie* entre les mains de ses frères, qu'il sentît que le devoir, et la gloire du roi d'un peuple libre, est de hâter le moment de n'être plus qu'un citoyen ordinaire.

"Ils ont voulu que *l'inutilité d'un roi,* la nécessité de chercher les moyens de remplacer *un pouvoir fondé sur les illusions,* fût une des premières vérités offertes à sa raison ; *l'obligation d'y concourir lui-même* un des premiers devoirs de sa morale ; et le désir, de n'être plus affranchi du joug de la loi, *par une injurieuse inviolabilité,* le premier senti-

ment de son cœur. Ils n'ignorent pas que dans ce moment
il s'agit bien moins de former un roi que de lui apprendre
à *savoir, à vouloir ne plus l'être.*[1] "

Such are the sentiments of the man who has occasionally filled the chair of the National Assembly, who is their
perpetual secretary, their only standing officer, and the
most important by far. He leads them to peace or war.
He is the great theme of the republican faction in England.
These ideas of M. Condorcet are the principles of those
to whom kings are to entrust their successors, and the
interests of their succession. This man would be ready to
plunge the poniard in the heart of his pupil, or to whet the
axe for his neck. Of all men, the most dangerous is a
warm, hot-headed, zealous atheist. This sort of man aims
at dominion, and his means are, the words he always has
in his mouth, "L'égalité naturelle des hommes, et la
souveraineté du peuple."

All former attempts, grounded on these rights of men,
had proved unfortunate. The success of this last makes a
mighty difference in the effect of the doctrine. Here is a
principle of a nature to the multitude the most seductive,
always existing before their eyes, *as a thing feasible in
practice.* After so many failures, such an enterprise,

---

[1] 'Until now, they (the National Assembly) have prejudged nothing.
Reserving to themselves a right to appoint a preceptor to the dauphin,
they did not declare that *this child was* to reign, but only that *possibly*
the constitution *might* destine him to it : they willed that while education should efface from his mind all the prejudices arising from the
delusions of the throne respecting his pretended birth-right, it should
also teach him not to forget, that it is *from the people* he is to receive
the title of king, and that *the people do not even possess the right of giving
up their power to take it from him.*

'They willed that this education should render him worthy by his
knowledge, and by his virtues, both to receive *with submission* the
dangerous burden of a crown, and *to resign it with pleasure* into the
hands of his brethren : that he should be conscious that the hastening
of that moment when he is to be only a common citizen constitutes
the duty and the glory of a king of free people.

'They willed that the *uselessness of a king*, the necessity of seeking
means to establish something in lieu of a *power founded on illusions*,
should be one of the first truths offered to his reason ; *the obligation of
conforming himself to this, the first of his moral duties ; and the desire of no
longer being freed from the yoke of the law, by an injurious inviolability, the
first and chief sentiment of his heart.* They are not ignorant that in the
present moment the object is less to form a king, than to teach him
that he should know how to wish no longer to be such.

previous to the French experiment, carried ruin to the contrivers, on the face of it; and if any enthusiast was so wild as to wish to engage in a scheme of that nature, it was not easy for him to find followers: now there is a party almost in all countries, ready made, animated with success, with a sure ally in the very centre of Europe. There is no cabal so obscure in any place, that they do not protect, cherish, foster, and endeavour to raise it into importance at home and abroad. From the lowest, this intrigue will creep up to the highest. Ambition, as well as enthusiasm, may find its account in the party and in the principle.

The ministers of other kings, like those of the King of France (not one of whom was perfectly free from this guilt, and some of whom were very deep in it), may themselves be the persons to foment such a disposition and such a faction. Hertzberg, the King of Prussia's late minister, is so much of what is called a philosopher, that he was of a faction with that sort of politicians in every thing, and in every place. Even when he defends himself from the imputation of giving extravagantly into these principles, he still considers the revolution of France as a great public good, by giving credit to their fraudulent declaration of their universal benevolence, and love of peace. Nor are his Prussian majesty's present ministers at all disinclined to the same system. Their ostentatious preamble to certain late edicts demonstrates, (if their actions had not been sufficiently explanatory of their cast of mind,) that they are deeply infected with the same distemper of dangerous, because plausible, though trivial and shallow speculation.

Ministers, turning their backs on the reputation which properly belongs to them, aspire at the glory of being speculative writers. The duties of these two situations are, in general, directly opposite to each other. Speculators ought to be neutral. A minister cannot be so. He is to support the interest of the public as connected with that of his master. He is his master's trustee, advocate, attorney, and steward—and he is not to indulge in any speculation which contradicts that character, or even detracts from its efficacy. Necker had an extreme thirst for this sort of glory; so had others; and this pursuit of a misplaced and misunderstood reputation was one of the causes of the ruin of these ministers, and of their unhappy

master. The Prussian ministers in foreign courts have
(at least not long since) talked the most democratic
language with regard to France, and in the most
unmanaged terms.

The whole corps diplomatique, with very few exceptions, leans that way. What cause produces in them a
turn of mind, which at first one would think unnatural to
their situation, it is not impossible to explain. The discussion would, however, be somewhat long and somewhat
invidious. The fact itself is indisputable, however they
may disguise it to their several courts. This disposition
is gone to so very great a length in that corps, in itself
so important, and so important as *furnishing* the intelligence which sways all cabinets, that if princes and states
do not very speedily attend with a vigorous control to that
source of direction and information, very serious evils are
likely to befall them.

But indeed kings are to guard against the same sort of
dispositions in themselves. They are very easily alienated
from all the higher orders of their subjects, whether civil
or military, laic or ecclesiastical. It is with persons of
condition that sovereigns chiefly come into contact. It is
from them that they generally experience opposition to
their will. It is with *their* pride and impracticability that
princes are most hurt; it is with *their* servility and baseness that they are most commonly disgusted; it is from
their humours and cabals that they find their affairs most
frequently troubled and distracted. But of the common
people, in pure monarchical governments, kings know
little or nothing; and therefore being unacquainted with
their faults, (which are as many as those of the great, and
much more decisive in their effects when accompanied
with power,) kings generally regard them with tenderness
and favour, and turn their eyes towards that description
of their subjects, particularly when hurt by opposition
from the higher orders. It was thus that the King of
France (a perpetual example to all sovereigns) was ruined.
I have it from very sure information (and indeed it was
obvious enough from the measures which were taken
previous to the assembly of the states and afterwards) that
the king's counsellors had filled him with a strong dislike
to his nobility, his clergy, and the corps of his magistracy.

They represented to him, that he had tried them all severally, in several ways, and found them all untractable. That he had twice called an assembly (the notables) composed of the first men of the clergy, the nobility, and the magistrates; that he had himself named every one member in those assemblies, and that, though so picked out, he had not, in this their collective state, found them more disposed to a compliance with his will than they had been separately. That there remained for him, with the least prospect of advantage to his authority in the states-general, which were to be composed of the same sorts of men, but not chosen by him, only the *tiers état*. In this alone he could repose any hope of extricating himself from his difficulties, and of settling him in a clear and permanent authority. They represented (these are the words of one of my informants) "that the royal authority, compressed with the weight of these aristocratic bodies, full of ambition and of faction, when once unloaded, would rise of itself, and occupy its natural place without disturbance or control": that the common people would protect, cherish, and support, instead of crushing it. "The people (it was said) could entertain no objects of ambition;" they were out of the road of intrigue and cabal; and could possibly have no other view than the support of the mild and parental authority by which they were invested, for the first time collectively, with real importance in the state, and protected in their peaceable and useful employments.

This unfortunate king (not without a large share of blame to himself) was deluded to his ruin by a desire to humble and reduce his nobility, clergy, and his corporate magistracy; not that I suppose he meant wholly to eradicate these bodies, in the manner since effected by the democratic power; I rather believe that even Necker's designs did not go to that extent. With his own hand, however, Louis XVI. pulled down the pillars which upheld his throne; and this he did, because he could not bear the inconveniences which are attached to everything human; because he found himself cooped up, and in durance, by those limits which nature prescribes to desire and imagination; and was taught to consider as low and degrading that mutual dependence which Providence has ordained that all men should have on one another. He is

not at this minute perhaps cured of the dread of the power
and credit likely to be acquired by those who would save
and rescue him.   He leaves those who suffer in his cause
to their fate; and hopes, by various, mean, delusive intrigues, in which I am afraid he is encouraged from abroad,
to regain, among traitors and regicides, the power he has
joined to take from his own family, whom he quietly sees
proscribed before his eyes, and called to answer to the
lowest of his rebels, as the vilest of all criminals.

It is to be hoped that the emperor may be taught better
things by this fatal example.   But it is sure that he has
advisers who endeavour to fill him with the ideas which
have brought his brother-in-law to his present situation.
Joseph II. was far gone in this philosophy, and some, if
not most, who serve the emperor, would kindly initiate
him into all the mysteries of this freemasonry.   They would
persuade him to look on the National Assembly, not with
the hatred of an enemy, but with the jealousy of a rival.
They would make him desirous of doing, in his own
dominions, by a royal despotism, what has been done in
France by a democratic.   Rather than abandon such enterprises, they would persuade him to a strange alliance
between those extremes.   Their grand object being now,
as in his brother's time, at any rate to destroy the higher
orders, they think he cannot compass this end, as certainly
he cannot, without elevating the lower.   By depressing the
one and by raising the other, they hope in the first place
to increase his treasures and his army; and with these
common instruments of royal power they flatter him that
the democracy which they help, in his name, to create, will
give him but little trouble.   In defiance of the freshest
experience, which might show him that old impossibilities
are become modern probabilities, and that the extent to
which evil principles may go, when left to their own
operation, is beyond the power of calculation, they will
endeavour to persuade him that such a democracy is a
thing which cannot subsist by itself; that in whose hands
soever the military command is placed, he must be, in the
necessary course of affairs, sooner or later the master;
and that, being the master of various unconnected countries, he may keep them all in order by employing a
military force, which to each of them is foreign.   This

maxim too, however formerly plausible, will not now hold water. This scheme is full of intricacy and may cause him everywhere to lose the hearts of his people. These counsellors forget that a corrupted army was the very cause of the ruin of his brother-in-law; and that he is himself far from secure from a similar corruption.

Instead of reconciling himself heartily and *bonâ fide*, according to the most obvious rules of policy, to the states of Brabant *as they are constituted,* and who in the *present state* of things stand on the same foundation with the monarchy itself, and who might have been gained with the greatest facility, they have advised him to the most unkingly proceeding which, either in a good or in a bad light, has ever been attempted. Under a pretext taken from the spirit of the lowest chicane, they have counselled him wholly to break the public faith, to annul the amnesty, as well as the other conditions through which he obtained an entrance into the provinces of the Netherlands, under the guarantee of Great Britain and Prussia. He is made to declare his adherence to the indemnity in a criminal sense, but he is to keep alive in his own name, and to encourage in others, a *civil* process in the nature of an action of damages for what has been suffered during the troubles. Whilst he keeps up this hopeful law-suit in view of the damages he may recover against individuals, he loses the hearts of a whole people, and the vast subsidies which his ancestors had been used to receive from them.

This design once admitted, unriddles the mystery of the whole conduct of the emperor's ministers with regard to France. As soon as they saw the life of the King and Queen of France no longer as they thought in danger, they entirely changed their plan with regard to the French nation. I believe that the chiefs of the revolution (those who led the constituting assembly) have contrived, as far as they can do it, to give the emperor satisfaction on this head. He keeps a continual tone and posture of menace to secure this his only point. But it must be observed that he all along grounds his departure from the engagement at Pilnitz to the princes, on the will and actions of *the king* and the majority of the people, without any regard to the natural and constitutional orders of the state, or to the opinions of the whole house of Bourbon. Though it is manifestly under the constraint of imprisonment and the fear of death, that this unhappy man has been guilty of all those humilities which have astonished mankind, the advisers of the emperor will consider nothing but the *physical* person of Louis, which, even in his present degraded and infamous state, they regard as of sufficient authority to give a complete sanction to the persecution and utter ruin of all his family, and of every person who has shown any degree of attachment or fidelity to him, or to his cause; as well as competent to destroy the whole ancient constitution and frame of the French monarchy.

The present policy, therefore, of the Austrian politicians is to recover despotism through democracy; or, at least, at any expense, everywhere to ruin the description of men who are everywhere the objects of their settled and systematic aversion, but more especially in the Netherlands. Compare this with the emperor's refusing at first all intercourse with the present powers in France, with his endeavouring to excite all Europe against them, and then, his not only withdrawing all assistance and all countenance from the fugitives who had been drawn by his declarations from their houses, situations, and military commissions, many even from the means of their very existence, but treating them with every species of insult and outrage.

Combining this unexampled conduct in the emperor's advisers, with the timidity (operating as perfidy) of the King of France, a fatal example is held out to all subjects, tending to show what little support, or even countenance, they are to expect from those for whom their principle of fidelity may induce them to risk life and fortune. The emperor's advisers would not for the world rescind one of the acts of this or of the late French assembly; nor do they wish anything better at present for their master's brother of France, than that he should really be, as he is nominally, at the head of the system of persecution of religion and good order, and of all descriptions of dignity, natural and instituted; they only wish all this done with a little more respect to the king's person, and with more appearance of consideration for his new subordinate office; in hopes, that, yielding himself, for the present, to the persons who have effected these changes, he may be able to game for the rest hereafter. On no other principles than these, can the conduct of the court of Vienna be accounted for. The subordinate court of Brussels talks the language of a club of Feuillans and Jacobins.

In this state of general rottenness among subjects, and of delusion and false politics in princes, comes a new experiment. The King of France is in the hands of the chiefs of the regicide faction, the Barnaves, Lameths, Fayettes, Perigords, Duports, Robespierres, Camus's, &c. &c. &c. They who had imprisoned, suspended, and conditionally deposed him, are his confidential counsellors. The next desperate of the desperate rebels call themselves the *moderate* party. They are the chiefs of the first assembly, who are confederated to support their power during their suspension from the present, and to govern the existent body with as sovereign a sway as they had done the last. They have, for the greater part, succeeded; and they have many advantages towards procuring their success in future. Just before the close of their regular power, they bestowed some appearance of prerogatives on the king, which in their first plans they had refused to him; particularly the mischievous, and, in his situation, dreadful prerogative of a *veto*. This prerogative, (which they hold as their bit in the mouth of the National Assembly for the time being,) without the direct assistance of their club, it was impossible for the king to show even the desire of exerting with the smallest effect, or even with safety to his person. However, by playing through this *veto,* the assembly against the king, and the king against the assembly, they have made themselves masters of both. In this situation, having destroyed the old government by their sedition, they would preserve as much of order as is necessary for the support of their own usurpation.

It is believed that this, by far the worst party of the miscreants of France, has received direct encouragement from the counsellors who betray the emperor. Thus strengthened by the possession of the captive king (now captive in his mind as well as in body) and by a good hope of the emperor, they intend to send their ministers to every court in Europe; having sent before them such a denunciation of terror and superiority to every nation without exception, as has no example in the diplomatic world. Hitherto the ministers to foreign courts had been of the appointment of the sovereign of France *previous to the revolution;* and, either from inclination, duty or decorum, most of them were contented with a merely passive obedience to the new power. At present, the king, being entirely in the hands of his jailors, and his mind broken to his situation, can send none but the enthusiasts of the system—men framed by the secret committee of the Feuillans, who meet in the house of Madame de Staël, M. Necker's daughter. Such is every man whom they have talked of sending hither. These ministers will be so many spies and incendiaries; so many active emissaries of democracy. Their houses will become places of rendezvous here, as everywhere else, and centres of cabal for whatever is mischievous and malignant in this country, particularly among those of rank and fashion. As the minister of the National Assembly will be admitted at this court, at least with his usual rank, and as entertainments will be naturally given and received by the king's own ministers, any attempt to discountenance the resort of other people to that minister would be ineffectual, and indeed absurd, and full of contradiction. The women who come with these ambassadors will assist in fomenting factions amongst ours, which cannot fail of extending the evil. Some of them I hear are already arrived. There is no doubt they will do as much mischief as they can.

Whilst the public ministers are received under the general law of the communication between nations, the correspondences between the factious clubs in France and ours will be, as they now are, kept up; but this pretended embassy will be a closer, more steady, and more effectual link between the partisans of the new system on both sides of the water. I do not mean that these Anglo-Gallic clubs in London, Manchester, &c., are not dangerous in a high degree. The appointment of festive anniversaries has ever in the sense of mankind been held the best method of keeping alive the spirit of any institution. We have one settled in London; and at the last of them, that of the 14th of July, the strong discountenance of government, the unfavourable time of the year, and the then uncertainty of the disposition of foreign powers, did not hinder the meeting of at least nine hundred people, with good coats on their backs, who could afford to pay half a guinea a head to show their zeal for the new principles. They were with great difficulty, and all possible address, hindered from inviting the French ambassador. His real indisposition, besides the fear of offending any party, sent him out of town. But when our court shall have recognized a government in France, founded on the principles announced in Montmorin's letter, how can the French ambassador be frowned upon for an attendance on those meetings, wherein the establishment of the government he represents is celebrated? An event happened a few days ago, which in many particulars was very ridiculous; yet, even from the ridicule and absurdity of the proceedings, it marks the more strongly the spirit of the French assembly. I mean the reception they have given to the Frith-street alliance. This, though the delirium of a low, drunken alehouse club, they have publicly announced as a formal alliance with the people of England, as such ordered it to be presented to their king, and to be published in every province in France. This leads more directly, and with much greater force, than any proceeding with a regular and rational appearance, to two very material considerations. First, it shows that they are of opinion that the current opinions of the English have the greatest influence on the minds of the people in France, and indeed of all the people in Europe, since they catch with such astonishing eagerness at every the most trifling show of such opinions in their favour. Next, and what appears to me to be full as important, it shows that they are willing publicly to countenance, and even to adopt every factious conspiracy that can be formed in this nation, however low and base in itself, in order to excite in the most miserable wretches here an idea of their own sovereign importance, and to encourage them to look up to France, whenever they may be matured into something of more force, for assistance in the subversion of their domestic government. This address of the alehouse club was actually proposed and accepted by the assembly as an *alliance*. The procedure was in my opinion a high misdemeanour in those who acted thus in England, if they were not so very low and so very base, that no acts of theirs can be called high, even as a description of criminality; and the assembly, in accepting, proclaiming, and publishing this forged alliance, has been guilty of a plain aggression, which would justify our court in demanding a direct disavowal, if our policy should not lead us to wink at it.

Whilst I look over this paper to have it copied, I see a manifesto of the assembly, as a preliminary to a declaration of war against the German princes on the Rhine. This manifesto contains the whole substance of the French politics with regard to foreign states. They have ordered it to be circulated amongst the people in every country of Europe—even previously to its acceptance by the King, and his new privy council, the club of the Feuillans. Therefore, as a summary of their policy avowed by themselves, let us consider some of the circumstances attending that piece, as well as the spirit and temper of the piece itself.

It was preceded by a speech from Brissot, full of unexampled insolence towards all the sovereign states of Germany, if not of Europe. The assembly, to express their satisfaction in the sentiments which it contained, ordered it to be printed. This Brissot had been in the lowest and basest employ under the deposed monarchy; a sort of thief-taker, or spy of police; in which character he acted after the manner of persons in that description. He had been employed by his master, the lieutenant de police, for a considerable time in London, in the same or some such honourable occupation. The revolution, which has brought forward all merit of that kind, raised him, with others of a similar class and disposition, to fame and eminence. On the revolution he became a publisher of an infamous newspaper, which he still continues. He is charged, and I believe justly, as the first mover of the troubles in Hispaniola. There is no wickedness, if I am rightly informed, in which he is not versed, and of which he is not perfectly capable. His quality of news-writer, now an employment of the first dignity in France, and his practices and principles, procured his election into the assembly, where he is one of the leading members. M. Condorcet produced on the same day a draft of a declaration to the king, which the assembly published before it was presented.

Condorcet (though no marquis, as he styled himself before the revolution) is a man of another sort of birth, fashion, and occupation from Brissot; but in every principle, and every disposition to the lowest as well as the highest and most determined villanies, fully his equal. He seconds Brissot in the assembly, and is at once his coadjutor and his rival in a newspaper, which, in his own name and as successor to M. Garat, a member also of the assembly, he has just set up in that empire of gazettes. Condorcet was chosen to draw the first declaration presented by the assembly to the king, as a threat to the Elector of Treves, and the other provinces on the Rhine. In that piece, in which both Feuillans and Jacobins concurred, they declared publicly, and most proudly and insolently, the principle on which they mean to proceed in their future disputes with any of the sovereigns of Europe; for they say, "that it is not with fire and sword they mean to attack their territories, but by what will be *more dreadful* to them, the introduction of liberty."—I have not the paper by me to give the exact words—but I believe they are nearly as I state them. *Dreadful,* indeed, will be their hostility, if they should be able to carry it on according to the example of *their* modes of introducing liberty. They have shown a perfect model of their whole design, very complete, though in little. This gang of murderers and savages have wholly laid waste and utterly ruined the beautiful and happy country of the Comtat Venaissin and the city of Avignon. This cruel and treacherous outrage the sovereigns of Europe, in my opinion, with a great mistake of their honour and interest, have permitted, even without a remonstrance, to be carried to the desired point, on the principles on which they are now themselves threatened in their own states; and this, because, according to the poor and narrow spirit now in fashion, their brother sovereign, whose subjects have been thus traitorously and inhumanly treated in violation of the law of nature and of nations, has a name somewhat different from theirs, and instead of being styled king, or duke, or landgrave, is usually called pope.

The Electors of Treves and Mentz were frightened with the menace of a similar mode of war. The assembly however, not thinking that the Electors of Treves and Mentz had done enough under their first terror, have again brought forward Condorcet, preceded by Brissot, as I have just stated. The declaration, which they have ordered now to be circulated in all countries, is in substance the same as the first, but still more insolent, because more full of detail. There they have the impudence to state that they aim at no conquest; insinuating that all the old, lawful powers of the world had each made a constant, open profession of a design of subduing his neighbours. They add, that if they are provoked, their war will be directed only against those who assume to be *masters*. But to the *people* they will bring peace, law, liberty, &c. &c. There is not the least hint that they consider those whom they call persons "*assuming to be masters*," to be the lawful government of their country, or persons to be treated with the least management or respect. They regard them as usurpers and enslavers of the people. If I do not mistake they are described by the name of tyrants in Condorcet's first draft. I am sure they are so in Brissot's speech, ordered by the assembly to be printed at the same time and for the same purposes. The whole is in the same strain, full of false philosophy and false rhetoric, both, however, calculated to captivate and influence the vulgar mind, and to excite sedition in the countries in which it is ordered to be circulated. Indeed it is such that, if any of the lawful, acknowledged sovereigns of Europe had publicly ordered such a manifesto to be circulated in the dominions of another, the ambassador of that power would instantly be ordered to quit every court without an audience.

The powers of Europe have a pretext for concealing their fears, by saying that this language is not used by the king; though they well know that there is in effect no such person, that the assembly is in reality, and by that king is acknowledged to be, *the master;* that what he does is but matter of formality, and that he can neither cause nor hinder, accelerate nor retard, any measure whatsoever, nor add to, nor soften the manifesto which the assembly has directed to be published, with the declared purpose of exciting mutiny and rebellion in the several countries governed by these powers. By the generality also of the menaces contained in this paper (though infinitely aggravating the outrage), they hope to remove from each power separately the idea of a distinct affront. The persons first pointed at by the menace are certainly the princes of Germany, who harbour the persecuted house of Bourbon and the nobility of France; the declaration, however, is general, and goes to every state with which they may have a cause of quarrel. But the terror of France has fallen upon all nations. A few months since all sovereigns seemed disposed to unite against her, at present they all seem to combine in her favour. At no period has the power of France ever appeared with so formidable an aspect. In particular the liberties of the empire can have nothing more than an existence the most tottering and precarious, whilst France exists with a great power of fomenting rebellion, and the greatest in the weakest; but with neither power nor disposition to support the smaller states in their independence against the attempts of the more powerful.

I wind up all in a full conviction within my own breast, and the substance of which I must repeat over and over again, that the state of France is the first consideration in the politics of Europe, and of each state, externally as well as internally considered.

Most of the topics I have used are drawn from fear and apprehension. Topics derived from fear or addressed to it are, I well know, of doubtful appearance. To be sure, hope is in general the incitement to action. Alarm some men—you do not drive them to provide for their security; you put them to a stand; you induce them, not to take measures to prevent the approach of danger, but to remove so unpleasant an idea from their minds; you persuade them to remain as they are, from a new fear that their activity may bring on the apprehended mischief before its time. I confess freely that this evil sometimes happens from an overdone precaution; but it is when the measures are rash, ill chosen, or ill combined, and the effects rather of blind terror than of enlightened foresight. But the few to whom I wish to submit my thoughts are of a character which will enable them to see danger without astonishment, and to provide against it without perplexity.

To what lengths this method of circulating mutinous manifestoes, and of keeping emissaries of sedition in every court under the name of ambassadors, to propagate the same principles and to follow the practices, will go, and how soon they will operate, it is hard to say—but go on it will—more or less rapidly, according to events, and to the humour of the time. The princes menaced with the revolt of their subjects, at the same time that they have obsequiously obeyed the sovereign mandate of the new Roman senate, have received with distinction, in a public character, ambassadors from those who in the same act had circulated the manifesto of sedition in their dominions. This was the only thing wanting to the degradation and disgrace of the Germanic body.

The ambassadors from the rights of man, and their admission into the diplomatic system, I hold to be a new era in this business. It will be the most important step yet taken to affect the existence of sovereigns, and the higher classes of life—I do not mean to exclude its effects upon all classes—but the first blow is aimed at the more prominent parts in the ancient order of things.

What is to be done?

It would be presumption in me to do more than to make a case. Many things occur. But as they, like all political measures, depend on dispositions, tempers, means, and external circumstances, for all their effect, not being well assured of these, I do not know how to let loose any speculations of mine on the subject. The evil is stated, in my opinion, as it exists. The remedy must be where power, wisdom, and information, I hope, are more united with good intentions than they can be with me. I have done with this subject, I believe, for ever. It has given me many anxious moments for the two last years. If a great change is to be made in human affairs, the minds of men will be fitted to it; the general opinions and feelings will draw that way. Every fear, every hope, will forward it; and then they, who persist in opposing this mighty current in human affairs, will appear rather to resist the decrees of Providence itself, than the mere designs of men. They will not be resolute and firm, but perverse and obstinate.

NOTES TO 'THE FRENCH REVOLUTION'

Page 1, line 3. *A very young gentleman.* This was **Mons. Dupont**, who had visited England and become acquainted with Burke. He afterwards translated the *Reflections* into French.

P. 1, ll. 6–7. *An answer . . . in October,* 1789. See Burke's *Correspondence,* III. 102. The letter was written with punctilious care, yet was withheld for fear it might be intercepted and bring Dupont into peril. The *reasons assigned* in the *short letter* will be found in the answer referred to.

P. 1, l. 17. *Early in the last spring:* i. e. in February 1790, when Burke had voiced his sentiments in a parliamentary speech on the Army Estimates and the *London Chronicle* had advertised the speedy publication of the *Reflections,* which was largely in proof, for Sir Philip Francis was reading the sheets (Burke's *Correspondence,* III. 128).

P. 2, l. 8. *Commodious:* convenient, serviceable.

P. 2, ll. 20–21. *Neither for nor from any description of men:* like the Constitutional Society and the Royal Society mentioned below. Burke claims to write from a detached and impartial standpoint, though he believes he has on his side the best English opinion. The *Constitutional Society* was founded in 1780 by John Cartwright (1740–1824), a naval officer, who afterwards became a major of militia. It included many Whig noblemen and circulated not only the works of earlier writers on liberty like Sidney and Locke, but more extensively those of contemporary pamphleteers. The abolition of slavery, the emancipation of Greece, and the liberation of Spain from its absolute government, were among the objects for which Cartwright worked.

P. 2, ll. 37–38. *The Revolution Society:* had been founded principally by Nonconformists in honour of the Revolution of 1688, and its chairman at this time was Charles Stanhope (third Earl Stanhope), brother-in-law of William Pitt. Lord Stanhope was a Fellow of the Royal Society, and his education in Switzerland had given him an intense love of liberty. His high qualities were marred by an impracticable disposition and his able speeches carried no weight with his fellow peers. He wrote a reply to Burke's *Reflections.* Burke says here (p. 3) that the members of the Society were not as well acquainted with the event that led to its foundation as they might have been. New recruits (p. 4) had joined it, and it had been re-modelled so as to co-operate with the French revolutionaries.

P. 3, l. 27. *As charitably read:* implying, of course, that they were really not worth reading.

P. 3, l. 33. *Meliorated:* improved. A more correct form than our "ameliorated."

P. 3, l. 40. *National Assembly:* sometimes called the Constituent Assembly, the first of the revolutionary parliaments in France. It sat 1789–1791, and was superseded by the Legislative Assembly.

P. 5, ll. 35–36. *Their signatures ought to have been annexed.* It was one of Burke's cardinal tenets that in political affairs men and measures should always be considered together.

P. 6, ll. 36–37. *The metaphysic knight,* etc.: Don Quixote, who freed the criminals (Part I. ch. 22), simply on the abstract or metaphysical (Burke often omits the "-al" in words of this type) ground that every man had a right to liberty.

P. 6, l. 40. *Wild gas:* Crabbe (*Tales of the Hall*), whom Burke had helped in his struggling days, takes up this illustration. He says of "the lighter gas"—

"Such is the freedom which when men approve,
They know not what a dangerous thing they love."

P. 6, l. 40. *The fixed air:* carbonic acid gas had been so called by Dr. Joseph Black (1728–1799), the great Scottish chemist, because of the readiness with which it fixed itself in many bodies. It is this gas which gives liquors their effervescence.

P. 7, ll. 7–9. *New liberty . . . combined with government:* Burke applies this test in detail in the second part of the book.

P. 7, l. 12. *Solidity:* safety, stability.

P. 7, l. 13. *Civil:* civic.

P. 7, l. 34. *Dr. Price:* Richard Price (1723–1791), a Nonconformist minister, who wrote largely on ethical and economical questions. His chief work was a *Review of the Principal Questions in Morals,* in which he criticized the position of Francis Hutcheson. He vigorously opposed the war with America in 1776, and was a close friend of Benjamin Franklin. He was now near the end of his life; Burke had a grudge against him for his attachment to Lord Shelburne, Rockingham's rival. His sermon, which Burke goes on to criticize, was "On the Love of our Country," and when published had as an appendix the Report of the Revolution Society's committee, an account of the people of France, and the National Assembly's Declaration of Right. The letter of the *Duke de Rochefoucault* was a private one to Dr. Price, that of the *Archbishop of Aix* (President of the National Assembly) an official communication to Earl Stanhope.

P. 8, l. 7. *Beginnings of confusion in England.* Burke was needlessly afraid that theoretical Jacobinism—and there was a good deal of it in England—would produce a revolution like that in France, where, however, very strong material causes had been the main factor in the upheaval.

P. 8, ll. 27–28. *The affairs . . . perhaps of more than Europe:* a prescient utterance. Through the Revolution the United States of America gained Louisiana, and both Africa and Asia came into the scope of Napoleon's plans and campaigns.

P. 8, ll. 30–31. *The most wonderful things,* etc.: cp. Johnson in *The Rambler,* 141 : "The greatest events may be often traced back to slender causes. Petty competition, or casual friendship, the prudence of a slave, or the garrulity of a woman, have hastened or retarded the revolutions of empire."

P. 8, l. 34. *Out of nature :* unnatural.

P. 9, ll. 6–7. *The secular applause of dashing Machiavelian politicians:* see p. 78. Niccolo Machiavelli (1469–1530) was secretary of the Republic of Florence, 1498–1512. In his great work, *The Prince,* he asserts that to preserve the integrity of the state, a ruler should not feel himself bound by any scruples of justice or humanity.

P. 9, l. 29. *Caballers:* plotters. The word is really from Cabbala or Cabala, a secret science of the Jewish rabbis for interpreting the hidden sense of the Hebrew scriptures. In English history the name Cabal is especially applied to five unpopular ministers of Charles II. (1672), whose initials happened to make up the word.

P. 9, l. 33. *Philippizes :* is on Philip's side or party—a reference to the great crisis in Greek history, when Philip of Macedon was seeking the friendship of Athens and was opposed by Demosthenes. Oracles were bribed to give utterances favourable to Philip.

P. 9, l. 39. *Rev. Hugh Peters* (1598–1660) : an Independent divine. He took his M.A. degree at Cambridge and lived for some years in New England as minister at Salem, Massachusetts. On his return to England in 1641 he allied himself with the Parliamentary forces and won many recruits to Cromwell's army by his preaching. He was made a chaplain to the Council of State in 1650, and preached regularly at Whitehall during the Protectorate. He was executed at Charing Cross in 1660 for having abetted the death of Charles I.

P. 10, ll. 4–5. *Your league in France :* the Holy Catholic League, organized in 1576 by the Duke of Guise to suppress Protestantism in France and prevent the accession of Henry IV.

P. 10, ll. 5, 6. *Our Solemn League and Covenant :* the agreement of the English Parliament with Scottish representatives, signed in St. Margaret's, Westminster, September 25, 1643, by which in return for assistance against Charles I. the Scots guaranteed the security of their own National Covenant to maintain Presbyterianism.

P. 10, l. 9. *Politics and the pulpit.* Dr. Price was not the only offender. Hardly three months after his famous sermon, *i. e.* on January 30, 1790, the Bishop of Chester preached to the House of Lords a violent attack on the French nation in general and the National Assembly in particular, for which thanks were voted him.

P. 10, ll. 27–28. *The hint given to a . . . lay-divine.* The (third) Duke of Grafton, who was Chancellor of the University of Cambridge, had about 1770 written a pamphlet (which Price said was "ascribed to a great name and would dignify any name") on the subject of the

Liturgy and the terms of subscription to the Anglican Articles. He did much to popularize Griesbach's famous edition of the Greek New Testament in England. In his retirement he wrote a defence of Unitarianism and an autobiography, first published in complete form in 1899. Among the other *lay-divines of rank* was Lord Shelburne, Burke's bugbear, who also favoured Unitarianism.

P. 10, l. 31. *Seekers:* inquirers for truth. Technically the "Seekers" were a sect of mystics (seventeenth century) which, according to Richard Baxter, included Roman Catholics and infidels as well as Puritans.

P. 10, l. 32. *Old staple.* The use of staple here seems to combine the nominal meaning "raw material," and the adjectival "established," "regularly produced for market."

P. 11, ll. 11–12. *The calculating divine.* Price wrote a good deal on public finance.

P. 11, ll. 15–16. *Hortus siccus:* a collection of dried plants.

P. 11, ll. 19–20. *Round of . . . dissipations.* In Burke's day the London season filled the winter months, lasting from November till May.

P. 11, ll. 20–21. *Mess-Johns:* an old Scottish term for clergymen. *Mess* is from *magister.* The *former blessed times* (l. 27) were those of Hugh Peters.

P. 11, ll. 35–36. *Utinam nugis,* etc. "Would that he had spent all that time of violence on trifles."—Juvenal, *Satires,* IV. 150.

P. 12, ll. 3–4. *Owes his crown to the choice of his people.* Price is here echoing Rousseau's theory of a primitive social contract, which was so repugnant to Burke.

P. 12, l. 7. *Meridian:* noonday, zenith. Innocent III. (1198–1216) in the same year excommunicated two of the most powerful sovereigns in Europe, John of England and the Emperor Otto.

P. 12, l. 14. *Solidity:* validity. Cp. note on p. 7, l. 12.

P. 12, l. 42. *Condo et compono,* etc. "I amass and arrange my stores, so that afterwards I may be able to bring them forth."—Horace, *Epistles,* I. i. 12.

P. 13, ll. 39–40. *An electoral college:* college is here used like the Latin *collegium,* an official board.

P. 14, l. 10. *Bottom in:* rest on.

P. 14, ll. 26–28. *Lives and fortunes . . . laws of their country.* Section 8 of the *Declaration of Right* (usually called the Bill of Rights) promises "that they will stand to, maintain and defend their said Majesties . . . with their lives and estates."

P. 15, l. 37. *Gipsy predictions:* random, fanciful utterances.

P. 15, l. 42. *A small and a temporary deviation,* etc. We must remember that all through this argument Burke is engaged in a piece of special pleading. He does not appear in the *rôle* of an impartial judge but as a warm and skilful advocate. As a matter of fact though there was very little deviation from formal law in the Revolution of 1688, there was a profound change in the spirit and disposition and sentiment of the nation towards the monarchy, and Burke fights shy of this very significant fact.

P. 16, ll. 4, 5. *Privilegium non transit in exemplum:* a special case must not be made a general rule.

P. 16, ll. 16, 17. *Eldest born of the issue . . . acknowledged as his:* i. e. of Mary and Anne. A prince, James Francis Edward (the Chevalier de St. George), was born in 1688, and rumour (quite groundless) threw doubt upon his legitimacy.

P. 16, l. 30. *Lord Somers* (1651–1716) : was the son of a Worcestershire attorney who rose to high station. In 1688 he was counsel for the seven bishops, and in 1689 asserted the virtual abdication of James II. and drafted the Bill of Rights. In 1697 he became Lord High Chancellor of England. He possessed great influence with William III., and later did much to bring about the union with Scotland in 1707. He was a greater lawyer than statesman, though his political tracts are models of lucidity.

P. 16, l. 32. *Address:* skill, adroitness.

P. 16, l. 33. *Solution:* dissolution, breach.

P. 17, l. 21. *Relax the nerves:* slacken the sinews.

P. 17, ll. 32–33. *As from a rubric:* This again illustrates Burke's emphasis on inheritance, custom and precedent, his regard for *law*. Rubric—directions for worship, so called because formerly printed in red ; hence, anything definitely settled.

P. 18, l. 12. *The limitation of the crown:* i. e. to those holding the Protestant faith.

P. 18, ll. 18–19. *For themselves and for all their posterity for ever:* Burke out-Herods Herod here. The Parliament of Elizabeth had a well-established right to regulate the succession to the Crown. It was pointed out by Joseph Priestley, one of Burke's most eminent contemporaries, that by denying this power to Parliament, Burke laid himself open to a charge of treason under an act framed by his own hero, Lord Somers. For the extreme Tory position here assumed by Burke, see Swift in the *Examiner*, No. 16 ; on the other side, Locke, *On Government*, Bk. II. ch. 8.

P. 18, ll. 21–22. *A better Whig than Lord Somers:* yet Somers wrote a work on the "Judgment of Whole Kingdoms and Nations," whose very title-page asserts "the rights of the people and parliament of Britain to resist and deprive their kings for evil government"!

P. 18, l. 28. *Aided with:* assisted by.

P. 18, ll. 37–38. *Limits of abstract . . . (and) . . . moral competence:* a distinction which Burke was always ready to draw, and had used in his reasoning on the American revolution. *Abstract* is always a term of depreciation with him ; statesmen have to deal with what is practically attainable, not with what is ideally perfect.

P. 19, ll. 2–4. *The House of Lords is not morally competent . . . to dissolve itself:* this dictum was quoted by Henry Grattan in his speech against the union of the Irish and English parliaments in 1800.

P. 19, l 26. *Communi sponsione reipublicæ:* the consent of the entire commonwealth.

P. 19, ll. 30–31. *Mazes of metaphysic sophistry:* another hit at the abstract. Sophistry (plausible but fallacious reasoning) takes its name from a Greek school of philosophy characterized by such methods. Burke here comes perilously near to advocating the slavery of absolute submission.

P. 20, ll. 13–14. *Ancient organized states:* (i. e. estates), the House of Parliament.

P. 20, l. 15. *Organic moleculæ:* the constituent parts of the nation, including the crown, nobility, gentry, clergy, local officials, traders, etc.

P. 20, ll. 27–31. *The law of inheritance . . . questions upon the legal principles of hereditary descent.* The germ of the hereditary principle can be traced in the time of the Witenagemote, who, while they had the sole power of electing the king, nearly always confined their choice to the royal family, and to the oldest male representative if of full age and capacity. The Norman Conquest strengthened the hereditary principle, for men argued to the crown from the analogy of a feudal fief. But the immediate descendants of William I. could not plead an hereditary title, and so the old elective theory was maintained. William himself went through a form of election, and Henry I. declared himself crowned by the general council of the barons of the whole realm of England. So with Stephen. In 1199 the election of John over Arthur shows that the hereditary principle was not yet established. Edward I. was the first English king whose reign dates from the death of his predecessor and commenced before coronation. The theory that the king never dies, thus adumbrated, was the accepted doctrine by the time of Edward IV.

The Lancastrian title, however, was purely Parliamentary, though Henry IV. showed his regard for hereditary right by claiming to be the lineal descendant of Henry III. Henry VII. claimed the crown by inherent right and by victory over his enemies, and though his title was debatable it is quite possible to maintain that he was king by hereditary right. As regards Parliament's power of deposition, it may be noted that in the case of James II., where the House of Commons declared that James had *abdicated* the government, the Scottish Parliament substituted the term *forfeited.*

P. 20, ll. 31–32. *Heir per capita . . . heir per stirpes:* terms borrowed from Roman law, though Burke has somewhat changed the original significance of the former. He uses it to denote the eldest and most worthy of the same blood, a reference to the Celtic system of "tanistry," a system which prevailed in Ireland to the time of James I., and in which the right of succession lay not with the individual but with the family in which it was hereditary, and by the family the holder of office or lands was elected. This system was partly in force in England in early days; gradually it gave place in the case of private possessions to that of inheritance *per stirpem* or *stirpes*, i. e. by direct descent, and the principle was extended to the Crown by the lawyers about the middle of the thirteenth century. While Edward I. in his proclamation refers to "hereditary succession and the will of the nobles," the last words were omitted in the proclamation of Edward II. Burke elsewhere says the heir *per capita* bases his right on consanguinity, the heir *per stirpes* on representation, from his standing in the place of his predecessor.

P. 20, ll. 37–38. *Multosque perannos, etc.* "For many a year the fortune of the house stands firm, and grandsires' grandsires swell the pedigree."—Virgil (speaking of bees), *Georgics*, IV. 208.

P. 21, ll. 11–12. *Dragged the bodies of our sovereigns.* At the dissolution of the monasteries under Henry VIII. the body of Stephen was disinterred at Faversham for the sake of the lead coffin. The Roundhead troops committed similar sacrilege in Winchester Cathedral. Burke naturally does not refer to the Restoration outrages on Cromwell's body.

P. 21, ll. 24–25. *Statute de tallagio non concedendo:* tallage was a tax on the towns and demesne lands of the crown, usually levied by a poll-tax, *e. g.* a tallage of 2000 marks levied from London in 1214. By this statute—really an unauthoritative extract from the *Confirmation of the Charters,* but held to be a statute by the *Petition of Right* (1628)—no tallage or aid is to be taken without the consent of all.

P. 21, l. 25. *Petition of Right:* eleven articles assented to by Charles I. in 1628.

P. 21, l. 26. *Habeas Corpus Act:* twenty-one articles passed under Charles II. in 1679, dealing especially with illegal imprisonment.

P. 22, ll. 26–28. *Sophia . . . daughter of the Princess Elizabeth:* others, nearer in blood, were passed over because of their Roman Catholicism.

P. 23, l. 42. *Illicit bottoms:* bottom is an old term for ship. "Illicit bottoms" refers to a contravention of the Act of Navigation (1651, repealed in 1849), by which it was sought to confine the carrying trade of England to English vessels.

P. 24, l. 25. *Exploded fanatics of slavery:* like Peter Heylyn (1600–1662), a great clerical upholder of the Stuart cause, and Sir Robert Filmer (*d.* 1653), who wrote *Patriarcha, or the Natural Power of Kings asserted.*

P. 24, l. 30. *New fanatics:* like Rousseau and Dr. Price.

P. 26, l. 5. *Aggravated:* piled up.

P. 26, l. 13. *Popular representative:* the representatives of the people.

P. 26, ll. 14–15. *The next great constitutional act:* the Act of Settlement (1701), which rectified some of the hastily drafted provisions of the Bill of Rights and dealt with abuses that had sprung up in the twelve years since that measure was passed.

P. 26, ll. 18–19. *No pardon . . . pleadable*, etc. The question arose out of the impeachment of the Earl of Danby for high treason in 1678. The Lords refused to commit him because the charge was general not specific. When the impeachment was revived in a new parliament Danby pleaded the king's pardon, but was, nevertheless, sent to the Tower (April 1679). There he remained until the Lords discharged him in 1685. His impeachment is of high constitutional importance on several grounds (see Feilden's *Constitutional History of England*, pp. 154, 155), among them that which is here mentioned. The Act of Settlement in making this ordinance provides that the Crown can pardon offenders *after conviction*: to allow it to do so before judgment was given would be to subvert the doctrine of ministerial responsibility.

P. 26, ll. 32–33. *Servant . . . sovereign*: one of the leading points in Rousseau's "Contrat Social." With his idea of an inalienable national sovereignty compare Burke's idea of king and people as *equal* contracting parties, whose compact creates government and is not to be broken by either as long as the original terms of the covenant are kept.

P. 26, l. 37. *The slave in the old play*: Sosia (Terence, *Andria*, I. i. 17) the steward who resents being reminded of his former slavery. "This reminder smacks of a reproach."

P. 27, l. 31. *Babylonian*: Babel-like.

P. 27, l. 36. *The Justicia of Aragon*: described in Hallam's *Middle Ages*, ch. iv. The office was founded early in the twelfth century, and about 1350 was endowed by the Cortes (the parliament of Aragon, then an independent Spanish kingdom and always noted for its stout defence of popular rights) with an authority which "proved eventually a more adequate barrier against oppression than any other country could boast." The Justicia's functions were in theory similar to those of the Lord Chief Justice of England, but in practice more important and extensive.

P. 27, l. 39. *In this he is not distinguished*, etc. No process can be granted against the king at Common Law.

P. 28, l. 22. *Justa bella quibus necessaria*: "Wars are righteous in so far as they are inevitable" (Livy, IX. 1). Livy goes on to say that they are inevitable in so far as there is no hope for safety except in arms.

P. 29, l. 35. *Sir Edward Coke* (1552–1634): solicitor-general, speaker of the House of Commons and attorney-general (1592), the great rival of Francis Bacon. In 1606 he was made Chief Justice of the Common Pleas. He quarrelled with James I. on questions of royal prerogative, was removed to the less lucrative office of Chief Justice of the King's Bench, 1613, and from the bench altogether in 1616. As one of the leaders of the parliamentary opposition he helped to draw up the Petition of Right in 1628. His writings (*Institutes of the Laws of England*) are distinguished for erudition and thoroughness rather than by method or order.

P. 29, l. 42. *Blackstone, Sir William* (1723–1780): a barrister whose fame was made by his *Commentaries on the Laws of England* (1765–1770), notable for the "way in which the author handles an immense mass of material and unloads it gently upon the reader in such quantities as the average man can bear." Like Coke, he sat on the Bench of Common Pleas and the King's Bench, but he was not a great judge.

P. 30, l. 15. *Rights of Englishmen:* similarly, it was the Americans' appeal to law and precedent that had influenced Burke in siding with them during their revolution.

P. 30, l. 16. *Selden, John* (1584–1654) : the famous jurist who wrote *History of Tythes, De Diis Syris, Table Talk,* and other works, and up to 1649 took a leading part in public affairs on the side of the Parliament. The "general theories concerning the rights of men" which Selden would know were those of Hooker and Grotius. Selden himself wrote *On the Law of Nature and of Nations according to the Teaching of the Hebrews.*

P. 30, l. 38. *Auspicate:* initiate or inaugurate with hope of good luck.

P. 31, l. 15. *A House of Commons and a people:* these were not so closely identified in Burke's day as in ours, when members are little more than delegates of the majority in their respective constituencies.

P. 31, ll. 19–20. *Following nature, which is wisdom:* cp. Burke's *Third Letter on a Regicide Peace:* "Never, no, never, did nature say one thing and wisdom say another," a favourite stoic maxim embodied in Juvenal's "Nunquam aliud Natura, aliud Sapientia dixit" (*Satires,* XIV. 321).

P. 31, ll. 20–21. *A spirit of innovation is generally the result of a selfish temper.* It was so with the Stuarts and with George III. at the beginning of his reign. Burke was never weary of insisting that innovation is not necessarily reform.

P. 31, l. 31. *Mortmain:* the transfer of property to a corporation, which is said to be a dead hand, or one that can never part with it again.

P. 31, ll. 37–38. *Our political system:* with this eloquent passage compare Bacon's *Essay on Innovations.*

P. 32, l. 25. *Freedom leading in itself to . . . excess.* The classical description of the vices of unfettered and intoxicated freedom is in Plato's *Republic,* VIII. 563.

P. 32, l. 26. *Awful:* awesome, awe-inspiring, solemn.

P. 33, l. 13. *Your old states:* the States-General, the name given to the representative body of the three orders (nobility, clergy, burghers) of the French kingdom.

P. 34, ll. 2–4. *Ancestors . . . a standard of virtue and wisdom:* especially in the reign of Louis IX. (St. Louis), 1226–1270, the Golden Age of France.

P. 34, l. 13. *Maroon slaves:* fugitive slaves living on the mountains in the West Indies (French, *marron;* Spanish, *cimarron,* wild ; *cima*, a mountain summit).

P. 35, ll. 4–5. *To lead your virtue not to overlay it:* i. e. smother, stifle.

P. 35, ll. 5–6. *A liberal order of Commons:* a middle class refined, educated, and broad-minded.

P. 35, ll. 36–37. *Foundations of civil freedom in severer manners:* cp. the Puritan *régime* of the Cromwellian commonwealth. We may remember here that if France " when she let loose the reins of legal authority, doubled the licence of a ferocious dissoluteness in manners and of an insolent irreligion in opinions and practices," England did exactly the same when, at the Restoration in 1660, she submitted to similar reins.

P. 36, ll. 4–5. *Disgraced:* displaced.

P. 36, l. 6. *Most potent topics:* strongest arguments.

P. 36, l. 30. *Medicine of the state:* cp. p. 60, ll. 27–30.

P. 37, l. 8. *Two great recognized species.* In the first days of the Revolution these were largely hoarded, but during 1791 much of both was invested in England, and three per cent. Consols rose from 75 to 88.

P. 37, l. 26. *The last stake reserved,* etc. : rebellion and bloodshed are the last desperate remedy, only to be used when all else has failed—not, as here, before trying legal measures.

P. 37, l. 30. *Their pioneers:* the revolutionary writers like Rousseau.

P. 37, l. 34. *Shoe-buckles:* were among the " patriotic donations " further referred to on p. 227. Cp. p. 52, l. 17.

P. 38, l. 23. *Engagement:* pledge, promise. Burke has in mind the theory of episcopal ordination and apostolic succession.

P. 38, l. 27. *Tiers État:* Third Estate—the Burghers or Commons section in the States-General. Here according to Burke there was a complete dearth of the statesman type.

P. 39, l. 24. *Six hundred persons.* This doubling of the *Tiers État* was advocated by the Abbé Sieyès and adopted by Necker, the financial adviser, in order to outweigh the privileged orders who were selfishly resisting necessary taxation.

P. 39, ll. 33–34. *Was soon resolved into that body.* The states met on May 5, and on June 17 the *Tiers État* resolved itself into the National Assembly.

P. 39, ll. 36–39. *A great proportion . . . of practitioners of the law.* These were very numerous in France (Montaigne said they almost constituted a Fourth Estate—as we to-day say about journalists), owing to the varied systems of common law that prevailed in different districts. But they were not in a majority in the *État;* out of 652 members the lawyers numbered 272. There were 162 magistrates of lower grades; the " distinguished magistrates " were represented in the Estate of the Nobility: and it was the lawyers who best knew the condition and need of the people. A Breton advocate, Le Chapelier, was President of the *Tiers État.*

P. 41, ll. 17-18. *Handful of country clowns . . . not a greater number of traders:* there were some seventy or eighty farmers and perhaps the same number of merchants. Of physicians instead of a "pretty considerable" number (l. 27) there were sixteen. Burke's slights on this profession remind us that his favourite French author was Molière. And why should we look for "the natural landed interest of the country" in the *Tiers État* when it was so abundantly represented in the nobility.

P. 42, l. 4. *The British House of Commons* was not, indeed could not be, regarded by Burke (or by any one in his day) as an example of "popular representation." Things have changed since the Reform Bill of 1832 and the extension of the franchise.

P. 42, l. 9. *Politic:* political.

P. 42, l. 42. *Breakers of law in India,* etc. A reference to Paul Benfield, an Indian trader and servant of the East India Company, who acquired a large fortune by trading and money lending. He was implicated in a very shady transaction with the Nawab of Arcot and was ordered home. His conduct occasioned one of Burke's strongest and most ironic speeches. Benfield became member for Cricklade in 1780, and had a number of other boroughs in his pocket. He afterwards lost his fortune in speculations, and died in needy circumstances in Paris in 1810.

P. 43, ll. 28-29. *Mere country curates:* curates is used here not in our sense of "assistants," but meaning curés, beneficed clergy. In the clergy *État* were 48 bishops, 35 abbots and canons, 208 parish priests. The lower clergy certainly, as Arthur Young points out, benefited by the Revolution.

P. 44, ll. 20-21. *Discontented men of quality:* Burke here intends not only such Frenchmen as the Duke of Orleans, Mirabeau, de Noailles and Talleyrand, but Englishmen of his day, like Lord Stanhope, Lord Lansdowne and the Duke of Bedford.

P. 44, ll. 25-26. *To be attached to the subdivision,* etc. But surely caste feeling does not always lead to universalism.

P. 44, ll. 37-38. *The then Earl of Holland:* Henry Rich (1590-1649), M.P. for Leicester 1610, who rose rapidly in court favour, negotiated the marriage of Charles I. and Henrietta Maria, and as Chief Justice in Eyre furthered the illegal claims of Charles. In 1642 he joined the Parliamentary party, went back to Charles in 1643, and then back again to the Parliamentary side. In 1648 he again took up arms for the king, was captured at St. Neots, July 1648, and beheaded.

P. 45, l. 34. *His kinsman, a favourite poet:* Edmund Waller, who was related to Cromwell through his mother, a sister of John Hampden. He wrote a "Panegyric to my Lord Protector."

P. 46, l. 10. *Guises:* a celebrated French ducal family deriving its title from the town of Guise in Aisne. The first duke (Claude, 1496–1550) distinguished himself in the service of Francis I.—his daughter married James V. of Scotland and was mother of Mary Queen of Scots. The second (Francis, 1519–1563) rose to high eminence as a soldier, and was virtual ruler of France under the feeble rule of Francis II., setting himself to crush Protestantism; in this he was helped by his brother Charles (1527–1574), Cardinal of Lorraine, perhaps the ablest of the family. Francis's son Henry (1550–1588) rigorously persecuted the Huguenots and was a party to the Massacre of St. Bartholomew; his designs on the French crown led to his assassination. His grandson (Henry II., 1614–1664) was the opponent of Richelieu, and finally became Grand Chamberlain to Louis XIV.

P. 46, l. 10. *Condés:* a collateral branch of the House of Bourbon. Louis I., Prince of Condé (1530–1569), a spirited soldier, who became a Protestant and opposed the Guises. The second Louis (1621–1686), "the great Condé," was equally distinguished in arms and in letters. Louis Joseph Condé (1736–1818) did all he could to save the monarchy at the Revolution.

P. 46, l. 10. *Colignis:* Gaspard de Coligny (1517–1572), a distinguished French admiral, who worked hard for toleration for the Huguenots and was the first victim of the St. Bartholomew Massacre.

P. 46, l. 11. *Richelieu, Cardinal* (1585–1642): minister of Louis XIII. and a great statesman, who strove (1) to ruin the Protestants as a political power; (2) to curtail the power of the nobles; (3) to humiliate Austria in the councils of Europe. He had a great genius for detailed administration and effected many reforms in finance, legislation, and the army. He founded the French Academy.

P. 46, l. 13. *Henry IV.:* 1553–1610, King of France from 1589. Better known as Henry of Navarre.

P. 46, l. 13. *Sully, Duke of* (1560–1611): the fellow campaigner and trusty minister of Henry IV. He did much to encourage agriculture as the true wealth of France.

P. 46, ll. 16–17. *How very soon France . . . recovered:* this has been illustrated since Burke's day, especially by the way France emerged from the burden of the great war with Prussia in 1871.

P. 46, l. 38. *Load:* overload; make top-heavy.

P. 47, l. 5. *Oratorical:* Burke wrote, quite correctly, *oratorial.*

P. 48, l. 1. *Woe to the country that rejects,* etc.: this is bombast. Burke himself supported the Test Act, which shut out many capable men from the service of their country, and he identifies religion with the Established Church.

P. 48, l. 10. *No rotation,* etc.: referring to the ideas of James Harrington (1611–1677) and the plan of Soame Jenyns (1704–1757) to have an annual ministry chosen by lot from among thirty picked peers and one hundred commoners.

P. 49, ll. 32–33. *Twenty-four million ought to prevail over two hundred thousand:* similarly to-day it is said that the seven million voters who elect the Commons ought to prevail over the six hundred peers who represent but themselves.

P. 49, l. 35. *The lamp-post:* referring to the street lynchings in Paris, when the mob hanged its victims with the ropes which were used to suspend the lanterns.

P. 52, l. 1. *Heroic fortitude towards the sufferers:* cp. Pope and Swift (*Thoughts on Various Subjects*): "I never knew any man in my life who could not bear another's misfortunes perfectly like a Christian."

P. 52, l. 11. *The House of Lords to be voted useless:* as it was by the Commons on February 6, 1649.

P. 52, ll. 17–18. *Land tax and malt tax:* these taxes brought in about two and a half millions, which was all that the navy then cost.

P. 53, l. 3. *Admire . . . the British Constitution:* not so much, however, for its theoretical and formal (which Bentham attacked in his *Fragment on Government* in 1775) as its moral basis—the good feeling and unity that prevailed among its component parts and which was impossible in the condition of things prevailing in France.

P. 53, l. 19. *Dr. Price . . . inadequacy of representation.* The events of the next generation and the Reform Act of 1832 proved Price to be justified in spite of Burke's sneer.

P. 53, l. 33. *Consistency of democratists:* this has always been the case. When the people favour a politician's views they are the enlightened source of all power, when they oppose him they are an uneducated mob. Even Milton often talks in the style of a Coriolanus.

P. 55, ll. 14–15. *A man . . . of great authority:* Dr. Priestley in his *History of the Corruptions of Christianity* (1782) strenuously attacked the state establishment of religion and its then chief supporter, Richard Hurd, Bishop of Worcester. His references to calamities appear to be based on the imagery of the Book of Revelation.

P. 55, ll. 37–38. *They have " the rights of men ":* the school which took this phrase for its watchword was founded by John Locke and Algernon Sidney, who argued that by nature certain rights belong to all men, and these rights have always been enjoyed by Englishmen.

P. 56, ll. 10–11. *Illa se jactat in aula,* etc. "In that hall let Æolus bluster, there let him reign when he has closed the dungeon of the winds."—Virgil, *Æneid,* I. 140.

P. 56, l. 12. *Levanter:* a strong easterly wind in the Levant. (*Levant* is really the point where the sun rises—hence the coasts of the Mediterranean east of Italy.)

P. 57, l. 41. *A power out of themselves:* i. e. outside themselves, an eternal power.

P. 58, l. 19. *Recruit.:* reinforcements.

P. 59, ll. 5–6. *Approved utility:* usefulness that has been " proved " or tested and found good.

P. 60, ll. 1–2. *Denominations:* denominators, numbers.

P. 60, l. 8. *Prudence:* the Aristotelian φρόνησις, practical wisdom, good sense, thoughtfulness.

P. 60, l. 11. *Liceat perire poetis:* let poets have the right to perish if they please.

P. 60, l. 13. *Ardentem frigidus Ætnam insiluit.* "He (Empedocles) leapt in cold blood into burning Etna."—Horace, *Ars Poetica,* 465 f.

P. 60, l. 15. *Franchises of Parnassus:* liberties or privileges accorded to poets, Parnassus being a mountain in Greece sacred to Apollo and the muses.

P. 60, l. 16. *Divine:* a reference to Dr. Price, who, Burke suggests, is like Empedocles (in the legend), discrediting a philosophical career by a piece of theatrical fooling.

P. 60, l. 37. *Cum perimit,* etc. "When many a class annihilates the cruel despots."—Juvenal, VII. 151.

P. 60, l. 41. *High-bred republicans:* like the Bedford, Grenville and Chatham houses—all these had gradually yielded to the seductions of the court.

P. 61, l. 2. *Those of us,* etc. : the Rockingham party.

P. 62, l. 29. *Still:* in the old adverbial sense of "always," "ever."

P. 62, l. 35. *Pisgah:* the hill from which Moses looked across Jordan to the land of Canaan (Deut. xxxiv. 1).

P. 63, l. 17. *Hugh Peters:* see note to p. 9, l. 39.

P. 64, l. 33. *Well born:* noble, high, liberal.

P. 64, l. 37. *Onondaga:* an Indian village in New York state near the site of the present town of Syracuse. The Onondagas were one of the Iroquois confederacy. Champlain attacked their fortress unsuccessfully in 1615. Burke had written an early book on *European Settlements in America,* drawing his information largely from the accounts of French Jesuits who had a mission in Onondaga.

P. 65, l. 16. *A foreign republic,* etc. : i. e. Paris, governed at this time by sixty departments, each of which like a Greek city state had full power within its own limits, and carried out the measures proposed in the clubs of the city.

P. 65, l. 19. *An army,* etc. : the National Guards, hastily raised at the beginning of July.

P. 65, l. 38. *Catiline:* an able but ambitious Roman, who formed an unscrupulous conspiracy against the state, the discovery of which by Cicero forced him to leave the city and attempt a rebellion. This was put down, and Catiline died in the engagement, 62 B.C.

P. 65, l. 38. *Cethegus (C. Cornelius):* one of Catiline's fellow conspirators, whose strangling in the Capitol dungeons, urged by Cato and Cicero, was opposed as illegal by Julius Cæsar.

P. 66, l. 10. *Embracing in their arms,* etc. In January 1790 two brothers named Agasse were condemned for forging bank-notes. While they lay under sentence their brother and cousin were made lieutenants of the National Guard and were publicly feasted and honoured.

P. 66. l. 20. *Explode:* cry down—the antithesis of applaud.

P. 66, l. 27. *Nec color imperii:* the quotation, paraphrased in the preceding context is from Lucan, *Pharsalia,* IX. 207.

P. 66, ll. 28–29. *A power . . . to subvert and destroy:* cp. Revelation xiii. 7.

P. 66, l. 35. *Institute:* institution.

P. 67, l. 5. *The vessel of the state,* etc. : Mirabeau's words quoted in the footnote on p. 71.

P. 67, l. 11. *The blood spilled,* etc. Barnave's remark on hearing of the hanging of Foulon and Berthier, two of the innocent gentlemen. Barnave was one of the best orators of the Revolution.

P. 67, l. 21. *Felicitation on . . . new year:* a deputation from the Assembly presented an address to the king and queen on January 3, 1790, in which they looked forward to presenting him as the friend of the people with a collection of laws calculated for his happiness and for that of all the French, etc.

P. 67, l. 34. *Frippery:* (1) second-hand clothes ; (2) a second-hand clothes shop.

P. 68, l. 3. *Ordinary:* a bishop or his deputy, here the prison chaplain.

P. 68, l. 10. *Leæe nation:* a phrase, modelled on the familiar lèse majesté (treason against the crown), applied by the Assembly to treason against the nation.

P. 68, l. 34. *Sentinel:* his name, de Miomandre, deserves to be recorded. Happily he recovered from his wounds.

P. 69, l. 13. *These two gentlemen,* of the king's bodyguard, were de Huttes and Varicourt.

P. 69, l. 27. *One of the two palaces:* the Tuileries.

P. 69, l. 32. *Theban and Thracian orgies:* Thebes was the chief city of Bœotia in ancient Greece and is associated in legend with the tragic story of Œdipus. The long Latin poem *Thebaid* is one steady record of horrors. Thrace was accounted the most barbarous state of Greece.

P. 69, ll. 35–36. *Apostle . . . revelations of his own:* as Paul in 2 Cor. xii. 1–4.

P. 70, l. 17. *Fifth monarchy:* certain fanatics at the close of the Commonwealth period looked for a coming universal kingdom of which Christ was to be the head. They were put down by Cromwell, and again soon after the Restoration.

P. 72, ll. 36–37. *A sovereign distinguished,* etc. : Maria Theresa, Empress of Austria.

P. 73, l. 3. *It is now sixteen or seventeen years:* Burke had seen the queen in 1774.

P. 73, l. 21. *Sophisters:* sophists ; captious, fallacious reasoners. Burke's lament over the departed age of chivalry is of a piece with the universal longing for "the good old times," a longing which is as old as it is untrue.

P. 73, ll. 32–33. *Vice lost half its evil . . . grossness.* Burke frequently expressed this view, but it is an opinion that challenges opposition.

P. 74, l. 16. *Bland assimilation:* easy digestion.

P. 74, l. 19. *The decent drapery of life:* Samuel Johnson was fond of saying that life was barren enough with all her trappings, and men should be cautious about stripping her of them.

P. 75, ll. 2–3. *Groves of their academy:* the philosophers of ancient Greece used to discourse with their pupils and followers in shady groves. Plato's school was in a grove on the Cephissus near Athens.

P. 75, l. 6. *Mechanic:* mechanical, soulless.

P. 75, l. 15. *Non satis est,* etc. "For poems to have beauty of style is not enough, they must have feeling too."—Horace, *Ars Poetica,* 99.

P. 76, ll. 9–10. *Two principles.* It did not suit Burke here to add to the spirit of gentleman (*i. e.* honour) and religion, a third great impulse that has guided human affairs, viz. Liberty.

P. 76, ll. 23–24. *Trodden . . . swinish:* from Matt. vii. 6.

P. 77, l. 17. *Gentis (in)cunabula nostræ:* the cradle of our race (Virgil, *Æneid,* iii. 105).

P. 78, ll. 5–6. *As it has long been observed:* i. e. by Aristotle in his definition of tragedy in the *Poetics,* ch. vi.

P. 78, l. 14. *David Garrick* (1717–1779): one of the most famous of English actors, born at Hereford, buried in Westminster Abbey. His impersonation of Richard III. was particularly good. He was one of Burke's intimate friends.

P. 78, l. 14. *Sarah Siddons* (1755–1831): England's greatest tragic actress, born at Brecon. She was sister of John and Charles Kemble, and played many parts, excelling in that of Lady Macbeth.

P. 79, l. 29. *To call his people to a share in government:* Burke is probably referring not so much to the parliament of Paris as to the institution of the provincial assemblies.

P. 79, l. 33. *Thought it necessary to provide force:* when he arrested certain magistrates.

P. 80, l. 7. *Listed with fortune:* enlisted in the army of fortune.

P. 80, l. 23. *Nero:* Emperor of Rome, 54–68. His reign was one incessant course of profligacy and crime.

P. 80, l. 23. *Agrippina,* mother of Nero, and murdered by him after she had incited him to all manner of evil.

P. 80, l. 23. *Louis XI.* (1423–1483): was a thorough despot, cruel and treacherous, and inaugurated the absolute tyranny that culminated in the Revolution.

P. 80, ll. 23–24. *Charles IX.* (1550–1574): was responsible for the Massacre of St. Bartholomew and the persecution of the Huguenots.

P. 80, l. 25. *Patkul:* the Russian ambassador at Dresden; had been surrendered to Charles XII. under a treaty by Augustus II., the deposed King of Poland, and was broken on the wheel in 1707 after a form of trial.

P. 80, l. 26. *Christina* (1628–1689) : Queen of Sweden, was the only child of Gustavus Adolphus. She abdicated after a capable rule, and spent her last years in artistic and scientific studies in Rome. Monaldeschi was an Italian whom she had favoured and then neglected. He published the story of her intrigues, and was assassinated in her presence, October 1657.

P. 81, ll. 10–11. *Attestation of the flower-de-luce:* some French courtiers (wearing the Royal *fleur-de-lis*) had sought refuge in England and were talking scandal about their queen.

P. 81, l. 12. *Lord George Gordon:* had been convicted in June 1787 of libelling the French queen. He evaded immediate arrest by going to the Continent, and on his return professed himself a convert to Judaism. He was arrested in Birmingham in December for contempt of court, and sent to Newgate. The mob that he raised was in 1780 in connexion with the "No-popery" riots.

P. 81, l. 23. *T(h)almud:* the Rabbinical exposition of and commentary on the Jewish scriptures.

P. 81, ll. 30–31. *Dr. Price has shown us,* etc. : a reference to Price's mathematical and economical treatises. The *thirty pieces of silver* are those given to Judas Iscariot by the Jewish officials. The *Gallican Church* is the Roman Catholic Church in France.

P. 82, ll. 14–15. *Slender dyke of twenty-four miles:* the Straits of Dover ; dyke=ditch.

P. 83, l. 1. *We formerly have had a king of France:* John, taken by the Black Prince at Poitiers, September 1356.

P. 83, l. 10. *Subtilized:* transformed, lit. spun or woven.

P. 83, l. 12. *Helvetius* (1715–1771) : a Parisian of Swiss origin, whose book, *De l'Esprit,* taught that man was a mere animal, guided altogether by self-love, the sole principle of morals being sensuous gratification.

P. 83, l. 28. *Blurred shreds:* i. e. scribbles.

P. 84, l. 29. *Prejudice,* etc. : these ideas were embodied in a collection of Essays by Lord Chesterfield and others, published about 1756, and no doubt familiar to Burke.

P. 86, ll. 41–42. *This people refused to change their law:* Parliament repudiated John's surrender of the realm to the pope, and in later days, by the Statute of Provisions, declared that the Court of Rome had no power to appoint English bishops or incumbents.

P. 86, l. 16. *Cabal calling itself philosophic:* "philosophic" seems here to imply free-thinking, the rejection of Christianity. Many of the leading thinkers in England (named below by Burke) during the eighteenth century had belonged to the "deistic" school, who had advocated a rationalist handling of the records and beliefs of Christianity. They never formulated any system, and indeed can hardly be called a "school" of thought, though much of their work was based on the teaching and spirit of John Locke.

P. 87, ll. 6–8. *Plainness and directness of . . . those men who,* etc. : men like Walpole, Chatham and Rockingham ; in our own day Salisbury and Campbell-Bannerman.

P. 87, l. 31. *The Armenian Church:* is not now given a place alongside the three great divisions of Christianity : Protestant, Roman Catholic and Orthodox Eastern (commonly called Greek, the religion of Russia, Greece, etc.). Like the Coptic and Abyssinian Churches it is treated as a branch of Eastern Christianity.

P. 88, l. 5. *Alembic:* a vessel used by the old chemists in distillation.

P. 88, l. 35. *In ancient Rome:* when the Decemvirate was founded, commissioners visited Athens, then at the height of its fame under Pericles.

P. 90, ll. 1–2. *To act in trust:* so it was said by *The Spectator* of Lord Cromer on his retirement from Egypt, that he had controlled all his conduct by the sense that he was a trustee.

P. 90, l. 42. *Quicquid multis peccatur inultum:* whatever wrong is wrought by the many, goes unpunished. The quotation is from Lucan (*Phars.* V. 260), and had been used before by Burke in pleading for the rioters of 1780.

P. 91, l. 20. *That eternal, immutable law,* etc. It was the "scholastic" theologians of the Middle Ages who laid down the doctrine that in the Divine mind reason and will are identical.

P. 91, l. 41. *Life-renters:* life-tenants.

P. 92, l. 3. *Entail:* the settlement of an estate on a series of heirs so that the immediate possessor may not dispose of it. "To cut off the entail" is to formally deprive such beneficiaries.

P. 92, l. 3. *Commit waste:* to depreciate the value of an estate by felling timber, allowing houses to fall into disrepair, etc.

P. 92, ll. 12–13. *No one generation could link with the other:* cp. what Burke says on p. 31.

P. 93, l. 18. *Hack that aged parent in pieces,* etc. On the advice of Medea, the daughters of Peleas, King of Thessaly, meted out to their father the treatment here described. Hobbes and Cowley had used the illustration in a similar way.

P. 94, l. 37. *Great name:* Scipio ; the *greater,* Cicero. The quotation is from Scipio's dream in Cicero's *De Republica,* Bk. VI.

P. 95, l. 4. *High origin and cast:* i. e. caste, descent, birth.

P. 95, l. 17. *Signiory:* seigniory—the power or authority of an overlord.

P. 97, l. 12. *As ample and as early a share,* etc. It may have been as ample, but it was certainly not as early. The revival of learning and all the new life associated with the Renaissance was very late indeed in reaching England.

P. 98, l. 1. *Identified the estate of the Church with private property.* A change from the position taken up by Burke in 1772 when, arguing for the repeal of the Act of Uniformity, he maintained that the Anglican Church was a voluntary society favoured by the State, and that the tithes were a species of public tax.

P. 98, l. 6. *Euripus:* the strait between the island of Euboea and the mainland where, contrary to most of the Mediterranean Sea, there is a considerable rise and fall of tides.

P. 98, l. 24. *The gospel's being preached to the poor:* see Matt. xi. 5.

P. 98, l. 42. *What imports men:* what it concerns men.

P. 100, ll. 22–23. *They can see a bishop of Durham . . .* Much of what Burke says is sound enough (*e. g.* on the value of a clergy not dependent on the offerings of those whom they may have to rebuke), but he does not touch the burning question of the inequality of clerical stipends, the vast discrepancy between the income of a bishop and that of a curate.

P. 103, l. 13. *Academies of the Palais Royal:* the courtyard of the Palais Royal was the favourite spot for gossip and tub-thumping oratory.

P. 103, l. 14. *The Jacobins* got their name from their meeting-place —the hall of the old monastery of St. James of Compostella, in the Rue St. Honoré.

P. 104, l. 2. *Dungeons and iron cages:* were much used by Louis XI. The iron cage was invented by the bishop of Verdun, and he was its first victim.

P. 106, l. 10. *The jus retractus:* the right of recovery, by which *e. g.* the lord could compulsorily repurchase alienated lands which had at any previous time formed part of his fief. The French law recognized a score of species of this *droit de retrait.*

P. 106, ll. 10–11. *Landed property held by the crown.* After the ordinance of Moulins in 1566, all private estates that became royal property were united to the crown lands and so became unalienable. In practice they were often alienated, but the *jus retractus* remained and largely nullified the alienation.

P. 107, l. 2. *Commendatory abbeys:* abbeys to which (as to sees) patrons had the right of presenting their nominees.

P. 107, l. 26. *The two academies of France:* (1) the Academy of Sciences (the French Academy) of forty members, founded by Richelieu in 1635; (2) the Academy of Inscriptions, whose function was to compose inscriptions in honour of the achievements of Louis XIV.

P. 107, l. 28. *The Encyclopædia:* was begun by Diderot and d'Alembert in 1751 with the avowed purpose of propagating rationalist and sceptical views of philosophy and religion. It was finished in thirty-three vols. by 1780, and contributed largely to fan the fires of the Revolution.

P. 108, l. 26. *Desultory and faint persecution.* This was on the part of the nobility and clergy. But the Jansenists and Jesuits could not unite against the common foe, and the committee of supervision appointed by the Parliament of Paris was equally helpless.

P. 109, ll. 2–3. *Late king of Prussia:* Frederick II. ("the Great"), who died in 1786 and was largely imbued with the French spirit, being a great friend of Voltaire.

P. 110, l. 41. *M. Laborde:* a Spaniard by birth and afterwards a prosperous Bayonne merchant, who became a financial contractor for the government of Louis XV. and received a marquisate. Under the Reign of Terror in 1794 he was condemned for exporting bullion and was guillotined.

P. 111, l. 6. *Duke de Choiseul* (1719–1795): Louis XV.'s "last substantial man" had done much to strengthen the Bourbon family compact and had greatly influenced European politics. He was dismissed from power through the jealousy of Madame du Barry, Louis XV.'s mistress.

P. 111, l. 13. *The Duke d'Aiguillon:* succeeded Choiseul as Minister for Foreign Affairs. He is remembered for his supineness in the partition of Poland. He was the wealthiest of all the French nobles, but took the side of the Revolution in the Assembly. The *protecting despotism* that saved him was Madame du Barry.

P. 111, l. 18. *Noailles:* several members of this old ducal family had distinguished themselves in Church and State, *e. g.* (1) Anne Jules (1650–1728), marshal of France, who persecuted the Huguenots; (2) Louis Antoine, his brother (1651–1729), Archbishop of Paris and Cardinal; (3) Adrien Maurice (1678–1760), also marshal, who was in the War of the Austrian Succession; (4) his son Louis was a private agent of Louis XVI.; (5) the Vicomte, Louis Marie (1756–1804), brother of (4), with the Duke d'Aiguillon took a leading part in the Assembly.

P. 111, l. 23. *The Duke de Rochefoucault:* was a famous political economist. The Cardinal (see footnote) belonged to another branch of the family and was President of the Order of the Clergy in the States-General of 1789.

P. 111, l. 39. *Crudelem illam hastem:* it was the custom of the Romans to stick a spear in the ground at public auctions, originally as a sign of booty gained in battle.

P. 112, l. 26. *Mariuses and Syllas:* Marius and Sulla were two prominent Roman generals of the first century B.C., whose strife one with the other involved the city in fearful slaughter for many years.

P. 112, l. 43. *Operose:* laborious, tedious.

P. 116, l. 40. *Offer of a contribution:* the clergy proposed to surrender the tithes, while retaining the Church lands.

P. 118, l. 14. *The Bank of Discount:* had been established by Turgot when he was comptroller-general.

P. 119, l. 22. *Arcanum:* mystery, secret.

P. 119, l. 31. *A sort of fine:* the sum paid by a tenant in return for the favour of a lease or renewal.

P. 119, l. 32. *Gift:* the technical term for a grant under the feudal system.

P. 120, l. 32. *Judicious check,* etc.: yet in Burke's day the House of Commons was largely nominated by the House of Lords.

P. 121, l. 8. *A direct train:* a straight course. The establishment of the Directory confirmed Burke's opinion.

P. 121, l. 13. *Purely democratic form,* etc. When Burke wrote the Republics of Genoa and Venice were in existence as well as the Swiss Confederation.

P. 122, l. 21. *I do not often quote Bolingbroke.* Yet to him Burke (like Pitt) owed more than he would confess, almost as much indeed as, in another way, to Addison. Viscount Bolingbroke (Henry St. John) (1678–1751) was Tory prime minister of Queen Anne and the friend of Swift and Pope (to whom he suggested the *Essay on Man*). He wrote "Letters" bearing on politics and literature, and his chief fame is that of a rhetorician. His *Ideal of a Patriot King* shows him at his best.

P. 123, l. 2. *These abuses accumulated,* etc. The existence of these abuses was fully known, and Jacques Robert Turgot (1727–1781), who was called by Louis XVI. to manage the national finances, had thoroughly probed them and planned a scheme providing for their gradual but complete removal. Unfortunately the vested interests were too strong for him, and he had to retire after less than two years of office. What he would have done peacefully only the shock of the Revolution could afterwards effect. And in what follows Burke is somewhat astray. The idea of a republic must have had its seeds long before 1789, it did not spring up and mature so swiftly as he makes out.

P. 123, l. 36. *Tahmas Kouli Khân:* Burke seems to have in his mind Mahmud, the inhuman Afghan conqueror of Persia who, between 1722 and 1725, almost depopulated Ispahan.

P. 124, l. 1. *Where the human race melts away,* etc.: as in the Congo State at the end of the nineteenth century.

P. 124, ll. 16–17. *Intendants of the generalities:* public officials at the head of the different districts, something like the English lords-lieutenant.

P. 125, l. 12. *Considerable tracts are barren:* e. g. the sandy tracts on the coasts of Gascony and Languedoc. About seventeen million acres out of a total area of 123 million are unproductive.

P. 125, l. 17. *Lisle:* the dense population of this district is due to its having been part of Flanders. Cp. the density of modern Belgium.

P. 126, l. 7. *Whole British dominions:* i. e. the United Kingdom or Great Britain and Ireland.

P. 127, l. 12–13. *Her spacious high roads:* these, made chiefly under Louis XIV. and XV., are still the admiration of Britishers.

P. 127, l. 13. *Opportunity:* fitness, suitability. The first canal in France was that which connects the Seine and the Loire, and was constructed early in the seventeenth century. The great canal of Languedoc connects Narbonne and Toulouse, the Atlantic and the Mediterranean, and was the work of Paul de Riquet under Louis XIV.

P. 127, l. 18. *Naval apparatus,* etc. As de Riquet made the canals so Jean Baptiste Colbert (1619–1683), one of the greatest ministers France ever had, made the navy, and the Marquis de Louvois the army, while Sebastien le Prestre de Vauban laid the foundations of modern fortifications and military engineering not only for France but for Europe.

P. 127, ll. 27–28. *Manufactures . . . not second (to ours):* this was especially the case with regard to silk fabrics.

P. 127, ll. 30–31. *The arts that beautify life:* music, architecture, painting—in all these France was leading the world.

P. 128, ll. 18–19. *Censurable degree of facility:* there is no doubt that the king made a good many rash promises (*with levity and want of judgment*) to the working classes, which excited opposition between them and the aristocracy.

P. 129, l. 15. *Circean:* Circe was the enchantress who, when Ulysses and his comrades landed on her island, first infatuated them and then changed them (except Ulysses) into swine.

P. 131, l. 10. *At the period when the Hanse-towns,* etc.: the Hanseatic League was a combination of towns in North-west Germany for the mutual protection (1) of their commerce against the Baltic pirates, (2) of their liberties against the encroachments of neighbouring princes. It was founded in 1241, and numbered at the time sixty-four cities, now dwindled to three—Hamburg, Lübeck and Bremen.

P. 131, l. 12. *Orsini:* better known in Italian history as the head of the Guelf party in the thirteenth century, and the opponents of Pope Alexander VI. at the end of the fifteenth.

P. 131, l. 12. *Vitelli:* this family governed the town of Citta di Castello (twenty-five miles from Perugia) in the fifteenth century. It is worth remembering that they were among the first to patronize the painter Raphael.

P. 131, ll. 14–15. *Mamelukes:* originally slaves from the Caucasus, who became the bodyguard of the Sultan in Egypt, and in time gained the supreme power there. They were defeated by Napoleon in 1798, and finally annihilated by Mehemet Ali, who became Viceroy of Egypt under the Sultan of Turkey.

P. 131, l. 15. *Nayres . . . of Malabar:* the Nairs are a military caste (claiming to rank next to Brahmans) who long held power on the Malabar or west coast of India. They were subjected by Hyder Ali (father of Tipu Sultan) in 1763.

P. 131, l. 18. *Statues of Equity and Mercy:* both these virtues were ranked among the goddesses of ancient Rome.

P. 132, ll. 8–10. *Triumph . . . over . . . a British constitution:* Maury and others really counselled a constitution on the British model. Burke is here really hitting at the English Jacobins, who, like the victorious revolutionary party, opposed the constitution.

P. 132, ll. 35–36. *Shed the blood . . upon the scaffold:* Henry IV. did this with Marshal de Biron.

P. 132, l. 39. *Merited:* received, earned.

P. 133, l. 22. *Officious:* not in our sense of meddlesome, but= full of good offices, kindly disposed.

P. 134, l. 4. *Partnership with the farmer.* Under this system, known as *métayage,* and still largely practised in India, the land-lord advanced stock, seed, etc., and received in return half the produce.

P. 134, ll. 13–15. *Civil government . . . not in the hands of the nobility:* It had passed to the central power, with the further result that the people grudged paying the old dues to those who had no responsibility of administration.

P. 135, l. 28. *Omnes boni,* etc. "True nobility is esteemed by every one of us."—Cicero, *Pro Sextio,* IX. 21.

P. 136, l. 7. *My inquiry concerning your clergy.* In these para-graphs Burke argues from the good character of the individual clergy to their corporate fitness in the administration of government, and so confounds two questions that should be considered independently. He resembles those apologists for Charles I. who say that because he was a kind husband and father we should overlook his faithless-ness, perjury and tyranny in public affairs.

P. 139, l. 4. *The Cardinal of Lorraine:* Charles, Duke of Guise (see note on p. 46), took a leading part in the Massacre of St. Bartholomew.

P. 139, l. 37. *Teachers of the Palais Royal:* see note to p. 103, l. 13.

P. 141, l. 26. *The two great parties:* the old faith and the new, Catholic and Protestant.

P. 142, l. 4. *Regulars of both sexes:* monks, friars, nuns—all who live under a monastic rule. The *seculars* are the clergy who are not so bound.

P. 142, l. 21. *Fénelon* (1651–1715): a famous French prelate and writer on historical, philosophical, theological and literary subjects. He was a remarkable preacher and a man of most benevolent dis-position. He became Archbishop of Cambrai in 1695.

P. 142, l. 27. *A provincial town:* Auxerre, capital of the depart-ment of Yonne, ninety miles south-east from Paris.

P. 143, ll. 15–16. *A hundred and twenty bishops:* bishops and arch-bishops numbered one hundred and thirty-one and were reduced to eighty-three, one for each department of the country. Of the one hundred and thirty-one, forty-eight had seats in the Assembly.

P. 143, l. 19. *Instances of eminent depravity:* e. g. Talleyrand, who was Bishop of Autun, and the Abbé of St. Germain des Prés, who under Louis XV. held 2000 benefices, which he sold to the highest bidders, spending his revenues in some very unecclesiastical directions.

P. 144, l. 24. *Ascertained:* made certain, determined, fixed.

P. 145, ll. 6–7. *Enlightened self-interest:* a reference to Helvetius (see note to p. 83, l. 12), who has some remarks on *Civic Education* at the end of his book *De l'Esprit.*

P. 146, l. 1. *Burnet, Gilbert* (1643–1715) : a native of Aberdeen, and professor of divinity in Glasgow. He supported William of Orange and was made Bishop of Salisbury. He wrote a *History of the Reformation,* and a *History of his Own Times.*

P. 146, l. 15. *Humour:* disposition, spirit.

P. 146, l. 36. *Justice and mercy,* etc. : see Micah vi. 8.

P. 147, l. 15. *A common enemy:* unbelief, atheism.

P. 148, ll. 3–4. *I see in a country very near us:* cp. what Burke said on p. 8 about a neighbour's house being on fire.

P. 148, l. 8. *Doctrine of prescription:* custom continued until it becomes a right or has the force of law.

P. 148, l. 9. *Domat, Jean* (1625–1696) : a great French jurist and friend of Pascal ; he regarded laws and customs as the reflex of political history.

P. 149, l. 19. *Anabaptists:* a fanatical sect which, originating in the Netherlands in the time of the Reformation, afterwards had their head-quarters at Münster in Saxony. Their excesses included community of goods and of wives.

P. 150, l. 16. *Tokens of confraternity and standards,* etc. The Revolution Society of London was presented by the Patriotic Society of Nantes with a banner that the latter had used in one of their festivals. It bore a representation of the flags of the two countries and the motto "Pacte Universel."

P. 152, l. 7. *Confederacies and correspondences.* The footnote shows that Burke is thinking of the secret society of the Illuminati, the discovery of which produced a panic out of all proportion to its importance. The society arose at Ingolstadt in Bavaria as a kind of political variety of freemasonry that aimed at combatting the obscurantism of the Jesuits. Certain malcontents betrayed the leaders, who were punished for infringing an electoral edict against secret societies.

P. 153, ll. 16–17. *As sophisters represent it:* i. e. as the next sentences show, as a dilemma between unreformed existence or absolute destruction. Burke's middle course would be "to mend," rather than to end or to continue the trouble. Cp. p. 155 : "It was your business to correct and mitigate everything noxious in this passion (superstition) as in all the passions."

P. 153, ll. 20-21. *Spartam nactus es; hanc exorna:* "your lot is cast in Sparta, be a credit to it"; "having made your bed, now lie on it as comfortably as you can." The proverb is frequent in Latin literature, being taken from the *Telephus* of Euripides, where it is addressed by Agamemnon to Menelaus.

P. 153, l. 40. *Purchase:* advantage in raising bodies, leverage.

P. 154, l. 11. *The winds blow as they list:* St. John iii. 8. A politician cannot always get his leverage when he wants it; he is as dependent *on the gifts of nature or of chance* as the sailing-ship was on the wind.

P. 154, ll. 33-40. *Steam, electricity, magnetism . . . most powerful and most tractable:* it would almost seem here that Burke foresaw the scientific triumphs of the nineteenth century.

P. 155, l. 34. *Munera Terræ:* the gifts of earth (Horace, *Odes,* II. xiv.); the things that pass away as opposed to the eternal.

P. 157, l. 4. *Commendatory abbots:* those who, like Abbé Clermont of St. Germain des Prés (note to p. 143, l. 19), held plural livings.

P. 158, ll. 35-36. *Petit maisons:* should be *petits maisons,* probably in the sense of chalets, small houses. Distinguish from *petites maisons* (mentioned, though wrongly spelt, in the footnote on p. 164), which means lunatic asylum.

P. 158, l. 36. *Petit(s) soupers:* little suppers (on which much money is often spent).

P. 159, l. 16. *Philosophic spoiler:* another hit at the Encyclopædists.

P. 160, l. 10. *This letter is grown,* etc. At this point Burke, after an interval of some months of absorption in parliament, in which he opposed several measures of political and religious reform, enters upon a distinctly new section of the work and sets himself to criticize (1) the capacity and policy of the National Assembly; (2) their achievements in the legislature, administration, the judicature, the army and finance.

P. 160, ll. 17-18. *My original purpose,* etc.: as outlined on p. 88 and never properly carried through.

P. 161, ll. 9-10. *They have assumed another (sanction and authority):* as they were obliged to by the political need of the situation. The Long Parliament did the same in the time of Cromwell.

P. 161, ll. 18-19. *Great majorities . . . near divisions:* Burke has some further remarks on the competence of majorities in his *Appeal from the New to the Old Whigs.* He says that to give authority to majorities it must be perfectly unanimously and generally understood by society that the act of a majority, however small, must be taken as the act of the whole.

P. 161, ll. 38-39. *Hardly a year . . . they have made a Revolution:* but the revolution was not the work of the Assembly: it had been growing more and more inevitable for nearly two generations.

P. 161, l. 40. *Prima fronte:* on the face of it.

P. 162, l. 15. *Pleader:* not in the sense of a barrister who argues in open court, but rather=draftsman, one who prepares the "pleas" in correct and formal terms. Burke refers to the set prosy speeches which were even more in evidence in the Assembly than the eloquence which he mentions at the beginning of the next paragraph.

P. 163, ll. 24–25. *Pater ipse colendi,* etc. "The great Father himself would not have the path of tillage an easy one."—Virgil, *Georgics,* I. 121.

P. 163, ll. 25–26. *He that wrestles with us,* etc.: an allusion to Jacob and the angel, Genesis xxxii. 24 ff.

P. 164, l. 25. *Expatiate:* in the original sense of "range at large" (now limited to speaking or writing).

P. 164, l. 39. *The Quinze-vingt(s):* a hospital in Paris for three hundred blind men.

P. 166, l. 9. *Excellence in simplicity:* i. e. in things regarded individually.

P. 166, l. 10. *Composition:* collectivity.

P. 166, l. 19. *Some of the philosophers:* the schoolmen of the Middle Ages.

P. 166, l. 29. *Empiric:* an experimenter whose experiments are not controlled by education and systematic knowledge, a quack.

P. 166, l. 36. *Declamations and buffooneries:* like those of Molière in *Le Médecin Malgré Lui,* and *Le Tartuffe,* satires on the doctors and the clergy respectively.

P. 167, l. 9. *Complexional disposition:* complexional here=temperamental, habitual.

P. 167, l. 11. *Quadrimanous:* or quadrumanous, "having four hands," monkeyish.

P. 167, l. 12. *Paradoxes of eloquent writers:* like Rousseau, as the succeeding sentences show.

P. 167, l. 24. *Pede nudo Catonem:* Burke quotes from Horace (*Epistles,* I. xix. 12), a gibe against those who think that wine drinking makes a poet. "Suppose a man with rough and stern countenance, *barefoot* and with the texture of a scanty toga, were to ape Cato, would he, therefore, reproduce the virtues and morals of Cato?" It takes something more than the philosopher's garb to make a philosopher.

P. 169, ll. 16–18. *The French . . . propose to divide,* etc. But the division when accomplished followed natural boundaries not geometrical lines.

P. 170, l. 3. *System of Empedocles and Buffon:* Empedocles (cp. p. 60) of Sicily (c. 490–430 B.C.) conceived the story of the universe as an everlasting evolution, a series of endless cycles in which the two motive principles, love and hate, alternately prevail over the four elements—fire, air, earth and water.

P. 170, l. 3. *Buffon* (1707–1780) : the great French naturalist who arranged the animal world in orders, genera and species.

P. 170, l. 27. *A third for her dower :* the fraction of a husband's real estate to which a widow is entitled.

P. 170, ll. 40–41. *But soft—by regular degrees, not yet :* from Pope's *Moral Essays,* IV. 129.

P. 174, l. 3. *Servius Tullius :* was the sixth king of Rome (578–534 B.C.), and divided the Roman territory into thirty "tribes," and the people into five "classes," from the richest to the poorest, and as any man became rich, so he had power in the state, though he were lowly born.

P. 174, ll. 30–31. *Eighteen livres a day :* the old French livre was about the value of a franc (9½d.), by which it was superseded in 1795.

P. 178, l. 29. *Hominem non sapiunt :* they do not take cognizance of man.

P. 179, ll. 4–5. *Such governments do exist in the world :* e. g. in the United States of America, in Switzerland and (in Burke's day) in Holland. In each case it was the revolt from an *external* despotism that was the necessitating cause.

P. 179, ll. 29–30. *The Romans freed Greece, Macedon,* etc. In 196 B.C. Rome having subjugated the Greek states proclaimed them free, giving them the opportunity to justify their old reputation for self-government. The difficulties became apparent when the liberated districts were distributed among existing political organizations. The degenerate Greeks failed to work out their own salvation, and in 148 B.C. their country was incorporated in the Roman province of Macedon.

P. 179, l. 39. *Civil habitudes :* civic manners.

P. 180, ll. 15–16. *Facies Hippocratica :* the consumptive face, so called because of the description of its symptoms (sunken eyes, sharp nose and ears, etc.) by Hippocrates, "the father of medicine," who lived in the fifth century B.C.

P. 180, l. 21. *The metaphysics of an undergraduate* were very different a century ago from what they are to-day.

P. 181, l. 17. *Montesquieu, Baron de* (1689–1755) : an illustrious French thinker, remembered chiefly by his *Esprit des Lois,* wrote also an able work on *The Causes of the Grandeur of the Romans and their Declension.*

P. 181, l. 34. *The troll of their categorical table :* i. e. the recitation of the table or list of categories—the classes under which objects of philosophy are systematically arranged.

P. 182, ll. 16–17. *If monarchy should ever again obtain ascendency :* the unfettered despotism of Napoleon proves the marvellous prescience of Burke's opinion.

P. 184, l. 6. *A trustee for the whole.* This is truer of the British House of Commons to-day than in Burke's time, when the interests of the industrial section of the community were subordinated to those of the agriculturists and especially the great landlords.

P. 184, ll. 10-12. *When did you hear . . . inequality of representation:* the cry was already beginning to be heard before Burke's death, it was answered by the Reform Bill of 1832.

P. 184, l. 21. *Out of some giddy clubs:* outside such fraternities as the Revolution Society.

P. 184, ll. 22-23. *Desire it on different ideas.* In Burke's day dissatisfaction was expressed not so much with the basis as with the method of representation—the buying and selling of seats in the House of Commons.

P. 185, l. 34. *Limbus Patrum* (the "limbo" of the fathers): an indefinite region in the intermediate state where the souls of those who had no opportunity to accept Christ (*e. g.* the good who died before He came, and unbaptized infants) are supposed to abide.

P. 185, l. 38. *Like chimney-sweepers.* Burke refers to the boys who went up chimneys before the introduction of the present long brushes. They were disqualified, of course, by growing too big.

P. 188, ll. 1-2. *They have reversed the Latonian kindness to . . . Delos:* Delos (in the Cyclades) in Greek legend was a floating island, and was first fixed in its place by Zeus that Latona (Leda) might have somewhere to give birth to her twin children Apollo and Artemis. *Oras et littora circum,* (floating) round coasts and shores, is from Virgil, *Æneid,* III. 75. Burke says that the Assembly instead of giving stability and permanence to landed property, have set it in fluctuation.

P. 188, ll. 8-9. *A holy bishop:* Talleyrand (1754-1838), Bishop of Autun, who espoused the revolutionary cause, and, being excommunicated by the pope, embarked on a statesman's career.

P. 188, l. 18. *Diis immortalibus sero:* "I sow to the eternal gods." —Cicero, *De Senectute,* VII. 25.

P. 188, l. 22. *Caisse d'Escompte:* Discount Bank.

P. 188, l. 25. *Carthusian monk:* one of an order founded by St. Bruno at Catorissium (Chatrousse) in Dauphiné in 1086, noted for their strictness.

P. 188, l. 37. *Beatus ille:* "Happy is the man"—the opening words of Horace's second Epode, in which a usurer praises the charms of country life, its freedom from worry and its simplicity, but soon finds his love of money overpowering his sentiment. *Hæc ubi,* etc., "So spake the money-lender Alphius; he was all but adopting a country life; he got in all his money at the middle of the month, but when the first comes round he wants to put it out again."

P. 189, l. 1. *Caisse d'Église:* the Church Bank.

P. 189, ll. 2-3. *Mississippi:* cp. p. 237. The Mississippi scheme was started in France in 1717 by John Law and the Government, nominally to develop the basin of that river, but really to ease the pressure on the exchequer. Over 600,000 shares were issued, and the demand was enormous; the crash came in 1720.

P. 189, l. 23. *South Sea:* the well-known English "bubble" of the same period.

P. 191, l. 5. *Ephemerous:* ephemeral.

P. 191, ll. 17–18. *He falls the value,* etc.: i. e. causes it to fall, depreciates.

P. 192, l. 1. *Serbonian bog:* a quagmire in Egypt in which armies were fabled to be swallowed up. See *Paradise Lost,* II. 592–594.

P. 193, l. 3. *Hackled:* hacked, rudely chopped up.

P. 195, l. 1. *Solon* (640–559 B.C.): the great Athenian lawgiver and one of the seven sages of Greece, famed for his maxim "Know thy self."

P. 195, l. 1. *Numa:* the second king of ancient Rome, revered as the organizer of the state and its civil and religious institutions.

P. 195, l. 33. *Bumbailiffs:* under-bailiffs. *Catch-pole* or catch-poll, a constable or petty officer of justice (old Latin, *chassipullus,* one who chases fowls).

P. 198, l. 8. *The business of the fifth and sixth of October* (1789): when the Parisian women marched to Versailles and brought the Royal family to Paris.

P. 200, l. 41. *Montmorin:* the French minister of Foreign Affairs.

P. 201, ll. 34–35. *Sed multæ urbes,* etc. "But a host of cities, with their public prayers, prevailed."—Juvenal, X. 284.

P. 203, l. 18. *Areopagus:* a tribunal of thirty-one members who judged criminal offences, and whose sentences were characterized by the strictest justice.

P. 208, l. 1. *Risum teneatis:* can you keep yourself from laughing?

P. 208, l. 24. *Comices:* the French equivalent of the Latin "comitia." See next note.

P. 210, l. 24. *Comitia:* the Assemblies of the Romans for electing magistrates, passing laws, etc. Burke introduces the Latin term to show what the use of the word *comices* implies.

P. 212, ll. 18–19. *Grand compounders,* etc. The allusion is to an old and now (except in some bogus American institutions) extinct university arrangement, by which in certain cases the degree could be obtained without going through the normal course.

P. 212, l. 33. *In my grand climacteric:* my sixty-third year. This age, being 7×9, has often been regarded as a critical one.

P. 212, ll. 36–37. *Si isti mihi largiantur,* etc. "But if any god would permit me to become young again and cry in my cradle, I would stoutly refuse."—Cicero, *De Senectute,* XXIII. 83.

P. 216, l. 6. *Some popular general:* a prediction fulfilled in Napoleon.

P. 216, l. 17. *Debauching:* in the (now rare) transitive sense, "to lead away from duty or allegiance."

P. 217, l. 11. *Marquis de la Fayette* (1757–1834): after aiding the Americans in their War of Independence, returned to France and was made commander-in-chief of the National Guard in Paris. He tried to model the new constitution on American lines. Burke refers to the revolution custom of dubbing every one "Citizen ——."

P. 220, l. 28. *Such unfeathered two-legged things:* Plato's humorous definition of man (ζῷον δίπουν ἄπτερον), a two-footed animal without wings. Dryden used the phrase in *Absalom and Achitophel* (l. 170) in describing the son of the Earl of Shaftesbury.

P. 222, l. 10. *Gabelles:* the excise duties upon salt. See p. 226.

P. 223, l. 7. *The systasis of Crete:* the union or confederation made by the cities of Crete (otherwise engaged in fighting each other) in face of a common foe.

P. 225, ll. 24–25. *Cedo qui vestram,* etc. "In what way, pray, did you lose your commonwealth which was so great?"—Cicero, *De Senectute,* VI. 20.

P. 227, l. 13. *John Doe and Richard Roe:* names of an imaginary plaintiff and defendant in old legal actions; the proverbial term for a legal fiction.

P. 227, l. 26. *St. Simon,* Louis de Rouvroy, Duke of (1676–1755), a French courtier and diplomatist in the reign of Louis XIV.; his *Memoirs* depict with remarkable sagacity the court life of his age. He was the grand-uncle of the Count St. Simon who is known as the founder of French Socialism.

P. 227, ll. 32–33. *A season for disposition and providence:* an opportunity for planning and providing.

P. 230, l. 21. *Hermetic:* belonging to alchemy, magical, secret.

P. 230, l. 23. *Mummy:* here used in the obsolete sense of a medicinal gum.

P. 231, ll. 5–7. *Mais si maladia,* etc. An adaptation of the closing scene of Molière's *Malade Imaginaire,* where a candidate for the degree of Bachelor of Medicine is examined in dog-latin. He is asked as to the remedy for various diseases, and gives the same answer: "Clysterium donare, postea segnare, ensuita purgare." So, says Burke, for all the evils in the state the one remedy of these quack legislators is assignats or paper currency.

P. 231, l. 19. *Pious and venerable prelate:* a sharp gibe at Talleyrand.

P. 237, l. 33. *Credat who will:* let him believe it who will. Horace in *Satires,* I. v. 100, refers to a Jew Apella who might be credulous enough to believe that at the entrance of the temple in Egnatia frankincense melts without fire. But, says Burke, no Jew would believe assignats to be as good as cash.

P. 237, ll. 36–37. *Fraudulent exhibitions of Mr. Law:* see note to p. 189, ll. 2–3.

P. 238, l. 16. *Nuzzling:* blindly following his nose.

P. 239, l. 37. *Cold, dry, petrific mace:* from *Paradise Lost*, X. 293—the weapon with which Death strikes the soil. "Petrific"—changing animal and vegetable substances into stone.

P. 241, l. 14. *Tontines:* a kind of life annuity, increasing as the subscribers die, loans raised with the benefit of survivorship. (From Lorenzo Tonti, a Neapolitan, who invented the system.)

P. 241, l. 30. "*All-atoning name.*" The quotation is from Dryden's *Absalom and Achitophel* (l. 179). He says Shaftesbury "usurped a patriot's all-atoning name."

P. 241, l. 42. *Fine raptures of Lucan.* Lucan (39–65 A.D.), a Latin poet, born at Cordova, was a nephew of Seneca. His poems contain so many "grand swelling sentiments of liberty" that they were withheld from the Dauphin.

P. 241, l. 42. *Corneille, Pierre* (1606–1684): "the father of French tragedy." Goethe said that he "delineated great men; Racine, men of eminent rank." Burke is perhaps thinking especially of his play *Cinna*.

P. 244, l. 17. *One of our poets:* Addison in his tragedy, *Cato*, V. i. The French constitution did indeed pass through "fire and blood."

EVERYMAN'S LIBRARY

By ERNEST RHYS

VICTOR HUGO said a Library was 'an act of faith,' and another writer spoke of one so beautiful, so perfect, so harmonious in all its parts, that he who made it was smitten with a passion. In that faith Everyman's Library was planned out originally on a large scale; and the idea was to make it conform as far as possible to a perfect scheme. However, perfection is a thing to be aimed at and not to be achieved in this difficult world; and since the first volumes appeared there have been many interruptions, chief among them Wars, during which even the City of Books feels the great commotion. But the series always gets back into its old stride.

One of the practical expedients in the original plan was to divide the volumes into separate sections, as Biography, Fiction, History, Belles-lettres, Poetry, Philosophy, Romance, and so forth; with a shelf for Young People. The largest slice of this huge provision of nearly a thousand volumes is, as a matter of course, given to the tyrranous demands of fiction. But in carrying out the scheme, publishers and editors contrived to keep in mind that books, like men and women, have their elective affinities. The present volume, for instance, will be found to have its companion books, both in the same class and not less significantly in other sections. With that idea too, novels like Walter Scott's *Ivanhoe* and *Fortunes of Nigel*, Lytton's *Harold*, and Dickens's *Tale of Two Cities*, have been used as pioneers of history and treated as a sort of holiday history books. For in our day history is tending to grow more documentary and less literary; and 'the historian who is a stylist,' as one of our contributors, the late Thomas Seccombe, said, 'will soon be regarded as a kind of Phoenix.'

As for history, Everyman's Library has been eclectic enough to choose its historians from every school in turn, including Gibbon, Grote, Finlay, Macaulay, Motley, and Prescott, while among earlier books may be found the Venerable Bede and the Anglo-Saxon Chronicle. On the classic shelf too, there is a Livy in an admirable translation by Canon Roberts, and Caesar, Tacitus, Thucydides, and Herodotus are not forgotten.

'You only, O Books,' said Richard de Bury, 'are liberal and independent; you give to all who ask.' The variety of authors old and new, the wisdom and the wit at the disposal of Everyman in his own Library, may even, at times, seem all but embarrassing. In the Essays, for instance, he may turn to Dick Steele in *The Spectator* and learn how Cleomira dances, when the elegance of her motion is unimaginable and 'her eyes are chastised with the simplicity and innocence of her thoughts.' Or he may take *A Century of Essays*, as a key to a whole roomful of the English Essayists, from Bacon to Addison, Elia to Augustine Birrell. These are the golden gossips of literature, the writers who learnt the delightful art of talking on paper. Or again, the reader who has the right spirit and looks on all literature as a great adventure may dive back into the classics, and in Plato's *Phaedrus* read how every soul is divided into three parts (like Caesar's Gaul). The poets next, and he may turn to the finest critic of Victorian times, Matthew Arnold, as their showman, and find in his essay on Maurice de Guerin a clue to the 'magical power of poetry,' as in Shakespeare, with his

daffodils
That come before the swallow dares, and take
The winds of March with beauty.

Hazlitt's *Table Talk* may help us again to discover the relationship of author to author, which is another form of the Friendship of Books. His incomparable essay, 'On Going a Journey,' is a capital prelude to Coleridge's *Biographia Literaria*; and so throughout the long labyrinth of the Library shelves one can follow the magic clue in prose or verse that leads to the hidden treasury. In that way a reader becomes his own critic and Doctor of Letters, and may turn to the Byron review in Macaulay's *Essays* as a prelude to the three volumes of Byron's own poems, remembering that the poet whom Europe loved more than England did was, as Macaulay said, 'the beginning, the middle and the end of all his own poetry.' This brings us to the provoking reflection that it is the obvious authors and the books most easy to reprint which have been the signal successes out of the many hundreds in the series, for Everyman is distinctly proverbial in his tastes. He likes best of all an old author who has worn well or a comparatively new author who has gained something like newspaper notoriety. In attempting to lead him on from the good books that are known to those that are less known, the publishers may have at times been even too adventurous. But the elect reader is or ought to be a party to this conspiracy of books and book-men. He can make it possible, by his help and his co-operative zest, to add still more authors, old and new. 'Infinite riches in a little room,' as the saying is, will be the reward of every citizen who helps year by year to build the City of Books. With such a belief in its possibilities the old Chief (J. M. Dent) threw himself into the enterprise. With the zeal of a true book-lover, he thought that books might be alive and productive as dragons' teeth, which, being 'sown up and down the land, might chance to spring up armed men.' That is a great idea, and it means a fighting campaign in which every new reader who buys a volume, counts as a recruit.

> To him all books which lay
> Their sure foundation in the heart of man . . .
> From Homer the great Thunderer, to the voice
> That roars along the bed of Jewish song . . .
> Shall speak as Powers for ever to be hallowed!

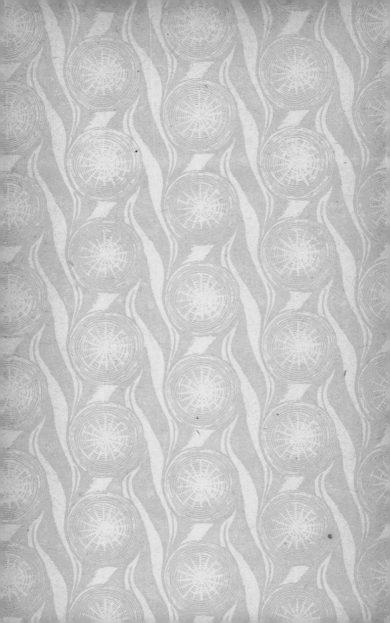